From Martyr to Monument

From Martyr to Monument: The Abbey of Cluny as Cultural Patrimony

By

Janet T. Marquardt

Cambridge Scholars Publishing

From Martyr to Monument: The Abbey of Cluny as Cultural Patrimony, by Janet T. Marquardt

This book first published 2007. The present binding first published 2008.

Cambridge Scholars Publishing

12 Back Chapman Street, Newcastle upon Tyne, NE6 2XX, UK

British Library Cataloguing in Publication Data
A catalogue record for this book is available from the British Library

ISBN (10): 1-4438-0004-X, ISBN (13): 978-1-4438-0004-4

Table of Contents

List of Illustrations ... vi
Foreword (Giles Constable) ... xii
Foreword (French) (Eric Palazzo) ... xiii
Preface and Acknowledgments ... xv

Chapter One ... 1
Background: An ending and a beginning

Chapter Two ... 28
Cluny in the Nineteenth Century I (1800-1848)

Chapter Three ... 60
Cluny in the Nineteenth Century II (1848-1900)

Chapter Four ... 107
Anticipating the Resurrection (1900-1928)

Chapter Five ... 150
American intervention: Kenneth Conant's vision I

Chapter Six ... 206
The "Resurrection" of Cluny: Kenneth Conant's vision II

Chapter Seven ... 253
Conclusions: From Martyr to Monument

Appendix ... 265
Kenneth J. Conant bibliography (Minot Kerr)

Bibliography ... 270

Index ... 282

LIST OF ILLUSTRATIONS

Chapter One

1. Postcard of Ancient Greek temple at Segesta, Italy (Author)
2. Toni Hambleton, *Spaces to Meditate In/On* (21.5" x 7" x 9"), 2001 (Toni Hambleton)
3. Postcard from around 1903 showing an engraving of Cluny before its destruction (Author)
4. Tintern Abbey, Wales, 2001
5. Le Corbusier, Monastery of La Tourette, 1953-1957 (Church tower visible in rear) (Simon Glynn: www.galinsky.com)
6. Palace of Jean de Bourbon with palace of Jacques d'Amboise in background (Ricard, *Cluny et les Environs,* plate XII)
7. Bruys de Charly project, 1808. (Musée d'art et d'archéologie, Cluny)
8. Undated photograph among Kenneth Conant's papers of carved medieval capitals reused on garden wall of local residence (Cluny Collection: Loeb Library, Harvard University)

Chapter Two

1. Alexandre Lenoir (designer), Tomb of Abélard and Héloïse in the *Jardin Élysée* of Lenoir's Musée des monuments français. From J.-E. Biet and J.-P. Brès, *Souvenirs du musée des monumens français* (Paris: l'auteur et al., 1821, pl. 38)
2. Rue de la Barre, Cluny, 2005 (Author)
3. Émile Sagot's view of Cluny from the South in Isidore-Justin-Séverin Taylor's *Voyages pittoresques et romantiques dans l'ancienne France* vol. 7 (McCormick Library of Special Collections, Northwestern University)
4. Émile Sagot's view of the ruined abbey church of Cluny in Isidore-Justin-Séverin Taylor's *Voyages pittoresques et romantiques dans l'ancienne France* vol. 7 (McCormick Library of Special Collections, Northwestern University)
5. Émile Sagot's view of the so-called façade of Pope Gelasius at the Abbey of Cluny in Isidore-Justin-Séverin Taylor's *Voyages*

pittoresques et romantiques dans l'ancienne France vol. 7 (McCormick Library of Special Collections, Northwestern University
6. Postcard of Bourbon Chapel, Cluny (Sébastien Pisano)
7. Émile Sagot's frontispiece to Lorain, *Essai historique sur l'Abbaye de Cluny,* 1839
8. Émile Sagot's 1838 illustration of Cluny's medieval houses in Lorain, *Essai historique sur l'Abbaye de Cluny,* 1839

Chapter Three

1. Porte d'honneur, Cluny, 2006 (Author)
2. Verdier's drawing of the door to the Bourbon Chapel (Ricard, *Cluny et les Environs,* plate XV)
3. Postcard showing restored doorway of so-called "Façade of Pope Gelasius", Cluny (Author)
4. Postcard of Sacré-Coeur, Paris around 1931 (Author)
5. Postcard of Grotto at Lourdes around 1910 (Author)
6. Postcard of Basilica at Lourdes around 1910 (Author)
7. Stereographic postcard of commercial area in Lourdes around 1910 (Author)
8. *L'Union républicaine* October 25, 1898, p. 2 (Archives départementales de Saône-et-Loire, Mâcon)
9. L'*Union républicaine*, November 9, 1898 (Archives départementales de Saône-et-Loire, Mâcon)
10. Musée Ochier before 1880 (Ricard, *Cluny et les Environs,* plate XIV)
11. Cover illustration, Forest, *Histoire d'un jubilé,* 1898
12. Plate VII, Forest, *Histoire d'un jubilé,* 1898

Chapter Four

1. *Le Vieux Paris*, Paris 1900 exhibition (Elizabeth Emery, image in public doman)
2. Program Cover, 1910 Millénaire de Cluny (Cluny Collection: Loeb Library, Harvard University)
3. Menu cover, 1910 Millénaire de Cluny (Millénaire proceedings, plate III)
4. Ecclesiastics assembled for 1910 Millénaire de Cluny (Millénaire proceedings, plate V)
5. Diagram of cortège for 1910 Millénaire de Cluny (Millénaire proceedings, plate VI)

6. First page of Delisle's resignation letter from 1910 Cluny Millénaire (Millénaire proceedings, plate II)
7. Portrait photo of Leopole Delisle (Millénaire proceedings, plate VII)
8. Postcard of cortège leaving fairground at Cluny for procession through city, Millénaire de Cluny, 1910 (Author)
9. Postcard of religious procession, Cluny 1910 (N. Roiné)
10. Postcard of pope and abbot awaiting arrival of king, Cluny Millénaire, 1910 (Author)
11. Postcard of crowd watching parade with medieval bells, Millénaire de Cluny, 1910 (Author)
12. Sculpted capital of fourth tone originally from ambulatory choir, abbey church of Cluny, ca. 1100 (Andrew J. Tallon 2002)
13. Postcard of Mayor and Minister Sarraut at Cluny for Millénaire events (N. Roiné)
14. Byzantine emperor and empress in cortège, Millénaire de Cluny, 1910 (Illustré soleil du dimanche 39 [September 25, 1910], 11. N. Roiné)
15. Queens of France in cortège reenactment, Millénaire de Cluny, 1910 (*Le Monde Illustré*, #2790 [17 Sep 1910], 181)
16. Postcard of king's arrival, Millénaire de Cluny, 1910 (Author)
17. Postcard of interior, Notre-Dame de Cluny, 1910 (N. Roiné)
18. Poster advertising 1910 Cluny Millénaire (Cluny Collection: Loeb Library, Harvard University)
19. Souvenir postcard, Millénaire de Cluny, 1910 (Cluny Collection: Loeb Library, Harvard University)
20. Postcard of commemorative medal for Millénaire de Cluny, 1910 (N. Roiné)
21. Area behind stables and between Bourbon Chapel and remaining abbey church ruins which Ventre called a "cesspool" in 1912, Loury photo from 1931 after Conant had dug excavation trenches here (Cluny Collection: Loeb Library, Harvard University)
22. Advertisement from Alfred Forest, *Cluny-Guide*, 1909
23. Kenneth Conant's photograph of abbey manuscript page once used to seal jam jar (Cluny Collection: Loeb Library, Harvard University)

Chapter Five

1. Kenneth Conant's thesis plan for "House of Studies for a Community of Canons Regular", front elevation of chapel and tower. 1919 (Cluny Collection: Loeb Library, Harvard University]
2. K.J. Conant, Sketches from European travels (Cluny Collection: Loeb Library, Harvard University)

3. Letter from Kinglsey Porter to Oursel introducing Conant in 1927 (Cluny Collection: Loeb Library, Harvard University)
4. Ground breaking, Medieval Academy excavations Cluny, July 29,1928. Conant is on the far left, Malo is wielding the pick. (Musée d'art et d'archéologie, Cluny)
5. Postcard advertisement for Conant restoration drawings of Cluny (Cluny Collection: Loeb Library, Harvard)
6. Advertisement for Conant's *Speculum* articles on Cluny, 1929 (Medieval Academy of America)
7. View of west portal of abbey church of Cluny before 1928 (Cluny Collection: Loeb Library, Harvard University)
8. Pit 1 at West portal, abbey church, Cluny, 1929 (Cluny Collection: Loeb Library, Harvard University)
9. Workers posing for photograph during Cluny excavations around 1928 (Cluny Collection: Loeb Library, Harvard University)
10. Men posing in excavation pit at Cluny, 1928 (Cluny Collection: Loeb Library, Harvard University)
11. K.J. Conant with excavation crew in *Haras* courtyard, May 1931 (Medieval Academy of America)
12. K.J. Conant with workers around pit IV in 1929 (detail) (Musée d'art et d'archéologie, Cluny)
13. K.J. Conant posing with team of workers after unearthing architectural fragment, 1931 (Cluny Collection: Loeb Library, Harvard)
14. Loury photographing pit during Cluny excavations (Cluny Collection: Loeb Library, Harvard University)
15. Typical documentation photograph of sculptural fragments including polychrome head, 1928 (Cluny Collection: Loeb Library, Harvard University)
16. View from transept tower of excavation area around Bourbon chapel with boxes of fragments, 1937 (Cluny Collection: Loeb Library, Harvard University)
17. K. J. Conant in excavation pit at Cluny, August, 1931 (Medieval Academy of America)
18. Bound page from Conant's 1928 daybook (Musée d'art et d'archéologie, Cluny)
19. K.J. Conant with sign indicating street closed for excavations showing Medieval Academy insignia in front of pit 1 before railing installed, 1928 (Cluny Collection: Loeb Library, Harvard University)
20. K.J. Conant with workmen in front of scaffolding used to photograph upper transept and towers, probably 1928 (Cluny Collection: Loeb Library, Harvard University)

21. Conant's 1929 photo of capital on great transept found under ivy (Cluny Collection: Loeb Library, Harvard University)
22. Photograph of an early phase of Conant's chalk layout drawn on floor for reconstructing fragments from the tympanum of west portal
23. Photograph of Marie Conant and their two sons, Kenneth and John in January, 1931 (Cluny Collection: Loeb Library, Harvard University)
24. Frederic Palmer and K.J. Conant in 1929 (Cluny Collection: Loeb Library, Harvard University)
25. K. J. Conant and Helen Kleinschmidt visiting Cluny in their later years (Cluny Collection: Loeb Library, Harvard University)
26. Photo of early excavation work in the *Haras* yard, 1929 (Cluny Collection: Loeb Library, Harvard University)

Chapter Six

1. Conant with workers during installation of Cluny choir capital casts in Fogg Museum, Harvard University, June, 1933. (Cluny Collection: Loeb Library, Harvard University)
2. Modified photo of Cluny choir capital casts in Fogg, Museum, 1933. Conant made a note on the right margin that the Fogg installation height was wrong, based upon a drawing of 1772. He has drawn over the photograph to lower the arcades and indicate the next higher wall level in the original church (Cluny Collection: Loeb Library, Harvard University)
3. Lead cover with inscription written by Conant over tomb he claimed to be that of Peter the Venerable, 1931 (Cluny Collection: Loeb Library, Harvard University)
4. Postcard of M. et Mme. Daclin in front of their pharmacy in Cluny around 1910 (Cluny Collection: Loeb Library, Harvard University)
5. Joan Evans (Cluny Collection: Loeb Library, Harvard University)
6. Interior view of remaining transept, Cluny abbey church, showing photograph of Conant drawing on closure wall where rest of church once stood (Cluny collection: Loeb Library, Harvard University)
7. Tour des Fromages before restoration (Cluny collection: Loeb Library, Harvard University)
8. Site of a 1944 bomb, Cluny (Cluny collection: Loeb Library, Harvard University)
9. Former granary and mill tower *(farinier)* at abbey of Cluny, exterior (Ricard,, *Cluny et les Environs,* plate VII)

10. Museum installed in *Farinier*, here seen in 1960 hosting a small concert under the direction of Conant's second wife, Isabel Pope (far left) (Cluny Collection: Loeb Library, Harvard University)
11. *L'Echo* (Lyon) 11 July 1049 (Medieval Academy of America)
12. *Le Progrès* (Mâcon) 11 July 1949 (Medieval Academy of America)
13. Deschamps lecturing in Farinier museum at Cluny, July 1949 (Cluny collection: Loeb Library, Harvard University)
14. Banquet held in Farinier museum, Cluny, July 1949. Conant is between the two women; Marcel Aubert is far right (Cluny collection: Loeb Library, Harvard University)
15. Women demonstrating Cluny lacemaking techniques, Cluny, July 1949 (*Le Progrès*, Mâcon)
16. Kenneth Conant in Cluny during 1949 Congrès (Cluny collection: Loeb Library, Harvard University)
17. Kenneth Conant posing in front of Pan Am flight to South America, 1940s (Cluny collection: Loeb Library, Harvard University)
18. Conant looking at the sign of street named after him in Cluny, 1948 (Cluny collection: Loeb Library, Harvard University)
19. Conant receiving the French Legion of Honor from the prefect of the Saône-et-Loire in the Farinier museum, 1966 (Cluny collection: Loeb Library, Harvard University)
20. Postcard showing choir of Paray-le-Monial abbey church which Conant used as a model to help recreate the larger east end of Cluny III
21. Radcliffe and Harvard students at Cluny with Conant during the early 1930s (Cluny collection: Loeb Library, Harvard University)

Chapter Seven

1. Postcard of Cathedral of Mâcon, built in 1860s and dedicated to St. Peter, around 1901 (Author)

FOREWORD

The history of Cluny is often treated as if it began with the foundation of the abbey in 910 and ended with the death in 1153 of its last great abbot, Peter the Venerable. Some scholars have recently begun to revise this approach and have given more attention both to ‘Cluny before Cluny’, on this basis of archaeological as well as documentary evidence, and to ‘Cluny after Cluny’, from the twelfth century to the dissolution of the monastery at the time of the French Revolution. The present book extends this view, beyond the Revolution, through the nineteenth century and into the twentieth. It is not simply a history of the town of Cluny or of the remains of the abbey. The author describes the book at different places as a study of Cluny as cultural patrimony, of ‘the factors contributing to the rise of a heritage site at the ruins of the monastery’, and of how ‘the ruined abbey began its new life as a memorial site and Burgundian tourist destination within the context of its “glorious” medieval past’. It is thus a study in the history of religious, national, and regional attitudes as well as in the history of taste, and it shows how over the years the remains of the abbey were used both as a revolutionary justification and as a source of romantic regret. The townsmen of Cluny were not invariably hostile to the abbey and its remains, as it is sometimes said, and they were not motivated exclusively by practical and pecuniary interests. The author studies in particular the shift in sentiment about 1820, when efforts began to save the ruins, the reverse of the ‘downward spiral’ in the 1830s, and the first serious efforts to finance the preservation in the 1880s. Later milestones were the elaborate anniversary ceremonies in 1898, 1910 – the millennium of the foundation of Cluny – and in 1949, which were not only, or perhaps even principally, scholarly celebrations of the history of Cluny but also significant events in the history of French nationalism and Catholicism. Along the way many important writers and scholars, including Lamartine, Michelet, and Guizot, contributed to the development of the myth of Cluny and its remains. Particular attention is given here to Kenneth John Conant, the American architect and archaeologist whose years of work at Cluny and many publications helped to bring the abbey to life and to put Cluny on the modern tourist map.

Giles Constable
Institute for Advanced Study

AVANT-PROPOS

Pour un médiéviste, le nom de Cluny résonne de façon si vive, si particulière, car l'abbaye bourguignonne, on le sait bien, compte parmi les hauts lieux du christianisme médiéval. Le livre que ici Janet Marquardt fera date à bien des égards d'abord et avant tout car il n'est en aucun cas un "livre de plus" sur l'abbaye de Cluny, sur son histoire ou l'importante production artistique de l'âge roman. Le lecteur s'apercevra dès le premier chapitre de ce beau livre qu'il s'agit d'un, ouvrage sur l'histoire intellectuelle, sociale et politique de la France du XIXe siècle jusqu'à nos jours vue à travers le prisme de la vie et de la recherche d'un architecte américain, véritable pionnier de l'archéologie moderne aussi, qui a vécu une véritable passion avec l'abbaye de Cluny, Kenneth John Conant. A n'en pas douter, le livre par plusieurs aspects si neuf et si original de Janet Marquardt devrait permettre de développer le dialogue entre médiévistes français et médiévistes américains dont la tendance est parfois – et on ne peut que profondément regretter cette situation – de s'ignorer mutuellement et réciproquement. Dans un certain sens, le livre de Janet Marquardt traite d'un sujet d'actualité : la notion de patrimoine et son histoire à partir du regard porté sur un monument phare du Moyen Age "français", l'abbaye de Cluny. Une grande part de l'originalité de ce livre réside dans le choix du monument. En effet, l'abbaye de Cluny n'est pas seulement un véritable symbole d'une certaine période du Moyen Age – ce que l'on a coutume d'appeler l'époque romane -, mais c'est aussi l'exemple parfait du "fantasme" moderne pour le Moyen Age. Car, comme chacun sait, l'abbaye de Cluny et son église ont pour une large part été détruites dans les suites néfastes de la révolution française, du moins pour le patrimoine médiéval en général.

Dans ce sens, on peut dire que la construction de la vision patrimoniale de l'abbaye bourguignonne s'est faite à partir du rêve de monuments disparus à jamais et nourrie par ce qu'il en reste encore aujourd'hui : une petite partie de l'un des transepts, quelques vestiges des bâtiments monastiques et une multitude de fragments sculptés. Dans les trois premiers chapitres de son livre, Janet Marquardt retrace avec une grande précision et une érudition sans faille le XIXe siècle mouvementé pour l'abbaye bourguigonne. Dans ces pages, Janet Marquardt offre au lecteur une magnifique vue d'ensemble de la sociologie du patrimoine en France et ses multiples implications et imbrications avec le monde politique au moment même où la notion fait véritablement son apparition, à une époque cruciale pour l'émergence de sciences historiques telle que l'archéologie. Le chapitre quatre du livre constitue l'articulation majeure de la pensée de Janet Marquardt. Dans ces pages, elle procède à une analyse fort pertinente des premières manifestations commémoratives de Cluny et de son patrimoine. Ici, il est fortement question de la structuration et de la mise en place du patrimoine clunisien à travers non seulement les diverses commémorations en tout genre reflétant la vie politique locale et nationale en même temps, tout autant que la mise en place d'une sociologie du patrimoine à l'échelle régionale, mais aussi du relais important dans ce processus pris par le monde savant des chercheurs universitaires et des recherches archéologiques naissantes.

Les chapitres cinq et six ainsi que, d'une certaine manière, la conclusion du livre proposent un enquête fort riche et inédite de la carrière de Kenneth John Conant et de ses travaux sur l'abbaye de Cluny. Dans ces pages, tout aussi savantes et très bien documentées que celles des chapitres précédents, Janet Marquardt retrace avec précision et une grand méticulosité la carrière du savant architecte et archéologue américain, ses origines intellectuelles et ses relations avec les milieux académiques de l'histoire de l'art médiéval dans la première moitié du XXe siècle, plus particulièrement avec les savants allemands exilés aux Etats-Unis au moment de la montée du fascisme en Allemagne. Janet Marquardt démontre avec beaucoup de pertinence et de façon convaincante le lien très étroit entre le contexte sociologique qui a vu naître et fait émerger la notion de patrimoine médiéval en France et les recherches archéologiques menées par Kenneth John Conant à l'abbaye de Cluny.

A tous égards donc, le beau livre de Janet Marquardt fera date non seulement dans le monde des spécialistes de l'abbaye de Cluny et, de façon plus générale, dans celui des médiévistes, mais aussi dans les cercles plus larges de la sociologie historique et de l'histoire culturelle.

Eric PALAZZO
Professeur à l'université de Poitiers
Directeur du Centre d'études supérieures de civilisation médiévale

PREFACE

Most of us who have taken or taught medieval art history classes study the abbey church of Cluny in the course of Romanesque architecture. We confront the remaining piece of the southeastern transept as a relic of the golden period of the abbey under St. Hugh and Peter the Venerable. Its vast size and decoration serve as a testament to Cluniac art and international patronage. Within such study, the current fragmentary condition of the abbey church is briefly attributed to its near total destruction caused by the French Revolution. Such an association conjures images of angry mobs, *sans-culottes* with pikes and torches, setting upon the monks and their possessions, smashing and burning the buildings. From our twentieth-century perspective, we poignantly try to imagine how the undestroyed portion would have fit into the overall form of the abbey church. We inevitably feel some form of regret that such a magnificent example of eleventh- and twelfth-century architecture was demolished. We secretly harbor a bit of righteous indignation at the ignorance of the revolutionary French.

Yet this version of events, when set against the facts of Cluny III's demise, reads like an ideal propaganda rendition of the affair, as if it had been disseminated by a guilty Restoration government. How convenient, to imagine the culpability of the general French populace, even specifically the very townspeople of Cluny, rather than the much more complex politics of multiple governments over a period of thirty years. I asked myself: Did such a polarization of town and abbey exist? Was the abbey actually destroyed during the Revolution? How, exactly, could they get this huge building down? Clearly, anyone thinking about it in technical terms cannot imagine that anything less than dynamite and wrecking balls could effect such a leveling today. So unless the French army was involved with cannons and mines, or employed a team of masons comparable to those employed in the leveling of the Bastille, I couldn't conceive of a revolutionary action—especially not spontaneous—which brought down the stone vaults and iron rebars.

What I found was a fascinating story of just such demolition, only long after the Revolution, and hotly contested by many local residents. I was also drawn into the politics of nineteenth-century historians and conservationists. All this led inexorably to Cluny's "resurrection" during the excavations sponsored by the Mediaeval Academy of America under Kenneth Conant in the twentieth century. The archival material he amassed presented a rich and unending source of study.

In this book I am concerned with ideas rather than the nuts and bolts of Cluny's "afterlife". I do not attempt to scrutinize the excavation programs, or do a comprehensive review of the scholarly literature on medieval Cluny or analyze Conant's architectural reconstructions. Rather, I try to follow larger trends and determine themes in the history of Cluny's development as a heritage site and as a modern touchstone for French notions of medieval monasticism. Anne Baud has made scientific measure of Conant's methods and conclusions in her analysis of the findings from the recent excavations at Cluny. I only wish to complement that scientific work with one of historiography.

Those larger trends raise broad questions about so many things: views on Romanesque art in the nineteenth century, the way that French identity is bound up with heritage and patrimony, the role of provincial scholarly societies, the decisions of the various patrimonial institutions established by the July Monarchy, the political shaping of medieval history, the relationship of cultural heritage to tourism, American philanthropy in France, the changing standards of archaeology, let alone the explosion of studies into the function of memory and memorials or my temptation to launch into a full biography of Conant's fascinating personal life! It seemed that the more I looked the greater the project became. Thus I have simply tried to introduce these issues as they arose within my specific investigation, then either send readers to those scholars who have made thorough studies of the questions or save it for a later work.

I am sure I missed things I should have read, resources I should have consulted, people I should have met. But in the end, one simply has to stop and get something out as grist for the mill. I welcome responses and look forward to critiques (within the spirit of scholarly advancement of course!) at: jtmarquardt@eiu.edu.

I am immensely grateful to the many people who have already assisted in some way with this project. Again, I'm probably missing someone along the way, but if so, know that you are thanked as well. Working for eight years on such a wide-ranging project, one finds some colleagues grow into friends. I feel I have been enriched many times over, first by strictly professional advice but also by the convivial meals where ideas were initiated in spirited discussions or in the conversations over tea that helped me retain some sanity after long hours in dusty archives. I hope that the final form of this book is not a disappointment to anyone.

Funding

National Endowment for the Humanities Fellowship 2003-2004
Sabbatical, Eastern Illinois University, 2004-2005
Eastern Illinois University College of Arts and Humanities travel grants 2001-2003
NEH Summer Seminar, 1998, "Gothic in the Île-de-France" (Stephen Murray, Columbia University)

Archives

Paris

Bibliothèque du Patrimoine, Ministère de la culture et de la communication (Jean-Daniel Pariset, Monique Pontet)

Cluny

Service de la Conservation (Hélène Tomaszczyk, Bénédicte Duthion, Veronique Bonin, Mary Sainsous)

Mâcon

Archives départmental
Académie de Mâcon (Georges Berthoud)

Cambridge, Massachusetts

Harvard GSD Loeb Library, Conant collection (Mary Daniels, Inés Zalduendo)
Harvard University Archives (Robin McElheny)
Harvard's Fogg Museum archives (Abby Smith)
Mediaeval Academy of America (Rick Emmerson, Jacqueline Brown, Mary Jo Arn)

Evanston, Illinois

McCormick Library of Special Collections, Northwestern University (Russell Maylone)

I am also grateful to the Interlibrary Loan and Circulation staff at Booth Library, Eastern Illinois University for their handling the enormous load of requests in support of this project over the past eight years (Sue Ebel, Christine Merllie) and to the dean of the College of Fine Arts (James K. Johnson) and the chair of the Art Department (Glenn Hild) for institutional support.

Individuals

The following people have provided either professional assistance or personal encouragement or both. Many read early drafts of the project and offered valuable comments. Others shared reminiscences of Kenneth Conant. Still others helped decipher and translate original documents or shared their photographs.

Bénédicte Berthelon, Kathryn Brush, Julie Campbell, Marie-Thérèse Camus, Marie-Thérèse Chauche, Stephen Canfield, Alice Meta Marquardt Cherry, Benjamin Marquardt Cherry, John Conant (Brother Gregory), Giles Constable, Elizabeth Emery, Stephen Eskilson, Peter Fergusson, Robert Gildea, Michelle and Jean Claude Gosse, Ara Guzelimian, Marcia Hadjimarkos, Ruth Hoberman, Dominique Iogna-Prat, Danielle Johnson, Ioli Kalavrezou, Minott Kerr, Terryl Kinder, Guy Lobrichon, Janice Mann, Pierre Martin, Max Marmor, Peter Mcphee, Christine Merllie, Lew Micklesen, Stephen Murray, Eric Palazzo, Robert Petersen, Sébastien Pisano, Nadine Roiné, Robyn Roslak, Conrad Rudolph, Donna Sadler, Elizabeth Sears and the readers for *Gesta* in 2000, Eduard Sekler, Mary Shepard, Christine Smith, Charles Sowerwine, Neil Stratford, David Walsh, Bailey Young.

Institutions

I am grateful to the following locations and/or session coordinators who allowed me to present preliminary portions of this book in the form of lectures and to the members of their learned audiences who made interesting and constructive comments:

Centre d'Etudes Supérieures Civilisation Médiévale, University of Poitiers (Eric Palazzo); L'Université d'Avignon and Le Palais des Papes, Avignon (Guy Lobrichon, Esther Moench); University of Illinois at Urbana-Champaign (Anne D. Hedeman, Karen Fresco, D. Fairchild Ruggles); The International Medieval Society, Paris (Meredith Cohen); The College Art Association (Lisa Pons and Anne-Marie Weyl Carr); Columbia University Branner Forum Lecture Series (Stephen Murray, Meredith Fluke); The International Medieval Congress at Western Michigan University (Rosemary Buck).

Preliminary portions of this work have appeared in the *Cahiers de la civilisation médiévale* (volume 48) and in the Medieval Academy of America newsletter and website. I appreciate these institutions' permission to incorporate that material into this larger study.
The Medieval Academy's name was originally spelled as "Mediaeval" and this was in effect during most of the years concerned in this study. I have kept that spelling except for references that specifically designate the current organization.

All translations are mine unless otherwise noted.

Dedications

This work is dedicated to my husband of twenty-six years, John Walter Cherry, who has been the epitome of patience and support and whose initial question in 1998 while standing at Cluny surveying the results of the 1988 nave floor excavation ("Just how DID they knock this building down, anyway?") sparked the entire investigation that led to this book.

In memory of my parents: Jacqueline Theresa (Paquin) Marquardt (1922-1996) and Wallace William Marquardt (1920-2004)

CHAPTER ONE

BACKGROUND: AN ENDING AND A BEGINNING

Tanta basilica…quam si centies videris, toties ejus majestatem obstupesces…
—Jean Mabillon on Cluny, 1682[1]

Dans ces lieux imprégnés d'histoire, la vue de telles reliques ne peut manquer de laisser une impression profonde.
—Emile Montégut, after 1840[2]

Cluny c'est ceci, et rien que ceci.
—Albert Thibaudet, 1928[3]

Imagining Space: An Introduction

The Greek temple Segesta stands stark against the sky, offering an open investigation of the outer wall construction and inner dimensions of a sacred precinct from the 5th century bce [fig. 1.1]. On first viewing, it is hard to tell whether these walls represent the demolished remains of a former complete monument or the vestiges of an unfinished project.

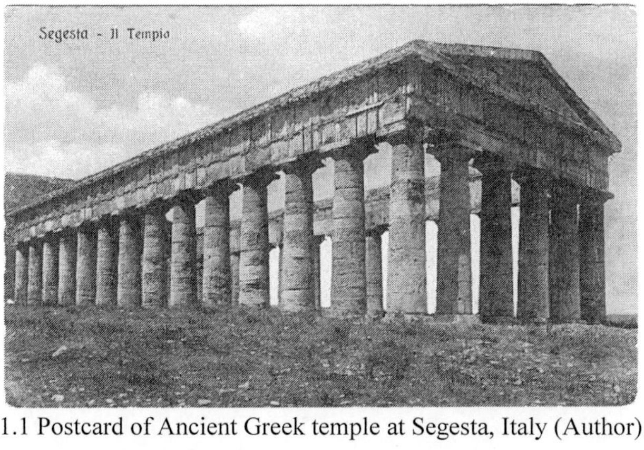

1.1 Postcard of Ancient Greek temple at Segesta, Italy (Author)

Partial buildings lead the imagination in many directions, especially after the romantic cult of ruins that swept Europe in the late eighteenth and early nineteenth centuries. Whether unfinished or unkempt, our view of them has been shaped to include nostalgia, regret, awe, and curiosity. Decaying remains of medieval architecture, once considered an annoying blight, much as we now regard deteriorating international-style concrete buildings, are recast in the light of beauty and mystery.

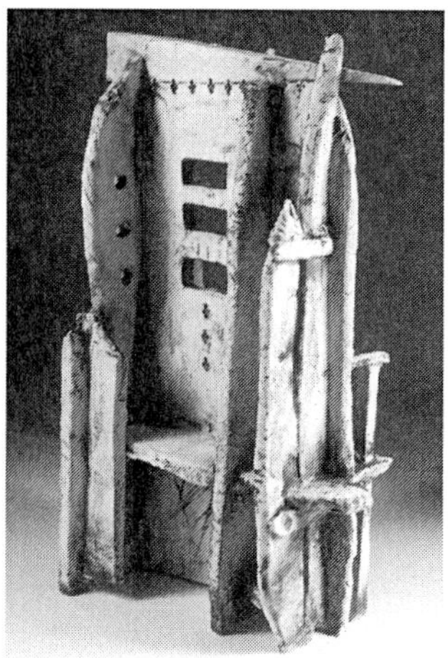

1.2 Toni Hambleton, *Spaces to Meditate In/On* (21.5" x 7" x 9"), 2001 (Toni Hambleton)

It is certainly easy to invoke these sensations; one does not need to visit a genuine Greek temple. An artwork from 2001 by ceramic artist Toni Hambleton, entitled *Spaces to Meditate In/On*, is a loose assemblage of white stoneware slabs up to two feet high in the form of walls—some have windows, doors, and gables [fig. 1.2]. As movable pieces, the little walls create new inner/outer spaces even as they suggest the history, secrets, and safety of old buildings. Both personal associations and social expectations are piqued for viewers, whose imaginations can wander between the walls like Alice through her mirror. The visual reading suggests the real experience of visiting ruins: sounds of silence, smells of decay, sensations of crumbling or coolness. Viewers increase their associations of mystery when the ruin they imagine is not from a passé ancient religion or a secular monument, but is that of a former temple, church, or monastery. The concept of sacred space is reinforced, especially for believers, and the imagined life of the building includes vague notions of symbolic furnishings, ritual movement, costume, and music.

An even deeper layer is created if the ruin is in England or France, where visitors know that many religious buildings were deliberately destroyed en masse in the sixteenth, seventeenth, and eighteenth centuries. But was the destruction of buildings so surprising? Certainly the original inhabitants of religious institutions had as actively pulled down and rebuilt buildings on their properties over the centuries past. Just as Cluny, the largest church on the European continent before the rebuilding of St. Peter's in Rome, eventually became a quarry for local builders, so too Abbot Odilo and his contemporaries had turned to Roman ruins for authentic, premium building elements in preparation for its construction.[4]

Many of the medieval monuments destroyed were as large, as ambitious, and as accomplished as architecture had been for quite a few centuries. For those who demolished them, the concept of the historic monument had not yet gained usage. These structures were still functional shelters or stages loaded with unpopular political associations. It was only in England during the eighteenth century (aftermath of the Dissolution) and France in the nineteenth century (aftermath of the Revolution) that the notion of buildings as monuments with historical value grew. The study and conservation of the outdated and/or damaged buildings began in the purview of the intelligentsia who revised stylistic prejudices and fought for recognition of regional architecture. Later, conservation and restoration moved into government politics with the rise of cultural heritage in the service of nationalism. Here the problem of the quality of intervention has been highly controversial. In the twentieth century nationalism shifted to cultural tourism and an industry developed that allowed the economic survival of numerous small communities throughout the world.[5]

Francoise Choay, in her study *The Invention of the Historic Monument (L'Allegorie du patrimoine, 1992),* makes a case for Alois Reigl's distinction between monuments (designed with a memorial purpose) and historic monuments (inadvertently memorialized by time)[6]. Yet in a way, the great church at Cluny can be seen in both roles. Cluny III began life as a monument to the success and power of the Cluniac order in the late eleventh and early twelfth centuries. Though the church was built for religious functions, it also stood as a symbol of strength, wealth, and artistic eminence [fig. 1.3]. This is especially evident when one examines the size compared to usage—it was designed to top the dimensions of the largest contemporary churches on the Continent (St. Peter's Basilica in Rome and Speyer Cathedral), a preview of the "world-record mentality" which would drive Gothic builders to ever greater heights.[7] After its near total destruction and subsequent conservation, the entire abbey but especially the fragment of the church became an historic monument, recalling the former glory of pre-Revolutionary Church and State as well as representing the Romanesque style—a style only truly appreciated in the early twentieth century with the rise of modern abstraction and minimalism.

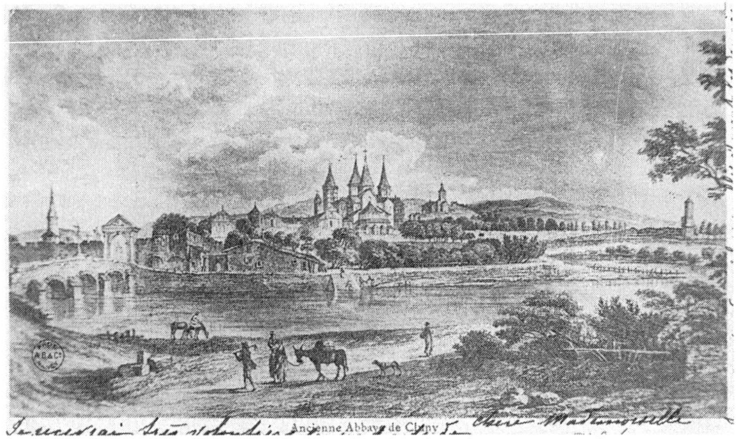

1.3 Postcard from around 1903 showing an engraving of Cluny before its destruction (Author)

In this book, I begin by outlining some of the issues that surround the study of Cluny's legacy and give a brief introduction to the abbey and its destruction from the 1790s to the early 1820s. In the second and third chapters, I explore the responses to the ruins and the initiation of conservation measures during the nineteenth century. It was in this period that the first modern histories of the institution were written. They established a "memory" of Cluny that influenced all later understandings of Cluny. Proceeding chronologically, Chapter Three ends with the first commemorative event hosted by the town, which grew out of the new historical awareness spreading across France at the end of the century. Chapter Four addresses the most elaborate of these festivals, held in 1910 to commemorate the founding of the abbey, and covers the growing scholarship on Cluny. In Chapters Five and Six, Cluny becomes the academic subject of Kenneth John Conant (1894-1984), the architect from Harvard who excavated the site and made detailed reconstructive drawings of the abbey his life work. Finally, in Chapter Seven, I summarize my observations about the construction of Cluny's past and its role as a key historic monument in French patrimony.

The destruction and subsequent conservation of the Abbey of Cluny was intrinsic to the development of the historic monument. Policies during the French Revolution removed the caretakers of the abbey thus initiating Cluny's demise. The loss of so many major monuments during and after this period engendered the creation of national awareness of the historic monument as well as desperate preservation measures. By the time the buildings came down at Cluny (1798-1824), decisions about the abbey were tangled between its role both as the ultimate symbol of repression destroyed and a place on the list of French national historic monuments. Since so much was gone, the church appeared on the list more as a token *lieu de mémoire* than a whole site and none of the government's *inspector generals* were interested in designating it for renovation or even conservation, In fact, the building was only formally declared off-limits to pilferers in 1887 when the *Monuments historiques* outlawed any modification of their classed sites.[8] Besides having little to work with, there was also little interest in the Romanesque style and even less knowledge about how to preserve such a large open relic. As Choay has written:

> It is one thing to wish to "list" monuments, and to know how to do so. To know how to conserve them physically and to restore them is another matter, which depends upon other realms of knowledge. They call for a specific praxis and specialized practitioners, the "architects of historic monuments" that it fell to the nineteenth century to invent.[9]

If one were to only *conserve* the ruin at Cluny, it would remain *heritage.*[10] It was by giving into the need to *restore* some portions of the abbey structures, as well as create a discourse about its original purpose and contemporary relevance, that it became part of national *patrimony.* Patrimony looks to the future, to the presentation of what is in-*herit*-ed from the past for national consumption.[11] Patrimony is the direct link between culture and tourism, between history and economics. The inherent changes necessary to the move from heritage to patrimony also re-imagine a site according to contemporary standards and thus change its collective memory, make it into a new monument that only remembers the past, but no longer houses it. More on this point appears in my conclusion.

Visitors feel conflicted about Cluny not only due to Revolutionary ideology or later renovation decisions, they also partake in a long tradition of aesthetic responses to the Picturesque coming out of the Romantic movement. The scars on these damaged buildings are real enough, but they also are evocative and affective. That is their attraction even as they cause *angst.* And the incomplete condition of the abbey church at Cluny lends itself to this effect better than buildings that could, and often were, renovated out of their ruined state. As I will show in the following chapters, those who studied Cluny during the nineteenth and early twentieth centuries were deeply affected by this *angst.*

Comparable to the poignant remains of other abbeys such as Jumièges or Tintern [fig. 1.4] where the essential shape remains, the fragment at Cluny is all the more evocative for the exercise it demands of the visitor to try to comprehend its original vastness. So much of the contemporary town lies within its original precinct, rather than a yawning ruin open to sky and imagination.

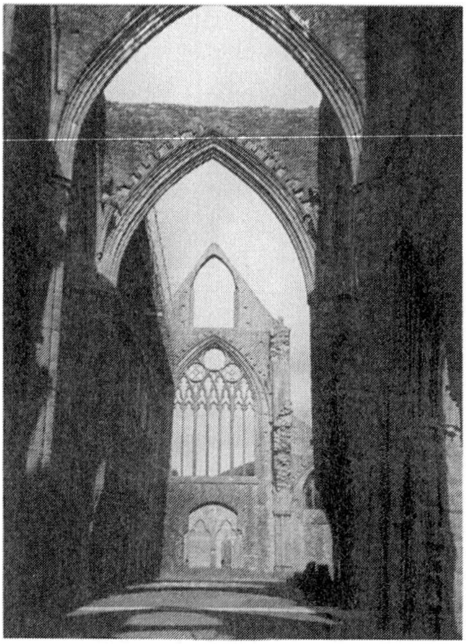

1.4 Tintern Abbey, Wales, 2001 (Author)

Cluny is a puzzle of pieces hidden within the new town which heavily markets the remains to tourists today. Although the former Romanesque abbey church is at the center of this industry, a Gothic chapel is attached and Renaissance structures serve as town hall and museum, while the eighteenth-century conventual buildings are now the *École des arts et métiers*, a national engineering school. Though the construction of these buildings may have been essential commerce for the little town when it lived in the abbey's shadow, the sumptuous late medieval palaces of the aristocratic abbots, appointed by the king and residing primarily in Paris, sharply contrasted with the humble lifestyles of the townspeople. One could easily conjure the resentment and spread of revolutionary furor suggested by Wolfgang Braunfels, who wrote in 1969:

> The townsfolk of Cluny began to break up the huge church immediately after the secularization in 1790. Their gall was roused by these witnesses to an archaic power… And though French archaeology has ever since laid stress on the grandeur of the original achievement that was so destroyed, the French public has up till now always sided with the Revolution.[12]

Braunfels was dramatic, but inaccurate. He applied unfounded Romantic notions to place blame for a destruction he mourned. In fact I will show in the second half of this chapter that the townsfolk did all they could to find a use for this giant complex of buildings in order to save the abbey from demolition. They were ultimately unsuccessful and in chapters two and three, I will describe the efforts made throughout the nineteenth century to conserve and revive interest in the ruins that remained.

These attempts concerned more than just the material condition of the remaining structures. Cluny also figured in the philosophical and political debates about the power of the Catholic Church in France. During the first half of the nineteenth century, an alliance between those who valued medieval art of the Church and those who supported the return of Christian ritual worked with historians and politicians who wanted to base the notion of a French national heritage upon an idealized Middle Ages. Later in the nineteenth century, French government politics and Church goals diverged. By the 1870s, Catholicism was embattled against Comte's positivism (personified most strongly by Jules Ferry), echoes of revolutionary dechristianizing, liberal Protestantism, and materialist or Kantian philosophy.[13] Ultramontane politicians and papal advisors instigated a revival of pilgrimage to sacred locations throughout France. They hoped to draw the French back to the Church, build resistance to the laicization campaigns of the Third Republic, and even replace the Bourbons on the throne. However, although nearby Paray-le-Monial drew vast crowds for the cult of the Sacred Heart,[14] Cluny had nothing to offer in the way of devotion. After the 1897 jubilee at Lourdes, which included pilgrimage and a festival of religious observations including elaborate processions, Cluny devised a similar event in 1898. But this was only a one-time event; the commemoration was of the creation of the Feast of All Souls by Abbot Odilo in the eleventh century. This was hardly the stuff of ongoing popular religiosity like innocent visionaries or miracle cures. In fact, everything about Cluny went against the currents of popular Catholicism in the nineteenth century. Cluny was neither a rural backwater, offering a pure and childish peasant spiritualism, nor an urbanized "religious resort" like Lourdes had become.[15] Cluny had always represented ecclesiastical power, not popular faith, so it could never be turned into a simple, pious place and the only poignant draw, casting the abbey as a "victim" of republican politics, implicated the local community and regional bishop. There was also no rich historical narrative, essential to the fate of religious sites. For a second time in her history, Cluny was unable to gain a foothold in the pilgrimage economy.[16] Never holding the major relics of a popular saint nor recording miracles on the site since the obscure tales of medieval abbots' graves, there was nothing at Cluny to inspire an outcry from Catholic believers, especially the women who made up the largest number of pilgrims, *miraculés,* and new clergy.[17]

Nevertheless, local authors wrote books on Cluny's history, trying to create a legendary presence and incorporate techniques found in Henri Lassere's wildly successful 1869 book on Lourdes such as evocative engraved illustrations and picturesque prose descriptions of the location.[18] Writers also tried to highlight use of primary historical documents, in an attempt to align themselves with positivist thinking, but they were unmasked by German scientific scholarship in the form of Ernst Sackur who, in 1892, showed the unreliability of their source cartularies and letters.[19] The town cultivated the cult of local memories, encouraged by governments throughout the nineteenth century, with ever grander commemorative events that included a historical pageant in 1910, fully documented by the popular new print medium, the postcard.

Cluny forged ahead in historical preservation during the twentieth century when Kenneth Conant's excavations for the Mediaeval Academy of America served to support his detailed reconstructive drawings. His architectural training and his vision of the medieval monastic contributions to architecture led him to produce numberless plans and elevations for churches and conventual buildings from the Early Christian Period through the Romanesque[20]. The discipline of historic monument conservation was still new and developing so that a trained architect, who was concentrating on excavation and drawn reconstruction rather than physical conservation and restoration, offered a fresh viewpoint while his Ecole de Beaux Arts-derived training at Harvard made his credentials acceptable to the French. Likewise, Conant's strong background in the history of architecture and his recent degree in the history of art gave him an edge in comparative analysis and imaginative breadth. At the same time, he returned to an earlier period's Romantic aesthetic conception of the religious past which, added to his American awe of ruins, made him venerate the fabric on which he worked more than many local practitioners.

Like the builders at the Holy Sepulchre during the Middle Ages,[21] the original stones at Cluny came to be seen as sacred relics to be conserved and then preserved—but only after its demise, not by the eighteenth-century remodeling monks. Although no additional religious building occurred in the nineteeth and twentieth centuries, the town itself grew around the fragmentary ruins like the Kariye Camii around the central Chora church or Nara around its pagoda and kondo. Conant contributed to this situation with his reverential and evocative drawings, making the parts whole again, resurrecting the buried body of the church from its stony grave.

He began his work at Cluny in 1927, at a time when the provincial landscape was strongly back in vogue as one of the results of the devastation of France during the first World War. Interest in decentralization and an appreciation of *la petite patrie* grew from what Romy Golan has characterized as the *retour à l'homme* movement between 1918 and the 1930s.[22] French painters increasingly portrayed the French landscape during this time, even moving away from some of the stronger avant-garde styles of the previous two decades towards more academic compositions. Although their works did not privilege the local ruin within that landscape, I would suggest that nevertheless the work of mid-nineteenth century artists, whose picturesque scenes of ruins were published as lithographs, underlay the reception of modern nationalist landscapes. Furthermore, beyond the general outgrowth of the maintenance work of the French historic monuments commission, the *retour à l'homme* awareness preconditioned sympathy for Conant's project. In particular, the fact that he was wounded on the battlefield in France in 1917 would have made him particularly welcome as a friend of the French countryside.

Much like the notion of France created after 1918, the third abbey church of Cluny always had to be imagined. Even when visiting in the Middle Ages, it was hard to see in its entirety all at once so that there was an element of envisioning the other parts necessary to all experiences of the building. In addition, most medievals were unable to travel to the site and resorted to the descriptions of awed visitors who waxed eloquent about its size and decoration. By the eighteenth century, the Romanesque style was often called "Greek Gothic" and its similarity to monumental classical structures stimulated other imagined comparisons.[23]

The term was not inapt. Romanesque could be called the Doric of Europe. Easily recognizable by their relative simplicity, solidity, and straightforwardness compared to later styles, neither Doric nor Romanesque is as monolithic in design as first appearances might suggest. Every building had its own problems and solutions; each application of the style was adapted and unique. One can find no "original" Greek temple with the template for all later buildings. Yet there was a conviction among early art and architectural historians that an early medieval *ur*-church existed, that one place applied the principles of Romanesque in the purest manner, forming a prototype by which both earlier and later buildings could be measured. With so little of the abbey church of Cluny remaining, it was easy for Conant to impose his dreams of finding this ideal application of Romanesque at the motherhouse of the largest monastic organization in Europe. His claims sparked debate that has kept the fragmentary ruin alive and whole in the academic mind ever since.

From Powerful Church to Plundered Ruin

Like any history of nineteenth-century France, the story of the remains of the abbey of Cluny during the nineteenth century must also begin with the first Revolution in 1789. However, although many authors have offhandedly referred to the abbey's demolition as coming during the Revolution, in fact the process was only begun with the dissolution of the monasteries and subsequent stripping of valuable materials to pay for the revolutionary wars. Auctioning of the buildings and their deliberate destruction for materials did not begin until 1798 and lasted until 1824.

Yet one could argue that the third church of the Abbey of Cluny was doomed from the start. An overly ambitious project, even as the largest basilica for the largest monastic institution in Europe was being finished in the early twelfth century, Abbot Peter the Venerable was fighting detractors and creditors.[24] The story of medieval Cluny has been told many times, but I briefly summarize the essence here for readers new to the subject.[25] Peter's famous predecessor, Abbot Hugh "the Great", had a vision, according to the chronicles a miraculous holy vision through the dream of an elderly dying monk named Gunzo, of an abbey church that would project his powerful place within the Church and European affairs. Under no Bishops or local lords, answerable only to the Pope, as abbot of Cluny for sixty years he not only controlled land holdings across much of contemporary Europe, he was a prime politician, diplomat, and advisor. He saw substantial annual gifts of gold, land, and other offerings in return for the intercessory prayer that Cluny made its primary business. If medieval society was divided, as Georges Duby has suggested, into those who worked, fought, and prayed, then the Abbot of Cluny was the European leader of the essential spiritual activity required for everlasting salvation. There was no reason to imagine this role would ever change, for who could suggest the end of heaven and hell?

So Hugh, with the help of contributors as distant and desperate as the kings of Leon and Navarre fighting the Islamic rulers of Spain, planned his enormous edifice as a new Rome dedicated to saints Peter and Paul and filled with various saints' relics distributed over twenty-five altars. Rents were collected all over Cluniac lands on their feast day, June 29. Hundreds of provincial abbots came home to the motherhouse in Burgundy on that day with stories of yet more monasteries being offered to Cluniac rule by local lords. Battles fought over key pilgrimage locations were seen as holy wars to place their revenue under the protection of the "best" Benedictine monks. The largest extension of Cluny's domain fell between the years 1080 and 1150, a time when the Church in general was benefiting from the accumulation of property donations. In addition, being untouched by the tradition to divide land among heirs, religious institutions found their domains increasing during the eleventh century as secular families' holdings weakened.

The last abbey church was begun in 1088.[26] Pope Urban II came to Cluny in 1095 to participate in the dedication ceremony of the main altar on his tour throughout France making similar dedications in other regions as he preached the first crusade.[27] The east end, the choir, was large enough to hold the entire ruling council of Cluniac abbots for meetings and services. To balance it, the nave stretched towards the west another 100 meters, making the original overall length nearly 150 meters. The nave was covered by a sophisticated form of the barrel vault, even as more complex forms of cross, groin, and rib vaulting were being fashioned elsewhere in Germany, France and Norman England. Conant suggested this was due to the fact that barrel vaulting provided the best acoustical amplification of the famed Cluniac intercessory liturgical performance, however this was only his conjecture. It also represented the architectural style these monks had been perfecting in their dependencies for over a century, a style derivative of the best structures produced by the powerful Romans, the last long-term leaders in Europe. To support the gigantic curve of the nave ceiling, the side aisles were vaulted as buttresses, comparable to the engineering of Norman churches. Sculptural decoration was minimal, carved by sculptors who worked for the order of Cluny at other building sites. The main entrance, the west portal, held a huge scene of Christ enthroned in heaven surrounded by lesser figures in its half-circle tympanum. Eight decorated capitals topped the columns which formed the outer aisle encircling the main altar at the east end of the church, called the ambulatory in pilgrimage churches for the pedestrian access it gave to the sacred relics often kept in this area. On these capitals were carved images symbolic of heaven and the sacred music of liturgical chant. Above, the half-dome in the apse was painted with a colorful fresco on the same subject as the sculpted west portal.

It was all very grand, but by the time Hugh died in 1109, trouble was already brewing for the order. Although not directed exclusively at the Cluniacs, the criticisms of Bernard of Clairvaux against monastic extravagance and the foundation of his order of austere Cistercians had begun to turn public opinion against the Benedictine order, especially the Cluniac empire.[28] The peak of Cluny's building expenses also unfortunately coincided with the effects of a European economic crisis growing during the twelfth century which hit large, landed estates the worst.[29] The story of the abbey's remaining centuries has been repeatedly told as a "decline and fall" narrative. Ultimately, everything changed. City markets were renewed and urban centers rebuilt. The Church allied with these new powers, leaving rural monasticism to its own devices. Cistercians and Franciscans preached a return to the basic precepts of poverty and charity. The king took over the selection of Cluny's abbots, gaining control of her resources for the Crown. The order was reformed more than once, and put under the control of other houses. By the end of the eighteenth century, only a handful of monks remained in the town of Cluny and most of the former treasures with monetary value were gone.

Rather than heralding an epochal revision of religion for the new Republican order, the decisions which led to the demolition of Cluny were the results of multiple directions people turned in order to adapt a difficult situation. In effect, they were facing a state comparable to short-term military rule and the war-time requisitioning of local resources. Most changes happened slowly, especially in the provinces, and decisions were exercised from a long line of government bodies. Actions varied upon the local representative's revolutionary fervor or inability to control small radical clubs.[30] In most cases, the general population was not quick to destroy its prized monuments. It remained to the later revolutions of 1830 and 1848 to see true popular uprisings across France.

The suppression of the buildings at Cluny can be cited as an example of the results of both the distant decisions of a bureaucratic government and local attempts to solve a municipal dilemma. There was never a short, fiery explosion of public vengeance against either the congregation or the structure. In fact, only one period (October 19, 28-29, and November 28, 1793) of serious vandalism occurred in Cluny—and it was by the revolutionary army—in a 30-year struggle over how to deal with this "white elephant."[31] The townspeople and local militia even increased vigilance in attempts to protect what they petitioned to become the town's largest parish church and took measures to halt the deteriorating effects of neglect and piecemeal recycling. Long after the revolutionary government had been replaced by Napoleon's reign, after the division and auction of the property in four sale lots, municipal Cluny continued to try to find viable uses for these giant buildings and legally stop new owners from destroying them.

Unfortunately, accounts of Cluny's later history contributed to a mythical polarization of clergy and townspeople. Most of these are the stories of regret published during the nineteenth century. However, twentieth-century authors carried on the tradition. Kenneth Conant repeated much of this bitterness when referring to a loss he so deplored. Louis Réau, in his exhaustive 1958 survey of "*vandalisme*" throughout the history of France, wildly condemned all destruction associated with or stemming from changes initiated during the revolution of 1789. He makes no distinction between mob activities, army detachments under orders, government appropriation of valuables, revolutionary club members' "civil" acquisitions, or sale of dangerously deteriorating structures for new functions or even for raw materials. All parties are referred to under the inflammatory terms "*sans-culottes*" or "Jacobins."[32] Even André Vauchez, writing for Pierre Nora's 1984-92 collection *Lieux de Mémoire* assigns the destruction of Cluny to the *bande noire*, a roving group of vandalizers.[33]

However, we must remember that the monks themselves had certainly not clung to their medieval past; they were the first to demolish old buildings in the ongoing spirit of renovation and expansion that had always characterized Cluny. Although Braunfels claims most remodeling work was done around 1720, as late as 1790 the monks were pursuing ongoing plans to remodel the entrance of the abbey into a monumental façade reminiscent of eighteenth-century chateaux. To accomplish this, they had purchased adjacent houses and begun a new portal between 1779 and 1784. During the years 1789-90, they constructed two symmetrical pavilions at the edge of the formal gardens.

Ultimately, plans suggest they would have replaced all the remaining abbey conventual buildings with eighteenth-century architecture matching the newer parts of the cloister area.[34] For all we know, the explosive powder they purchased for this work was stored on site and may have been the very stuff employed later by post-Revolutionary secular purchasers to level the church! To imagine that without the revolution Cluny's abbey church would still look today like the images in Kenneth Conant's reconstructive drawings is both romantic and naive. Buildings are particularly discursive sites and none more so than centers of power. How likely is it that this building would have remained Romanesque at all? It is more probable that it would have resembled the neoclassical Panthéon in Paris by 1820 or if remodeling had taken place even later, the monastery of Sainte Marie de la Tourette in nearby Lyon designed by Le Corbusier [fig. 1.5]![35]

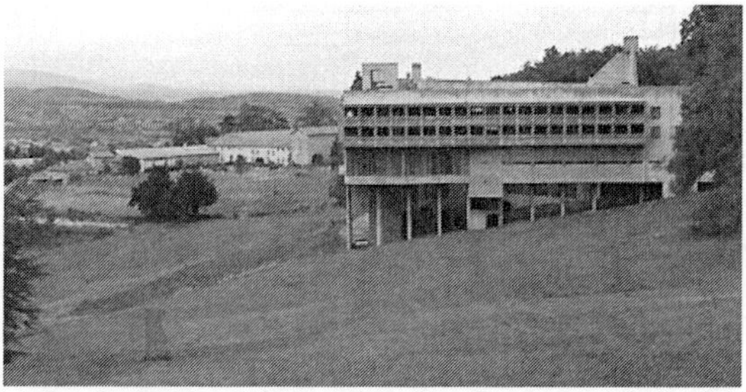

1.5 Le Corbusier, Monastery of La Tourette, 1953-1957
(Church tower visible in rear) (Simon Glynn: www.galinsky.com)

Art historical investigation has traditionally focused on disentangling the stories behind the construction of great monuments. It is the history of things appreciated, the tale of the victors, the process of creation and design that has held our attention. Thus any threat presented now or in the past to these favorite subjects is seen as barbaric. Yet equally fascinating must be the process by which precious and sacred can turn overnight into useless and expendable. This has occurred in a constant cycle throughout the history of the visual arts and, in the overall scheme of things, there have been many more monuments and artworks destroyed than saved. One imagines Walter Benjamin's "Angel of History" with all the former buildings, monuments, and artworks piling up at his feet.[36] For all the methods of digging, casting, molding, carving, painting, raising, and so on which have been perfected, there are equal techniques for filling in, melting down, breaking apart, scraping off, and knocking down. These are necessary to renewal and recycling. However, the techniques are also used by those whose motives are purely destructive. Is it really so easy to distinguish these intentions?

The most common destruction that occurred to churches during the revolution throughout France came in three phases. Initially, the new government simply needed funds; in particular to support the constitutional clergy who were now promised state salaries after the divorce from Rome. As war was declared outside France on monarchical enemies, specific materials were in high demand for armed warfare. Thus the first phase of *physical* dechristianization came in the official requisition of valuable objects in church treasuries and structural decoration such as precious metals, gemstones, and cash assets. At the same time, the ideological direction of the revolution demanded a symbolic severance from the *ancien regime* with the removal of so-called "feudal" imagery. This led to the type of physical destruction and removal that the Abbé Grégoire and subsequently the collector, Alexandre Lenoir, denounced.[37] In order to remove symbols of aristocratic and royal families, many objects were defaced or destroyed, the most famous instance being the demolition of the royal tombs in the abbey church of St. Denis. A word, which had been in some use before but which now became a contemporary catch-word rife with political baggage, was coined for this action: *vandalisme*. By making a historical reference to acts of destruction by enemies of the State, the champions of conservation pointed their finger at the royalists. They claimed that the removal of many valuable artworks, and their sale outside France, was not merely for the benefit of the revolutionary government, but, on the contrary, was also done illegally by émigrés and other counter-revolutionaries trying to get ready cash for their goods.[38]

The second phase of destruction was enacted primarily under the Terror during Year II of the Revolutionary calendar (1793). In the case of churches, it involved the entrances, usually the west facades, and easily breakable statuary and windows. It was effected by Réau's famous Jacobin mob members who belonged to revolutionary clubs and societies, or workers hired by the local *representatives en mission* of the government, or army detachments under general orders to seize valuables. The latter either got out of hand or were specifically directed to stir up a little trouble in order to remind the provincial populations of the new political climate. This was most likely the case in Cluny where both the capital of the new department, Mâcon, and the town of Cluny itself were suspected of being too moderate.[39] There are numerous examples of revolutionary destruction being limited to just this relatively cosmetic damage, such as we see at Notre-Dame and S. Germain-des-Prés in Paris, as well as the cathedrals and abbey churches in Noyon, Sens, Beaune, Vézélay, Strasbourg, Senlis, Beaune, and many others. At that point, if Christianity had been tolerated and funds available, the losses could have been easily replaced with little or no substantial permanent damage to the structures themselves.

According to Albert Soboul, there was a third and worse phase of destruction.[40] Even under Robespierre, the government had been primarily interested in stamping out visual associations with religion or feudalism and the destruction was limited to easy targets such as statues, windows, and church furniture. Under the Directory (1795-1799), however, the very property and the fabric of church foundations were sold. By this time, of course, without any clergy in residence, most of the value of this property had already been lost to the local community. Some of the buildings had been sitting unused and without maintenance long enough to severely undermine their structural integrity. Add to this the fact that most of the roofs had been removed in the initial requisitioning of valuable materials and the windows may have been broken out for their lead cames. Mortar that is exposed to wet and freezing weather deteriorates quickly and many vaults were on the verge of caving in before explosives were even applied. Yet the sheer scope of the demolition undertaken from the beginning of the Directory through Napoleon and then even under Louis XVIII belies any further attachment to the notion that revolutionary rioting and army raids did more than surface damage. No one really imagines that the Bastille was physically demolished on the same day its defenses were breached. Simon Schama tells us that the demolition of this massive structure was the effort of large masonry crews, working for over four months on the project after the events of July 14th.[41] Interestingly, for the first national "consecration" of the Bastille site, an open pavilion was built along its original contours, mimicking a gaping ruin much like Cluny's church would appear less than two decades later.[42]

In the case of Cluny, pulling down the prodigious church was a long, slow process that the town fought every step of the way. Already in 1789, when peasants ravaged nearby chateaux and were stopped by the local militia on their way towards Cluny, the municipal leaders sent a letter to the prefecture at Mâcon, asking for reinforcements in view of their greater exposure as the site of the huge abbey. Some of these "brigands," who had been imprisoned during the fighting, were tried in the narthex of the abbey church. Seven were condemned to death.[43] Similar to the situation in other nearby abbey towns, this swift reaction must be seen as an outward sign of an old partnership between the monks and the town burghers, who, in spite of their differences over the centuries, knew that the economic stability of both institutions rested upon their mutual support.[44]

Once the monastic community was dispersed by the revolutionary government during 1790-91, the abbey was left vacant. On the 5th of February, 1791, in response to government requisitioning, Cluny sent a huge chest of valuables from the abbey to Paris. Yet, in December of that same year, the commune fought the department's requisitioning of the abbey church's bells even though it did send those of the three smaller parish churches.[45] In response to ongoing government demands, an inventory was drawn up on November 15 listing the value of the remaining goods held on the abbey's grounds. From January 7, 1793, the general council of the commune (revolutionary form of the municipal council) paid for a guard at the abbey church. This was ordered with a view to protecting what was now national property, and all the valuables from the other local churches were transported here as well. Some of the debris from the destruction of the mausolea was sold as building material shortly after this.[46] The guard, named Laurent, complained to the commune of Cluny in February 1793 that he could not singlehandedly provide enough protection. In response, he was granted two assistants.

In May of 1793, the Saône-et-Loire and three neighboring departments united to resist the ideas of the radical Montagnards in the revolutionary government and to propagate federalist politics. This caused the government representative, Javogues, who was an ardent Montagnard, to visit Mâcon from Paris. As one aspect of his repressive measures against the department's rebellion, he took all the rest of the valuables in the abbey, including the remaining bells, which were yanked out of their towers at the cost of architectural decoration around the openings.[47]

Requisitions of precious materials continued to be made by the government. Thus on March 16, 1794, two local appraisers were hired to make a thorough assessment of the abbey's total value at this time. They reported back that, overall, the estate was worth 6,624,761 francs, but made a notation that this did not mean it could yield more than 100,000 to 150,000 francs if it were to be sold at that time.[48]

In June 1795, the French government granted permission for the nation to resume religious celebrations. The townspeople in Cluny petitioned for the designation of the abbey church as their largest parish church, claiming that even if the local Notre-Dame and St. Marcel were reopened (St. Mayeul had been destroyed), they would not begin to hold more than half the population (this was clearly an exaggeration of expected church attendance). On the other hand, they described the "vaste et curieux monument" at the abbey as able to contain the town's entire population 6 times and more.[49] This request was not granted, so a resident of Lyon, by the name of Gros, proposed to turn the abbey buildings into a factory to process silk,[50] but the demand for luxury textiles was down after a free trade agreement with England in 1786 and the trade blockages during the revolutionary war beginning in 1792.[51] The textile industry would continue throughout the nineteenth century, but remain in larger cities with greater workforces.

Other Lyonnais approached the municipal council in spring 1796 with plans to use the site to produce wallpaper. This idea was approved with the proviso that no structural changes be made to degrade the artistic quality of the monuments and that the buildings be purchased rather than leased.[52] Apparently these terms were too steep and the plan was never implemented. During the years 1796 and 1797, Bouché de la Bertelière, a local doctor, recorded in his journal that small sales of raw materials began.[53] The iron trellises from the vineyards, a stable, the mill, buildings whose descriptions suggest the abbot palaces of Jean de Bourbon and Jacques d'Amboise, and some land all went to private citizens.

Then Pierre Jean Guillemot, chief engineer of the Saône-et-Loire, divided the remaining abbey property into four sections for eventual sale by piercing two streets; one through the middle of the nave (north/south axis) and the other through the west end of the property up to this north/south street. The total value of the four lots was estimated at 114,313 francs, plus the value of the land and buildings taken up by the new streets.[54] The sale was held in April, 1798 with a minimum bid advertised of 85,584,82 francs. The purchasers, a group of businessmen from Mâcon, in fact won with a bid of only 2,014.000 francs and that was levied against public tax funds.[55] Margery-Melin records an undocumented oral tradition in his 1985 account that these men passed around 7000 francs worth of wine to bribe away other bidders.[56]

Thus from July 1798, dismantling of the abbey began in earnest. Some work was done by secondary purchasers of specialized materials. Other work was contracted to obtain materials that could be recycled in further sales such as roofing tiles, water pipes, wood paneling, marble slabs from the altars, or flagstone from the floor.[57] Since the completion of new thoroughfares was a condition of the sale, a private house, the abbey refectory and guesthouses as well as various smaller structures were removed to open the necessary space. The city had not put the abbey furniture in the 1798 auction. In 1799 they sold the choir stalls, prize workmanship made in 1781 and valued at 40,000 francs, to three local men—a grocer, butcher and ex-priest—for 2000 francs. These men later resold them to other religious establishments; some of the stalls are now in Lyon.[58]

Alexandre Lenoir was one of two commissioners sent down from Paris to investigate the sculptures in the mausoleum built by Cardinal Bouillon (which had also not been included in the auction sale) in August 1800. He was horrified at the condition of the abbey church and wrote back to Chaptal, the Minister of the Interior, about its importance and beauty ("le style de l'architecture est un mélange de l'art grec avec le goût arabe.")[59] He also recounted a brief history of its sale, claiming it was sold illegally and for a loan sum allotted against tax funds of 1790 which had equaled only about 50,000 francs in cash (plus the wine!) Claiming the townspeople wanted to make it into a school and would pay for repairs, he begged the minister to order an annulment of the sale and the conservation of what remained. In lieu of this, he asked that at least detailed documentation be made in the form of a ground plan and elevations of all sides appropriate for copper and marble engravings. It is unknown if Lenoir received a response. In any case, he returned to Paris with some sculptures from the tomb.

After also receiving letters from both the department préfect and the mayor of Cluny that fall, Chaptal gave the prefect authority to stop further demolition and take whatever legal proceedings against the new owners he felt were germane. The mayor communicated the order on December 22 and all work stopped for the time being.[60] The order was renewed until June 10 1801, but in the meantime the owners demanded their legal right to their property and the matter raged until the commune of Cluny finally petitioned the government to annul the sale altogether. A written statement was prepared, outlining the consequences of the destruction as well as the uses to which such a building might be put. Distracted by other problems and unclear where to find the funds to replace the vaults which had already been torn down for the new street, the government in Paris, the finance minister, and the prefect all concluded it was impossible to save the building. The new owners went ahead and completed access through the nave to the cloister area in an attempt to make the area available for commercial use.[61]

Another attempt Cluny made to save the abbey was in September of 1801, when a legal exchange of some common meadows for regained city title to part of the monastic buildings was arranged. These included the huge eighteenth-century building off the east aisle of the cloister, the inner gardens, the orchard, a terrace of chestnut trees, and all the parts of the church situated to the east of the new street that had been pierced through the nave. All of this sat untouched for many years. The community had no financial base upon which to make plans for its use.

Besides these central parts of the abbey, there were buildings that had been purchased previously. The palace of Jean de Bourbon was sold to a private individual and was eventually donated back to the city to become a museum, while the palace of Jacques d'Amboise was also resold to Cluny to become the *mairie* [fig. 1.6]. The chapel of the Virgin had been resold early on to a merchant who turned it into a profitable store. Though partially torn down in 1799, it reappears in the 1801 exchange between the town and the purchasers of the 1798 auction. Parts of the walls from the kitchen and refectory for the lay brothers remain, one arch exposed by a bomb in 1944 and the rest incorporated into modern buildings.

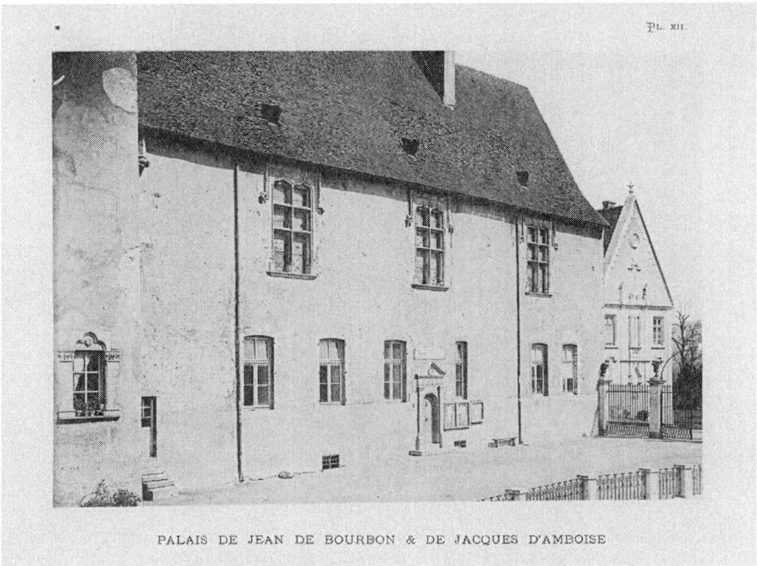

1.6 Palace of Jean de Bourbon with palace of Jacques d'Amboise in background (Ricard, *Cluny et les Environs,* plate XII)

No demolition activity is recorded between 1801 and 1808. A high school was founded in 1803 in some of the later buildings; letters from the middle of the century attest to the problems with student destruction of the remaining abbey library materials (they entered through a building with open storage stacks) and architectural sculpture.[62] In April 1808, the 1798 purchasers sold the section of the church narthex, the two western towers, the main room of the old hostelry and contiguous land to some brothers from Mâcon. On May 16, one of the original buyers was in the process of dismantling a pier further west, in the nave, when block of stone fell and killed him. The surviving owners hired Italian workers to complete the removal of the last four piers on June 7-8.[63]

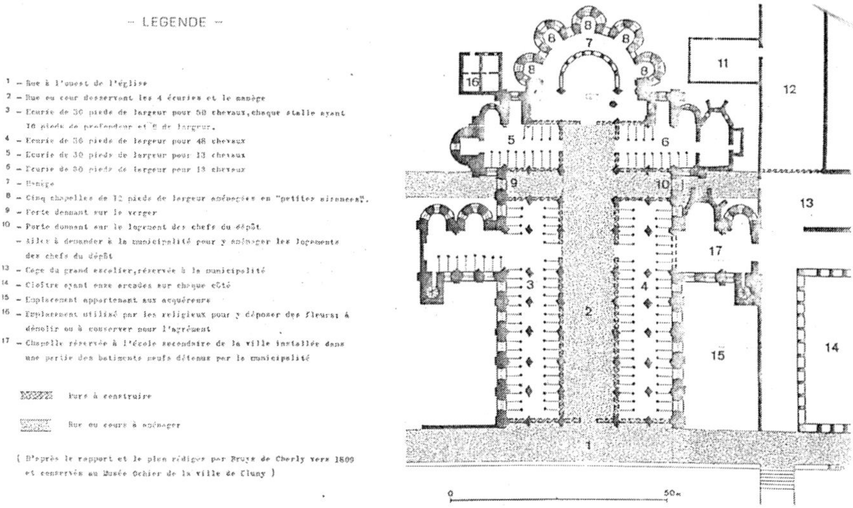

1.7 Bruys de Charly project, 1808. (Musée d'art et d'archéologie, Cluny)

Around 1805, the government and the city began to entertain ideas for Cluny to house a stable for imperial stallions. Since the only remaining stable building of the abbey was not sufficiently commodious, a number of suggestions were made for additional locations. A letter to the prefect dated November 16, 1808 details a proposal to partition the church into 124 stalls to stable stallions with an equitation ring in the apse (fig. 1.7), comparable to the way that St. Sernin at Toulouse was used by the army until 1865.[64] However, only four months later the crossing tower fell and the truly ruinous condition of the building must have become evident.[65] Nonetheless, the idea remained current with both private citizens and the city deeding over parts of the former church and gardens to the State in anticipation of an agreement. In 1811 the State set up a construction site and began to dismantle major areas of the nave for materials to reuse in the construction of stables.[66] From 1814-1817 negotiations continued, with the government putting pressure on the town to help pay for the new facility which would be an administrative center for the breeding of stallions used by the military and thus more appropriately called by its French name, *haras*, than the limited English term, stable. Cluny grumbled about the clause that required the town to clear and level the site of the former church,[67] but the city leaders knew the presence of the national stables would benefit them in the end and agreed to do all except provide the wood. The stone was easy, more than enough became available as they completed demolition of the church's east end.[68] Apparently it was unclear how much existing construction would be utilized since a petition went from the Saône-et-Loire to

Paris in February 1820 to stop destruction of the monastic buildings citing their usefulness as lodgings for the horses and employees. The final sale was dated January 21, 1822.

Part of the creaking bureaucracy of revolutionary government, subject to the whims of changing allegiances and commercial enterprise, distant from the direct supervision of Paris, the dechristianization of Cluny was effected in small doses. As Jean de Viguerie stated in 1986:

> Dechristianization was not an order coming from Paris. It was an action conducted throughout the entire country by all the revolutionary powers—the Committee on Public Safety, the Convention, the Jacobins, the "*representatives en mission*", local societies and local administrations.[69]

In spite of local attempts to protect it, there were still vigorous attacks against the abbey from its neighbors. The revolutionary army's progress south from Paris to Lyon in fall 1793, looking for pockets of "fanaticism," was pointed towards Cluny by the Mâcon *societé populaire*, some of whom joined in the action.[70] One can easily imagine some spiteful glee in Mâcon, seeing their neighbors in the former elite abbey town scrambling for cover. The huge abbey, defined by its historical relationship to the pope who was outside France, ended up dependent upon the goodwill of only a tiny, powerless, provincial town and thus was doomed to be sold from the start of the Revolution. It could not escape notice like some of its smaller, more remote, dependencies. Yet to fight back with the critical mass of opposition like Toulouse exhibited in support of S. Sernin was not feasible with such a small rural population. The abbey was too well known as a centuries-old repository of wealth and power and the long arm of the government reached down into Burgundy to lay claim to its treasure. Once emptied, the buildings themselves were so colossal, so out of proportion to the needs of the little town, it could never hope to absorb such a facility. Even the provincial seat, the city of Mâcon, though providing nearly all the purchasers and contractors, struggled with the scale of the project. None of the citizens who bought parts of the site really knew how to turn an impressive profit from them; we read over and over of buildings purchased and then left to deteriorate or bought, partially dismantled, and then resold. The population in the region was too small and predominantly agrarian to support a manufacturing facility or large commercial enterprise. Unlike Lenoir, who wanted the materials in their original condition for artistic value, these middle class businessmen, who were learning a new entrepreneurship after the Revolution, did not think like the gentrified classes and were not collecting when they went to the auctions. Rather they were looking at the entire site as a vast resource to be culled for the raw materials used in new construction, renovation, even minor repairs. Thus someone who bought twenty columns, capitals, and voussoir stones was not planning on reassembling them à la the Cloisters at New York's Metropolitan

Museum! They probably stored them in the corner of some work yard until a customer came in needing fine stonework. There is evidence all over the town of such reuse; one can find stones from the abbey everywhere from garden walls to the carved capital Conant later found holding up the grain cellar at the stables [fig. 1.8].

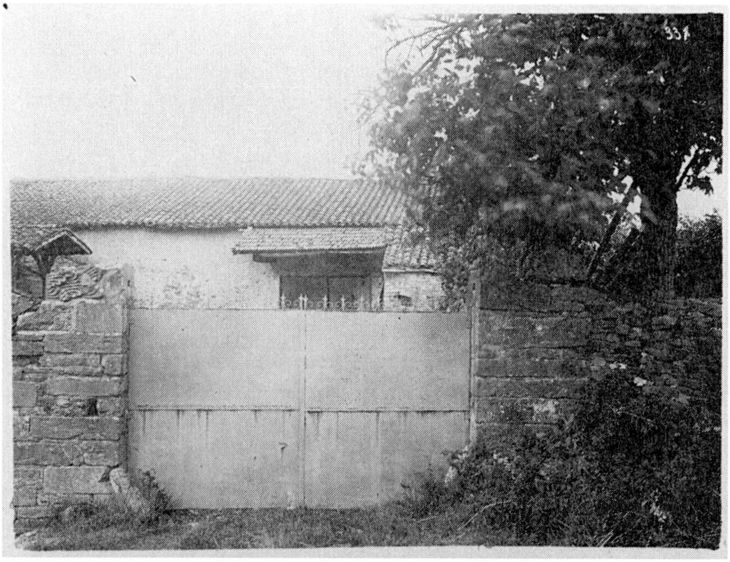

1.8 Undated photograph among Kenneth Conant's papers of carved medieval capitals reused on garden wall of local residence (Cluny Collection: Loeb Library, Harvard University)

The importance of Cluny's place within tradition, as a representative of a grandeur that had surprised so many by being vulnerable, made its end more important as a symbol than its true history in the new department of the Saône-et-Loire. The further one gets from the destruction, the more compacted the events appear, eventually all being attributed to "revolutionary" causes when in fact the revolution only began the process by removing the abbey caretakers. If not for the existence of the single transept, standing as testimony to such a loss, the historical account may have become as shadowy in time as other locations which did not survive in any part such as Arras and Cambrai cathedrals or the abbeys of Longchamp in Paris, Alet in Languedoc and Hautvilliers, Champagne.

For the contemporary French public, the Revolution has become a popular historical event and was purged of much of its horror during the nineteenth century in favor of being the origin of the nationalistic slogan "liberté, egalité, et fraternité." National patrimony grew with successive governments, both royalist and republican, as a claim to an imagined independent and accomplished French past. During the event, however, choices were not so clear and the townspeople of Cluny clung to what they had. Contrary to later myth, they did *not* begin to break up the church right away after 1790. Rather they guarded the buildings against looting. Likewise, Braunfel's suggestion of their "gall" being raised by the abbey's existence is romantic hindsight. Such Parisian revolutionary jingoism had no place in the small Burgundian town's self-image, so intimately linked with the fortunes of the much larger industry to which it was attached. Like many other dependent provincial towns, the majority of the burghers of Cluny did not join the rural revolutionary band of discontented farmers or Mâcon's urban club of political opportunists and turn on their greatest asset.

Notes

[1] [Such a great basilica…which [even] if you see it a hundred times, you will still be astounded by its grandeur every time…] Original quoted in Kenneth John Conant, *Cluny: les églises et la maison du chef d'ordre*, *Mediaeval Academy of America. Publication no. 77* (Mâcon: Impr. Protat Frères, 1968). 37

[2] [In these places impregnated with history, the view of such relics cannot fail to leave a profound impression.] From Émile Montégut, *Souvenirs de Bourgogne* and quoted in. 6

[3] [Cluny is this and nothing but this.]. 4

[4] Françoise Choay, *The Invention of the Historic Monument* (Cambridge: Cambridge University Press, 2001), 17-18.

[5] Ibid. 17-18.

[6] Ibid. 13.

[7] The phrase is from Jean Gimpel, quoted in André Vauchez, "The Cathedral," in: Pierre Nora and Lawrence D. Kritzman, *Realms of memory: rethinking the French past*, 3 vols., *European perspectives.* (New York: Columbia University Press, 1996). 49. Conrad Rudolph has pointed out that though Kenneth Conant and others have repeatedly claimed Cluny was the largest church before the rebuilding of St. Peter's in Rome, that distinction in fact belongs to Canterbury. See: "Bernard of Clairvaux's *Apologia* as a Description of Cluny and the Controversy Over Monastic Art," *Gesta* 27 (1988), 129.

[8] Choay, *The Invention of the Historic Monument*, 98.

[9] Ibid. 99.

[10] Claude-Maire Bazin, "Industrial Heritage in the Tourism Process in France," in: Marie-Françoise Lanfant et al., *International tourism: identity and change*, Sage studies in international sociology 47 (Thousand Oaks, Calif.: London: Sage Publications, 1995), 119-123.

[11] André Desvallées, "A l'origine du mot "patrimoine", in *Patrimoine et Modernité*, ed. Dominique Poulot (Paris: L'Harmattan, 1998). Desvallées discusses the problem with the English translation of the word *patrimoine* as "heritage", page 104.

[12] From the English translation. 52

[13] Jean Marie and Madeleine Rebérioux Mayeur, *The Third Republic from its origins to the Great War, 1871-1914*, trans. J.R. Foster, The Cambridge history of modern France; 4 (New York/Paris: Cambridge University Press; Maison des sciences de l'homme, 1984). 84

[14] Suzanne K. Kaufman, *Consuming visions: mass culture and the Lourdes shrine* (Ithaca, N.Y.: Cornell University Press, 2005). 12

[15] Ibid. 10-11

[16] For a discussion of the medieval struggle to control sites on the pilgrimage routes see: O. K. Werckmeister, "Cluny III and the Pilgrimage to Santiago de Compostela," *Gesta* XXVII, no. 1/2 (1988).

[17] Ruth Harris, *Lourdes: body and spirit in the secular age*, 1st American ed. (New York: Viking, 1999). Chapters 7-10; Kaufman, *Consuming visions: mass culture and the Lourdes shrine*. Introduction; Ralph Gibson, *A social history of French Catholicism, 1789-1914, Christianity and society in the modern world* (London; New York: Routledge, 1989). 104-107; Laura Morowitz and Elizabeth Emery, *Consuming the past : the medieval revival in fin-de-siècle France* (Aldershot, England; Burlington, VT: Ashgate, 2003). Chapter 6. Cluny had dozens of fragments, but could claim to hold no one large relic of a saint unavailable elsewhere.

[18] See Lorain, Cucherat, Champly, Penjon, and Chaumont in the bibliography.

[19] Ernst Sackur, *Die Cluniacenser in ihrer kirchlichen und allgemeingeschichtlichen Wirksamkeit bis zur Mitte des elften Jahrhunderts* (Darmstadt: Wissenschaftliche Buchgesellschaft [Halle an der Saale, 1892-4], 1965).

[20] See his Penguin series monograph: Kenneth John Conant, *Carolingian and Romanesque Architecture 800-1200*, ed. Nikolaus Pevsner and Judy Nairn, Second ed., *The Pelican History of Art* (Harmondsworth: Penguin, 1959; reprint, 1974).

[21] Robert Ousterhout, "Architecture as Relic and the Construction of Sanctity: The Stones of the Holy Sepulchre," *Journal of the Society of Architectural Historians* 62, no. 1 (2003).

[22] Romy Golan, *Modernity and nostalgia: art and politics in France between the wars* (New Haven: Yale University Press, 1995).

[23] Jean Nayrolles, *L'invention de l'art roman à l'époque moderne (XVIIIe-XIXe siècles), Collection "Art & société,"* (Rennes: Presses universitaires de Rennes, 2005). 66.

[24] For Cluny's finances during the construction of the third abbey church, see Georges Duby, "Le budget de l'abbaye de Cluny entre 1080 et 1155. Économie domaniale et économie monétaire (1952)," *Hommes et structures* (1973).

[25] A longer, most recent summary, can be found in Anne Baud, *Cluny, un grand chantier medieval au coeur de l'Europe*, *Espaces mediévaux* (Paris: Picard, 2003).

[26] Numbering the last church as the "third" comes from Kenneth J. Conant (*Cluny: Les églises et la maison du chef d'ordre.* Cambridge, Mass./Mediaeval Academy of America. Imprimerie Protat Frères, Mâcon, 1968) and has been rethought but the term has entered common usage. Regarding the likelihood that Conant's "Cluny I" was not a separate church, see Baud, p. 49. For general background on the history of the order of Cluny see Marcel Pacaut, *L'Ordre de Cluny: 909-1789* (Paris: Fayard, 1986).

[27] For instance, St. Martin at Tours and the abbey church of Montierneuf in Poitiers were both dedicated by Urban in 1096. See also chapter 4, note 52.

[28] Conrad Rudolph, "Bernard of Clairvaux's *Apologia* as a Description of Cluny and the Controversy Over Monastic Art," *Gesta* 27 (1988) 125-132; *The "Things of Greater Importance": Bernard of Clairvaux's* Apologia *and the Medieval Attitude Toward Art"* Philadelphia: University of Pennsylvania Press, 1990, 161ff.

[29] Noreen Hunt, *Cluny under Saint Hugh, 1049-1109*, 1st American ed. (Notre Dame, Ind.: University of Notre Dame Press, 1968). 79ff.

[30] See John Black Sirich, *The Revolutionary Committees in Departments of France 1793-1794,* New York, Howard Fertig, 1971

[31] Richard Cobb, *Les armées révolutionnaires*, vol. 2 (Paris: Mouton, 1963). 664.

[32] Réau's book was republished posthumously in augmented form in 1994. Two colleagues, Michel Fleury and Guy-Michel Leproux, added a final chapter on the "Cinquième République" which applies Réau's fanaticism from 1958 on. For example, the wonderful 1985 Daniel Buren sculpture, which decorates the courtyard of the Palais Royale in lieu of the earlier ugly carpark, is referred to as an act of vandalism by two successive ministers against the advice of the Commission supérieure des monuments historiques. Louis Réau, Michel Fleury, and Guy-Michel Leproux, *Histoire du vandalisme: les monuments détruits de l'art français*, Ed. augm./ed. (Paris: R. Laffont, 1994).

[33] Vauchez's assertion is possibly based upon a reading of Chaumont (241), who associated the men working for the Mâconnais purchasers with these *bandes noires.* André Vauchez, "The Cathedral," in *Realms of Memory: rethinking the French past*, ed. Pierra Nora and Lawrence D. Kritzman (New York: Columbia University Press, 1996). 37.

[34] Cluny, Archives municipales : "L'Abbaye de Cluny Utopie et Realité" I.3, 7

[35] Christopher M. Greene argues that the popular taste for severe neoclassicism presented the greatest threat to France's medieval national art in "Alexandre Lenoir and the Musée des monuments français during the French Revolution," *French Historical Studies* 12 (1981): 200-222

[36] Quoted in Benedict R. O'G Anderson, *Imagined communities: reflections on the origin and spread of nationalism*, Rev. and extended, 2nd ed. (London ; New York: Verso, 1991). 161-2 from Walter Benjamin, *Illuminations,* ed. Hannah Arendt (New York: Schocken Books, 1986).

[37] Gabrielle Sprigath, "Sur le vandalisme révolutionnaire," *Annales historiques de la Révolution française.* 52 (1980). 510-535

[38] Ibid.

[39] Réau, *op.cit:* 426; Bruno Marguery-Melin, *La Destruction de l'Abbaye de Cluny 1789-1823* (Cluny: Centre d'Études Clunisiennes, 1985). 28; Cobb, *Les armées révolutionnaires*.

[40] Albert Soboul, *Mouvement populaire et gouvernement révolutionnaire en l'an II (1793-1794)* ([Paris]: Flammarion, 1973).

[41] Simon Schama, *Citizens: a chronicle of the French Revolution*, 1st ed. (New York: Knopf: distributed by Random House, 1989). 412-414

[42] Richard A. Etlin, *Symbolic Space: French Enlightenment Architecture and Its Legacy* (Chicago and London: University of Chicago Press, 1994). 38

[43] Marguery-Melin, *La Destruction de l'Abbaye de Cluny 1789-1823*. 14-15. This small book gives the most complete account of the abbey's destruction. Marguery-Melin goes

into detail that I have found unnecessary for my purposes here but which coordinates more source material and is highly recommended.

[44] The monks themselves were quick to recognize the gravity of the situation that had arisen in Paris. Only two weeks after the fall of the Bastille, on July 28, 1789, the Chapter met and drew up a preemptive offer they made to the municipal council the next day which granted the townspeople greater access to abbey land resources (Cluny, Archives municipales: BB 6 and 7; Philibert Bouché de la Bertelière, "Description historique et chronologique de la ville, abbaye et banlieue de Cluny," (1787-1817). Cluny, Archives municipales: VII, 46-57; also covered in Marguery-Melin, *La Destruction de l'Abbaye de Cluny 1789-1823*. 10-12.

[45] Th. Chavot, "Destruction de l'église de l'abbaye de Cluny," *Annales de l'Academie de Mâcon* (1869). 291

[46]:Marguery-Melin, *La Destruction de l'Abbaye de Cluny 1789-1823*. 25-27

[47] Cluny, Archives municipales: 69 Série M10.

[48] The monetary values assigned here are taken from Marguery-Melin. He believed that this appraisal proves the government's intention to sell the building rather than lease it, as was more common, in spite of the city's attempts to save it (29-31).

[49] Cluny, Archives municipales: D1

[50] Proposal dated 3 Juin 1809, Cluny, Archives municipales: P8 Série 37.

[51] Peter McPhee, *A social history of France 1780-1880*, Routledge social history of the modern world (London; New York: Routledge, 1992). 55

[52] Cluny, Archives municipales: P8 Serie 37, *Extrait des pieces deposée...Deyrieu frères*...The fact that this plan was never carried out contrasts significantly with the abbey of Fontenay which was actually saved by leasing for a paper factory.

[53] Bouché de la Bertelière, "Description historique". I, 264.

[54] Cluny, Archives municipales: 152, M1

[55] Dom G. Charvin, "La fin de l'Ordre de Cluny (1789-1791)," *Revue Mabillon* 40 (1950).

[56] Marguery-Melin, *La Destruction de l'Abbaye de Cluny 1789-1823*. 36

[57] Ibid. 39-40

[58] Chavot, "Destruction de l'église de l'abbaye de Cluny." 293

[59] K. Conant, *Cluny: les églises et la maison du chef d'Ordre*, Mâcon: Imprimerie Protat Frères (Mediaeval Academy of America), 1968, 11-12. For a complete list of the objects Lenoir conserved in Paris see: Alexandre Lenoir, *Description historique et chronologique des monumens de sculpture réunis au musée des monumens français*. Paris, 1806. The process by which France came to do this is outlined by Emmet Kennedy, *A Cultural History of the French Revolution*. New Haven: Yale UP, 1989 (chapter VIII) and the contradictions inherent in it are discussed by Stanley J. Idzerda, "Iconoclasm during the French Revolution," *American Historical Review* 60 (1954) 13-26.

[60] Chavot, "Destruction de l'église de l'abbaye de Cluny." 294

[61] L. Chaumont, *Histoire de Cluny depuis les origines jusqu'à la ruine de l'Abbaye* (Paris, 1911). 242-3

[62] Cluny, Archives municipales: L11, Série 1

[63] Marguery-Melin, *La Destruction de l'Abbaye de Cluny 1789-1823*. 56-57

[64] Cluny, Archives municipales M.44, letter from Bruys de Charly "...pour donner au local du dêpot d'Étalons à Cluny l'accroissement qui lui convient pour rendre cette etablissement vaste commode et compter...nous avons regretté si souvent d'être arrivé trop tard dans ce département pour le conservation entier du plus beau monuments de Saone et Loire, que vous ne vous refuserez pas..." Mérimée describes the 500 horses housed in St. Sernin in a letter to Ludovic Vitet from 1845, quoted in: Christian Amalvi, *Le goût du moyen age*, Civilisation et mentalités (Paris: Plon, 1996). 147-148.
[65] Lorain, writing in 1839, stated that there were those in Cluny who still remembered the horrible noise that shook the town when the tower fell: "...l'on souvient encore à Cluny de l'effroyable bruit qui secoua la ville à la chute de la plus grande tour." Prosper Lorain, *Histoire de l'Abbaye de Cluny depuis sa fondation jusqu'à sa destruction à l'époque de la Révolution française* (Paris: Sagnier et Bray, 1845). 278.
[66] *Guide pratique de Cluny:* Cluny Office de Tourisme, 1998; Marguery-Melin, *La Destruction de l'Abbaye de Cluny 1789-1823*. 61, 63, 66, photos in appendix.
[67] Cluny, Archives municipales: D6
[68] Chaumont dramatically points to the sacrilegious irony of building walls for stables out of stones from the church, *Histoire,* 242 (1): "On dit qu'elles furent employées pour les toits du grand bâtiment des haras qui fut élevé précisément sur la place de la grande nef et dont les murs ont été édifiés avec les pierres de l'église!"
[69] "La déchristianisation n'est pas un ordre venu de Paris. C'est un action conduit dans tout le pays par tous les pouvoirs révolutionnaires, le Comité de Salut Public, la Convention, les Jacobins, les représentatives en mission, les sociétés populaires locales, les administrations locales." Jean de Viguerie, *Christianisme et Révolution.* Nouvelles Editions Latines:, Paris, 1986: 152 (He also makes the interesting suggestion on this page that of all the steps towards the secularisation of the French religion, it was the change of the calendar which initiated the greatest impact.)
[70] R. Cobb, Ibid.

CHAPTER TWO

CLUNY IN THE NINETEENTH CENTURY I (1800-1848)

> The eighteenth century was the age of criticism and of destructions; the nineteenth century must be the age of intelligent rehabilitations.
> —Victor Cousin, 1817[1]

> It is then the work of imagination and reason to reconstruct the demolished edifice, to resuscitate the being destroyed by the scientific scalpel. But it is absolutely necessary to pass through this process of dissection: such are the demands made by the weakness of the human mind.
> —François Guizot, 1829-32[2]

> Nous ne sommes plus ici dans l'histoire médiévale, et la seule image de vie perçue est une image archétypale de l'histoire construite en fait au XIXe siècle.
> —Arlette Farge, 1997[3]

Cluny could not become an historical monument until the generation that remembered its unbroken and overpowering presence—threatening, decadent, or simply venerable—had passed to one for which the ruins were poignant, romantic, and powerless. As Roland Barthes wrote in 1980: "History does not exist until one observes it, and to observe it, one has to be excluded from it."[4] The past recalled by each historical monument may not always be one that contemporaries are ready to remember, or collective memory may need to adjust that past to fit current needs. Certainly the years of the Terror must have made sentimental retention of old buildings seem meaningless—even more so than the books and art advocated by Abbé Grégoire—as over 200,000 people died in civil fighting and that many again outside the country in the ongoing war. Even Grégoire, with his colleague the Abbé Sieyès, advocated regeneration rather than rehabilitation which would not help the case for ruins.[5] More war and the invention of empire during the Napoleonic years also precluded concern for the recently rejected past. Yet the revolution had piqued interest in defining a national patrimony, especially when defense of historical records and precious works of art were threatened by destruction.

The first appearance of a shift in perception at Cluny comes in 1813 from Alphonse de Lamartine, a local noble who visited the partially demolished and decaying site and was moved to write poetry upon it (*Sur les Ruines de Cluny*) He was both young and aristocratic, so revolutionary readings of the abbey as oppressor were not his concern. He was also among the first wave of French Romantics, regarding the past with nostalgia. However, he did not see the *ancien régime* as a prescription for future government as did many of his generation. In fact, Lamartine later briefly served as a minister in the Second Republic, championing the rights of the working class. He was also one of the generation that would rewrite the history of the Revolution, offering an alternative to the Restoration's horror tale of Robespierre with one of justification for 1789 and an emphasis on the reformulation of ideals in 1792 after compromises with the king had failed.[6]

The dozens of plans formulated in Paris for republican monuments to the new France were designed as alternatives to the old symbols of power. Thus the idea of Cluny being a national treasure was slow to gain currency, too slow in fact as we have seen, since by the time real interest in preserving the site had grown, the buildings had been sold for materials that the new owners were removing even as awakened authorities tried to stop them. Cluny was only one example of the curious concurrence that took place during these years when revolutionary fervor to erase the monuments of former powers met head-on with rising awareness of the artistic patrimony being destroyed. Although many other church lands had been sold after November 1790 to try to balance the national budget, as shown in chapter one, throughout the 1790s the government sought uses for the buildings at Cluny and only upon failing to secure a commercial contract began to sell off them off to individuals in 1798.

Repair work at Cluny began in 1821 as the municipal council reacted to final demolitions on the church during 1818-1819. Neil Stratford corrects the record on this chronology, redating interpretations of a lithograph showing the apse being pulled down with 1823 written on it.[7] The city paid to have some repairs made to the "only tower which remains from the Abbey, as well as a few extant walls and vaults."[8] However, it is still true that even as their interest in saving some of the abbey structures was building, the site for the stables was still being cleared and stones from the church piled up for the new construction.

Stratford has also recently uncovered documents in the municipal archives at Cluny which show little known work done early on. According to his research, the department chief engineer, Francois Vaillant, took a plan of action for Cluny to Paris on behalf of the city council at the end of 1821. This resulted in Cluny receiving government funds for repairs to the large transept and its tower in 1823 and 1825. The radiating apse chapel was conserved, the transept turned into a functioning chapel for a local secondary school (collège) now using the eighteenth-century cloister buildings, and a partition wall was erected on the open north side of the transept to protect it. Meanwhile the mayor of Cluny (Furtin) ordered work already in 1820 on the Bourbon Chapel and was in correspondence with the prefect to try to get Vaillant to add it to his work plan. This came to fruition in 1825 when Charles X's Minister of the Interior approved such an allocation of resources. Work on the Bourbon Chapel was carried out between 1826-1827 when the prefect released funds for this purpose. Vaillant renewed his requests in 1832, now to Louis-Philippe's government.

Although the town leaders in Cluny began considering conservation of the remaining south transept tower during the 1820s, the official national motivation to reevaluate aristocratic and religious architecture only arose with the generation that came into power under Louis-Philippe after the 1830 revolution. Using the notion of national treasures to build patriotism, sites that would have been targets of the early republicans were now passive carriers of artistic accomplishments rather than symbols of the abuses of the First and Second Estates. This government was filled with men too young to have been involved in the political upheavals of the first revolution yet who considered it their birthright and fought for bourgeois control against regained noble privileges under the Bourbon rulers. A similar class battle occurred within the Church; the Restoration meant both rechristianization and a need for new clergy at all levels. The rather heavy-handed reassertions of clerical power were short-lived and associated with the royal agenda, however, so popular opposition to the Church does not seem to have extended to the physical centers of religious activity unlike 1789-1795. Under the Restoration and July Monarchy governments, monuments associated with the ruling class were no longer anathema and it was finally conceivable to identify and restore them as symbols of French power.

This generation of leaders, which included historians and artists such as Victor Hugo, Eugène Delacroix, Prosper Mérimée, and Jules Michelet (who was the first to write a history of France using primary source material) was faced with a legacy of historical monuments in ruinous condition while no great replacements had ever materialized. Although Catholic writers as early as Chateaubriand in 1802 (*Génie du christianisme*) and later Montalembert (*Lettre sur le vandalisme en France*, 1833) called for the preservation of churches by making an association between sacred architecture and an idealized medieval Church, it was Victor Hugo who offered an opportunity to whitewash these associations with a secular fantasy, championing Notre-Dame in Paris as a living document of history rather than a symbol of the alliance between king and bishop.[9] In particular, Hugo's claim that the cathedral could be read as a democratic stone book preserving French history would have appealed to people in small towns like Cluny, which had lost prestige with the demise of "their" abbey. It was during this time that we see the first constructive approach to French patrimony and Cluny's downward spiral is reversed. The central government's interest in the site would begin slowly but continue to grow throughout the nineteenth and twentieth centuries.

Hugo and Chateaubriand were not alone and it was not only statesmen in Paris who wanted to recover France's historical identity. As Stéphane Gerson has shown so comprehensively in his study *The Pride of Place: Local Memories and Political Culture in Nineteenth-Century France*, they were part of a larger movement to redefine the nation's patrimony (after the disruption of the Revolution) that was equally intense at the local level.[10] A sentimental attachment to the provincial *pays* and its history in a distant and rose-colored past arose after 1820 with an intense interest in "scientific" studies on every aspect of local culture. Certainly these investigations were encouraged by government initiatives such as the Commission des Travaux Historiques, but they also gave local elites a sense of ownership.

The difference between Cluny and many of the towns that Gerson studied in the Nord, however, is important. Unlike cities whose histories included secular relationships with the government and the growth of commerce and independence during and after the Middle Ages, Cluny was in the central zone of France that did not flourish agriculturally or commercially in the twelfth and thirteenth centuries and its economy remained associated with the abbey.[11] The town had grown only in relationship to the service it provided the larger institution and once the Revolution had removed this *raison d'être*, it had little to celebrate from its history that fit post-revolutionary France. In other words, while other cities, such as those Gerson cites in the Nord like Cambrai or Valenciennes or even further south, Poitiers or Montfauçon, could stage historical festivals commemorating the Middle Ages as the crucible of bourgeois self-government or the cradle of celebrities from all walks of life who had contributed to the greatness of the nation-state, Cluny had only its claim as the home of Lamartine and the painter Pierre-Paul Prud'hon.

Gerson's archival research reinforces my own observations that serve as the starting point for this study; the government-sponsored examination and compilation of historical artifacts within a general interest for the Middle Ages as an ideal past and the fresh view of ruins as attractive and liminal sites. His ideas regarding historical spectacles and literary pursuits will inform elements of Cluny's modern development in later chapters as well. In addition, I see a neoclassical foundation to the nineteenth-century fascination with open ruins like Cluny, resting in the power of architecture to evoke paradoxes, which Richard Etlin describes as "the space of absence."[12] This carried over into early nineteenth-century projects such as Alexandre Lenoir's Elysium Garden in his Musée des Monuments Français, the original site of his tomb for Helöise and Abélard [fig. 1].[13]

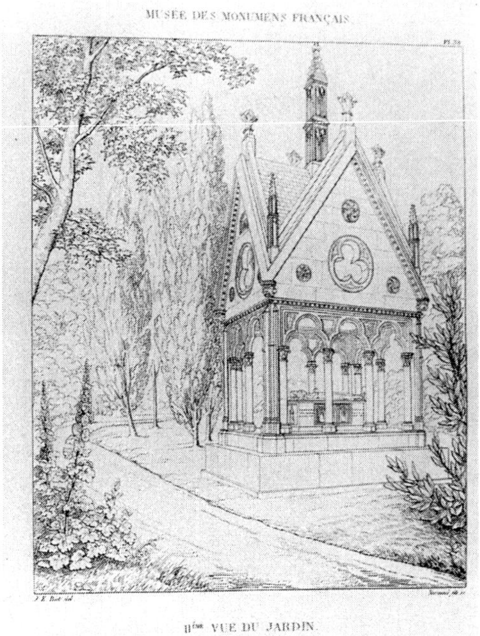

2.1 Alexandre Lenoir (designer), Tomb of Abélard and Héloïse in the *Jardin Élysée* of Lenoir's Musée des monuments français. From J.-E. Biet and J.-P. Brès, *Souvenirs du musée des monumens français* (Paris: l'auteur et al., 1821, pl. 38)

It is important to closely examine this rise of the "picturesque" in nineteenth-century thought, since it plays a seminal role in the development of tourism and heritage management—encompassing both conservation and restoration. Looking specifically at France, one of the earliest and most important manifestations is the twenty-three volumes published from 1818 to 1878 under the direction of Isidore-Justin-Séverin Taylor entitled *Voyages pittoresques et romantiques dans l'ancienne France.*[14] This work encapsulates contemporary assessments of medieval architecture as repositories of sensory impressions and, in a staggering number of lithographs of drawings by Émile Sagot, documents scenes of "old" structures in such a way as to encourage appreciation and conservation. The work clearly references earlier volumes by Lamy published under the name *Voyage pittoresque en France* from 1787 but Taylor's additional use of the adjectives "romantique" and "ancienne" are significant for a work begun only 21 years later. Lamy's first volume was on Burgundy (in turn based upon Mabillon's *Voyage in Bourgogne* from 1682) and included two engravings of the undamaged abbey of Cluny after sketches by Lallemand.[15]

There are seven images of Cluny, including three of the former abbey, in volume nine of Taylor's work, which he produced in partnership with Charles Nodier. This volume introduces the Burgundian region to readers with evocative words of the wide ranging styles of the remaining buildings, as well as harsh condemnations of those who destroyed others (whether in the religious wars of the seventeenth century or the more recent Revolution):

> [The abbey church at Cluny] formed the most picturesque and imposing ensemble. The immense buildings of the monastery and its church, one of the most magnificent in the Christian world, were slowly torn down between 1791 and 1811, under the hammer of modern iconoclasts who took nearly twenty years to accomplish this work of destruction. All that remains of the abbey basilica is a portion of the side aisle surmounted by a bell tower, some sculptural debris, sections of columns and a fifteenth-century chapel built by the abbot Jean de Bourbon. Besides these desolate ruins, whose appearance inspires a profound sense of sadness, the city of Cluny also includes two parish churches, the oldest constructed in 1159 and dedicated to Saint Marcel, which is not without interest.[16]

One scene is taken from the south edge of town, at the top of the hill (today rue de la Barre [fig. 2.2]) where parts of the outer wall still stand, across the view of the parish church, Notre-Dame de Cluny, and the Tour des Fromages to the remaining transept towers with the Tour Ronde barely visible behind [fig. 2.3].

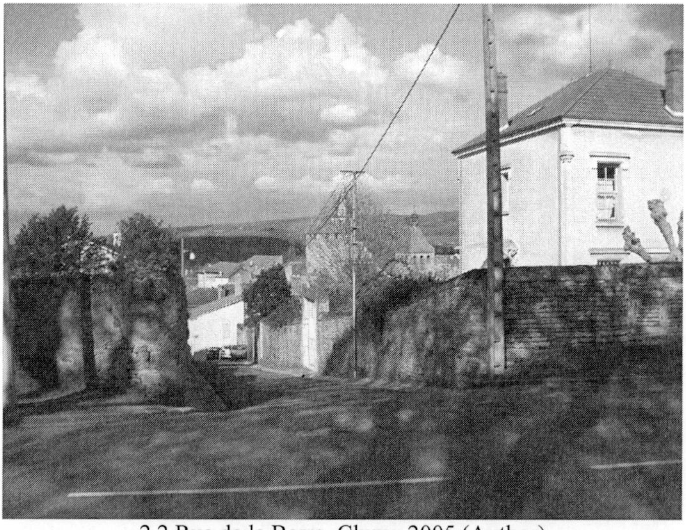

2.2 Rue de la Barre, Cluny, 2005 (Author)

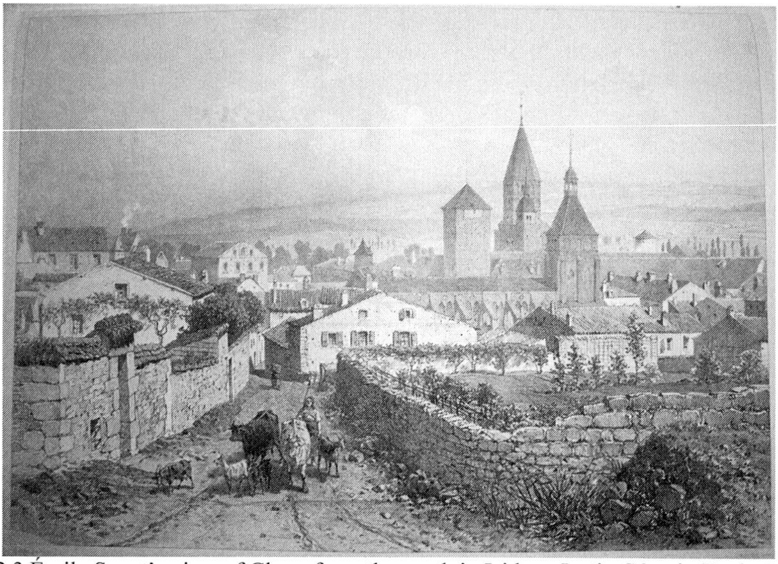

2.3 Émile Sagot's view of Cluny from the south in Isidore-Justin-Séverin Taylor's *Voyages pittoresques et romantiques dans l'ancienne France* vol. 7 (McCormick Library of Special Collections, Northwestern University)

The effect is of a grouping of Romanesque buildings, suggesting an impression of the original complex. The picturesque aspect is underlined by chimneys spiraling smoke against the distant hills and billowing clouds, by a woman herding cows and goats up the street towards us in the foreground, by the espaliers decorating visible walls, and by artfully arranged rubble. A closer view of the abbey church remains is framed by the left side of the northern arch from the west entrance, again artfully softened with plant material and people milling in the road [fig. 2.4].

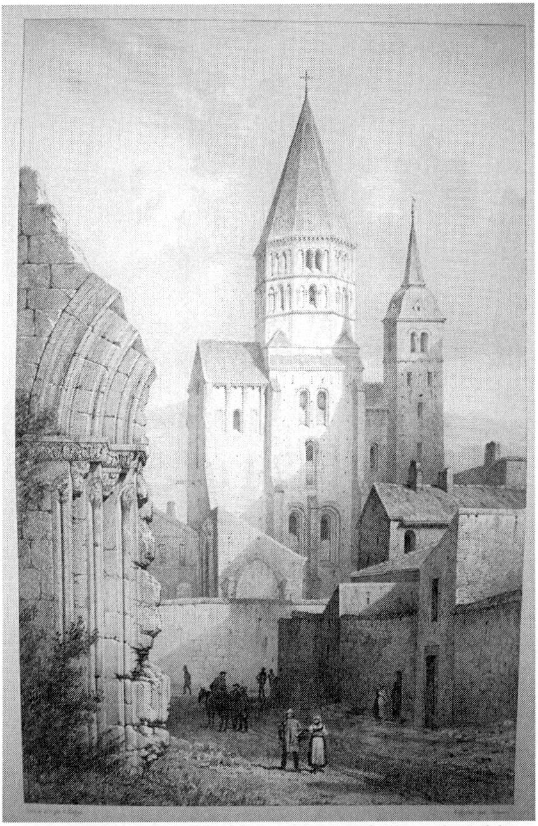

2.4 Émile Sagot's view of the ruined abbey church of Cluny in Isidore-Justin-Séverin Taylor's *Voyages pittoresques et romantiques dans l'ancienne France* vol. 7 (McCormick Library of Special Collections, Northwestern University)

Little deterioration of the roofs or stones of the exterior transept is visible which is bright against grey clouds and sharply lit from the south so as to create a pattern duplicating the form of the small tower on the larger one. Artistic license must account for the similarly located shadow on the small tower and lower walls, since nothing tall was near enough to cast it.

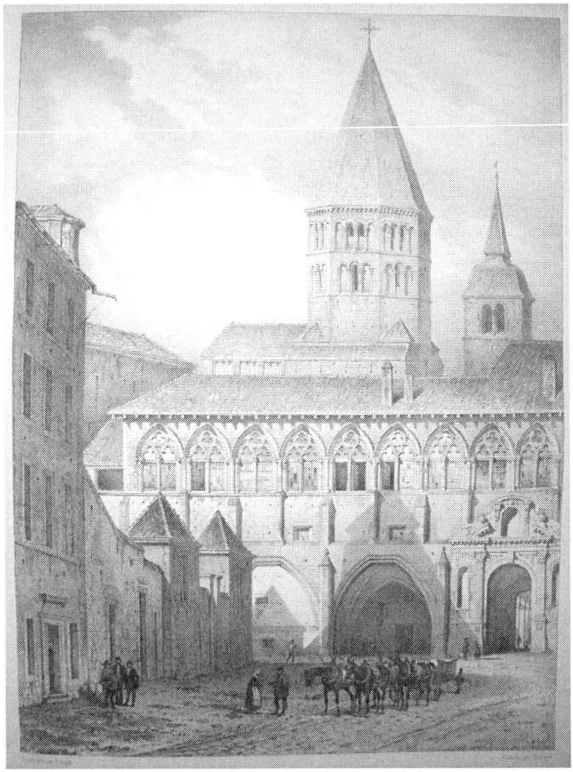

2.5 Émile Sagot's view of the so-called façade of Pope Gelasius at the Abbey of Cluny in Isidore-Justin-Séverin Taylor's *Voyages pittoresques et romantiques dans l'ancienne France* vol. 7 (McCormick Library of Special Collections, Northwestern University)

The third view of the abbey represents a building that has been greatly modified. It is the façade of the late medieval "palace of Pope Gelasius" with its famous upper row of Gothic windows and Baroque entryway [fig. 2.5]. Now the lighting comes from the west, allowing the old "stable of St. Hugh" to cast a shadow on the lower façade as well as the people and team of horses in the courtyard. The most dramatic sky of the series sets off the two transept towers looming in the background. Other images of Cluny include the interior of Notre-Dame, the exterior of S. Marcel and two views of streets with Romanesque houses. Volume nine also includes a large collection of scenes of Paray-le-Monial with reference to its new role as a small sample of the original appearance of Cluny III.

Volume nine thus reflected the contemporary concerns of the government's "Bureau of Historic Works" in urging readers, which would have been the elite and governmental subscribers, to appreciate their architectural patrimony. It opened with a straightforward manifesto:

> Beautiful and noble province of Burgundy, which held such a brilliant and dramatic place in our history, your monuments added to your glory, hardly spoiled by a few ruins. It is perhaps you who has suffered the most from our devastating passions. God grant that the misfortunes of the past be but lessons for your children so that they save the final archeological joys that you possess! These magnificent remains contribute not only to your celebrity but also to that of all France.[17]

Susan Stewart, in her semiotic study of art and narrative entitled *On Longing*, reminds us that the picturesque was the "domestication" of the "sublime."[18] The concept of the sublime in architecture was developed by Edmund Burke in the middle of the eighteenth century as different from "beautiful" because it was astonishing, terrifying, vast, difficult to realize, and magnificent.[19] The sublime was associated with pain whereas the beautiful with pleasure. For early eighteenth-century viewers, Cluny had always been vast, astonishing, difficult to construct, magnificent, and associated with the terrifying power of the Church.

Taylor uses Sagot's images to "tame" this perception and to change Cluny into the harmonic and user-friendly nature of the picturesque. The remaining fragments of the abbey are treated as "souvenirs" of the past, or what Stewart calls "traces of authentic experience."[20] The creation of narratives makes souvenirs carry our desire for the past. "The souvenir is by definition always incomplete," writes Stewart, referring to its abstract reference to lost events and its fragmentary state, a condition which demands narrative discourse from the viewer.[21] In this case, the transept arm stands as a metonymic prompt for the entire church building, the abbey complex, the Cluniac community, the Benedictine order, monastic life, medieval piety, even feudal organization of society. It serves to engender the medieval past in a way that even Pre-Raphaelite paintings or modern performances of Gregorian Chant can never do, for it is a relic, it had a real place in the past; we simply did not experience it ourselves. We need a way in, a way to "see" it whole again, up and running in its original setting. Stewart defines the souvenir replica in a way that the preserved heritage site also serves: "It will not function without the supplementary narrative discourse that both attaches it to its origins and creates a myth with regard to those origins."[22] Or, as Françoise Choay put it: "The very essence of the monument lies in its relationship to lived time and to memory, in other words, in its anthropological function." Robert Gildea agrees in *The Past in French History* (1994): "What matters is myth, not in the sense of fiction, but in the sense of a construction of the past elaborated by a political community for its own ends."

Sagot's views give us a picturesque narrative by softening the ruins, cleaning up the rough parts, adding simple people and plant material, lighting the stones and beautifying the skies. The narrative text accompanying the images made the ruins into poignant victims, rather than terrifying monumental symbols of oppression. The sublime was reduced from public and vast to private and fragile. Taylor's Burgundy is, like the imagined medieval past, a conceptual region which its inhabitants have slowly defined out of natural boundaries and political traditions.[23] This province is not the medieval kingdom or dukedom of Burgundy, nor are its four *départements* (Yonne, Côte d'Or, Saône-et-Loire, and Nièvre) exactly the same as those before the 1789 revolutionary government redrew the map of France. Taylor was working with a new set of borders and his book helped define cultural and architectural signs that would unify the area's identity and create a communal past. The descriptive voyage was a popular writing conceit.[24] Another writer, Jean-Baptiste Bouché, also published a *Voyage en Bourgogne* in 1845 with an entire chapter on his "ville natale" [birth city] of Cluny (no illustrations).[25] His tone of historical reverie is comparable to that of Taylor, including detailed depictions of powerful abbots and of rich treasures lost since the Revolution.[26]

Finding a national architectural style for France was not self-evident. Writers at the turn of the nineteenth century struggled to separate the medieval edifices they saw around them from the assumed superiority of Classical and Italian design. Like many others, J.-C. Huet, writing in 1809, imagined a judicious fusion of "Catholic" styles (the many "Gothic" forms of medieval churches) and the Antique. For instance, he wrote:

> But will one always think it impossible to reconcile the knowledge of the gothic builder with the spirit of the Greek architect? … If one took the trouble to study these bold monuments, wholly worthy of their object perhaps by mixing with the delicious conceptions of the Greeks some ideas that belong to the gothic constructions, one would arrive at creating a genre of architecture particularly appropriate for Christian temples: and is it not true that by diversely combining the Greek orders, the Romans managed to give their monuments a type of characteristic physiognomy? Why will we not have the same ambition? Is it necessary to always languish in the same routine, and will we still remain for a long time Greeks or Romans when we are French?[27]

When Alexandre Lenoir visited Cluny in 1800, he wrote a persuasive letter to the government calling for conservation measures. Possibly to raise the importance of the church building in the eyes of First Consul Napoléon's Mediterranean successes, he describes the style as a "mélange of Greek art and Arab taste,"[28] using the exotic East to qualify the types of "Gothic" style represented there. The designation of the Romanesque style ("roman(e)") only came into usage in France in 1818 and was popularized by de Caumont during the second quarter of the century.[29] So Lenoir was making a distinction between the rounded arches of the twelfth-century buildings (what he terms "Greek", meaning Byzantine, something he later changes in his compilation of these letters and calls "Lombard")[30] and the pointed design of such later additions as the Bourbon Chapel or abbots' palaces ("Arab").[31] In fact, as Mary Shepard will show in her forthcoming book on Lenoir, the synonymous use of "Arab" and "Gothic" for Lenoir was closely interwoven with his Masonic beliefs and, thus, an origin in the East –specifically coming from Syria under the aegis of Louis IX.[32] That same year, Napoléon had reportedly made the connection himself when visiting the Musée des monumens français. Later, Bonaparte would compare his forays into the east with both army and artists to those of the saintly crusading king. Lenoir also made a point of saying that the Cluny abbey church was as grand as anything of the Greeks but built by the French—his classic justification for keeping religious and aristocratic monuments as historical achievements

The function of the picturesque can be traced to multiple sources—certainly there was the aforementioned desire among early nineteenth-century artists to rescue the great monuments falling down around them, but the movement also encapsulated a morality similar to the Protestant ethic in the Lowlands during the seventeenth century with the striking visual evidence of mortality. Ruins could be beautiful but their Romantic attraction was the poignancy in their reminder of decay and death.

> Beyond the very immediate and pure pleasure it offered, the picturesque image could also give rise to that feeling of anxiety or angst that the Romantic soul reveled in when it transformed the traces left by time on human constructions into scars of stigmata.[33]

Cluny was in many ways the perfect candidate for the picturesque moral; ruined by both human hands and the passage of time, there was a mixture of styles from many ages as well as the desolation involved in the persecution of the original inhabitants. As I mentioned in my Introduction, the fact that Cluny III did not remain whole, in fact was too fragmentary to suffer modern attempts at rebuilding, gives it an emotional impact still experienced by today's visitors. The Romantic movement initiated the conflict that tourists, particularly French, confront at sites like Cluny. Aesthetic and technological awe, replete with regret for the demolition, is difficult to reconcile with popular nationalism, so heavily based upon French pride for their collective memory of the Revolution bringing democracy to Europe. Thus the remaining transept functions as a religious and political relic both for the Catholic *Ancien Régime* and the secular cult of France's artistic heritage. As such this architectural arm can be related to the qualities Cynthia Hahn has suggested for the precious arm reliquaries of the medieval relic cult where the part is more powerful because of its evocation of the saint's whole body, whether in historical life or in heavenly glory.[34] It was consecrated through veneration; a state to which Cluny moved as the ruin was classed by the Monuments Historiques and then marketed as a tourist destination. Likewise, Linda Nochlin has spoken to the increased imagery of body fragments in the nineteenth century as a form of modern "signals of destruction of an unjust past,"[35] applicable to the role of Cluny's transept arm for the post-Revolutionary period in France.

Finally, the picturesque movement has also been attributed to reactions against industrialism, articulated by Hugo and Balzac as the threat of industry destroying art (Hugos' famous chapter 2 of Book 5 "This will kill that" [Ceci tuera cela] in *Notre-Dame de Paris* epitomizes this fear). This is not to say that this generation was against modernity—quite the opposite. But they wanted to include a conservation of the past in their ideal of history as progress. This conception of history was in direct opposition to that of *Ultra* and legitimist conservatives for whom the past was a prescription of a static social organization to which France was bound to return.[36]

A member of the group of this generation of educated bourgeois who became liberal historians and politicians, François Guizot also wanted to reclaim the French past from the conservatives and reconcile both the order of the Middle Ages and the tension over the two revolutions of 1789 and 1793, His powerful educational and political positions would allow him to implement many of his ideas.[37] Along with Augustin Thierry, Guizot believed in freedom under an ordered government and regretted the excesses of the Terror. This allowed an appreciation for the progressive events between 1789 and 1793 while restoring the importance of the artistic heritage to French national culture. Liberals linked themselves to the moderate Revolution, to the Girondists who had fallen under the oppressive acts of the Jacobins (Guizot's father was guillotined when he was six years old.)[38] Like these people, the monuments from the past were seen as victims whose destruction was not essential to the principles of the new political order. Both Thierry and Guizot turned to archives which the Enlightenment scholars had ignored.[39] Their rescue of French history from royalist dynastic accounts began a type of critical thinking which launched Michelet's opus, *Histoire de France* (1831).

Guizot's history lectures at the Sorbonne were well attended and he was called the most important historian of France by Sainte-Beuve[40] and, more recently, Larry Siedentop, in his introduction to the Penguin edition of Guizot's *History of Civilization in Europe,* concludes that he was a key influence on Tocqueville, Karl Marx and John Stuart Mill.[41] During the July Monarchy (1830-1848), Guizot became an important politician and his role in the creation of a national identity for the country benefited from his study of English government, his collection of old legal documents, and his association with writers and artists. Architecture encapsulated his preoccupations with the rise of European civilization and his conviction that France was the best representative. Unlike earlier appreciation of Antique architecture for the formal models it presented to practicing architects, the rising interest in the Gothic that Guizot and his friends supported was based upon its sensory evocation of the Middle Ages. Ceri Crossley has made a distinction between the first group of Romantic historians and this later, better known one.[42] The former turned to the Middle Ages as a time of perfect religious harmony and feudal hierarchy. Many were legitimists, for whom the Gothic period represented a royal ideal to which France should look to resolve its contemporary conflicts. Later liberals, such as Guizot, used the idea of repeating history to soften the aberration of the Revolution but asserted that the Middle Ages were not idyllic. In fact, spokesmen like Trognon attacked the Romantic writers for clouding the truths of history.[43] First Thierry and then Ludovic Vitet and Viollet-le-Duc developed the stance that it was in the twelfth century that townspeople began agitating for communes and struggling against Church oppression and feudal bondage.[44] Rather than hoping to negate the effects of the Revolution, Guizot wanted to keep middle-class rights which he saw as merely regained during the struggle. (Victor Cousin held that the sixteenth, seventeenth, and eighteenth centuries of French history only served to undo the society built in the Middle Ages.)[45] If Guizot could help form a representative government sustained by a higher moral law, he felt he could help generate a society whose individual freedoms were protected by central authority.[46]

From this basis came Guizot's interest in identifying and protecting the national architectural patrimony as a symbol of social accomplishment and an ideal order from the historical past. Rather than the results of individual men, monuments from the Middle Ages were particularly easy to attribute to society at large since they were rarely signed or finished in a single building campaign. Undocumented, the working processes and artistic conceptions of medieval artisans could be regenerated to fit a new conception of history where the individual and the sensory responses of the audience were paramount, rather than the programmatic ideological messages of the patrons or celebrants. This allowed nineteenth-century viewers to imagine experiencing responses similar to their ancestors and to see those very ancestors as contributors to the development of historical change.

Guizot served as Minister of Education, Foreign Minister, and finally, Prime Minister for Louis-Philippe. As an historian turned statesman, Guizot wanted to use the past in service of the "new France". He imagined a society able to appreciate its recent Revolutionary past as progress toward basic individual rights held up by a constitutional monarchy. Nationalistic pride of heritage would be engendered by restored medieval and Renaissance monuments of France's heyday.[47] Under Guizot, the government formed committees of historians, artists, and writers to evaluate the artistic detritus left after Revolutionary and Napoleonic neglect. As a Protestant, he believed in a morality which transcended both king and popular sovereignty and which could best be effected by a representative government of intelligent men whose recognition of divine will directed their actions. The ultimate result would be an ordered society led by a privileged group of lawmakers.[48] Since it was the inner reality of individuals, their collective spirituality that made up a principled society, the Church no longer had a place in this system so the associations of the Catholic oppressors with religious monuments was now irrelevant. (Montalembert was meanwhile carrying on an active literary campaign to keep the religious association but idealize it for a new spirituality).[49] Instead, these monuments represented the achievements of the talented French people; their commerce and industry which first appeared in the twelfth century to begin the bourgeoisie's progress towards emancipation. This opened up a new interpretation of colossal projects like Cluny III. Rather than reading the building as a statement of the political power and religious authority of the Benedictine order, Guizot would encourage the French to see it as an example of the artistic skills and engineering superiority of their ambitious twelfth-century ancestors. This Protestant's ability to distance himself from the enemy Catholic Church as well as from the excesses of the Terror which took his own father, show us how time had served to smooth over the sharp edges of the Revolution for the "generation of 1820."[50]

The creation of the post of a general inspector of historic monuments (*Inspecteur général des monuments historiques*) in 1830 was part of Guizot's attempt to restructure the past for a collective sense of national history. For one thing, it allowed the regions to rediscover their local attractions without conflicting with the notion of a national culture.[51] The government could work with prefects and mayors to bring French heritage under state control at the same time as bestowing state funds in a way that would build political support for the July monarchy. Guizot's younger colleague, Ludovic Vitet, first held the position. Vitet was also an aristocratic intellectual from this generation of 1820 who had worked on the influential liberal newspaper, the *Globe* with Guizot. He was a vibrant Romantic writer, eventually elected to the Académie Française due to his dramatic representations of historical events and was credited by Alexander Dumas with influencing the literary renaissance of 1830.[52] His interest in historical monuments was thus less scientific than literary, although he was only twenty-eight at the time of his appointment so the post helped form his professional direction, eventually leading to further political appointments (in 1834 to the Chamber of Deputies and to the Council of State in 1836). Like Guizot, Vitet became a lifelong supporter of the Orléans family after this formational period under the July Monarchy and denounced the 1848 Revolution. His work as inspector general led to the formation of the

Commission of Historic Monuments (*Commission des Monuments historiques*) in 1837.

The story of the Monuments historiques has been critically chronicled by both Françoise Choay in *L'Allegorie du patrimoine* (1992) and Kevin Murphy in his 2000 publication: *Memory and Modernity.*[53] Murphy stresses the shift between seeing a monument as a functional building used in the present to its becoming a precious relic from the past. As Choay also shows, the term "historic monument" denotes a break in time periods. Historians of this generation of 1820 such as Guizot used it as part of their vocabulary to demarcate the post-Revolutionary, industrialized period as "modern". Everything that had come before was now historical, and part of the past that they could use to construct their new France. Already Aubin-Louis Millin, one of the first to use the term "monument historique" already in 1790, petitioned the prefect on October 25, 1811 to save the apse fresco in Cluny III for posterity.[54] Murphy also quotes a ministerial bulletin from 1837 that makes this separation of time periods clear;

> …the devotion to those memories associated with the arts or with the annals of the country is unfortunately too neglected in the departments . . . all of these memories, all of these living remains *at a time that is no longer*, belong to the national patrimony and to the intellectual treasury of France [my italics].[55]

Dominique Poulot underlines the importance of Guizot's conception, which "established a national legitimacy for conservation."[56]

It is not necessary here to tell the entire story of the development of the Commission of Historic Monuments again, however, it is important to understand how a government body charged with finding and conserving the important historical monuments in France, could list and then ignore something as significant as the largest and most important abbey in the history of the country. What exactly was the focus of the heritage program of the July Monarchy?

Since the Revolution, committees overseeing the arts and monuments were put under the aegis of the Minister of Education and linked to the nation's patrimony.[57] Under the Bourbons, an initial link between politics and historic monuments was made with the linking of the term 'restoration' (monarchy and buildings.)[58] However, it was only with the programs of the moderate government of Louis-Philippe and Guizot that real progress was made. Funds were allocated toward the maintenance of initial sites. The inspector general was assisted by a group formed in 1834 under Guizot as Minister of Education called the "Comité des travaux historiques", which was responsible for inventorying all types of historical works, including documents relating to French history.

Yet business was not easily carried out. Between 1830 and 1840 there were fifteen different ministers and their cabinets, while elections were constantly necessary to replace parliaments that did not last.[59] With so many changes of government, political intrigue and instability were rampant. Political parties were fluid and fragmented, coalitions formed and dissolved. It is actually amazing that anything constructive got accomplished during these years.

The official creation of the Commission of Historic Monuments, headed by the Minister of the Interior and targeting physical monuments, was made in August 1837, four months after Guizot had resigned in protest from the government then in power. Nonetheless, the philosophy behind the Commission is still Guizot's: France's physical heritage would move from local curiosities to national treasures and support an interpretation of the history of France as that of the most highly cultured nation in Europe. The members of the commission demonstrated a strong desire to centralize control of national patrimony and to lift the treatment of historical artifacts out of the plethora of methods practiced in the provinces. As a result, from the beginning, there was tension between local historical preservation societies and the roving government inspectors. Although everyone wanted government funding to save monuments, both sides suspected the knowledge and intentions of the other.[60] The task was enormous and exhausting. Vitet only lasted four years and his successor, Prosper Mérimée, was sustained by his close friendship with the indefatigable architect, Viollet-le-Duc.

The Commission of Historic Monuments was directed by men who distrusted both the Church and the provinces and thus sought to remove architectural monuments from their control. As mentioned above, Guizot himself was a Protestant and other important men in the formation of these policies included Mérimée and Viollet-le-Duc, both cosmopolitan Parisians educated with a healthy disdain for naïve religious sentiments.[61] Another anti-clericalist, Victor Hugo, not only published *Notre Dame de Paris,* he also took direct action in essays such as "Guerre aux démolisseurs!" pamphlets which appeared in 1825 and 1832.[62] The Catholic comte de Montalembert took up Hugo's crusade in print as well, adding a more conservative voice to the cause but also specifically targeting provincial municipalities for their role in vandalizing historic property.[63]

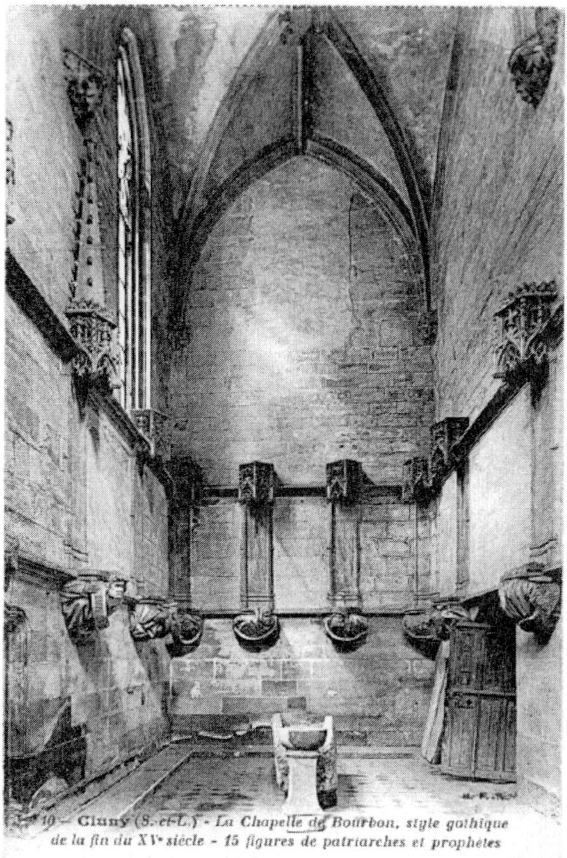

2.6 Postcard of Bourbon Chapel, Cluny. (Sébastien Pisano)

The Bourbon Chapel was of the most interest to both local and early inspectors of historic monuments because it was both intact and of the Gothic style [fig. 2.6]. Since sculptural fragments were being stored in there as well (first mentioned by Mérimée in 1834), it seemed to represent an early sort of museum for abbey remains and later was officially designated as such. In 1837, the year of the formation of the Commission of Historic Monuments, we find Louis Ochier—a local doctor who inherited, and whose widow will later leave to the town, important buildings from the abbey—writing to Mérimée and Vitet for their help in securing the support of the Minister of the Interior for its further restoration.

Cluny had its share of other supporters, who wrote passionate accounts of Cluny's legacy with dramatic portrayals of the abbey's demise under the

Revolution providing a castigating theme. In 1839, the first edition of Prosper Lorain's *Essai historique sur l'Abbaye de Cluny* came out.[64] It was reprinted in 1845 as *Histoire de l'Abbaye de Cluny.*[65] This is the first published work of substantial length on the history of the abbey after the Revolution.[66] The Introduction to the first edition is over forty pages of polemic against the new France of the generation of 1820. Lorain was concerned about the leveling effect of the national unification being undertaken during the July Monarchy. He wanted to preserve the rich cultures of the provinces with their special languages, customs, and folklore. He described the dangers of equalizing all the parts of France into a common patrimony:

> I do not wish to offend, but I believe that it is not merely a matter of true liberty, of real representative government, in these narrow ideas which leave nothing in the wake of legal expansion that compresses and does not budge, paralyzing more than stimulating, impoverishing the entire circumference without enriching the center, and making all of France the capital—a capital of a single location to which all ambitions aspire, asserting themselves, mocking themselves, overturning themselves, at the risk of constantly applauding this tightly condensed governmental power; so that the provinces burn out and die without energy, without hope, living by imitation and loan, becoming stars in a firmament growing more and more similar, continually losing the taste and ambition of beautiful and good things such as literature, science, and arts; sleeping without dignity in moral turpitude, and surrendering periodically to the sins of Babylon the few souls of the elite who can only doze off in an existence without food or purpose.[67]

He compared nationalizing to the policies of the Roman Empire and warned against falling into the same demise, a downfall toward which he saw the current governmental policies heading. He asked:

> Is there a cure for this sickness in the future of our representative government?[68]

Lorain claimed that outside of a few curious and sad souls who loved to dig around in the debris of the past, the remains of strong and beautiful institutions that once covered French territory were lost to memory: "The spirit of the masses is separated from our national memories by a thousand years."[69] *Essai historique sur l'Abbaye de Cluny* was an attempt to begin studies of important features of the past poorly known in his day. As a Burgundian, he naturally commenced with the ruins in which he had played as a child; those of the abbey of Cluny. A poetic description of the wreckage began his justification of the topic, which turns into a lament for the destruction of both the physical site and the chronicles of the institution. Claiming no one "in this century of forgetting"[70] had any interest in the history of a place that had been effaced only twenty years before, he compared the abbey to the exiled Bourbons "...already killed in the heart and memory of the new generation…"[71] He saw his study of this single important abbey standing for the sad destiny of all French monasteries after 1789, grand Catholic institutions which had played such an important role in Christian civilization—a remark pointed toward Guizot and other Protestant administrators. He reminds the reader that without the "poor monks" the historical accounts of many centuries would not exist, as well as the progress of agriculture, the achievements of architecture and fine arts, the conservation of antique books, the model for communal living, and so on.

The first edition of Lorain's text was a much richer publication than the second. Leather bound, it included fine lithographs by Émile Sagot of the abbey before its demolition. Though similar locations, these are not the same images that were included in Taylor's *Voyages Pittoresques.*[72] The lavish frontispiece, also by Sagot, set the expansive mood of Lorain's undertaking [fig. 2.7]. Within a romantic and elaborately carved tripled-arched architectural frame, complete with Gothic turrets, flags, and crenellations suggesting defensive city walls, Sagot placed a view from the east end of the intact basilica behind statues of the Madonna with saints Peter and Paul to either side. Below them are the emblem of the city and the Latin phrase: SUM QUOD ERAM NEC ERÃ QUOD SUM NUNC DICOR UTRUMQUE ("I am [not] what I was nor was I what I am, now they say I am both"). Weeds grow out of cracks in the stone base and vines wind up the columns of the frame, much like Sagot had used plant material to soften ruins for the views published in Taylor's *Voyages*. Thus before even opening the first page of Lorain's text, the reader understood that this was going to be a paean to Cluny's past. Lorain was the dean of the faculty at Dijon and the first edition was published there. The second, reduced quality edition, was published in Paris six years later. It does not include any of the illustrations and the text was reset to fit more words on each page, shortening the overall work by 68 pages.

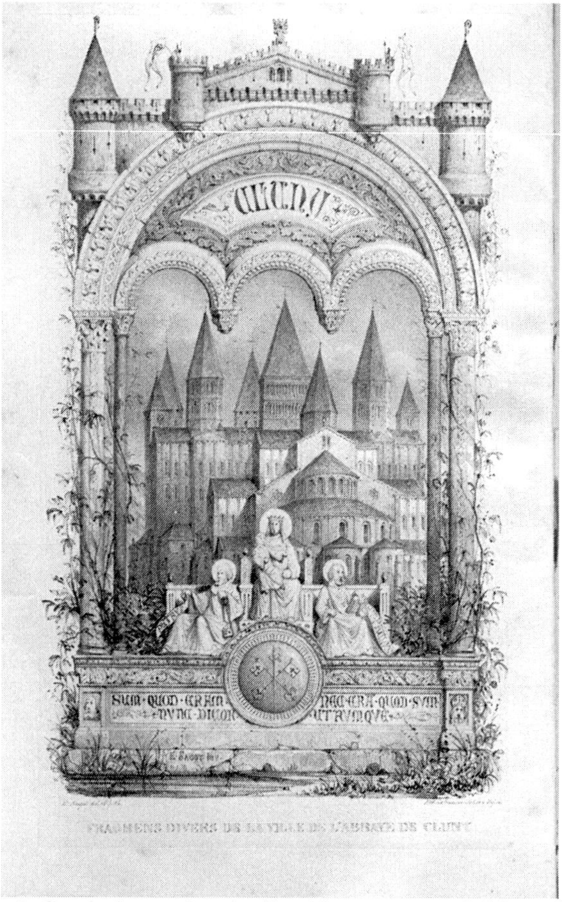

2.7 Émile Sagot's frontispiece to Lorain, *Essai historique sur l'Abbaye de Cluny,* 1839

Lorain's study reaches back to the foundation of the abbey and recounts all the highlights of Cluny's history, then surveys its decline. The writing is flamboyant, histrionic, and filled with colorful metaphors. He quotes dedicated monastic administrators, such as Bernard of Clairvaux and Peter the Venerable, at length to prove that they were aware of the pitfalls of the rich and splendid monastic life but could eloquently combat them from within the system. Lorain is oratorical and persuasive, championing the cause of religious monuments throughout France but personally dedicated to reclaiming the lost history of his beloved local ruin. He qualifies his approach with a disclaimer from the beginning, telling the reader that although he had the advantage of remaining source material at Cluny, he was not going to use citations, that specialists could easily verify his statements for themselves. Rather he was simply following the lead of the great scholar, Montalembert, and felt that this was an opportune time to bring out a study of the greatest Benedictine monastery in history when the monks at Solesmes were just beginning their renewal of monastic life.

In fact, since Lorain's book would become the model for nineteenth- and early twentieth-century histories of Cluny, it is important to recognize that he was following an historiographic model already established in the late seventeenth and early eighteenth centuries by Luc d'Achery (with the publication of Ulrich's eleventh-century customary in 1661), Jean Mabillon (1691), and his followers Jean Hermant (1710) and Pierre Hélyot (1718).[73] In essence, the general assessment of the abbots and their contributions, the role of the abbey in European society, and the decisions about what periods to emphasize and which to ignore from the institution's history all come from these initial sources. The dedication of an entire chapter to a description of Abbot Hugh's church follows the model of Michel Félibien on Saint-Denis.[74] Lorain also provided a tenor of dismay and regret for the post-revolutionary period that will be conveyed nearly unchanged by later authors. It is uncanny to see, via Lorain, some of the same statements made in the early eighteenth century still echoing in presentations during the Congrès held at Cluny's millennial commemoration in 1910 (see chapter 4).

Other lithographs reproduced in Lorain's text are illustrations of Cluny's most picturesque sites, as he tied into this aspect of attracting sympathy for his subject. Many of the same locations reappear that were in Taylor's work, yet these are different scenes that Sagot made of Cluny. For instance, we see another version of the façade of Pope Gelasius, another view of the remaining transept towers, another S. Marcel. The final image is of some medieval houses [fig. 2.8]. In the *Voyages pittoresques*, there were two scenes, both showing timber roofs covered with tile and cobblestone streets. This version is less refined, showing wood and straw roofs and a dirt street. One wonders if Lorain preferred the rougher, older look to fit his contrast between neoclassical architecture of the recent past and the authentic medieval period of Cluny.

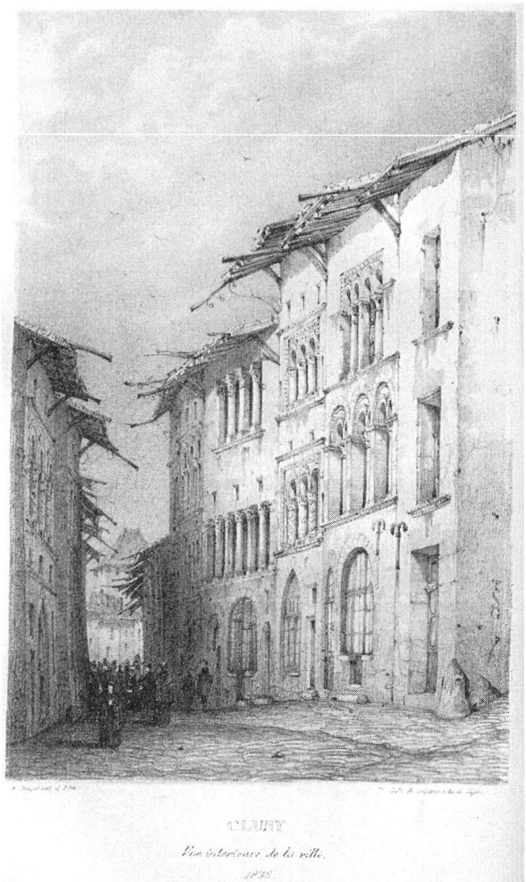

2.8 Émile Sagot's 1838 illustration of Cluny's medieval houses in Lorain, *Essai historique sur l'Abbaye de Cluny,* 1839

In the final chapters, Lorain records the last years of Cluny's history, blaming its degeneration on the rapacious policies of the monarchy under Richelieu and Mazarin, working hand in hand with the papacy. The richness of the abbey was reduced to a source of income for clerical administrators who resided in Paris and the monastic observance was put under the congregation of St. Maur. Although construction was undertaken in the eighteenth century, Lorain is dismissive of its value: "…grands, vastes, mais sans caractère architectural, sans mérite artistique."[75] He is critical of the last abbot, cardinal Dominique de la Rochefoucauld, but he rather ironically cites his visits to the abbey as the final period of happiness for the little city.

Lorain reminds us that most of Cluny's valuables had already been sold during the period from the thirteenth to the sixteenth centuries to keep the abbots in fine living and the buildings maintained. What was left disappeared in the wars of religion so that only "la moins précieuse et la plus moderne"[76] were left in 1789. This will be one of the few points that is not followed by later authors, who want to blame the Revolution for everything. He cites inventories from the fourteenth and sixteenth centuries to list just what riches Cluny had lost from her spectacular history, blaming the mismanagement of the abbots and speaking of the institution overall as a sort of passive victim. He describes how he imagines the monastic residents to have been (as opposed to the administrators living decadently in Paris):

> There are no longer the thin and pale figures of austere monks, roaming their cloister, passing their lives in the service of the poor and God, singing day and night the praises of the Lord, kneeling at the foot of altars; there are no more holy souls purified by mortifying the flesh, uplifted by contemplative meditations, knowing nothing of the noise and dissoluteness of the world, and serving as models of Christian piety, even like the Ark of the Covenant between earth and heaven.[77]

This is the romantic imagination writing; this is the Middle Ages which the nineteenth century wished to reclaim and the benevolent local Catholic clergy wanted to believe they had lost. This sort of image would serve to repopulate the monastery in visitors' minds through the nineteenth and twentieth centuries. Lorain's description of the years of Revolutionary demolition, although replete with facts which correspond to those in the aforementioned journal kept by a local elite named Philibert Bouché de la Bertelière,[78] is the partisan and condemnatory grand finale he has been building towards all along, throwing about terms like "stupides iconoclastes", "aussi ignorante que barbare". He is the first historian of Cluny to publish the legend of Napoléon replying to a request to visit Cluny with "You have allowed the sale and destruction of your huge and beautiful church, go away, you are Vandals, I'm not going to visit Cluny."[79] He bitterly reports that the remaining tower and chapel were kept only because they threatened the stability of adjacent buildings and that the only imperial benefit Cluny saw was the establishment of Napoléon's departmental stud-farm "less as consolation for the splendors lost as due to the abundance of good quality fodder on the prairies of the Grosne."[80] He bemoaned the industrial age and left the ruins of Cluny to the contemplation of scholars.[81]

Théodore Chavot, a member of the Academy of Mâcon who wrote his own version of the story of the destruction of Cluny, took issue at an Academy meeting with Lorain's account. His critique was published in the proceedings of 1869.[82] He felt that he had to address "a number of errors" in Lorain's text, especially his accusations against the city inhabitants that they only made verbal protests when in fact Chavot said that they had written numerous documents to try to save the abbey, which were preserved. He graciously attributed Lorain's indictments to legitimate regrets but faults him for not consulting original sources. Chavot corrected the record regarding the attempts by the City Council to find a use for the site and to stop demolition. Ultimately he calls for his audience to recognize that both Napoléon and Lorain did a great injustice by blaming the commune in this matter and to realize that only through local efforts was the abbey saved from being a *complete* ruin.

In spite of all the vacillations of governmental policies, the members of Guizot's Commission on Historic Monuments did their jobs. By 1840, Guizot was back in power, this time as Prime Minister. He now had the opportunity to oversee the implementation of his policies regarding historical monuments in specific restoration projects such as that at Vézelay, begun by Viollet-le-Duc in 1840 and renewed after a review by Mérimée in 1842.[83] Although Mérimée had visited Cluny in 1834, he was most impressed with what he called the"sixteenth-century cloister" by then ringed with shops and cafés.[84] This dating was perhaps due to the view of the Baroque façade inserted into the so-called Palace of Pope Gelasius from the fourteenth century. Cluny did not present an ideal work site to Guizot or the commission, since there was no complete monument that could be restored as evidence of healthy national patrimony. Thus only small stopgap measures continued to be funded, some locally and some by the government, for a few thousand francs every two to three years—one of the largest allotments being 8000 francs from 1823 to 1825.[85] Since the initial allotment for the restoration at Vézelay was 40,000 francs, it is clear that Cluny was not of primary interest to Paris.

Guizot's government came under increasing criticism, earning a reputation for the Orleanists as philistines, protestant atheists, and upper-bourgeois plutocrats.[86] Guizot's foreign policy as Prime Minister matches his earlier interest in building unified French patriotism, but he also stood as a pacifist which angered many investors and imperialists who did not wish the country to appear soft on the European stage. Tocqueville was thinking about France's affairs outside the country, not her heritage management inside, when he wrote against the Orleanist "ruin of national honor."[87] Thus the programs of the Commission of Historic Monuments from the 1830s, though continuing, were now serving a less popular, longer-term goal than mere propaganda for Louis-Philippe.

The widespread use of electoral favors under the July Monarchy also meant that many of the higher local officials and department representatives would have naturally supported Guizot's policies, including funding the work of the Commission of Historic Monuments. But after an initial boom from 1840-45, an economic slump not only made this difficult, it also reinforced the claims of opponents that Guizot's government had not been responsible for the upturn and were now reaping the results of their myopic infighting.[88] Bankruptcies, riots, banks closing, abandoned building programs…how could the Commission of Historic Monuments expect to fund repairs to old, often little-used structures in outdated styles?

Radicals began to encourage the disenfranchised to demand social reform and the right to vote, hoping to then gain control of their electoral power.[89] In Burgundy this appeared already in 1847, as the ground swell to another revolution grew. Outside of Paris, the largest group of organized workers was in Lyon—only fifty miles south of Cluny. Lyon was also a center of anti-clericalism during the July Monarchy. The sentiments of many young intellectuals during these years were still as harsh as some of the generation of 1789. Gustave Nadaud (1820-1893) for instance, wrote in the 1840s that he would die happy “to the sounds of the churches crumbling under the hammers of the people.”[90] Although one must assume this is more metaphorical than it would have been in the 1790s, especially since we know Nadaud was not adverse to historical patrimony as his most famous poem is about wishing to visit the citadel of Carcassonne, nonetheless such revolutionary attitudes would certainly have made the work of the Commission of Historic Monuments more difficult.

In 1847, Aymar Verdier (1819-1880), a young architect in the employ of the Commission of Historic Monuments, was assigned to Cluny. Records in the Culture Ministry in Paris begin with the administration in power after the revolution of 1848. The first letter in the Cluny file is from Verdier, undated, reporting to the Commission of Historic Monuments on his evaluation of the site after a visit of two weeks. He seemed to have been particularly interested in the twelfth-century houses and the thirteenth-century parish church but also proposed that the remaining abbey transept be measured and used to calculate the architectural plan of the monastery in comparison with an oil painting from 1809.[91]

So as much as Guizot’s foundation of the Commission of Historic Monuments was of great significance for the future of French architectural patrimony in general, and Cluny in particular, the site did not directly benefit during his tenure in government. The period of the July Monarchy was more important for the ideological formulation of a political relationship between French historical buildings and national pride. This concept would prove central to the development of Cluny as a heritage site.

Notes

[1] Victor Cousin, 'Discours prononcé à l'ouverture du cours le 4 décembre 1817' in *Du vrai, du beau et du bien* (Paris: Didier, 1881), 9. Quoted and translated in Ceri Crossley,

---

French historians and romanticism : Thierry, Guizot, the Saint-Simonians, Quinet, Michelet (London ; New York: Routledge, 1993). 34-35

[2] François Pierre Guillaume Guizot, *Histoire de la civilisation en Europe depuis la chute de l'Empire romain jusqu'en 1789* (Brussels: Vandooren, 1829-32). Quoted and translated in Crossley, *French historians and romanticism : Thierry, Guizot, the Saint-Simonians, Quinet, Michelet*. 84

[3] [We are no longer in the Middle Ages, and the only perception we have of that time is a model actually constructed in the nineteenth century.] Arlette Farge, "Des historiens Bouvard et Pécuchet," *Des lieux pour l'histoire* (Paris: Editions de Seuil, 1997). 138

[4] "[L'histoire] ne se constitue que si on la regarde –et pour la regarder, il faut en être exclu." Roland Barthes, *La Chambre claire*. (Paris: Cahiers du Cinema, Gallimard-Le Seuil, 1980), 102. Quoted and translated in Françoise Choay, *The Invention of the Historic Monument* (Cambridge: Cambridge University Press, 2001). 9. Choay goes on to say "The formulation conveys in a nutshell the shift in meaning, and the inverse role of the monument, charged by its presence as a metaphorical object with recalling to life a privileged past and with reimmersing the observer in that past."

[5] Pierre Birnbaum, *The idea of France*, 1st American ed. (New York: Hill and Wang, 2001). Chapter 2.

[6] Maurice Agulhon, *The Republican experiment, 1848-1852*, trans. Janet Lloyd, *The Cambridge history of modern France; 2* (Cambridge: Cambridge University Press; Editions de la Maison des sciences de l'homme, 1983). 3-4

[7] Neil Stratford, Brigitte Chabard and David Walsh, *Corpus de la sculpture de Cluny*, vol. I (Paris: Picard, forthcoming). I. 3 (d), 1

[8] "…seul clocher qui reste de l'Abbaye, ainsi que les quelques murs et voûtes subsistants." Ibid. 1. 3 (d), 1

[9] For earlier writers who first revived interest in medieval architecture and invented the term "Romanesque", see: Tina Waldeier Bizzarro, *Romanesque Architectural Criticism: A Prehistory* (Cambridge: Cambridge U Press, 1992). A more recent study has just appeared: Jean Nayrolles, *L'invention de l'art roman à l'époque moderne (XVIIIe-XIXe siècles)*, *Collection "Art & société"* (Rennes: Presses universitaires de Rennes, 2005). An excellent general introduction to the historiography of medieval art has also been written by Conrad Rudolph as the first essay in his collection *A Companion to Medieval Art: Romanesque and Gothic in Northern Europe,* Blackwell companions to art history 2 (Malden, MA: Blackwell Publishing, 2006).

[10] Stéphane Gerson, *The pride of place: local memories & political culture in nineteenth-century France* (Ithaca: Cornell University Press, 2003).

[11] Vauchez describes the lines of division in "The Cathedral," *Realms of Memory: rethinking the French past*. 2, ed. Pierra Nora and Lawrence D. Kritzman. *European perspectives.* (New York: Columbia University Press, 1996). 40

[12] Richard A. Etlin, *Symbolic Space: French Enlightenment Architecture and Its Legacy* (Chicago and London: University of Chicago Press, 1994). 172

[13] Andrew McClellan, *Inventing the Louvre: art, politics, and the origins of the modern museum in eighteenth-century Paris* (Berkeley, Calif.: University of California Press, 1999). 180

[14] Charles Nodier and Isidore-Justin-Séverin Taylor, *Voyages pittoresques et romantiques dans l'ancienne France* (Paris: P. Didot l'aîné, 1820). Vol. 9 (Bourgogne)

[15] Viewable on line from the Bibliothèque Nationale site at http://gallica.bnf.fr/ark:/12148/btv1b7742596x and http://gallica.bnf.fr/ark:/12148/btv1b77425943.

[16] "...formoient l'ensemble le plus pittoresque et le plus imposant. Les immenses bâtiments du monastère et son église, une des plus magnifiques du monde chrétien, sont tombés lentement, de 1791 à 1811, sous le marteau des modernes iconoclasts, qui mirent ainsi vingt ans à accomplir cette oeuvre de destruction. Il ne reste plus, de la basilique abbatiale, qu'une portion d'un des collatéraux, surmontée d'un clocher, quelques débris de sculpture, des tronçons de colonnes et une chapelle du xve siècle, bâtie par l'abbé Jean de Bourbon. Outre ces ruines désolées, dont l'aspect inspire un profond sentiment de tristesse, la ville de Cluny possède encore deux ég1ises paroissiales; la plus ancienne, construite en 1159, et dédiée à saint Marcel, n'est pas sans intérêt." Ibid. 176-177.

[17] "Belle et noble province de BOURGOGNE, qui tiens un rang si brillant et si dramatique dans notre histoire, tes monuments venoient ajouter à ta gloire, et il en reste à peine quelques ruines. *C'est peut-être toi qui as le plus souffert de nos passions dévastatrices*. Dieu veuille que les malheurs du passé soient pour tes enfants un enseignement, afin de conserver les derniers joyaux archéologiques que tu possèdes! Ces débris sont magnifiques; ils contribuent non seulement à ton illustration, mais encore a celle de toute la France." Ibid. 177

[18] Susan Stewart, *On longing: narratives of the miniature, the gigantic, the souvenir, the collection* (Baltimore: John Hopkins University Press, 1984). 75

[19] Burke's ideas grew out of the writings of Joseph Addison, who in 1711, pitted the beauty of Classical art against the greater awe associated with Gothic architecture. See: Conrad Rudolph, *A companion to medieval art: Romanesque and Gothic in Northern Europe*, Blackwell companions to art history 2 (Malden, MA: Blackwell Pub., 2006). 11

[20] Stewart, *On longing: narratives of the miniature, the gigantic, the souvenir, the collection*. 135

[21] Ibid. 136

[22] Ibid. 136

[23] Joseph A. Conforti, *Imagining New England: explorations of regional identity from the pilgrims to the mid-twentieth century* (Chapel Hill: University of North Carolina Press, 2001).

[24] The Bibliothèque nationale has an entire searchable site set up on this theme.

[25] Jean-Baptiste Bouché, *Voyage en Bourgogne; Suivi de Mélanges littéraires* (Paris: Martinon, 1845).

[26] Much of the information was drawn from Prosper Lorain, *Essai historique sur l'Abbaye de Cluny : suivi de pièces justificatives et de divers fragmens de la correspondance de Pierre-Le-Vénérable avec Saint Bernard* (Dijon: Popelain, 1839).

[27] Quoted and translated in Bizzarro, *Romanesque Architectural Criticism: A Prehistory*. 131

[28] Entire letter is quoted in *Kenneth John Conant, Cluny: les églises et la maison du chef d'ordre,* Mediaeval Academy of America. Publication no. 77 (Mâcon: Impr. Protat Frères, 1968). 11

[29] Bizzarro, *Romanesque Architectural Criticism: A Prehistory*. Chapter 5.

[30] See difference between original letter (as quoted by Conant, note 17 above) and that appearing in his later compilation: Alexandre Lenoir. Musée des Monumens Français, ou Description Historique et chronologique des Statues en marbre et en bronze, Bas-reliefs et Tombeaux des Hommes et des Femmes célèbres, pour server à l'Histoire de France et à celle de l'Art. 8 vols. Paris: Guilleminet-Nepreu, year IX-1821. Vol. 2, 5-7

[31] This distinction had already been made by Jean-Francois Félibien des Avaux in 1687 but did not gain general usage in France. See Rudolph, *A companion to medieval art: Romanesque and Gothic in Northern Europe*. 20

[32] Mary B. Shepard, "L'oeuf sacré: Alexandre Lenoir's Courtyard of the Thirteenth Century and the Pointed Arch," in *Medieval Art and Architecture After the Middle Ages*, ed. Alyce Jordan and Janet Marquardt (Newcastle-upon-Tyne: Cambridge Scholar's Publishing, 2008 [forthcoming]).

[33]Choay, *The Invention of the Historic Monument*. 88

[34] Cynthia Hahn, "The Voices of Saints: Speaking Reliquaries," *Gesta* XXXVI, no. 1 (1997). 28 (My thanks also to Donna Sadler for initially linking the arm reliquary to Cluny's transept in her response to my paper at the Sewanee medieval colloquium in April, 2002.)

[35] Linda Nochlin, *The Body in Pieces: The Fragment as a Metaphor of Modernity* (New York: Thames and Hudson, 1995). Quote from review by C.K. in *The Journal of Aesthetics and Art Criticism* 54/4, 410.

[36] Ceri Crossley, *French historians and romanticism: Thierry, Guizot, the Saint-Simonians, Quinet, Michelet*. 4-10

[37] For an important analysis of Guizot's notion of *patrimoine*, see: Dominique Poulot, "The Birth of Heritage: 'le moment Guizot'," *Oxford Art Journal* 11, no. 2 (1988).

[38] Robert Gildea, *The Past in French History* (New Haven and London: Yale U Press, 1994). 255

[39] Stanley Mellon, *The Political Uses of History: A Study of Historians in the French Restoration* (Stanford, CA: Stanford University Press, 1958). 15

[40] Karl Joachim Weintraub, *Visions of culture* (Chicago: University of Chicago Press, 1966). 94

[41] François Pierre Guillaume Guizot, *The history of civilization in Europe*, ed. William Hazlitt and Larry Siedentop. Penguin classics. London; New York, N.Y.: Penguin Books, 1997. xxx-xxxvii

[42] Crossley, *French historians and romanticism: Thierry, Guizot, the Saint-Simonians, Quinet, Michelet*. 8

[43] Mellon, *The Political Uses of History: A Study of Historians in the French Restoration*. 14

[44] See: André Vauchez, "The Cathedral." In *Realms of Memory: rethinking the French past*, ed. Pierra Nora and Lawrence D. Kritzman. New York: Columbia University Press, 1996. 37-68

[45] Victor Cousin, "Cours de l'histoire de la philosophie," (1829). 35-36 as discussed in Mellon, *The Political Uses of History: A Study of Historians in the French Restoration*. 17

[46] Crossley, *French historians and romanticism: Thierry, Guizot, the Saint-Simonians, Quinet, Michelet*. 71-74

[47] "The conservation of the past thus formed part of an intellectual strategy of the Nation-State." Poulot, "The Birth of Heritage: 'le moment Guizot'." 50

[48] Crossley, *French historians and romanticism: Thierry, Guizot, the Saint-Simonians, Quinet, Michelet*. 71ff. I believe Crossley would disagree with Pierre Birnbaum's assessment of Guizot as a "doctrinaire Catholic" (Idea of France, 101), a claim based upon the bitter years after 1848 when Guizot condemned democracy and turned to theological writing. In spite of this, Guizot's interest in the English revolution and his earlier belief in a middle-class liberalism eschewed notions of Church control for belief in the guiding principles of a higher "Providence." He never supported the Counter-Revolution. See also Crossley, 94 ff.

[49] See Vauchez, "The Cathedral." 58-59.

[50] Alan B. Spitzer, *The French generation of 1820* (Princeton, N.J.: Princeton University Press, 1987). 105

[51] However, Gerson qualifies this general situation much more precisely in his study (*The pride of place: local memories & political culture in nineteenth-century France*), asserting that successive governments during the nineteenth century were conflicted about both the benefits and the drawbacks of provincial ownership of their local monuments. See especially Chapter 7, "The Quandary of Local Initiative".

[52] Godefroy, Frédéric, Histoire de la littérature française depuis le XVIe siècle jusqu'à nos jours. (Paris: Gaume, 1878-1881) II, 10

[53] Françoise Choay, *L'allégorie du patrimoine*, Couleur des idées (Paris: Editions du Seuil, 1992). Translated as *The Invention of the Historic Monument* (Cambridge: Cambridge University Press, 2001); Kevin D. Murphy, *Memory and Modernity: Viollet-le-Duc at Vézelay* (University Park, PA: The Pennsylvania State University Press, 2000). 22-53

[54] Listed in Stratford, Chabard and Walsh, *Corpus de la sculpture de Cluny*. Full text available from Cluny, Archives municipales: 78 P5 8.

[55] "...[L]e culte des souvenirs qui se rattachent à l'histoire des arts ou aux annales du pays est malheureusement trop négligé dans les départements...tous ces souvenirs, tous ces débris vivant des temps qui ne sont plus, font partie du patrimoine national et du trésor intellectuel de la France." Bulletin of 10 August 1837 found in *Circulaires ministérielles relatives à la conservation des monuments historiques* quoted and translated in: Murphy, *Memory and Modernity: Viollet-le-Duc at Vézelay*. 23

[56] Poulot, "The Birth of Heritage: 'le moment Guizot'." 50

[57] For a discussion of revolutionary arts committees and Abbé Grégoire, who led the way on educational reform, see: Emmet Kennedy, *A cultural history of the French Revolution* (New Haven: Yale University Press, 1989).

[58] Murphy, *Memory and Modernity: Viollet-le-Duc at Vézelay*. 40

[59] Douglas Johnson, *Guizot; aspects of French history, 1787-1874,* Studies in political history (London: Routledge & K. Paul, 1963). 159-161

[60] Choay, *The Invention of the Historic Monument*. 97-100; Murphy, *Memory and Modernity: Viollet-le-Duc at Vézelay*. 41. See also Françoise Bercé, "Arcisse de Caumont et le sociétés savants," in Pierre Nora, *Les Lieux de mémoire*, (Paris: Gallimard, 1984). Vol. 2 (*La Nation)*, 536-45

[61] Murphy, *Memory and Modernity: Viollet-le-Duc at Vézelay*. 38

---

[62] Victor Hugo, *Littérature et philosophie mêlées*, Bibliothèque du XIXe siècle 2, ed. Anthony R. W. James (Paris: Klincksieck, 1976). 135-177

[63] Montalembert, *Du vandalisme et du catholicisme dans l'art* (Paris: Debecourt, 1839). See also Choay, *The Invention of the Historic Monument*. 95

[64] Lorain, *Essai historique sur l'Abbaye de Cluny: suivi de pièces justificatives et de divers fragmens de la correspondance de Pierre-Le-Vénérable avec Saint Bernard.*

[65] Prosper Lorain, *Histoire de l'Abbaye de Cluny depuis sa fondation jusqu'à sa destruction à l'époque de la Révolution française* (Paris: Sagnier et Bray, 1845).

[66] Gerson (*The pride of place: local memories & political culture in nineteenth-century France*) discusses the pros and cons of elites from provincial learned societies chronicling their local histories in answer to government requests and in the hopes of securing government funding and notice in his fourth chapter "Local Memories and the Governing of Minds."

[67] "Je ne sais si je m'abuse : mais je crois qu'il n'y a point de vraie liberté, de vrai régime représentatif, dans ces idées étroites qui ne laissent à nulle chose sa force légitime d'expansion, qui compriment et ne dirigent point, paralysent plutôt qu'elles n'excitent, appauvrissent sans fin la circonférence sans ennoblir le centre, et font de la France entière une capitale, et de la capitale un point unique, où toutes les ambitions aspirent, se pressent, se heurtent, se bouleversent, au risque de faire éclater à chaque instant la force gouvernementale trop condensée; tandis que les provinces s'éteignent et meurent sans énergie, sans espoir, vivant d'imitation et d'emprunt, laissant s'étioler de plus en plus ce qui végète au milieu d'elles, perdant sans cesse le goût et l'ambition des belles et bonnes choses, des lettres, des sciences, des arts; s' endormant sans dignité dans leur inaction morale, et livrant périodiquement aux perditions de la grande Babylone le peu d'âmes d'élite qui n'ont pu s'assoupir tout à fait dans une existence sans aliment et sans but." Lorain, *Histoire de l'Abbaye de Cluny depuis sa fondation jusqu'à sa destruction à l'époque de la Révolution française*. iv

[68] "Y a-t-il une guérison à tant de mal dans les destinées du gouvernement représentatif?" Ibid. iv

[69] "L'esprit des masses est séparé par mille siècles de nos souvenirs nationaux." Ibid. vi. Lorain compares the "forgetting" of national patrimony with the easy erasure of the Bourbons, yet he is living within the period of the formation of the Commission of Historic Monuments by Guizot under the government of Louis-Philippe. So in spite of his hatred for this reign, his awareness of the problem coincides with contemporary efforts—which are more effective than his writing!—by his self-proclaimed enemies.

[70] "…dans ce siècle d'oubli…" Ibid. vii

[71] "L'abbaye tout entière avait déjà péri dans le coeur et dans le souvenir de la génération nouvelle, comme ces Bourbons exilés, qui, revenus en France quelques années plus tard, ne devaient pas rencontrer un seul jeune homme qui sût qu'ils existaient et qu'ils allaient régner." Ibid., viii

[72] Sagot's view of the west façade of the abbey church done for Lorain is studied by David Walsh in "An Image of Cluny by Emile Sagot" in *Medieval Art and Architecture after the Middle Ages*, ed. Alyce Jordan and Janet Marquardt (Newcastle-upon-Tyne: Cambridge Scholar's Publishing, 2008 [forthcoming])

[73] Daniel-Odon Hurel, "La représentation de Cluny chez les auteurs des XVIIe et XVIIIe siècles," *Revue Mabillon* 72 (2000). 115-28

[74] See an analysis of Félibien's *Histoire de l'abbaye royale de Saint-Denys en France* in the article by Kerry Boeye, "Reframing Saint-Denis for the Sun King: A Spectacular History" in *Medieval Art and Architecture after the Middle Ages*, ed. Alyce Jordan and Janet Marquardt (Newcastle-upon-Tyne: Cambridge Scholar's Publishing, 2008 [forthcoming])

[75] Lorain, *Histoire de l'Abbaye de Cluny depuis sa fondation jusqu'à sa destruction à l'époque de la Révolution française*. 263

[76] Ibid. 276

[77] "Ce ne sont plus les maigres et pâles figures de moines austères, errant dans leurs cloîtres, passant leur vie à servir les pauvres et Dieu, à chanter jour et nuit les louanges du Seigneur, agenouillés au pied des autels; ce ne sont plus de saintes âmes purifiées par les macérations corporelles, élevées par des méditations contemplatives, ne connaissant rien des bruits et des dérèglements du monde, et servant de modèles exaltés de la piété chrétienne, et comme d'arche d'alliance entre la terre et le ciel." Ibid. 264

[78] Philibert Bouché de la Bertelière, "Description historique et chronologique de la ville, abbaye et banlieue de Cluny," (1787-1817). Cluny, Archives municipales.

[79] "Vous avez laissé vendre et détruire votre grande et belle église…allez, vous êtes des Vandales, je ne visiterai pas Cluny." Lorain, *Histoire de l'Abbaye de Cluny depuis sa foundation jusqu'à sa destruction à l'epoque de la Révolution française*. 278. See also discussion of the first use of the term *vandalisme* and the Revolutionary government in my Chapter 1.

[80] "…moins pour la consoler de ses splendeurs perdues, que parce que les fourrages étaient abondants et de bonne qualité dans les prairies de la Grosne." Ibid. 279

[81] After Lorain's model, an anonymous "priest of the diocese" published a pamphlet about the abbey in 1846 which included a description of the church and other lost treasures, especially manuscripts, in the same chastising tone: *Description historique de l'abbaye de Cluny*, (Chalon sur Saône: Imprimerie et lithographie Montalan, 1846).

[82] Academie de Mâcon, *Annales*, vol. VII (Mâcon: 1869). 288-299

[83] Murphy, *Memory and Modernity: Viollet-le-Duc at Vézelay*. 91-131

[84] Stratford, Chabard and Walsh, *Corpus de la sculpture de Cluny*. I, 3 (d), 3

[85] Ibid. I, 3 (d), 1

[86] Roger Magraw, *France, 1815-1914: the bourgeois century* (New York: Oxford University Press, 1986). 78-88

[87] Ibid. 73

[88] Ibid. 74-76

[89] Ibid. 77-78

[90] Ibid. 139

[91] Paris, Bibliothèque du Patrimoine: Cote 81/71, 181/1, Box 17

CHAPTER THREE

CLUNY IN THE NINETEENTH CENTURY II (1848-1900)

La vérité est un besoin de notre temps.
—Viollet-le-Duc, 1845[1]

Le Moyen Age devient un folklore, une sorte d'enfance de la nation…
—Jacques Le Goff, 2002[2]

Nostalgia is often for past thoughts rather than past things. People flock to historic sites to share recall of the familiar, communal recollection enhancing personal reminiscence. What pleases the nostalgist is not just the relic but his own recognition of it, not so much the past itself as its supposed aspirations, less the memory of what actually was than of what was once thought possible.
—David Lowenthal, 1985[3]

On July 28, 1848, a letter was delivered to the prefect of the Saône-et-Loire from the Ministry of the Interior in response to letters from the Minister of Public Instruction and Léopold Niepce, the president of the Historical and Archeological Society of Châlons-sur-Saône, requesting the new government of the Second Republic take an interest in Cluny.[4] The prefect was asked to send a complete description of the monument as well as all the information he had on its historical value. Eleven months later, the Minister of Public Instruction again wrote to the Minister of the Interior suggesting that the "superb" chapel (Bourbon) be made into a "truly unique" museum. He suggested that the building could also hold fragments gathered up from where strewn around the site "which could even be sold should the occasion arise." He asked that a halt be put to further losses and sale of abbey fragments and for the government to actually purchase the ruins as a "special destination, useful to study." During 1849 the Minister of Agriculture directed the *Haras* director to deposit all objects taken from the ruins of the church into the Bourbon Chapel. Verdier, who was making drawings of the remains, moved a capital and other "interesting debris" from the former church apse to the chapel and filed detailed reports that prompted the government to allocate 300 francs for window repair in the chapel, 200 francs to repair the *porte d'honneur* "forming entry to the abbey" [fig. 3.2], and 300 francs to buy and transport interesting fragments of the abbey from elsewhere in the town.[5]

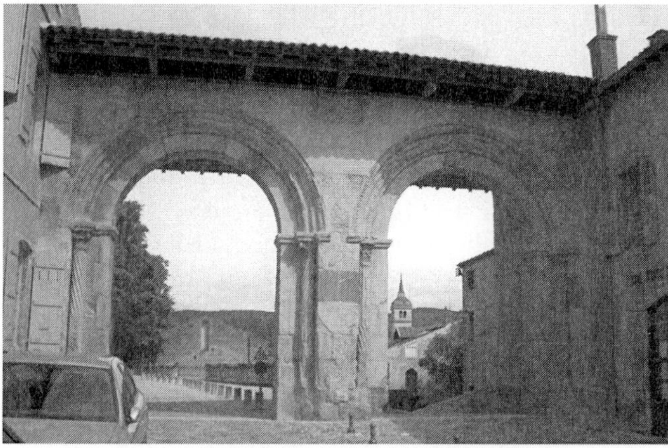

3.1 Porte d'honneur, Cluny, 2006 (Author)

By 1850, letters flying between Paris and the Saône-et-Loire show that there was great interest at both ends in getting something done about the continued deterioration of the abbey remains. When Verdier didn't show up to oversee the work for which the 800 francs was allocated, the prefect wrote the minister who immediately contacted Verdier and told him to get on with it. Verdier replied within two days with his apologies; only the grave illness of his mother precluded his leaving Paris to travel to Cluny. In this letter, he mentioned that the repair work awaiting him was insignificant and would be accomplished in a few days; it was the purchase of the fragments (sculptures) that was the main reason he must go.

Meanwhile, Dr. Ochier was also writing from Cluny to the prefect.[6] Apparently, the ministry's repair allocation was not used in 1850 and students were about to return to the collège on the site so he was asking help to approach the Minister of the Interior about rolling over the funds to 1851, and adding some as well. Ochier refers to the poor condition of the abbey buildings as resulting from "dévastation du vandalisme révolutionnaire". Both Verdier and the prefect wrote to the ministry with a new bid for repair of the chapel window and arcades, as well as sculpture purchases. The amount requested (2188.50 francs) was considerably higher than the previous allotment, which had been nearly entirely used just for the floor, something that had to come first if sculpture were to be moved into the new Bourbon Chapel museum.[7]

On the 15th of November 1850, the Commission des Monuments Historiques met. Mérimée states that the members' felt Verdier was asking too much and that Cluny should cover half of the cost since "in the final analysis [the city] would profit."[8] A special session of Cluny's municipal council was called for January 10, 1851 but the minutes (*extrait du registre*) record that unless the town's tax income was increased, with all the expenses of the *collège*, the members did not see how they could afford the 1,094 francs. Nevertheless, in the hopes that they would find the money later, the prefect wrote asking that the inability of the commune to absorb this huge amount in their budget not deprive them of the funds the minister was disposed to give and the necessary conservation work the Commission thought necessary. Mérimée tabled the issue until the following year and held 1000 francs in reserve.[9]

In February, Verdier submitted a new bid for 415.50 francs, saying other work could wait until the town could afford to split the cost. If the work was approved, he wanted to use the original contractor who was familiar with the job, M. Jacquelin. At the end of the month, Mérimée reported that the Commission approved the new request but regretted that this pittance would only prepare the chapel to receive fragments of the abbey. Miraculously, upon hearing that the minister would not accord half the amount, the municipal council decided that they could afford to take 1094 francs out of their budget of 1854 francs to begin more extensive repairs to the Bourbon chapel.

These exchanges demonstrate a shift in responsibility from the elite members of government to the local community for creating a historical museum. Verdier's work for the government gave the municipal council members professional validation of the worth of their medieval remains and the value of investing in these monuments. It seems it was the intention of the Interior Ministry and Commission of Historic Monuments to force some of this awareness in order to shift a portion of the financial burden of the buildings' maintenance. They must have been pursuing the same course in many other French communities.

And so the long and laborious process of conserving the last pieces of the abbey and the fragment of the church began at Cluny. The French economy was on the upswing and a stable rule of twenty years was beginning with the accession of Louis-Napoléon (president December 1848, *coup d'état* 1851, Second Empire 1852). This period of industrial growth and capital investments coincided with the rule of a leader whose attitude about the use of monuments was influenced by Guizot's legacy of nationalistic pride. Despite the slump of 1856, government spending for both new and conserved monuments rose sharply during Napoléon III's reign. The rebuilding of Paris under the Second Empire is well known, yet the emperor also looked elsewhere in the country to enrich his patrimony. Although Cluny was still not the Commission of Historic Monuments' idea of the perfect project, it is apparent from correspondence during this period that local administrators and others interested in preserving the abbey felt that they now had a better chance to prevail upon the government for help. Louis-Napoléon continued the Commission's programs to spotlight architectural patrimony begun under the July Monarchy. Although attention to Cluny was complicated by the ruined state of the church and the presence of both the school and the *Haras*, there was movement toward classing the various parts as official *monuments historiques.*

Interestingly, in January of 1852, Verdier obtained permission from the minister of the Interior to exhibit his drawings of Cluny in the annual *Salon*. Thus the Romanesque houses, parish churches, and parts of the abbey that Verdier had studied went on view in Paris for the general public during the Second Empire, greatly surpassing the number of viewers Baron Taylor's book would have reached [fig. 3.2]. One wonders if this little place in Burgundy, certainly still well known as a historical name all over France, captured some imaginations during this exhibition. It would not be long before rail travel would become generally accessible and an interest in tourism would rise as the economy under the Second Empire improved.

Pl. XV.

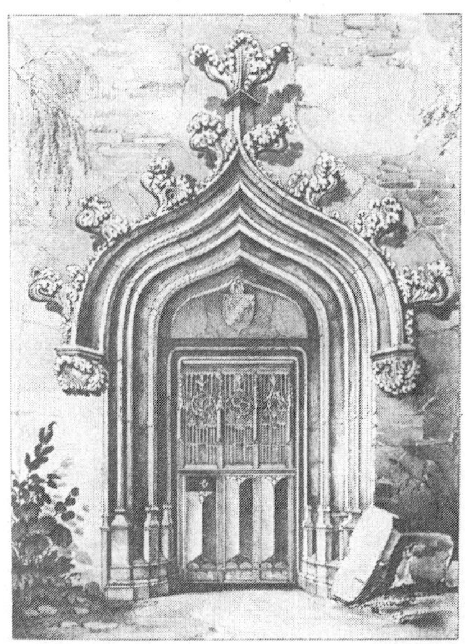

PORTE DE LA CHAPELLE BOURBON

3.2 Verdier's drawing of the door to the Bourbon Chapel (Ricard, plate XV)

On January 11, 1853, Dr. Ochier advanced 100 francs which the Société française had allocated for Bourbon Chapel repairs during a conference at Dijon. Apparently, the state of the roof was so bad that he did not feel it could wait for the funds to arrive. He employed a local architect for an estimate and was going to undertake the work immediately. Ochier's letter requesting reimbursement is an eloquent example of the descriptions of Cluny that would be used to justify funding for the next century:

> ...You have no doubt not forgotten, Monsieur, the importance of this chapel from the artistic point of view, being a church of the Gothic style. It is from the same period as the *hotel* de Cluny in Paris and the abbot's palace in Cluny. It is the sole monument of our city that remains complete and, in spite of the deplorable mutilations subjected to the interior, still merits conservation as a beautiful example of 15th-century art, but it needs to be restored. It is destined to become a repository for the sculptures saved during the demolition of the great church, notably the eight Byzantine capitals of the apse...the government has already allocated a small sum which is entirely entailed in the paving of the chapel under the direction of M. Aymer Verdier. But much still remains to be done....
>
> Now that the vaults are open to rain and bad weather, we can only wish that our honorable president continues to protect them and list it (this monument) in the *monumens historiques*, as well as the fragment of the transept from the great church which was already destroyed. If no repairs are made to both the bell tower and the roof of this section, it is certain that those vaults will shortly deteriorate and will break up under the weight of the bells which will fall down, as already happened to the other one.
>
> I beg you, Monsieur, to make account of my mission to M. de Caumont...and beg him on my part to intervene with the minister that he give the necessary orders and grant funds toward the conservation of the remains of the antique basilica of Cluny...[10]

Ochier signed as a "Member of the society for the conservation of monuments" which gave his letter the weight of a national organization and it was retained in government files concerning the Commission of Historic Monuments. The *Société pour la conservation des monuments de la France* had been founded in 1834 by the Arcisse de Caumont, a lawyer from Bayeux who dedicated himself to the study of patrimony, originally founding an antiquary society in Normandy in 1824. He took a national role in promoting provincial organizations and held scientific congresses for regional representatives.[11] His circle of supporters was often critical of government measures regarding historical patrimony and tried to influence policy.[12] Membership validated Dr. Ochier's role as a provincial elite interested in the history of his region and added to his credibility.

In early 1858, the ministry, the prefect, and Cluny's city council jointly agreed to make the entire remaining transept space into a museum, rather than just the Bourbon Chapel. It was a good decision at the right time; the Commission of Historic Monuments placed the "Ancienne Abbaye et ses dépendances" on their list of classed sites in 1862.[13]

In 1866, the eighteenth-century abbey buildings received a boost in status. Under Victor Duruy, Napoléon III's education minister, the communal collège at Cluny was turned into an *école normale de l'Enseignement secondaire spécial*. This was part of an initiative coming from Duruy's law of 21 June 1865 to create a four-year education program directed toward the *classes moyennes* consisting of practical subjects such as modern languages and science, as well as Republican approaches to geography and history that would emphasize the ideals of 1789 over that of the Terror and reinforce notions of nationhood among the disparate provinces of France.[14] At Cluny, Duruy hoped to train faculty for this new program by recruiting students from the provincial teacher training schools.[15] The community was perfect for such an institution, since Duruy targeted the type of *petite bourgeoisie* who populated the area as shopkeepers, artisans and farmers.[16] He liked the idea of an education center away from Paris and installed a new *collège* (a local high school) under the same roof in order to have local students in training classrooms for the nascent professors.[17] C. R. Day writes:

> [Duruy] believed that Cluny, the ancient symbol of medieval learning and science, would become a revivified intellectual center from which would issue a new breed of simple, austere men of learning—'missionaries of modern science'— to seek a reconciliation between the sciences and the arts in the form of a new scientific humanism for modern times.[18]

Thus Duruy was not only creating a progressive new center to train lower middle class students as teachers, but he was attempting to shift the traditional associations of the abbey into a modern paradigm. The choice of Cluny's former abbey buildings was not merely practical but also ideological.

At Cluny, the contrast between Duruy's modern training to traditional instruction by religious orders would have been striking, set among the ruins of the largest Catholic abbey in France's history. Associations with its medieval stature were never far from mind and reinvesting the buildings with this new concept for education must have been significant. In Robert Gildea's study of rural education in nineteenth-century France, he tell us: "For the Catholics, the Middle Ages symbolized a chivalric, Christian, and paternalistic world, while for the republicans it was characterized by feudal strife, serfdom, and intolerance, relieved only by the emergence of the towns, *Tiers Etat*, and Estates General."[19] For someone like Duruy, the underutilized abbey buildings would not only have been perfect for his institution but the only answer to champions of their conservation whose proposals represented an unnecessary drain on monetary resources.

Cluny's city council offered Duruy the eighteenth-century cloister buildings plus 70,000 francs to re-situate those uprooted by the change (people were living in apartments and running businesses installed in the portions not used by the collège); the département of the Saône-et-Loire gave 100,000 francs to purchase subsidiary structures and renovate the site; 90 scholarships of 800 francs were arranged; the museum put together an experimental garden of 5 hectares for the school's use, professors sent equipment and industrial companies sent materials.[20] All in all, though the national government did not allocate funds to help with this new project, the local region was more than willing to find resources in order to convert the abbey into Duruy's special training school.

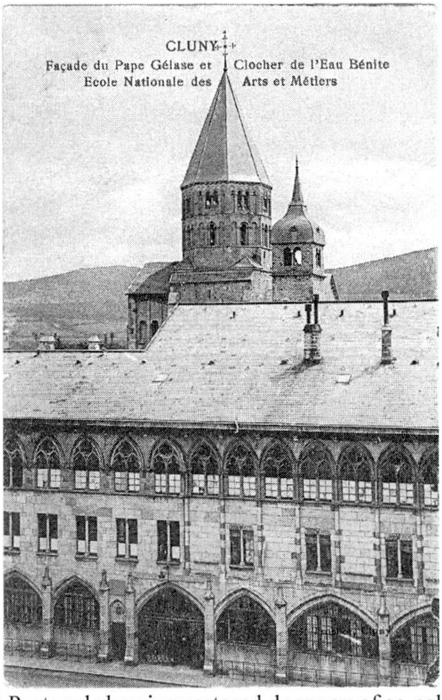

3.3 Postcard showing restored doorway of so-called "Façade of Pope Gelasius", Cluny (Author)

In revamping the buildings for the new school, Duruy restored the so-called "façade of Pope Gelasius" closer to its original construction style of

1295-1308 by removing the Baroque doorway (compare fig. 2.5 to fig. 3.3). We are told by Léopold Chaumont that at this time Duruy took care to mark on a stone pillar the width of the south wall of the church.[21] In this same year, 1866, Duruy also wrote to ask the Minister of Fine Arts (who oversaw the Monuments historiques) that the chapel be classified among the *monuments historiques* in order to receive funds for repair and maintenance.[22] The minister responded that the chapel was already classed and had received funds but now that it belonged to the new *école normale*, the costs should be borne primarily by that institution (i.e., under the Education ministry).

The architect Laisné was in charge of the renovations necessary to the installation of the new school. Due to the transfer of the abbey buildings to the government for the *école normale,* the 1858 plans to turn the transept into a sculpture museum were dropped, however in 1864, Dr. Ochier's widow had donated their sculpture collection, along with the Palais Jean de Bourbon to house it, so the city had an alternative space and in 1866 opened the Musée Ochier.[23] Laisné remodeled the transept into a more commodious chapel for the larger student body at the new school by having the walls whitewashed, the floor paved, and furniture installed.[24] However, serious structural problems with the tower remained.

In 1867, correspondence began between the departmental prefect, Minister of Fine Arts and Minister of Education regarding responsibility for maintaining the school buildings. The prefect took the stance that the chapel was an integral part of the abbey ceded by the city to the State on the third of March, 1866 and thus it was no longer in the local budget.[25] The ministers ordered an investigation by the Commission's Inspector-General on the importance of funding repairs. The report, from April 1868, estimated that the architect needed 30,000 francs. Fine Arts concluded that the expenses should be borne by those who made principal use of the building.[26] The news must have been doubly frustrating for Duruy since the government had allowed him no funds towards this project in the first place and he knew the town had done more than its fair share.

The continual disagreement over financial responsibility for the maintenance of a historical monument was only partly a matter of 'passing the buck'. There was real confusion in the French government about Cluny because it was no longer serving its original purpose, and, unlike many other medieval structures, it had not been rededicated to a single function such as the abbey of Clairvaux, turned national prison. Rather, it was divided between ministries of agriculture (*Haras)*, education, and offices for the city of Cluny. Even though the building that most interested nineteenth-century enthusiasts was the Bourbon Chapel, once classed, the entire historical site was technically under the ministry of Fine Arts. As a school space, the transept needed only to be safe and dry, but as an historical monument—which could benefit the city more than the school—more expensive preservation measures were entailed. Thus the desire of each organization to convince the other to assume funding responsibility.

After 1869, when Duruy retired from his ministry, there was little ongoing interest in *enseignement spécial* and Cluny's school lost support.[27] Enrollments declined and graduates were treated as second-class scholars. Day tells us that the former normal school became little more than a glorified *lycée* (preparatory high school). Concern for the structures returned to those most interested in their historical value—the Commission on Historic Monuments and the city of Cluny.

By 1881 a new administration was in power, dominated by Jules Ferry who served as Minister of Education three times and Prime Minister twice. In 1882, Ferry initiated compulsory primary education. He was a powerful instigator of the laic movement in education, removing clerical control from schools, opening access to primary instruction in the provinces, and cultivating political support of the popular classes.[28] Ferry was more interested in the primary level than rehabilitating the deteriorating *enseignement spécial* begun by Duruy. Nevertheless, he made a speech promising the graduates of Cluny equal pay in their teaching positions with those holding the classical diploma and he proposed a new studies program in applied science to renew the Cluny curriculum.[29] It was Ferry's turn, with his Director of Secondary Education, Charles Zévort, to get embroiled with Fine Arts ministry about the ongoing, dangerous deterioration of the bell tower at Cluny. Laisné's estimate for work on the entire transept equaled 33,890.70 francs, entailing the "…old buttresses, cornices, stringcourses, posts and stone steps; restoration of the framework and repair of the cover of the large and the small bell-towers as well as the part of the old transept which is associated with worship."[30]

1882 was a difficult year for France. Gambetta's government fell in January and he died at the end of the year, thus ending the "Great Ministry" of the Third Republic.[31] Implementation of the Freycinet Plan, to buy up private rail companies, caused stock to fall and the *Union Générale*, a merchant bank, collapsed. The triple alliance of Germany/Austria-Hungary/Italy, which would lead to the First World War, was formed in May and the French-Indochine war of conquest began. An economic recession began that would continue into the 1890s. Political allegiances were shifting, and towns like Cluny with a predominance of small vintners became strongholds of democratic republicanism.[32] The phylloxera disease, which began in the 1870s and affected production throughout the 1880s and 1890s while waiting for the new vines imported from the United States to mature, must have made it difficult for many small wine proprietors around Cluny to pay their taxes. In spite of all this, the

Third Republic was a period of relative stability and modernization and the government's budget did not reflect these setbacks.[33]

This did not mean the government honored all bills with prompt remittances; telegrams held in the Archives Nationales regarding work done in the *Haras* contain urgent requests for payment from the contractor.[34] The mayor of Cluny wrote to the new Education minister's secretary, Logeratte, telling him of the city's decision to construct a little building to protect the precious stones of their former abbey in spite of the poverty of their budget—"this glorious debris once part of a barely appreciated historical monument…these remains of [Cluny's] early architectural glory…these precious vestiges of her past..."[35] He indicated that this was necessary to protect sculpture fragments from damage by the students and reminded him that Cluny had given up a lot for the sake of national education. The expenses were around 4500 francs; the town wanted 2000 francs aid from the government. Nothing was granted.

Finally, in May of 1883, Ruprich-Robert, Inspector-general, broke through the red tape and stated that all the work done by Laisné in 1881 and 1882 was absolutely necessary and that the expense could simply be divided in two parts: half covered by the Commission and the other by the school in a request to the Education minister.[36] These were the first serious funds to be allocated from any government since the Revolution to Cluny's monuments. Although it may seem ironic that this support came from the secular Third Republic, we must remember that the cloister buildings were still in use for the *enseignement special* with the church transept as the adjoining chapel. Thus these funds were given as much to maintain a state institution as to repair the historic abbey basilica.

Ferry's promises to the graduates of 1881 were never realized. In fact, he and Zévort tried to transfer the school to Versailles in 1883 and convert the old abbey buildings into a home for soldier's children, "…but these negotiations leaked to the press, and protests in the city of Cluny, the Department of the Saône-et-Loire, the alumni association, and several Paris newspapers (notably Clemenceau's *La Justice*) eventually forced Ferry and Zévort to back down."[37] Nevertheless, the writing was on the wall and by 1890 Léon Bourgeois, Minister of Education, deemed that "practical training and intellectual culture were irreconcilable."[38] He transferred the Cluny students to the applied science programs in Rouen, Lyon, and Paris and gave the site to the Ministry of Industry and Commerce.[39] For a brief time (1891-1901), this ministry utilized the space to train labor supervisors (*École national pratique d'Ouvriers et de Contremaîtres*)[40] and take in overflow from *arts et métiers* schools in Châlons, Angers, and Aix while waiting for the construction of a fourth institution at Lille. In 1901 the current *École nationale d'Arts et Métiers* was installed at Cluny, part of the same network of engineering schools, responding to the growth of mechanical industry, under the Ministry of Commerce. Enrollment slowly grew to the level once held by the *école normale.* Workshops and residential facilities were added in the twentieth century and it has become a respectable and advantageous resource for the town.[41]

Once Laisné's work had been paid for in 1883, the town did not forward any new requests for repair projects for a decade. After 1885 there was little point in such petitions. Ferry fell out of favor and the government was so unstable and ministries changed hands so often it would have been difficult to secure new funding. Political concerns were not centered on cultural patrimony during this period; rather nationalism took the form of militarism around Boulanger. Economic stresses complete with strikes and shortages were met by rising Guesdism and other forms of radical socialism.[42] The department of the Saône-et-Loire consistently maintained political orientation toward the republican left and the area around Cluny, in particular, was pro-trade union and anticlerical through the end of the nineteenth century when the Dreyfus Affair polarized the country. The Church, under Pope Leo XIII, effected the *Ralliement,* which emphasized patriotism and acceptance of the Republic among Catholic voters, thus giving up a century of support for the monarchy's return.[43]

In the final decade of the 1800s, letters from the rector of the Academy of Lyon to the Education and Fine Arts ministers concerned the conservation of sculpture found in the Bourbon Chapel.[44] The suggestion was to move it to the city museum. However, what they thought were fifteenth-century statues from the chapel were actually correctly identified by the drawing instructor, Legrand of the same academy, who knew that these were twelfth-century pieces that had been found between 1866 and 1888 in the gardens and simply deposited in the chapel. He recommended keeping all the abbey sculpture together in the museum where "artists and tourists could more easily admire and study Cluniac Romanesque art."[45] The matter was sent to the Commission of Historic Monuments (since a law of 1877 prohibited any modifications to classed monuments without their approval) whose members approved the move but retained the right to molds for the Trocadéro Museum in Paris.

The Jubilee of 1898

Major commemorative events were held at Cluny beginning in the years 1898, 1910 and 1949 and then at regular intervals throughout the twentieth century. These public demonstrations of the town's identification with the past demonstrate consciously constructed yet shifting collective memories about medieval Cluny. The first is discussed in this chapter, the other two appear in chapters 4 and 6. We will see that the events at Cluny changed over the years but fundamentally remained commemorations of its medieval past in order to draw visitors to the site—a past that was as much formed upon *forgetting* unwanted parts as in *remembering* others.[46] These events were part of the nineteenth-century popularity for reviving provincial history mentioned in Chapter Two.

As Gerson quotes from the Parisian *Journal des departments et colonies* in 1858: "[Every town] as small as it may be…dream[s] of a pageant or tournament."[47] Many towns had old *fêtes* to revive, others like Cluny no longer had the infrastructure that had hosted them so the towns had to invent new festivals. Cluny would respond to growing popularity for the secular historical pageant and medieval fair only in the twentieth century. At the end of the nineteenth century, the growing movement in France to reinvigorate Catholic participation in public life helped generate interest for an event at Cluny that would highlight the site's rich religious history.

As the generation reared on the anti-clericalism of the Revolution was gradually replaced by their children, Catholic observance began to reestablish in most parts of France during the 1830s.[48] The battle over France's identity as a Catholic or Republican nation, seen as mutually exclusive, furthered the country's historical self-definition. We saw in Chapter Two that liberal politicians and historians like Guizot and Thierry reclaimed the past by designating medieval France as the initiator of middle class rights and artistic culture for Europe. Meanwhile religious conservatives, following Montalembert, also turned to the past in attempts to thwart the Republic. Their version of France's history emphasized the inspired spirituality of public devotional practices and the protective guidance of an infallible Church hierarchy. At the heart of both arguments were the medieval churches that had been such targets during the 1789 revolution. Both sides claimed them as evidence of France's great historical heritage, liberals from the technological aspect and conservatives for their original religious function.

The local cults of saints was particularly revitalized in the wake of the cholera epidemics of 1832 and 1849.[49] In addition, Napoléon III returned France to the alliance between Church and Crown upon which the country had been founded under the Carolingians and which partnership had endured up to the Revolution of 1789. Although he was not as pious as his wife, the empress Eugénie, nor as ultramontane as the authoritarian pope Pius IX would have liked (since he also supported Enlightenment science and philosophy), he did reinforce Catholicism as a cultural identity of France under the Third Empire.

It was, however, Napoléon's fiasco with the Franco-Prussian war and the events of 1870, "l'année terrible", which most helped the Church regain supporters. The rise of the railway system after 1860 made distant pilgrimage possible for the masses and charitable organizations were formed to help even the poor afford such trips. New churches, such as the Sacré Coeur in Paris, were built as "destination shrines" with which the populace associated an anti-Republican cultural identity, reclaiming Catholic symbols and rituals for France [fig. 3.4].[50]

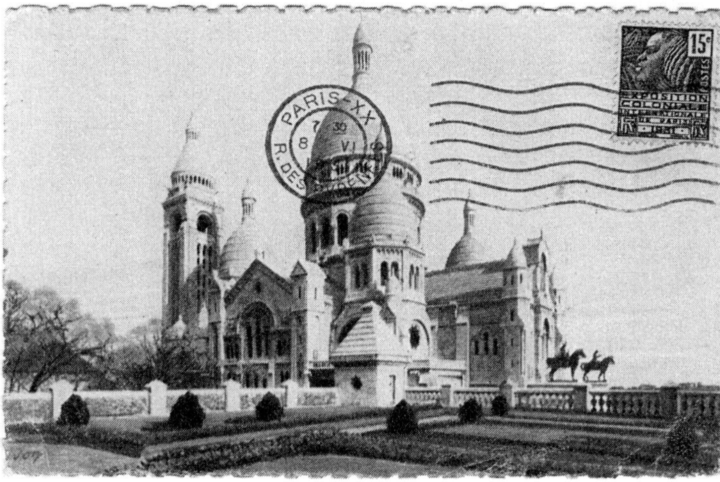

3.4 Postcard of Sacré-Coeur, Paris around 1931 (Author)

The Third Republic, so-called the "moral order government", polarized religious and secular adherents, pushing royalists to rally one last time around the pretender, the Comte de Chambord, and republicans to nearly canonize Léon Gambetta, who in his 1877 election campaign made the famous statement "Cléricalisme, viola l'ennemi."[51] Visible, public methods of bringing people together to show God their renewed commitment and of healing a wounded nation were needed. Public demonstrations of Church adherence were called upon as antidotes to republican festivals. The pilgrimage movement grew in response, popularizing medieval traditions and providing wide entertainment with religious festivals as well as other consumer-oriented elements of tourism. The clerical organization of these pilgrimages with ceremonial processions, administration of the sacraments, and homilies[52] corresponds to the way short-term "missions", popular earlier in the century, had been held regularly around France. Although the latter were closely associated with the Restoration, they continued under the radar during the July Monarchy and were slowly replaced by the rising revival of the pilgrimage. A new religious order, the Augustinians of the Assumption founded 1843-1850, made pilgrimage their mission, calling the holy sites "stations of faith" and claiming public prayer would appease God's anger at France's secularism.

Close to Cluny was the cult of the Sacred Heart at Paray-le-Monial, where national pilgrimages were organized in the 1870s. Paray-le-Monial is only about 50 kilometers from Cluny and since the nineteenth century has been within the same diocese (Autun) and *département* (Saône-et-Loire). In 1873 a large festival enticing 20,000 pilgrims was organized by the political right to underline ultramontane and monarchist affiliations and that same year, over one hundred conservative deputies from the Assemblée Nationale met at Paray-le-Monial to dedicate France to the Sacré Coeur.[53] The most famous vision of the Sacré Coeur had occurred in the seventeenth century to Marguerite-Marie Alacoque. The symbol was popularized by the Royalist Chouans in the Vendée during the Revolution and Alacoque was beatified in 1864. In 1856, Pope Pius IX proclaimed the Sacré Coeur as a sort of totem against liberal politics and the cult of the Sacred Heart came to symbolize the struggle of the Catholic Church against the Third Republic.[54] Paray's bicentennial in 1889 served as an alternative for Catholics who wished to avoid the anniversary celebrations for the Revolution.[55] However, the cult flourished through World War I as a symbol of the moral and political reform many felt was needed for France to survive what seemed like endlessly recurring disasters.

According to Joseph Byrnes in his work on religion and national identity in France, the most popular attraction for pilgrimage was the Virgin Mary.[56] This is why La Salette was successful in spite of unattractive visionary children. Cardinal Pie declared the first modern national pilgrimage to the Virgin's relics at Chartres also in 1873, promoting its cathedral as a "historic center of French Catholic life" in the words of Byrne.[57] Chartres is particularly instructive in our study of Cluny, because it was the only one of these nineteenth-century sites that had been a thriving medieval shrine. The local clergy also inaugurated its modern cult without any blockbuster miracles or papal intervention. They had a huge medieval church building that required restoration and repairs so its artistic and historical value were emphasized along with the spiritual. However, the two sites are in a more important sense quite different—Cluny had never been a pilgrimage center and even in the modern period, had no claim to become one.

Most successful was Lourdes with "authenticated" visions only four years after the dogma of the Immaculate Conception had been proclaimed from Rome in 1864. Modern methods of marketing and tourism were brilliantly mustered at Lourdes in the presentation of a both medieval values and commercial culture.[58] Bringing together the sacred and the profane in one travel destination, Lourdes appealed to the religious traveler, especially women, by offering multiple attractions: home of the docile visionary Bernadette Soubirous, who only died in 1879 and was styled by church administrators as a pure and pious peasant child; center for Marian worship at a grotto near the

Pyrenees (barely even France at that time and certainly not so to Parisians for whom the inhabitants' customs and *patois* would have been entirely foreign) that had begun in the wild tradition of southern French folk religion but was subsequently shaped by the Church to include a huge basilica with processional ramps; natural spring with reportedly curative waters; and resort town with hotels, restaurants, and souvenir shops lending an atmosphere of lively entertainment [figs. 3.5, 3.6, 3.7]. A "jubilee" was held here in 1897 to commemorate twenty-five years of national pilgrimage to Lourdes with huge processions, public cures, high services, and much press.

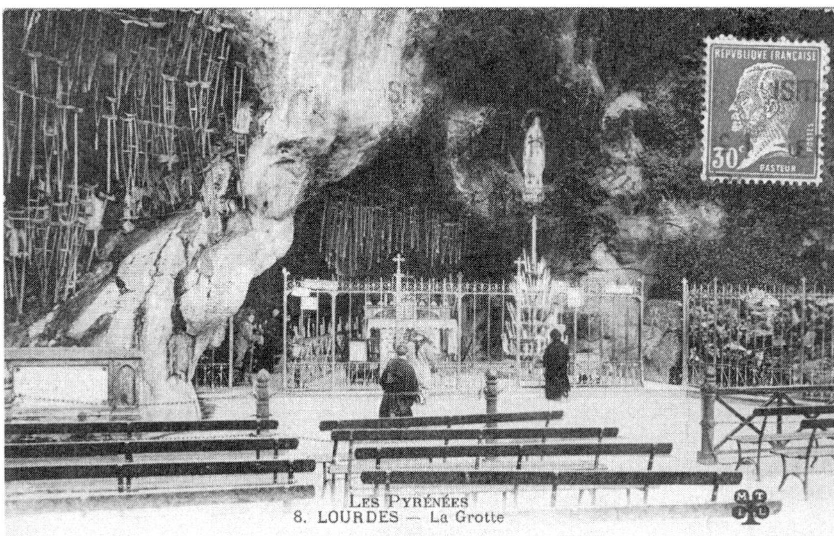

3.5 Postcard of Grotto at Lourdes around 1910 (Author)

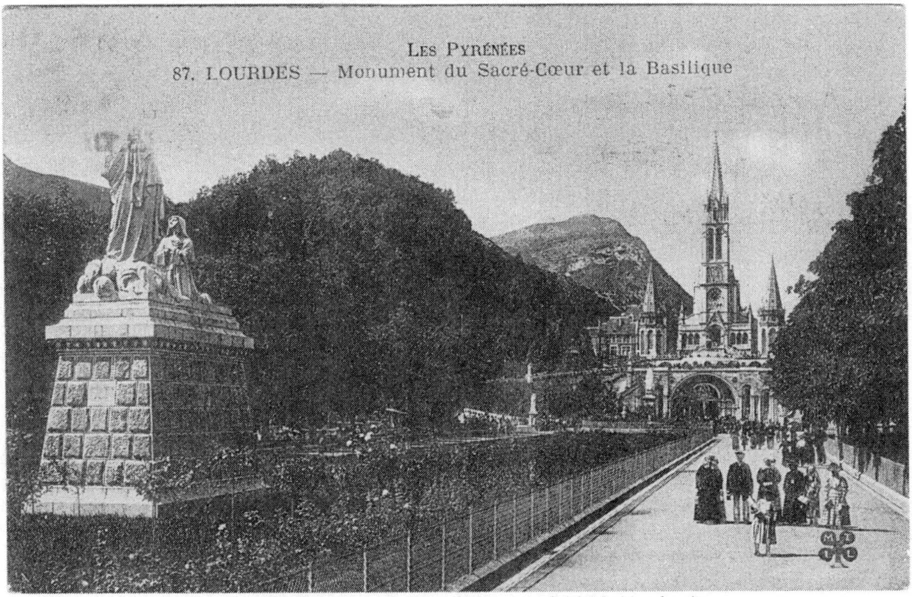

3.6 Postcard of Basilica at Lourdes around 1910 (Author)

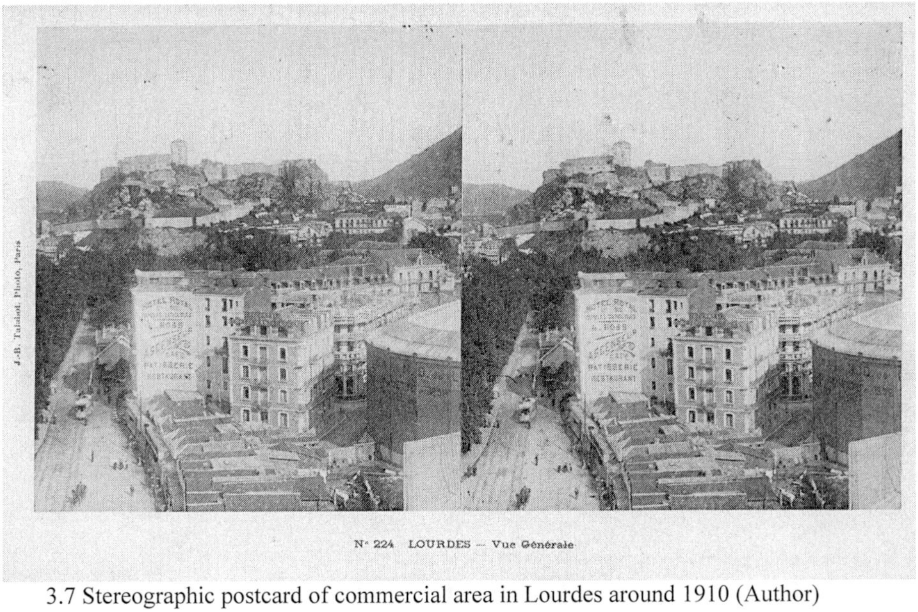

3.7 Stereographic postcard of commercial area in Lourdes around 1910 (Author)

In 1898 the town of Cluny organized its first historical event with a jubilee for the 900th anniversary of Odilon's foundation of the "*Commémoraison de tous les fidèles trépassés*" (faithful departed), now the Church's annual feast called, in English, All Souls Day. Activities were held throughout the year but culminated October 31 to November 9, determined by a joint committee of clerics and lay folk from the town and surrounding area. The celebration consisted primarily of religious ceremonies and a colloquium, designed to recollect the medieval Christian origins of the town and the period in which it had seen its heyday.

Cluny's jubilee was a direct reference to the jubilee held at Lourdes in 1897 and ties into the revival of local pilgrimage in Burgundy, within the tradition of medieval travel to a holy site. Unlike Lourdes or Paray, Cluny had no spiritual attraction to offer outside of the temporary association with Odilo's intercessory cult of the dead. Even the site of his grave was unknown.[59]

We know a great deal about the plans, preparations and outcome of this project from a little booklet written by Abbé Auduc, chaplain at Cluny's *Hôtel-Dieu.*[60] Initiated in February by Cardinal Perraud, Bishop of Autun, (who also administered the sees of Châlons-sur-Saône and Mâcon, his territory comprising the entire département after the Revolution) and approved by Pope Leo XIII, the year 1898 was dedicated by the Catholic leaders to intercessory prayers for the dead—the primary occupation of the monks of Cluny during the Middle Ages and the activity by which the institution gained so much power and property. Commemorations on the Feast of All Souls had already grown over the course of the nineteenth century as the day during which the French made small pilgrimages to their local cemetery to lay token memorials on family members' graves.[61] By using the theme of intercessory prayer for the 1898 events, contemporary practice and historical reference to the abbey of Cluny were joined and people were able to participate in what appeared to be "authentic" medieval religious performance at a time when the sentiments surrounding the Dreyfus Affair were at their peak (he was only pardoned by President Loubet the following year). The Church was apparently trying to pull an area back into its orbit where up to twenty percent of the population voted for the extreme Left,[62] and where religious observation was "indifferent".[63] The faithful were urged to fulfill requirements to acquire the plenary indulgence of the Jubilee, "...applicable to the suffering of souls in Purgatory."[64] These consisted of confession, communion, and a visit to one of the two parish churches in Cluny to pray for the pope's current intentions, to wit: peace between Christian leaders, extermination of heresy, conversion of sinners, and the aggrandizement of the Church.[65] In addition, the faithful were "strongly urged"[66] to add a donation if they wanted to gain the indulgence, either "into the hands of one of the priests of Cluny" or deposited in the church alms-boxes.[67] Visits from those outside the town were literally organized as "pilgrimages" from three directions: Mâcon, Saint-Gengoux, and Paray-le-Monial. The *Pélerin*, published in Paray, was designated to be the official centennial bulletin. For six months the history of Cluny was published in installments and donations were solicited through its pages.

Another impetus for this year of commemoration in Burgundy may have been the growing popularity of the traditional ceremonial religious pardons held in Brittany.[68] According to Patrick Young, Anatole le Braz published his first edition of the wildly popular *Au pays des pardons* in 1894. By combining such attractions as travel, spectacle, and religious piety, Perraud must have felt he was also bringing these current fashions to his region.

In the culminating festival during the fall, a series of liturgical services were celebrated for ten days from Monday through the next Wednesday.[69] These were solemn and elaborate observations of traditional Catholic liturgical practice, including two high masses approved by the pope. The festival was inaugurated Monday afternoon, October 31, with a reading of the Papal brief and address by Cardinal Perraud. Tuesday November 1, the Feast of All Saints, a High Mass was celebrated at 10 a.m. with vespers for the dead at 3 p.m. The next day was Odilo's feast of All Souls with a homily at mass by the resident superior of the Jesuits at Paray-le-Monial; there was a 2 p.m. meeting at the cemetery and solemn absolution. After this, every day began at 9 a.m. with a funeral mass commemorating, in order, all the former monks of Cluny, all the benefactors of the abbey and churches of Cluny, all the former bishops of the diocese, all the priests and faithful of Cluny, all those dead in the armed service of France and, finally, all the faithful departed of the entire diocese. Every day ended with a 5 p.m. sermon by the bishop and benediction. On Sunday there was a pontifical mass with the inauguration of an archconfraternity of priests for the repose of the souls in purgatory and at vespers. At closing, the vicar general gave a eulogy for Saint Odilo, then the bishop closed the jubilee and everyone sang the *Te Deum.* Here we see the application of the medieval Cluniac intercessory prayer towards a revival of sympathy for the monks and other religious folk of the past. The entire jubilee is reactionary in tone, considering the anti-clerical stance of the contemporary government and a century of republican whitewashing of the Revolution. Clerical participants were drawn mostly from the diocesan seat at Autun and the stronghold of ultramontane revival at Paray-le-Monial. Commemorating those who had donated to the abbey or the monks from the abbey was certain to raise regret for loss of the institution among devotees, not to mention reminders of the monks' unhappy demise in the 1790s.

The press mentioned the events, calling the jubilee a "centenaire"—an inaccurate shortening of the explanatory "neuvième centenaire" listed on the program and an increasingly popular event in France—but did not devote much space or personnel to coverage. Abbé Auduc wrote summaries for the *Journal de Saône-et-Loire.* On October 25th, L'*Union républicaine* reported that the socialist mayor, Julien Simyan who was also owner of the newspaper, had posted notices on the walls of Cluny reminding citizens that all religious processions outside the churches on city grounds were prohibited [fig. 3.8].[70]

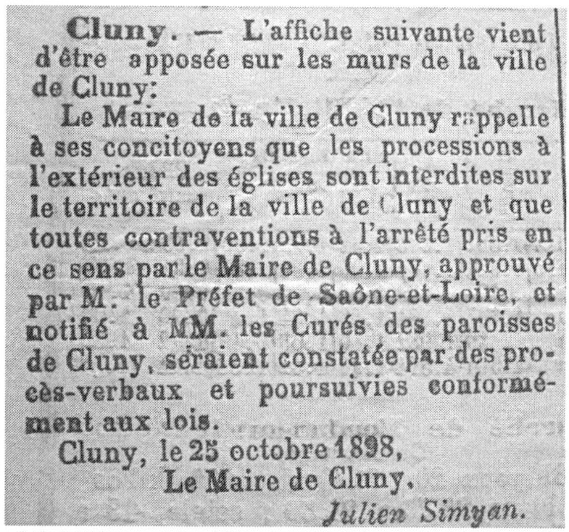

Cluny. — L'affiche suivante vient d'être apposée sur les murs de la ville de Cluny:

Le Maire de la ville de Cluny rappelle à ses concitoyens que les processions à l'extérieur des églises sont interdites sur le territoire de la ville de Cluny et que toutes contraventions à l'arrêté pris en ce sens par le Maire de Cluny, approuvé par M. le Préfet de Saône-et-Loire, et notifié à MM. les Curés des paroisses de Cluny, seraient constatée par des procès-verbaux et poursuivies conformément aux lois.

Cluny, le 25 octobre 1898,
Le Maire de Cluny.
Julien Simyan.

3.8 L'*Union républicaine* October 25, 1898, p. 2
(Archives départementales de Saône-et-Loire, Mâcon)

Although the conservative paper *l'Autunois* had a small serious column on November 9th, most journalists found the petty thefts that occurred in the churches while services were being held to be of more interest. Again, the *L'Union républicaine* took a cynical view. On November 3rd, one writer asked whether St. Odilo couldn't intercede with God to help the police end the problem?[71] On the same day, *Le Progrès* covered a banquet held in Autun for a leftist senator where Simyan is shown in attendance, but no mention is made of the pilgrims praying in his city's churches. And on the 9th his paper really poked fun at the whole affair by running irreverent verses written to a well-known tune by "an old Cluny native" entitled *La Complainte de Saint Odilon* [fig. 3.9].[72]

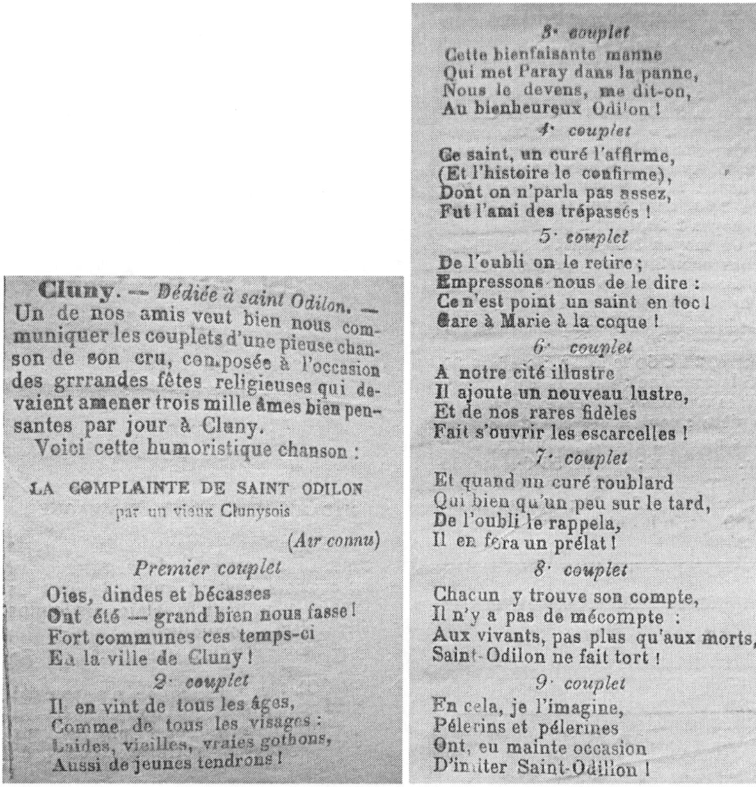

Cluny. — *Dédiée à saint Odilon.* — Un de nos amis veut bien nous communiquer les couplets d'une pieuse chanson de son cru, composée à l'occasion des grrrandes fêtes religieuses qui devaient amener trois mille âmes bien pensantes par jour à Cluny.

Voici cette humoristique chanson :

LA COMPLAINTE DE SAINT ODILON

par un vieux Clunysois

(*Air connu*)

Premier couplet

Oies, dindes et bécasses
Ont été — grand bien nous fasse !
Fort communes ces temps-ci
En la ville de Cluny !

2e couplet

Il en vint de tous les âges,
Comme de tous les visages :
Laides, vieilles, vraies gothons,
Aussi de jeunes tendrons !

3e couplet

Cette bienfaisante manne
Qui met Paray dans la panne,
Nous le devons, me dit-on,
Au bienheureux Odilon !

4e couplet

Ce saint, un curé l'affirme,
(Et l'histoire le confirme),
Dont on n'parla pas assez,
Fut l'ami des trépassés !

5e couplet

De l'oubli on le retire ;
Empressons-nous de le dire :
Ce n'est point un saint en toc !
Gare à Marie à la coque !

6e couplet

A notre cité illustre
Il ajoute un nouveau lustre,
Et de nos rares fidèles
Fait s'ouvrir les escarcelles !

7e couplet

Et quand un curé roublard
Qui bien qu'un peu sur le tard,
De l'oubli le rappela,
Il en fera un prélat !

8e couplet

Chacun y trouve son compte,
Il n'y a pas de mécompte :
Aux vivants, pas plus qu'aux morts,
Saint-Odilon ne fait tort !

9e couplet

En cela, je l'imagine,
Pélerins et pélerines
Ont, eu mainte occasion
D'imiter Saint-Odillon !

3.9 *L'Union républicaine*, November 9, 1898
(Archives départementales de Saône-et-Loire, Mâcon)

Publications

"Faire l'histoire de l'abbaye, c'est écrire l'histoire de Cluny…"
—Louis Henri Champly, 1866

Cluny's history has followed the Romantic historians' teleological model (Guizot, Thiers, Michelet) which separated the past into pre- and post-Revolutionary periods.[73] Cluny was an obvious candidate for this division, yet such a perspective discounts the importance of her later history in our understanding of the site. Although the monks left, buildings were taken down, and property changed hands, the history of Cluny continued—both of the town and the former abbey. Yet visitors have read Cluny only in terms of its glorious medieval past, decline in the sixteenth to eighteenth centuries, and final demise in the early nineteenth. This vision was predicated upon the writing of the nineteenth and early twentieth-century authors reviewed here, who saw the Romantic trajectory of an institution being formed out of early France, growing through the work of saintly agents, faltering in the forecasting of royal manners which would lead to both its and the country's conflagration, and then culminating in the event of the Revolution. Readers can be misled into assuming the abbey disappeared sometime between 1789 and 1797 when in fact, a great deal of the buildings' "history" struggled on through demolition up to the 1820s and then re-usage of the remaining buildings up to the present. Part two of Cluny's story for these authors was merely the Romantic church ruin seen via the tourist guide; a stroll through the past, completely driven by nostalgia and the collective memory of Cluny's role in Burgundy's status.

These accounts (except for one exception at the end of the century which I cover last) were neither self-reflexive nor did they attempt to deconstruct the received notion of the past promulgated by their predecessors and the town leadership in favor of the real-time process in which they lived with the ongoing site. Nonetheless they provide us with coherent pictures of how nineteenth-century historians wanted to formulate their history and how they tried to maneuver the difficult terrain of revolutionary justification versus romantic regret. In this, they were following the lead of their teachers, applying moderate leftist principles which treated the course of French history as a series of events leading to the great invention of a Republic, treating the Terror as a lamentable misstep in that process. They were thus able to praise the powerful role of Cluny in the Church-dominated medieval past and admire its artistic achievements as indications of the advances of early French society,[74] even as they confused their own role in Restoration or Republican governments that upheld the legend of the Revolution as a watershed in France's progress toward modernity. Linda Orr reminds us in *Headless History* (1990) that these histories are only reflections of the "duplicities and paradoxes that define postrevolutionary society" and as such are both "highly stable and unstable."[75]

Michelet's model was the more recent and affective influence seen in these works. For one thing, unlike Tocqueville, who wanted to underplay the Revolution, Michelet's history predicts the violent end of a struggle between two opposing powers (Christianity and Revolution) and thus serves well as a schema by which to comprehend the abbey's demise.[76] Prosper Lorain, discussed in the previous chapter, was the first to take up the task of Cluny's history and therefore represents the model for later authors. Writing in 1839, his work preceded the French histories of Michelet, Tocqueville, Lamartine and Quinet but his method also grew out of their teachers—Guizot, Thierry, Thiers, and Henri Martin (*Histoire de France*, 15 volumes, 1833-36)—who used archival sources even as they reformulated history to fit their political or literary needs and treated events in a highly peppered style. However, unlike these liberal historians whose self-imposed purpose was to justify the Revolution and/or reconcile it with constitutional monarchy or fledgling republican governments, those writers who felt strongly enough about Cluny to take up her history came from a position of anger at the destruction and sacrilege of the sacred institution. Similar to Lorain, who the reader will remember was motivated by his concern for lost patrimony, many were born in or had made Cluny their home. They felt a proprietary melancholy at the ruined condition of once-great architectural monuments surrounding them. And akin to Lamartine's poetry on the ruins, it was this melancholy which drove them to undertake a study of Cluny rather than some larger literary or scholarly purpose.

Stéphane Gerson reports that over eighteen thousand book-length publications appeared on local history in France between 1825 and 1877, more than five times that of the preceding three centuries, and made up more than twenty percent of the Bibliothèque Nationale's 1897 catalog.[77] Products of elites who belonged to scientific societies, they both hoped for recognition by the government and labored to separate their provincial histories from that of the centralized State. Three works on Cluny after Lorain, appeared before the end of the nineteenth century, which together established a firm narrative tradition for the abbey's popular history.

At mid-century the second major book on Cluny's history appeared.[78] François Cucherat, chaplain at the hospital in Paray-le-Monial and canon of Autun, was awarded first place by the Academy of Mâcon for his answer to the question of the Cluniac order's influence in the eleventh century raised at their 1849 meeting. As a result, the Academy paid for the publication of his work at the end of 1850. The eleventh century was considered the peak of Cluny's powers and Cucherat's focus would underscore the tendency already apparent to privilege the tenure of Abbot Hugh above all other abbots of Cluny.

In his presentation of Cluny's origins, Cucherat emphasized two things: the importance of the decision by William of Aquitaine and Pope John XI to put the abbey directly under the Holy See and the insistence that the monks elect their own abbot. The first point would be echoed in the literature on Cluny for over a century as something extraordinary contributing to the order's greatness, until 1970 when Cowdrey would prove that it was common to other foundations during the Carolingian period.[79] In spite of this, one can still find the point stressed in publications written after that date.

Cucherat's considered Mabillon an authority for general historical facts and he believed in the ultimate goodness of the Church in spite of the condition of monastic institutions in the ninth century and the political machinations of abbots and popes evident in the tenth. He also took charters, chronicles, and vitae at face value, believing their pious formulae, and repeating some of the hagiographic stories.[80] He defended Cluny against the austerity of the Cistercians.[81] He championed Cluny as the Church's greatest force for the reform cause "which was that of God and civilization".[82] Cucherat was writing in the tradition of older, more famous French Catholic scholars such as Montalembert and Albert de Broglie.[83] Cucherat took their model of the Church transforming dying Classical culture after the fall of Rome and updated the period of decline to that of the ninth century. He then made Cluny, a French institution, into the source of medieval European civilization. He underlined this point in Part I with Chapter V, which emphasized the diffusion of the order into countries outside of France.

The rest of Cucherat's little volume does not proceed chronologically through the abbots of the eleventh century, rather he was only interested in Hugh ("C'est saint Hugues qui est regardé comme le vrai fondateur de la congrégation de Cluny") and claimed the second half of the century was superior.[84] The original question posed at the Academy meeting specified Cluny's intellectual and political influences. Cucherat divided the second two sections of the text into these two categories. The first contains three chapters, beginning with a review of education at the monastery and moving into overall monastic studies, then concluding with the short sketches of the most famous eleventh-century scholars to come out of Cluny. The writing is very suggestive throughout, even conflating the arches of the contemporary surviving cloister (from the eighteenth century) with those of the eleventh century.[85] Naturally, Cluny's school produced the greatest minds of the century and those detractors of the century before him who reviled all medieval accomplishments were simply following the narrow fashions of their time.[86] Cucherat attempted to address the topic put the case rather simplistically; early medieval society was Christian, and its civil and claustral aspects were so interrelated that each had brought the other down.[87] Cluny led the crusade to rebuild culminating in the period of Hugh's abbacy which included the powerful Pope Gregory VII, a former monk of Cluny. Cucherat listed the wide-ranging fields pursued in Cluniac studies in an effort to support his claim that these monks maintained knowledge of the ancient world at a time when the rest of Europe had forgotten. Under the Arts, Cucherat described the third abbey church in superlative terms as evidence of the progressive thinking of Hugh, even though he believed it was built around 1220, and referred the reader to Lorain's book for further details. The conclusion returns to an introductory quote by Urban II, calling the Cluniac community a sun shining on the earth; the light of the world. Cucherat writes: "Thus Cluny relit the sacred fire of monastic perfection through the wisdom of her reform. She preserved the last glimmer of the sciences, letters, and arts by the character and renown of her schools. She saved the world through the nobility and consequences of her political concepts."[88]

In 1866, the first edition of a more complete history of the abbey appeared by Louis Henri Champly.[89] He would publish a second edition in 1878 and then his son, René Champly, added drawings and an introduction for a third printing in 1930. In the introduction to the second edition, Louis notes that he expanded his material by referring to Bouché de la Bertelière, the *Bibliotheca Cluniacensis,* the *Gallia Christiana*, and the annals compiled by Bergier and Leronde, making one wonder what were his initial sources. René tells us that his father used the abbey's archives as much as possible, but their destruction had occurred less than sixty years earlier and thus they were incomplete. To supplement, Louis had consulted old residents who had witnessed the abbey's demise and thus included oral history. He also footnoted Lorain and Cucherat (once each).

Oral history gives us an interesting angle on Cluny; although subject to apocryphal tales and exaggerations, it also allows the reflection of collective memory to appear. In other words, the things that residents wanted to tell Louis Champly and the tales they remembered were sifted through a screen of opinions about the former abbey and the ways the buildings had since been used by the city or their personal attitudes toward French politics and the Church. Peer pressure and local pride may have caused the Clunysois to champion the lost monks, even if they would not have been in sympathy with eighteenth-century monasticism. Thus stories about virtuous abbots, monastic alms, the power of relics or other flattering tales of religious piety were repeated and recorded, forming an oral and written tradition that would appear in accounts of Cluny's history for generations. It seems ironic today to realize all the French went through at the end of the eighteenth century to rid themselves of feudal class differences, only to find such authors as these in the mid-nineteenth century praising the creation of privileges, listing the names of titled visitors, and generally using all the terms of the *ancien régime* to convey former glory. Yet perhaps we can understand this in terms of the battle against modernism.[90] Linda Nochlin has potently described how, after the revolution of 1789, fragments became metaphors for the destruction of the old world and the subsequent creation, upon the ruins, of a new order.[91] Those who resisted, or at least regretted, this change looked back, holding on to the most powerful language and imagery from the past. At Cluny, the fragment of the church stood as a stark reminder that the *ancien régime* was gone and the modern world had little place for abbeys and feudalism. Champly's style of writing evidences the tension for those classes of people who are traditionally assumed to have benefited from the Revolution yet who lived in towns they felt had lost their status, and economic base, when their best products were destroyed as symbols of oppression.

Champly's conception of monasticism was intensely Romantic—rose-tinted with a retrospective notion of peace and calm that dogged the heels of most nineteenth-century historians in the counter-revolutionary nostalgia that became prominent after 1830. Introducing the picturesque location of the town and the impressive past of the medieval monastery, he quoted Lamartine's portrayal of the Cluny region from his text on Héloïse and Abélard written during the height of the Romantic literary movement. Describing the garden, he made reference to the Linden tree where Abélard meditated and to the paths where "cenobites dreamed while reading holy books."[92] Regretting the loss of the abbey church, he recalled the celebrated events that brought princes of the Church and kings of Europe to visit.[93] He echoed the calls of Victor Hugo and Viollet-le-Duc to save medieval monuments when he mentioned the damage of the "rains of autumn and the deferred maintenance which each year threatens the [walls'] stability".[94] And, in spite of his apparent debt to his local sources, Champly complained about the indifference of the resident population, saying that the Bourbon Chapel or museum were not generally open to the public and that the guard who made them available was only doing a favor to tourists who had traveled across Burgundy to pay homage to a faded grandeur.[95]

Histoire de l'abbaye de Cluny proceeded chronologically in the same manner as the *Histoire* written by Lorain and echoed by Cucherat that Cluny's reform movement saved Europe. Champly covered more history than any former author, taking the reader back before William the Pious and explaining the politics of the region at the time of the charter. He included apocryphal stories and legends.[96] In the following chapters, Champly concentrated on the abbots to tell the history of the abbey and he emphasized those who had been canonized, relying upon formulaic panegyrical biographies (mostly written by their successors) for facts about their lives. Thus he recorded without critical assessment such material as the visions of Mayeul, the miracles of Odilo and the legend behind his institution of the Feast of All Souls, or the forbearance of Hugh in the face of ever fiercer battles over Cluny's exemption from ecclesiastical control. When not using chronicles, surviving letters, or religious biographies, Champly's favorite secondary source was Henri Martin's *Histoire de France*. He also relied heavily upon Lorain's similar chapters about each abbot, but rarely credited this source.

Champly admitted that there had been a "bad" abbot (Ponce) and went so far as to link the collapse of vaults in the third abbey church in 1125 with its violent desecration during the conflict between warring factions, while Peter the Venerable asserting his abbacy, did not censure those Cluniac monks who vengefully burned a Cistercian abbey years later.[97] In general, Champly tried to stay true to his sources written by religious authors, and to validate the history of the Church as written by its victors.[98] This led to contradictions in his text, such as when he turned around after denouncing Ponce and, based upon the fact that he was later buried in the abbey church, recounted legends of miracles performed at his tomb as proof of his ultimate saintliness.[99]

Chapter VI, entitled "Cluny au douzième siècle", summarized the accomplishments and importance of Cluny during her heyday. The remainder of Champly's 367-page text, nearly two thirds of the entirety, covered the later periods in detail by following Lorain very closely. The difference between the two studies is more in tone than in content, for both men drew the same material from the same sources. For Lorain, everything that was done to the abbey, as a sort of entity in and of itself, was bowdlerizing the original as founded by William of Aquitaine, sullying its pure essence and leading to the eventual "forgetting" that he was trying to combat. Champly, on the other hand, tried to understand the reasoning behind those who did things that could be perceived as detrimental to Cluny's wellbeing but which were, ultimately, simply the unavoidable ongoing life of an old institution. For instance, Lorain strongly denounced Richelieu's reforms and forcible fusion of Cluny with Saint-Maur. Champly tried to set out Richelieu's plan as an administrator's logical approach to Cluny's troubles, even though he clearly regretted the outcomes. Both men ended their histories with the Revolution, but Lorain's account is the more poignant since he told of having visited Cluny just before the upheavals with his Cardinal uncle. In both cases, the descriptions of destruction and demolition became listings of lost relics, treasures, and the progress of demolition. Champly painted a picture of the little city council trying desperately to hold on to its monument via petitions and monetary allocations. However, the revolutionary fervor was too strong and his final paragraphs of Chapter 19 described a macabre scene of mobs dancing around the auto-da-fé in the *place*, where "the most superstitious recounted that in the midst of the flames images of the old saints, protectors of the monastery, writhed with eyes full of menace casting anathema on the city, portentous of the most sinister misfortunes."[100] He ended this penultimate chapter with the Cluniac's "blood payment to the Terror" when the last superior-general and three other monks mounted the scaffold and fulfilled a legend that predicted the abbey would be destroyed when a native son became prior (The last prior was Dom Roltet of Cluny).[101] In the end, after bemoaning the demolitions, Champly injected admiration for the efforts over the previous forty years to begin repairs and to find uses for the remaining structures, concluding on an upbeat note about the return of learning to the buildings.

A massive three-volume study on the order of Cluny by J. H. Pignot appeared in 1868.[102] Pignot limited his study to the period from Cluny's foundation to the death of Peter the Venerable, entirely avoiding the decline and destruction. He extended the nationalistic premise by emphasizing how Cluny expanded French influence on religious and political life all over the continent. He must have been deep in the writing of it when Champly's study came out but he claimed to have only relied upon primary sources, eschewing anything written from the eighteenth-century onward. The text was organized in three parts, corresponding to the three volumes. After an 83-page introduction tracing the creation of Saint Benedict's *Rule* and its early applications in Europe, the breakdown of order and reform by Benedict of Aniane, the ups and downs of the Carolingians and the invasions, Pignot followed the early history of the abbey by dedicating whole chapters to the major abbots. He thus prepared the groundwork from manuscript sources for later biographers and shaped a thematic organization around reformers, showing the great Cluniac abbots carrying the torch of the early Benedicts.

Pignot used the same cartularies, letters, early biographies, and Mabillon's annals that Champly consulted. In spite of his caution against dramatic biographies in his foreward[103] and although Pignot went into much greater detail, his essential approach did not differ from Lorain, Cucherat, or Champly. Some of the abbot chapters could stand as small books on their own: 144 pages on Odo, 175 pages on Odilo, 372 on Hugh (the latter comprises sixty-five percent of the second volume). The increased amount of text in Pignot's study is not due to new ideas, rather he simply increased the amount of material he reported from pre-eighteenth-century sources.[104]

After covering Saint Hugh, Pignot recorded the customs of Cluny used throughout all of her houses, both monastic and civil. Then he devoted two chapters to "L'art Clunisien," beginning with the construction of the third church. Pignot repeated Hildebert's legend from his *Vita S. Hugonis* of 1121 about saints Peter, Paul and Stephen specifying the church measurements in a dream to the old monk, Gunzo, and that another, Hézelon, was the architect. This hagiographic device, which Hildebert himself took from two previous authors, would be expanded, justified, and reused as fact for over a century by other Cluny scholars, including Conant.[105] Pignot followed with a minutely detailed description of the church. He depended primarily upon Lorain for this, as well as the drawing published by Viollet-le-Duc in his *Dictionnaire* among firsthand accounts. He linked "local taste" to a severity of style in the "temple" interior that allowed for a "unique grandeur", mentioned the "remarkable sonority" of the form and he tried to write a chronological description of the various forms of Cluniac architecture throughout Europe and the Middle East.[106] Viollet-le-Duc was also his source for observations about sculptural decoration. Pignot included a list of Cluniac dependents, as well as those with Cluniac architecture, at the end of Volume Two and ends his work after the long third volume on Peter the Venerable, saying that after him, Cluny was no more than a great feudal institution of no interest to the history of the Church.[107]

Wider histories of France also appeared around this time, incorporating the material about Cluny found in Lorain, Cucherat, Champly, and Pignot. For instance, Louis Chaumont wrote a popular history of Burgundy for "schools and families" which first appeared in 1881 and was reissued in 1887.[108] More focused work also proceeded from these origins. The first modern biographical study of St. Hugh was published in Germany in 1869.[109] Richard Lehmann worked in what would become recognized as German academic style to painstakingly analyze primary sources (vitae, chronicles, and letters) which had been mostly compiled in the seventeenth and eighteenth centuries and then correlate them to devise some authoritative facts which he included in part II as "Research on Hugh's Life and Work up to the year 1072" (Hugh died in 1109). In Lehmann's first footnote, he cited the 3-volume work by Pignot, which had just appeared, saying that it was certainly the most definitive study on Cluny thus far, but faulted Pignot for sloppy research.[110] Their approaches could not have been more different. Lehmann's goal was to sift through the available primary sources on Hugh's life in order to separate fact from reused hagiographic tradition, determine errors and personal biases, and elicit material that could contribute to a modern understanding of Hugh as a real person. His entire study is 113 pages. Pignot, on the other hand, produced a three-volume work of over 1700 pages on the history of the Cluniac order as a major factor in French civilization, heavily depending upon the veracity of primary sources.

Lehmann's work was the true academic foundation stone for an entire genre of writing on Cluny—the abbot-saint biography. Unlike Lehmann, however, most of the work would be done by religious men, wishing to extol their forebears and please their superiors in the Church. Already an early study of Peter the Venerable had appeared in 1862 which belongs to this type of scholarship and Pignot's long chapters are essentially the same thing.[111] These were followed by those who paid little attention to Lehmann's critical model. L'Huillier, a Benedictine monk at Solesmes, produced an exhaustive study of Hugh, complete with transcriptions of sermons and other primary documents, in 1888. In 1898, Jardet, abbé and canon of Autun, published an equally long work on Odilo to coincide with that year's commemoration of Odilos's Feast of All Souls. Many more would follow in the twentieth century. The interest they show and elicit in Cluny is only tangential to this study—the factors contributing to the rise of a heritage site at the ruins of the monastery—and most of their material was directly derivative from the primary sources and conformed to partisan assessments of Cluny's role in the medieval world.

One of the most important scholars from this period is the art historian Jean Virey. In 1892, Virey published his dissertation on Romanesque churches in the diocese of Mâcon.[112] Central to his thesis was the role of Cluny in Burgundian architecture of the eleventh and twelfth centuries, in fact a second edition published in 1935 adds Cluny into the subtitle.[113] It was the first systematic and detailed analysis of this period's architecture applied to provincial examples. Virey began with the written material of Viollet-le-Duc but differed from him in asserting the innovation and regional differences evident within Cluniac influences, constituting the lack of a specific Cluniac "school" per se. Virey found independence among architects working for Cluny's dependencies, demonstrating their fusion of local styles with overall guidelines from the motherhouse. Even those in the direct region of Cluny showed distinguishing features, attributable to differing stone and terrain, while remaining a "Burgundian School".

Virey's treatment of the remains of the abbey church at Cluny comprises 86 pages. Based upon the plan described by Mabillon in the seventeenth century and stating that the remains give us the scale by which we can imagine the whole (a challenge Conant would take up 35 years later), Virey laid out the structural features of the abbey church.[114] He also consulted the drawings of Etienne Martellange, a description in yet another Voyage pittoresque de la France from 1784, Viollet-le-Duc's interior view from his *Dictionnaire*, and the drawings of Aymar Verdier. However, most of this section is taken up by a brief history of the order, based almost exclusively upon the work of Pignot from 1868, and thus privileging the biographies of the most important abbots. For the periods after Peter the Venerable, where Pignot ends, Virey relied upon Champly's second edition of 1878 and then quoted Chavot for six pages regarding the destruction of the abbey after the Revolution. Within his detailed description of the structure, Virey also carefully notes where Philibert Bouché de la Bertelière's journal cites specific elements that were broken or removed after 1789.

Virey's work, both in this 1892 text as well as his 1926 study of Paray-le-Monial and the churches of the Brionnais, provided important background material for Kenneth Conant, showing him where to look in existing regional churches for comparable architectural features.[115] Virey's meticulous analysis of the abbey church, complete with authoritative dimensions and decoration, must have served as Conant's primary descriptive source. He wrote imaginatively of original visual effects of the building that could have inspired Conant's reconstructive drawings. He also ended by asking which parts of the building were eleventh century, which twelfth century, and which were additions from later centuries. These were questions that helped pique Conant's inquiry. Virey went on to devote an entire monograph to Cluny which appeared while Conant was beginning his measurements in 1927.[116]

Tourist Guides

In 1874, one of the first tourist guides to Cluny, since the description by the anonymous priest of 1846, was published by Auguste Penjon.[117] Such guides would serve as the modern histories of Cluny. Taking the same title as an earlier, longer work on the history of Cluny by the same author, this little piece is called a "*Notice*" and includes full-page drawings. Penjon's taste were still nineteenth-century Romantic, in that he preferred Gothic to Romanesque and neoclassical to both. He was a former professor at the Cluny school and on the faculty at Douai. Included in the booklet are 15 illustrations by the drawing instructor at Cluny (apparently the same Legrand from Lyon who identified the twelfth-century sculpture fragments in the chapel). Penjon began the text with the familiar romantic evocation of the scene ivy- and moss-covered walls and the great bell tower of the church…"harmonizing with the quiet countryside and giving the impression of a little city from the Middle Ages which has been preserved up to our day".[118] His admiration for picturesque views is reminiscent of Sagot's scenes of Cluny from Taylor and Lorain, which he most likely knew.

Unlike the 186-pages in the first full edition, where Penjon wrote separate chapters on each part of the town and abbey,[119] the second and third editions simply pull some of the facts and arrange them as a twenty-page guide into the early and late periods in Cluny's famous history. He relied upon the research from his full earlier study which was itself dependent upon Bertelière. Penjon shaped the "*Notice*" to give a brief history of the abbey at the same time as he described the remaining buildings for the tourist.

Beginning with the abbey church, Penjon called the remaining transept tower "one of the strangest monuments imaginable…giving the odd sensation of both admiration and uneasiness."[120] He told readers that one must suppress one's thought of the "brutal" wall that suddenly cut off from view the five naves with their gigantic pillars. In other words, Penjon was directing visitors to imagine the church whole again by refusing to see what was there in front of them, thus offering an evocative and Romantic tour complete only in their mind's eye. He was also acknowledging this "malaise" of feelings that the ruins generated for both visitor and inhabitant; validating that impression by admitting the single tower was a bizarre sight. As such, he tapped into the older Romantic tradition of the somewhat macabre attraction to ruins.

Penjon credited Cluny's monks with the perfection of the Romanesque style, directing tourists to the remaining twelfth-century houses in town "which give this little town, especially in certain neighborhoods, the most genuine effect".[121] However, he preferred those dating from the thirteenth and fourteenth centuries and was equally enamored of the Gothic parish church, Notre-Dame, saying that it merited being classed among the best products of the late thirteenth century, except for its plain tower which he wrote did not give the slightest indication of the lightness or elegance of the interior.[122] He reserved his highest praise for the fifteenth-century Palais de Bourbon, now the museum. In describing its contents, a note was added in the 1882 edition to indicate that the remains of the monastic library had been moved to the Bibliothèque Nationale.[123]

Penjon did not skimp on flattering adjectives when describing the chapels added to the "severe" Romanesque church. Nonetheless, he compared the scale of these subsidiaries to the main church as the contrast between the eleventh and fifteenth centuries in Cluny's history.[124] In his final section, Penjon listed the depredations suffered under the Wars of Religion and was critical of how slowly reconstruction proceeded in the eighteenth century ("Ils prenaient bien leur temps!")[125] He spoke highly of the neoclassical structures, saved under Napoléon's reign. He called them imposing, admiring the breadth of the vaulted two-story galleries, the proportions of the cloister, and the stairs and balconies fashioned by a monk called "frère Placide." Nevertheless, Penjon thought they came at a price:

> But the monks themselves erased all the vestiges of the past; they gave the first example of this vandalism which would destroy, a few years later, the only monument which was fully respected and as well as a great number of the newer buildings.[126]

He ended with a note of hope similar to that of Champly; the new life of the town surrounding the double establishment of the *collège* and the *école secondaire spécial* had restored the Benedictine buildings and thus changed the "physiognomy" of the town for the better.[127]

Another early guide to Cluny, with a short (14 page) text by E. Ricard, began with yet another derivative *Notice Historique.*[128] In this way, the information about Cluny that was published by French clergy and nationalist historians is uncritical and circular, forming a set of legends that will be repeated for the next century.[129] Ricard described each remaining abbey building, public statue, enclosure wall, and original house as well as the nearby chateaux of Lourdon, Berzé, and Lamartine's at St. Point. A great number of images were reproduced from old engravings and contemporary photographs. Plate XIV shows the interior of the Musée Cluny when it still was the only sculpture depository; four of the ambulatory capitals are grouped with smaller colonnettes in the center of a room [fig. 3.10].

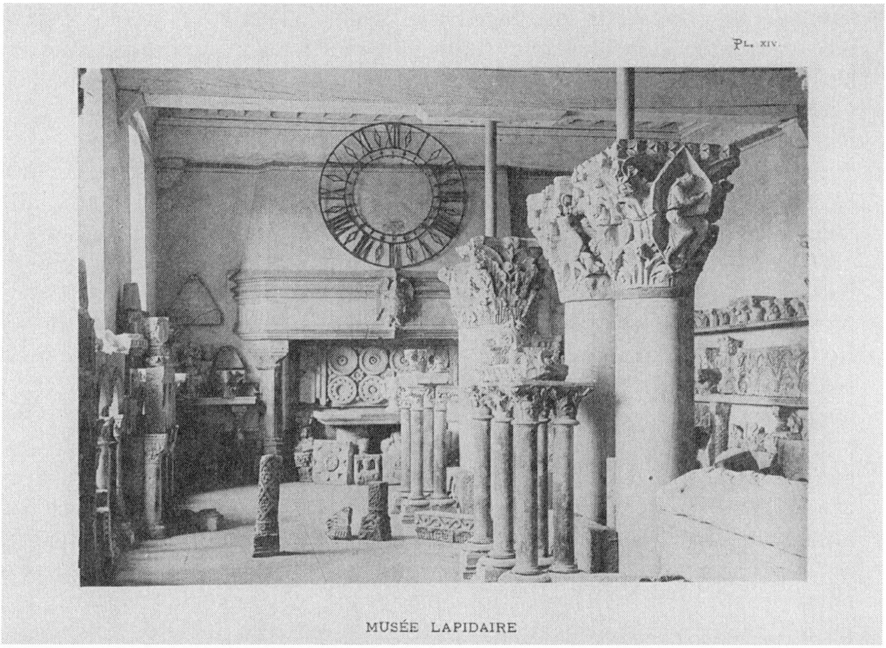

3.10 Musée Ochier before 1880 (Ricard, plate XIV)

A more important contribution to the scholarly studies of Cluny was published in 1892-4. Ernst Sackur, an editor of the *Monumenta Germaniae Historica*, wrote a new history of the abbey up to St. Hugh. He turned to primary sources such as the recently published charters.[130] As Barbara Rosenwein has shown in her 1982 review of the literature on Cluny,[131] Sackur also believed that Cluniac reform led to the rise of the Romanesque and the revitalization of France after the Viking invasions. He claimed Hugh's politics led him to champion the papal reform under Gregory VII and move the abbey into the outer secular sphere of the Church. Sackur acknowledged that the sources showed not all of Europe was under Cluniac influence yet as a model he felt it served a unified monastic reform movement in medieval Europe.[132]

Although comprehensive, historically-documented, and well-organized, Sackur's work would remain unnoticed by the French for some time: relations between the two countries had reached an all time low in 1870 and would not improve in the first half of the twentieth century. During the Third Republic, studying medieval French culture became a patriotic pastime.[133] Exhibitions of French art and recovery of neglected monuments brought the past to life and created new collective memories. Guidebooks, such as those written about Cluny, were only one facet of this popular movement. The kind of narrative they create re-interpreted the Middle Ages as a wholly French precursor to the Third Republic. A new phase of Romanticism reached further into the general public than previously, coming to a head in the 51 million visitors who took home souvenirs from Albert Robida's *Vieux Paris* at the 1900 Paris World's Fair.[134]

Finally, there was a dissenter who is worth reviewing for the contrast offered to the laudatory tradition already formed about Cluny. A bizarre little volume on the 1898 jubilee written by a local man, Alfred Forest, appeared in 1899 from the publishers V. Giard and E. Brière in Paris. In contrast to Lorain's "poor monks", Forest was bitterly anti-clerical, a radical Republican who saw socialism and the Church as direct enemies. In this, he is also a sort of Romantic, firmly holding to the idealism of the Revolution. His 224-page book is a total rant against the events in Cluny ("The Jubilee of Cluny is nothing but a humiliating farce!")[135] cast in the light of an enlightened Parisian scoffing at the primitive Catholic provincials who let the Church control their lives and steal their money. It came out of the contemporary climate of hatred between conservatives and republicans over the role of the Church in France, which had been particularly intense since battle lines were drawn in 1889 over the centenary commemoration of the Revolution.[136] Then the Sacré Coeur was pitted against the Eiffel Tower; pilgrimages and religious festivals substituted for revolutionary commemorations. Everything was seen in these terms: Pierre Birnbaum even describes a fierce struggle over control of the ringing of village bells.[137]

Within the unbridled style of anticlerical ridicule rampant since the 1880s, Forest painted the Church as both the greatest feudal power and the ultimate capitalist venture, raking in funds for the pope's coffers in Rome while the little people slaved and starved. ("…the Church, like a huge octopus, has entwined our country in its countless tentacles").[138] He used the occasion of the jubilee to refute the sixty-year tradition of pro-clerical writing on Cluny and, without directly mentioning it, implied a wider critique of the Lourdes phenomenon.

Forest asked, "Should the republican state authoritatively substitute reason for all these religious lies?"[139] and reminded the reader that the excesses of the Revolution were nothing compared to the centuries of abuse by the First and Second Estates. He described the "yet visible" prisons and torture chambers in local castles, used by both lords and monks, calling the "martyring of people on earth to assure them eternal bliss above" cowardly.[140] Forest claimed that the Revolution abolished torture in France and called it an "act of justice."[141] He endorsed Ferry's old program to laicize the schools but lamented that private religious education had only grown; he saved his worst venom for the Jesuits and other teaching orders, accusing them of sexual crimes due to the unnatural condition of celibacy, even listing in his Epilogue all such crimes published in the newspapers from 1897 through 1899, and went so far as to recommend they all be castrated.

In spite of all this, Forest claimed he did not intend to offend anyone and was only attacking underlying hypocritical principles that he hoped influential, intelligent, and rich people would join together to reverse. He felt it was his duty to point out the collective ignorant state of souls "under the demonic ferule of clerical tyranny."[142] Describing each event in the program of the "comédie jubilaire,"[143] Forest mocked the piety and devotion of churchmen and faithful alike. Regarding tableaus at the convent and hospital chapel, he called them "lyrico-dramatico, opéra-comico-cléricalo de la grande pièce en neuf journées du Jubilé cafardo-frocardo de Cluny."[144] Admiring the music, especially the organ as played by a young priest in the church of Notre-Dame, he irreverently reminisced about a time twenty years prior when he was a fresh soldier meeting his Italian mistress in a Roman church. Describing the little statuettes of Abbot Odilo being sold around town, he suggested the young and handsome physiognomy was a smart marketing decision in light of the lack of a true portrait. He made up raucous conversation among imaginary visitors in the streets and rated Cardinal Perraud of Autun a rhetorician rather than an orator since his quiet, precise style was more dangerous than fiery eloquence.

Forest did not disparage the citizens of Cluny for the demolition of the abbey or even for their simple belief in the religion of the past. Rather, he tried to dispel the oft-repeated myth that revolutionary hordes destroyed the great church saying that it was a story propagated by the clergy to keep people sympathetic to their cause. To him, the people were simply being duped by their "gangrenous clerical-capitalist"[145] leaders and the buildings were victims of "commercial greed, shameful dealings."[146] Forest admitted that it had been impossible for the little community to maintain these immense structures "which for so long had pressed upon their shoulders and their purses,"[147] but he attributed responsibility for the "pillaging" of building parts to business men who found it an excellent occasion for "lucre" and profits.[148]

Some of the sarcasm is ribald, even crude, and spares no one. Forest called for four jubilees rather than just one since there were four abbot-saints at Cluny. He claimed dismay at not receiving the pastoral letter about the festival sent out from the episcopal office at Autun, writing that he had gone to the postmaster to see what was wrong. He pretended to misunderstand the term 'pastoral'; he asked why no one can sit on the left hand of God; he joked that if he changed faiths he would not become a Jew because he didn't like their cuisine but rather would prefer to be Muslim in order to take part in the joys of the harem; he ridiculed the countertenor as a "*demi-homme*"; he made fun of the pope's list of tasks to gain the plenary indulgence especially the condition for donations saying "Heaven isn't for the poor!" [149] as well as of those who performed them by renaming the *Ligue de Pèlerinards* the "*Ligue des Poires*" ('poire' is French slang for a sucker or gullible person) and he asked if, since the "faithful departed" could be moved up from purgatory to heaven through prayer, could not the "unfaithful departed" like Freemasons and Socialists move up from hell to purgatory? Forest even concluded one chapter by saying that of all religions, Catholicism was incontestably the most stupid. Though blatant slander in the guise of humorous political satire, and certainly not alone in its genre, Forest's text is refreshingly entertaining to read today among the saccharine positivist nineteenth-century histories of Cluny and shows us how divided was opinion about revivals of medieval customs.

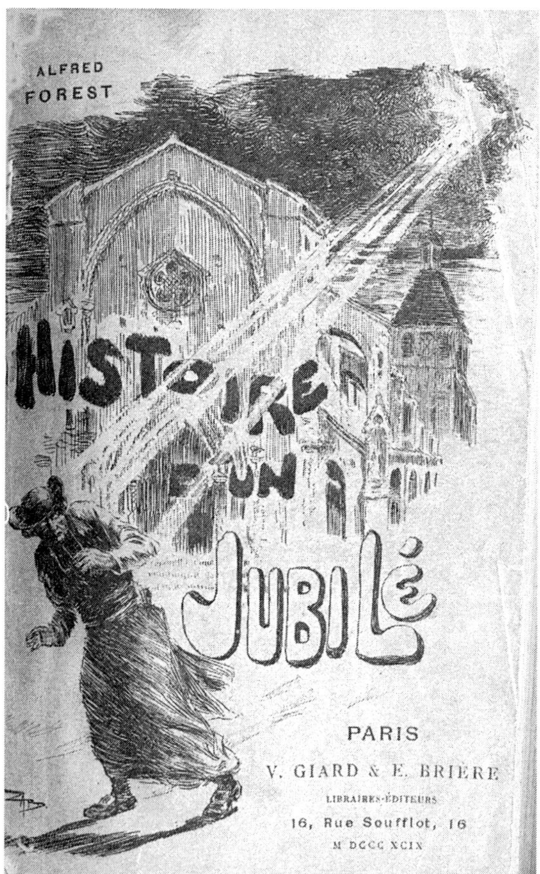

3.11 Cover illustration, Forest, *Histoire d'un jubilee,* 1898

Pen-and-ink illustrations intensified Forest's denunciatory style. They were attributed simply to "ZARD" and range from lovely little scenes around Cluny heading each chapter to full-page dramatic illustrations worthy of Victor Hugo's wildest plots. The cover set the mood for Forest's text, with a background drawing of Notre-Dame de Cluny setting the location for a shadowy, skulking figure of a cleric complete with "the soutane, broad-brimmed hat and buckled shoes habitual to the French curé"[fig. 3.11].[150] He is being struck by rays of light streaming down through a break in dark, ominous clouds. The whites of his eyes overwhelm the tiny irises turned downward so that he has a macabre and menacing appearance. The title of the book, *Histoire d'un jubilé*, was lettered by the artist in large, primitive and dark undulating letters.

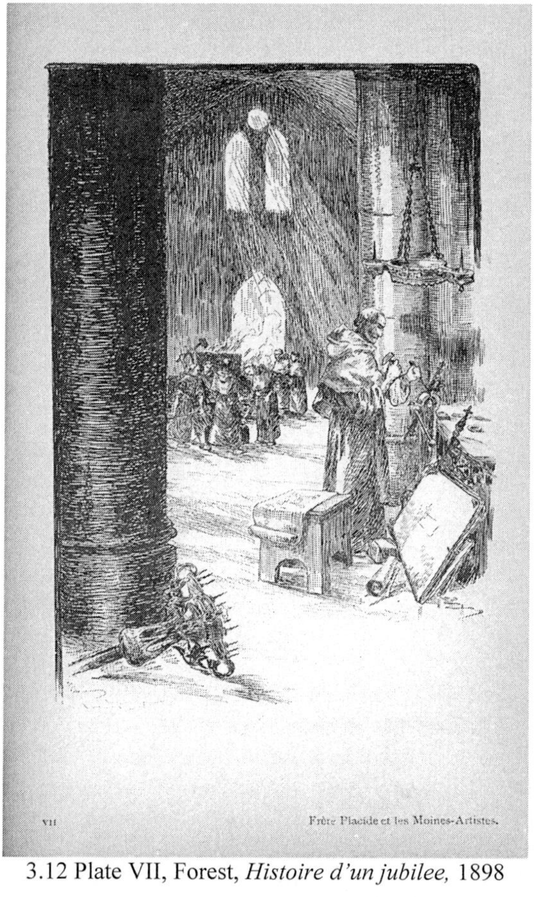

3.12 Plate VII, Forest, *Histoire d'un jubilee,* 1898

Other images illustrated Forest's imaginary notion of artisan monks working in a large church-like studio [Fig. 3.12], bogus church miracles, and other stories in his text. The copy I read, which belongs to Yale University Library, contains a handwritten dedication on the flypage from the author presenting the volume to Émile Zola, "indefatigable defender of rights and justice," under the imprinted quote from Gambetta: "Le Cléricalisme, voilà l'ennemi." Zola, who was most famous for his defense of Dreyfus in 1896, figured prominently in Forest's account ("this master among all the master writers").[151] He used Zola's fictional novel, *Rome*, as an illustration of how far the pope was from the pure religion of truly spiritual men. However, rather than merely describing the story as Zola told it, or quoting directly from the novel, Forest chose to invent his own dialogue between Louis XIII and the main character, the humble priest who tried to write a book about true faith. Forest concluded: "It is incontestable that all clerical acts are motivated by the question of money."[152] One wonders how the colorful little volume was received by Zola, particularly since it ended up in an American university library.

As caustic and unprofessional as Forest's polemic was, he gave us a good sense of the republican distance from the clerical estimate of Cluny's worth and made it easier to see why the government would not have been eager to throw funds at the repair of her ruins. The fact that the ruins at Cluny which the Commission of Historic Monuments was asked to save were from the most powerful medieval monastic institution in France was not forgotten, and must have served to give a few Parisian functionaries pause when reading documents extolling the past grandeur of the great abbey and requesting national funds to repair the damage wrought in its downfall. They were, after all, in the midst of a bitter political struggle against Catholics that would end only seven years later with the legal separation of Church and state.[153]

Forest showed us provincial clergy taking themselves too seriously and local populations becoming caught up in their ideas. Criticism of Catholic ceremonies was not limited to anti-clericalists; Ralph Gibson describes growing concerns about the "infantilism" or "feminization" of ultramontane piety during the later nineteenth century.[154] Observance drew increasingly upon emotional and aesthetic devotional practices rather than intellectual content, characterized for example by the popularity of such saints as Thérèse of Lisieux (the "Little Flower") or so-called *Saint-Sulpicean* style statues of the Virgin Mary.

Forest's book brings up one more issue for the end of the nineteenth century which Zola targeted in his novel *Lourdes*, the first of the trilogy on pilgrimage which included *Rome.* There, in a "scientific" investigation of Lourdes written in his characteristically naturalistic style, Zola exposed credibility gaps in the spiritual experience and described the seamier side of trainloads full of the sick, pools of grotto water fetid from their bodies, and the commerce of tourism. Yet his writing project was undertaken in the midst of the positivism and science of the late nineteenth century when a new need for spiritual outlets was felt by many, not only Catholics. Zola's trilogy demonstrates this with its shift away from narratives of working life under the Second Empire and toward questions of religious faith. Like Lourdes, which many French people regarded as a tiny corner so remote and impoverished that it was free of the materialism and secularism they feared was contaminating old beliefs, the writers of the various guides to Cluny tended to emphasize the idyllic setting of Cluny's valley and the genuine medieval appearance of town streets with the most Romanesque houses left standing. Forest demonstrated that the "nostalgic fantasies" of the organizers at Lourdes had spread across France but his heavy critique of the Jubilee was really overstated.[155] The event had no obvious sequel since there was no sacred pilgrimage cult at Cluny to revive. Paray was near enough to serve that function for the entire area. After 1905, it was historical patrimony, rather than revived Catholicism, which the Clunysois emphasized, as local leaders saw their town unable to compete with the kind of Marian cult Lourdes and other towns could attract and instead began to target the advantages of rail travel for the broader tourism industry.

Notes

[1] [Truth is a necessity for our times] Quoted in Janine Dakyns, *The Middle Ages in French Literature, 1851-1900* (London: Oxford U Press, 1973). 87

[2] [The Middle Ages became a folktale, a sort of childhood of the nation…] (refering to the nineteenth-century renewal of interest in the past.) Jacques Le Goff and Jean-Maurice de Montremy, *A la recherche du Moyen Age* (Paris: L. Audibert, 2003). 48

[3] David Lowenthal, *The past is a foreign country* (Cambridge; New York: Cambridge University Press, 1985). 8

[4] 28 juillet 1848: Paris, Bibliothèque du Patrimoine: Cote 81/71, 181/1, Box 17

[5] 26 juillet 1849 and 14 Août 1849. This amount is negligible; a laborer's daily wage was about 3 francs. [Thank you to Peter McPhee for this information.]

[6] 21 août 1850: Paris, Bibliothèque du Patrimoine: Cote 81/71, 181/1, Box 17

[7] "Grâce aux savantes recherches du docteur Ochier qui habite Cluny il nous sera facile de classer tous les objets déposés dans la Chapelle Bourbon et d'avoir un musée des plus intéressants."

[8] "…en dernière analyse leurs sont profitables".

[9] Merimée, Rapport à la Commission, 15 Novembre 1850: Paris, Bibliothèque du Patrimoine: Cote 81/71, 181/1, Box 17

[10] "…Vous n'avez pas oublié sans doute, Monsieur, l'importance de cette chapelle pour le point de vue artistique et de l'élégance du style gothique. Elle est du même temps que l'hôtel de Cluny de Paris et la maison abbatiale de Cluny. C'est le seul monument de notre ville qui reste entier et malgré les déplorables mutilations qu'il a subi dans son

intérieur, il mérite sans doute d'être conservé, comme un joli spécimen de l'art du 15éme siècle, mais [il doit] être restauré. Il est en outre destiné à servir de Dépôt aux sculptures qu'on a pu sauver de la démolition de la grande église, notamment aux huit chapiteaux byzantins de l'abside si justement estimés des amateurs. Le gouvernement avait déjà accordé une faible somme qui a été consacré au pavage de la chapelle sous la direction de M. Aymar Verdier, mais il reste encore beaucoup à faire.

Maintenant que les voûtes sont à l'abri de la pluie et des intempéries, il serait bien à désirer que notre honorable président continue de les protéger et le fit classer (ce monument) dans le monumens historiques, ainsi que le morceau du transept de la grande église qui est encore détruit. Si on ne fait pas bientôt des réparations soit au clocher, soit à la toiture de cette partie, il est certain que les voûtes seront dans peu de temps altérées et cèderont sous les poids du clocher qui s'écroulera de même que cela est déjà arrivé pour l'autre.

Je vous prie, Monsieur, en rendant compte de ma mission à M. de Caumont…et le supplier de ma part d'intervenir au près du ministre pour qu'il donne les ordres nécessaires et accorde des fonds pour la conservation des restes de l'antique basilique de Cluny…" Paris, Bibliothèque du Patrimoine: Cote 81/71, 181/1, Box 17. (My thanks to Stephen A. Canfield and Christine Merllie who helped me decipher this nearly illegible script.)

[11] http://www.antiquaires-de-normandie.org

[12] Stéphane Gerson, *The pride of place: local memories & political culture in nineteenth-century France* (Ithaca: Cornell University Press, 2003). 163

[13] Detailed in report of André Sallez to the Minister of Education, 20 December 1946. Paris, Bibliothèque du Patrimoine: Cote 81/71, 181/2, Box 18

[14] Roger Magraw, *France, 1815-1914: The Bourgeois Century* (New York: Oxford University Press, 1986). 218; Peter McPhee, *A social history of France, 1789-1914*, 2nd ed. (New York: Palgrave Macmillan, 2004). 253; and Robert Gildea, *Education in provincial France, 1800-1914 : a study of three departments* (Oxford; London; New York: Clarendon Press; Oxford University Press, 1983). 198-199

[15] C. R. Day, "Education, Technology, and Social Change in France: The Short, Unhappy Life of the Cluny School, 1866-1891," *French Historical Studies* 8 (1974). 428

[16] Patrick J. Harrigan, *Mobility, elites, and education in French society of the second empire* (Waterloo, Ont.: Wilfrid Laurier University Press, 1980). 28-29

[17] Celestin Roubaudi, "l'Ancienne école normale spéciale de Cluny" (paper presented at the Millénaire de Cluny: Congres d'histoire et d'archéologie, Cluny, 1910). 320

[18] Day, "Education, Technology, and Social Change in France: The Short, Unhappy Life of the Cluny School, 1866-1891." 433-434

[19] Gildea, *Education in provincial France, 1800-1914 : a study of three departments*. 116

[20] Cluny, Archives municipales : Sèrie 70 II M 1 (Expropriation d'immeubles détachés de l'Ancienne Abbaye); Roubaudi, "l'Ancienne école normale spéciale de Cluny". 319

[21] Louis M. J. Chaumont, *Nouveau guide de Cluny, ou Explications historiques des cartes postales et vues de la ville et de l'ancienne abbaye* (Domois-Dijon,: Impr. de l'Union typographique, 1905). 20 (1)

[22] Patrimony was under Fine Arts in these years but this position merged with Education in 1870. See Hollis Clayson, *Paris in Despair* (Chicago: University of Chicago Press, 2002). 201.

[23] Neil Stratford, Brigitte Chabard and David Walsh, *Corpus de la sculpture de Cluny* (Paris: Picard, forthcoming). I. 3 (d), 6

[24] Ibid. I. 3 (d), 7

[25] "…la restauration aux frais de l'Etat de la Chapelle de l'Ecole normale d'enseignement spécial de Cluny, qui faisait partie des bâtiments de l'ancienne abbaye et qui est déja classée au nombre des monuments historiques… chapelle fait partie intégrante des bâtiments que la ville a cédés à l'Etat par acte du 3 Mars 1866, et cette ville n'y entretient aucun service."

[26] 23 Avril 1868: Paris, Bibliothèque du Patrimoine: Cote 81/71, 181/1, Box 17

[27] Day, "Education, Technology, and Social Change in France: The Short, Unhappy Life of the Cluny School, 1866-1891." 434-437

[28] Roger Magraw, *France, 1815-1914: the bourgeois century* (New York: Oxford University Press, 1986). Chapter 6

[29] Day, "Education, Technology, and Social Change in France: The Short, Unhappy Life of the Cluny School, 1866-1891." 438-439

[30] "…reprises de contreforts, de corniches, de bandeaux, de colonnettes et de marches en pierre; la restauration de la charpente et la réfection de la couverture du grand et du petit clocher ainsi que de la partie de l'ancien transept qui est affecté aux exercices du culte." 4 juillet, 1881: Paris, Bibliothèque du Patrimoine: Cote 81/71, 181/1, Box 17

[31] Jean Marie and Madeleine Rebérioux Mayeur, *The Third Republic from its origins to the Great War, 1871-1914*, trans. J.R. Foster, *The Cambridge history of modern France; 4* (Cambridge; New York/Paris: Cambridge University Press; Maison des sciences de l'homme, 1984). 80-81

[32] McPhee, *A social history of France, 1789-1914.* 251

[33] Charles Sowerwine, *France since 1870: culture, politics and society* (New York: Palgrave, 2001). 62-64 and an email message dated September 29, 2004 in which he stated: "… I am not aware of any work suggesting that there was a decline in public expenditure."

[34] Paris, Archives Nationales de France: F21 1406

[35] "ces glorieux débris ayant appartenu à un monument historique tant apprécié…ces restes de son [Cluny's] ancienne gloire architecturale…ces vestiges precieux". 14 August 1882

[36] According to a letter from Director of Secondary Education to the Director General of the Fine Arts the work was completed by May 9. 1882. Notes on the report claim that the work was done under the direction of the Education ministry (again headed by Jules Ferry who was simultaneously serving as Prime Minister). Paris, Bibliothèque du Patrimoine: Cote 81/71, 181/1, Box 17

[37] Day, "Education, Technology, and Social Change in France: The Short, Unhappy Life of the Cluny School, 1866-1891." 439

[38] Ibid. 441

[39] Ibid. 441

[40] Bruno Marguery-Melin, *La Destruction de l'Abbaye de Cluny 1789-1823* (Cluny: Centre d'Études Clunisiennes, 1985). 72; Jean-Denis Salveque, "Les batiments conventuels du XVIIIe siecle," *Dossiers d'archeologie* 269 (2002). 91

[41] However, in 2005, discussion about transferring the school to Lyon took up a suggestion first broached in 1946. In spite of all the construction that has taken place around Cluny for its purposes, this shadow of possible empty cloister buildings seems to keep hanging over the town. See article in *La Gazette de Cluny* 88 (December, 2005) and letters of 1946: Bibliothèque du Patrimoine, Paris: Cote 81/71, 181/2, Box 18.

[42] Mayeur, *The Third Republic from its origins to the Great War, 1871-1914*. Chapters 3-6

[43] Ibid. 147-155; see also Pierre Leveque, "Le "Déchristianisation" en Maconnais à l'époque contemporaine: Quelques problèmes," *Mémoires de la Société pour l'histoire du droit et des institutions des anciens pays bourguignons, comtois et romands* 37 (1880). 293-313

[44] October 1891 to June 1892.

[45] Letter of 9 November, 1891: "Il s'y retrouveraient en famille et cet ensemble permettrait aux artistes et aux touristes d'admirer et d'étudier plus facilement l'art roman Clunisien."

[46] Paul Ricoeur, *Memory, history, forgetting* (Chicago: University of Chicago Press, 2004).

[47] Quoted in Gerson, 40

[48] Ralph Gibson, *A social history of French Catholicism, 1789-1914*, *Christianity and society in the modern world* (London; New York: Routledge, 1989). 228-231

[49] Ibid. 141

[50] On the cult of the Sacré Coeur see: Raymond Anthony Jonas, *France and the cult of the Sacred Heart: an epic tale for modern times*, *Studies on the history of society and culture 39* (Berkeley: University of California Press, 2000).

[51] Pierre Birnbaum, *The idea of France*, 1st American ed. (New York: Hill and Wang, 2001). 118; Joseph F. Byrnes, *Catholic and French forever: religious and national identity in modern France* (University Park, PA: Pennsylvania State University Press, 2005). 93

[52] Gibson, *A social history of French Catholicism, 1789-1914*. 145

[53] Ruth Harris, *Lourdes: body and spirit in the secular age*, 1st American ed. (New York: Viking, 1999). 255-256; Gibson, *A social history of French Catholicism, 1789-1914*. 148

[54] Jonas, *France and the cult of the Sacred Heart: an epic tale for modern times*.

[55] Birnbaum, *The idea of France*. 113

[56] Byrnes, *Catholic and French forever: religious and national identity in modern France*.

[57] Ibid. 99

[58] On Lourdes see: Suzanne K. Kaufman, *Consuming visions : mass culture and the Lourdes shrine* (Ithaca, N.Y.: Cornell University Press, 2005).

[59] Both of these "jubilees" used the word in the sense of a "holy year" established by the popes in 1300, rather then the strict Old Testament meaning from Leviticus 25: 8-10 of the "sabbath of sabbaths," or 49 years, when slaves were freed and land returned to the commune. E. J. Hobsbawm and T. O. Ranger, *The Invention of tradition* (Cambridge;

New York: Cambridge University Press, 1983). 281, n. 34; *Oxford Dictionary of the Christian Church*, ed. Elizabeth A. Livingstone (Oxford: Oxford U Press, 1977). 245-6, 281

[60] Emmanuel Auduc, *Les fêtes de jubilé de Cluny: Leur preparation, leur célébration, leur conclusion* (Cluny: J. Lamante, 1898).

[61] Daniel J. Sherman, *The construction of memory in interwar France* (Chicago; London: University of Chicago press, 1999). 265

[62] Georges Dupeux, *French society, 1789-1970* (London/New York: Methuen; Barnes & Noble, 1976). 180, Fig. IV.2

[63] Mayeur, *The Third Republic from its origins to the Great War, 1871-1914*. 105, diagram

[64] "...applicable par voie de suffrage aux âmes du purgatoire." Cardinal Perraud, "Le Jubilé de Cluny," (Autun: 1898). 6

[65] "...la concorde entre les princes chrétiens; l'extirpation des hérésies, la conversion des pécheurs, l'exaltation de notre sainte mère l'Église." Ibid. 7

[66] "...vivement exhortons..." Ibid.

[67] "Remises entre les mains d'un des prêtres de Cluny, ou déposés dans des troncs qui seront placés dans les deux églises de Notre-Dame et de Saint-Marcel, les offrandes jubilaires seront employées à faire célébrer des messes pour le soulagement des âmes du Purgatoire." Ibid.

[68] Patrick Young, "Of Pardons, Loss, and Longing: The Tourist's Pursuit of Originality in Brittany, 1890-1935," *French Historical Studies* 30/2. 269-304

[69] Ibid. 9-11

[70] L'*Union républicaine* #306, 28 October 1898. 2

[71] "On se demande si Saint Odilon ne va pas intercéder auprès du grand Maître pour fournir les indications nécessaires à la gendarmerie pour mettre fin à cette série de vols." L'*Union républicaine* #300, 3 November 1898. 2.

[72] Ibid. #312, 9 November 1898. 2-3.

[73] Linda Orr, *Headless history: nineteenth-century French historiography of the Revolution* (Ithaca: Cornell University Press, 1990). 37-73

[74] Ceri Crossley, *French historians and romanticism: Thierry, Guizot, the Saint-Simonians, Quinet, Michelet* (London ; New York: Routledge, 1993). 71-74

[75] Orr, *Headless history: nineteenth-century French historiography of the Revolution*. 20

[76] Ibid. 44, 53

[77] Gerson, p. 35

[78] François Cucherat, *Cluny au onzième siècle: son influence religieuse, intellectuelle et politique*, 2e éd. corr., complétée, enrichie de documents inédits. (Mâcon: M. Dejussieu, 1873).

[79] H. E. J. Cowdrey, *The Cluniacs and the Gregorian reform* (Oxford: Clarendon Press, 1970). 3-15 as cited in Barbara H. Rosenwein, *Rhinoceros bound : Cluny in the tenth century* (Philadelphia: University of Pennsylvania Press, 1982). 43

[80] Cucherat, *Cluny au onzième siècle: son influence religieuse, intellectuelle et politique*. 40-44

[81] Ibid. 45, 100

[82] "...qui était celle de Dieu et de la civilisation..." Ibid. 13

[83] See G. P. Gooch, *History and historians in the nineteenth century*, [2d] rev., ed. (London, New York: Longmans Green, 1952)., 506-510
[84] Cucherat, *Cluny au onzième siècle: son influence religieuse, intellectuelle et politique.*, 29
[85] Ibid. 101. Note that between the first and second editions (1850 and 1873), Cucherat remarks that this area *had been* the open square for the public market.
[86] Ibid. 112-113
[87] Ibid. 165
[88] "Ainsi Cluny a rallumé partout le feu sacré de la perfection monastique par la sagesse de sa réforme. Il a conservé les dernières lueurs de la science, des lettres et des arts, par la force et la renommée de ses écoles. Il a sauvé le monde par l'élévation et la suite de ses conceptions politiques." Ibid. 218
[89] Louis Henri Champly, *Histoire de l'abbaye de Cluny* (Macon: Legrand/Mme. Ve Félix, 1866).
[90] See Linda Nochlin, *The Body in Pieces: The Fragment as a Metaphor of Modernity* (New York: Thames and Hudson, 1995).
[91] Ibid.
[92] "Voilá les sombres allées où les cénobites de Cluny allaient rêver en lisant les livres saints!" Louis Henri Champly and René Champly, *Histoire de l'abbaye de Cluny*, 3. éd., rev., ed. (Paris: Librairie centrale des sciences, 1930). 8
[93] Ibid. 7
[94] "...il ne reste plus que quelques pans de murs dont les pluies d'automne et le défaut d'entretien altèrent chaque année la solidité." Ibid. 7
[95] "...et si, parfois, le gardien de ces reliques les exhume aux regards d'un visiteur, ce n'est qu'en faveur d'un touriste étranger who, traversant la Bourgogne, vient saluer ce souvenir d'une grande éteinte." Ibid. 10
[96] For instance, Cucherat writes about Bernon and the establishment of the institution culled from the abbey chronicles (*Bibliotheca Cluniacensis)* and recorded a legend about Saint Odo said to have been only one of many in the oral tradition about his extraordinary life (Ibid. 21-31).
[97] Champly, *Histoire de l'abbaye de Cluny*. 87-99, 116-117
[98] For an interesting comparison between Champly's nineteenth-century scholarship and more modern critical analysis on this and the next issue I discuss, see chapter 6 of Marcel Pacaut, *L'Ordre de Cluny : 909-1789* (Paris: Fayard, 1986).
[99] 99-100. The desire to hold true to official Church history returned, and was even less appropriate, in Champly's coverage of the schism between the two popes: Anaclet II and Innocent II. Although he informed the reader that Anaclet II was elected by a large majority of the College of Cardinals and that Innocent II was mainly supported by Benedictines, the fact that Peter the Venerable, and later Bernard of Clairvaux, Suger of St. Denis and Louis VII all ratified his election in France, convinced Champly that he was the legitimate holder of the papal chair (101-103). Nevertheless, he does not avoid Champly's censure either, since he was horrified to report that Innocent IV later supported the Cistercians at the expense of the Cluniacs (104-106). The book is clearly partisan to its subject. Likewise, Peter the Venerable's medieval attitudes about Jews and Muslims was regarded by Champly as part of his admirably relentless efforts on behalf

of the Church. He also conflated Abélard's panegyrical with that of Peter the Venerable, the former gaining in Champly's estimation by his association with the abbot of Cluny. Bernard of Clairvaux's discipline and austerity in the face of Cluny's wealth and comforts was a difficult issue for Champly to resolve in Cluny's favor, however he managed to make Bernard appear to act more from a "sour grapes" position with Peter the Venerable than that of a reformer. In all, Peter the Venerable could do no wrong. Champly erased the debts that mounted during Peter's rule with the story of Henry of Winchester's gifts upon his entry into the abbey and ended his account with a long quote from Lamartine's *Héloïse and Abélard..* The reader was thus left with a dramatic and Romantic tribute whose tone was the model for Champly's own text.

[100] "Les plus superstitieux racontèrent qu'au milieu des flammes les images des vieux saints, protecteurs du monastère, se tordaient avec des yeux pleins de menaces et lançaient sur la ville l'anathème, présage des plus sinistres malheurs." Champly and Champly, *Histoire de l'abbaye de Cluny.*, 351

[101] Ibid. 351 (*)

[102] J. Henri Pignot, *Histoire de l'Ordre de Cluny depuis la fondation de l'abbaye jusqu'à la mort de Pierre-le-Vénérable (909-1157)*, ed. Société éduenne des lettres sciences et arts (Autun, France) (Autun/Paris: Michel Dejussieu/Libraire Durand, 1868).

[103] Ibid. 3

[104] Again, like the others, Pignot took contemporaries who were writing eulogizing biographies as objective chroniclers. He also added odd things. For instance, at the end of volume one, after Odilo, there is a chapter recording the *vita* of William of Dijon as written by Rudolf Glaber. William fit into Pignot's theme as another reformer. In the final notes of volume one, there was an attempt at objectivity when Pignot championed the opinion of Moulinet that something attributed to Odo was not in fact written by him (*Notes additionnelles I)*. This, in spite of evaluations to the contrary by all the foremost authorities such as Mabillion, was due, in Moulinet's mind, to the many errors implicit in the text. Pignot, believing in Odo's peerless intelligence and sanctity, agreed and went on to credit musical writings to Odo which had previously been assigned to others, again basing his argument upon that of a specialist whom he quotes at length (*Notes additionnelles II*). Finally, he disagrees with earlier authors whom he names (Lorain, Cucherat, Duparay) that Casimir I of Poland became a Cluniac monk (*Notes additionnelles III*) and rests his objections upon Polish historians who considered the story no more than a fable, conflated with events in the life of the fourteenth-century Casimir the Great.

[105] On these monks not being architects see: Janet Marquardt, "The Original Significance of the Gunzo Legend at Cluny," *Comitatus* IX (1978).; Carolyn M. Carty, "The Role of Gunzo's Dream in the Building of Cluny III," *Gesta* XXVII, no. 1 and 2 (1988).

[106] "Mais cette ornementation, prodigué dans d'autres Églises clunisiennes, sous l'influence du gout local, avec une plus grande profusion, ne s'éloignait pas dans la basilique d'une certaine sévérité. Ce qui est frappant, avant tout, c'était la grandeur unique du temple, l'harmonie de ses proportions qui lui donnaient une sonorité remarquable, son heureuse disposition pour les cérémonies religieuses." Pignot, *Histoire de l'Ordre de Cluny depuis la fondation de l'abbaye jusqu'à la mort de Pierre-le-Vénérable (909-1157)*. Vol. 2, 505

---

[107] Ibid., 508-509

[108] Louis M.-F. Chaumont, *Histoire populaire de Bourgogne, à l'usage des écoles et des familles* (Cîteaux: Librairie Saint-Joseph, 1881).; Louis M. F. Chaumont, *Histoire populaire de Bourgogne : les faits, les institutions*, 3e ed. (Lyon: Librairie et imprimerie Vitte et Perrussel, 1887).

[109] Richard Lehmann, *Forschungen zur Geschichte des Abtes Hugo I von Cluny (1049-1109)* (Göttingen: Vandenhoeck & Ruprecht, 1869). Though admittedly incomplete, this is earlier than the work Barbara Rosenwein cited as the first modern biography: Albert L'Huillier, *Vie de Saint Hugues : abbé de Cluny, 1024-1109* (Solesmes: Imprimerie Saint-Pierre, 1888).

[110] Lehmann, *Forschungen zur Geschichte des Abtes Hugo I von Cluny (1049-1109)*. 1 (*)

[111] Benoit Duparay, *Pierre-le-Venerable, abbe de Cluny, Sa vie, ses oeuvres et la societe monastique au 12e siecle* (Chalon-sur-Saône: P. Mulcey, 1862).

[112] Jean Virey, *Les églises romanes de l'ancien diocèse de Mâcon* (Paris: Picard, 1892).

[113] Jean Virey, *Les églises romanes de l'ancien diocèse de Mâcon, Cluny et sa région* (Mâcon: Protat, 1935).

[114] "Tout le monde sait que ce monument magnifique est presque entièrement détruit : il ne subsiste que…précieux restes qui nous donnent l'échelle de l'édifice, et qui permettent à l'imagination de se représenter l'ensemble." Virey, *Les églises romanes de l'ancien diocèse de Mâcon*. 31

[115] Jean Virey, *Paray-le-Monial et les églises du Brionnais* (Paris: H. Laurens, 1926).

[116] Jean Virey, *L'abbaye de Cluny* (Paris: H. Laurens, 1927).

[117] A. Penjon, *Cluny : notice sur la ville et l'abbaye,* 2 ed. (Cluny: Imprimerie J.-M. Demoule, 1874).

[118] "…s'harmonisent avec ce calme paysage et font de loin l'impression d'une ville du moyen âge qui se serait conservée jusqu'a nos jours." A. Penjon, *Cluny; notice sur la ville & l'abbaye*, 3. éd. (Cluny: Renaud-Bressoud, 1884). 2

[119] A. Penjon, *Cluny la ville et l'abbaye* (Cluny: Mme. Ve. Félix etc., 1872), microform.

[120] "…un des plus étrange monuments qu'il soit possible d'imaginer… causent une impression singulière d'admiration et de malaise à la fois." . 5-6

[121] "pour donner à la petite ville, dans certains quartiers surtout, l'aspect le plus original." Penjon, *Cluny; notice sur la ville & l'abbaye*. 9

[122] "…est la partie la plus médiocre de l'édifice, et ne peut fair soupçonner ni la légéreté, ni l'élégance de l'intérieur." Ibid.

[123] "…débris de la bibliothèque des moines" Ibid. 15, note ***

[124] "Le xie siècle et le xve se résument dans ce contraste." Ibid. 16

[125] Ibid. 19. Penjon explained the building history of the Pope Gelasius façade, saying that only the revolution saved the entire area from a major remodeling by the monks. Instead, he recounted that the façade was demolished and rebuilt in the same Gothic style merely a dozen years before he wrote this, with 19 ogive windows on the second level which he found a rare blessing in its perfection.[125] The drawing by Legrand on page 12 shows the original state of the façade with the Baroque portal they removed at that time; it is today stored in the basement of the Farinier.

[126] "Mais les moines ont effacé eux-mêmes tous les vestiges du passé; ils ont donné les premiers l'exemple de ce vandalisme qui devait détruire, quelques années plus tard, le seul monument qu'ils eussent entièrement respecté et une grande partie des bâtiments nouveaux." Ibid. 29

[127] Ibid.

[128] This work is something of a bibliographical puzzle. Copies cataloged by libraries as a second edition from 1880 include reference to the École Nationale de Contre-Maîtres replacing the École Normale in 1891 as the current institution in the cloister buildings. In fact, the Bibliothèque Nationale, Paris lists the date as 1895, no edition specified. Other publications appeared by E. Ricard in the 1890s as well. Some designate him as "Abbé".

[129] Ricard, for instance, quoted the little ditty that everyone loved to repeat about everywhere the wind blew Cluny collected rents, mentioned the story of the 1245 visit that the abbey was so large it could accommodate any number of important guests in the abbatial palace without disturbing regular monastic life, and after a statistical description of the church wrote that it was said the grills of the chapels weighed more than 11,000 pounds and were turned into weapons in 1794.

[130] Auguste Bernard and Alexandre Bruel, eds., Recueil des chartes de l'abbaye de Cluny, 6 vols. (Paris: Imprimerie nationale, 1876).

[131] Rosenwein, Rhinoceros bound : Cluny in the tenth century.

[132] Ernst Sackur, *Die Cluniacenser in ihrer kirchlichen und allgemeingeschichtlichen Wirksamkeit bis zur Mitte des elften Jahrhunderts* (Darmstadt: Wissenschaftliche Buchgesellschaft [Halle an der Saale, 1892-4], 1965).

[133] Laura Morowitz and Elizabeth Emery, "From the living room to the museum and back again," *Journal of the History of Collections* 16, no. No. 2 (2004). 290-291

[134] Elizabeth Emery, "Protecting the Past: Albert Robida and the *Vieux Paris* Exhibit at the 1900 World's Fair," *Journal of European Studies* (2005). 80-81

[135] "Le Jubilé de Cluny ne fut qu'une humiliante arlequinade!" Alfred Forest, *Histoire d'un jubilé; neuvième centenaire de l'institution par Saint-Odilon, abbé de Cluny (962-1049) de la commémoraison de tous les fidèles trépassés (31 octobre--9 novembre 1898) a Cluny* (Paris: V. Giard, E. Brière, 1899). 14

[136] Birnbaum, *The idea of France.* 115ff.

[137] Ibid. 117

[138] "...l'Eglise, comme une pieuvre gigantesque, a enlacé notre pays dans ses innombrables tentacules." Forest, *Histoire d'un jubilé; neuvième centenaire de l'institution par Saint-Odilon, abbé de Cluny (962-1049) de la commémoraison de tous les fidèles trépassés (31 octobre--9 novembre 1898) a Cluny.*, 22

[139] "L'État républicaine doit-il faire acte d'autorité en substituant la raison à tous ces mensonges religieux?" Ibid. 15

[140] "...martyriser l'homme sur cetter terre pour lui assurer....[sic] là haut....[sic] une éternelle béatitude..." Ibid. 162

[141] Ibid. 45

[142] "...sous la démoniaque férule de la tyrannie cléricale." Ibid. 32

[143] Ibid. 100

[144] Ibid. 120

[145] "gangrène clérico-capitaliste" Ibid. 137

[146] "convoitises commerciales, de trafics honteux" Ibid. 38
[147] "...qui si longtemps avait pesé sur leurs épaules et leur bourse..." Ibid. 39
[148] "Mais le responsibilité de cette vente revient aux hommes d'affaires de cette époque qui trouvèrent là une excellente occasion de lucre et de profits." Ibid. 39
[149] "Le paradis n'est pas pour les pauvres!" Ibid. 68, 138, 73
[150] Baroness Orczy, *The Scarlet Pimpernel* (1905), chapter 24. This popular novel, though written a few years later, is set during the French revolution and evokes similar macabre figures in clerical garb associated with victimizing poor citizens.
[151] "...ce Maître entre tous les Maîtres écrivains..." Forest, *Histoire d'un jubilé; neuvième centenaire de l'institution par Saint-Odilon, abbé de Cluny (962-1049) de la commémoraison de tous les fidèles trépassés (31 octobre--9 novembre 1898) a Cluny*. 79
[152] Ibid. 79
[153] The intense hatreds and radical violence this struggle provoked is one of the primary subjects in Birnbaum, *The idea of France*.
[154] Gibson, *A social history of French Catholicism, 1789-1914*. 265-67
[155] Harris, *Lourdes : body and spirit in the secular age*., 24, 253

CHAPTER FOUR

ANTICIPATING THE RESURRECTION (1900-1928)

> ...car l'histoire de nos monuments est un long martyrologe, et jamais nation n'a gaspillé plus follement son patrimoine artistique.
> —Le Comte de Lasteyrie, 1910[1]

> Tout Clunysois naît pour l'histoire avec un péché original: celui d'avoir détruit la basilique de saint Hughes....Le Cluny d'aujourd'hui n'est pas Cluny: c'est l'absence de Cluny.
> —Albert Thibaudet, Cluny 1928[2]

> The human project of memory, i.e., commemoration, is basically a religious project to secure some form of immortality.
> —Avishai Margalit, 2002[3]

The end of the nineteenth century in France saw a return to political concerns about the power of the Church to influence the government. The moderate leader Méline had tried to stave off radical agitation for complete separation of Church and State by following a policy of appeasement and what his minister of Education, Spuller, called a "new spirit" of good sense, justice and charity.[4] By 1897 Léon Bourgeois was claiming that the Church was controlling the Right and that the *notables* (local elites), whose power had been defeated, might use this to regain influence.[5] Mayeur and Rebérioux summarize the philosophical union of the Left this made possible with the statement: "Anti-clericalism was democratic and made people equal."[6] Thus Leo XIII's efforts at *Ralliement* failed and were replaced by growing political alignments against conservative defense of the Church.[7] The passions aroused during the Dreyfus Affair brought out the worst side of the Church and left it vulnerable to criticism by Republicans after the conspiracy between judges and Army was known.[8] In 1901 a law was passed that limited associations to those whose members had no foreign attachments, forcing clerical institutions to cut their ties with the Vatican.[9] The government now had the leverage to close private Catholic schools, which had flourished after Ferry had removed the teaching orders from public schools in 1881. The monastic orders were disbanded and their members exiled in 1903. Peter McPhee suggests that resulting inventories of church property brought out strong responses according to regional political preferences.[10] Pressure grew until Church and State were finally legally separated in France on December 9, 1905, effective December 11, 1906.[11]

Ultimately, the preservation of the abbey remains at Cluny during the twentieth century would be seen in terms of historical monumental architecture rather than about the religious functions of specific buildings as chapels for the school or as symbols of a monastic medieval past. Guizot's Romantic associations for the sake of a liberal nationalism gave way to practical plans for maintaining the old buildings in their original form as much as possible while keeping them in use as museum, town hall, school, and stable. The rise of tourism had made such a course evidently advantageous. Although this time around Cluny was remote from struggles over church property and papal influence, nonetheless, lingering associations with the powerful medieval abbey would have colored funding requests which did not make clear references to their contemporary secular utility.

The Millénaire of 1910

> Like monuments themselves, ceremonies convey meaning in many different ways, but they function most notably as idealizing representations of the communities they seek to shape.
> —Daniel J. Sherman, 1999[12]

In spite of the secular justifications for maintenance of the remaining abbey buildings, 1910 was the millennial anniversary of the foundation of the abbey in 910 and it was commemorated with events that, like those of 1898, emphasized the medieval Church. Dominique Iogna-Prat has shown that Cluny's *millénaire* was planned within a French "culte du centenaire" and served as the first example of a French millennial anniversary event, just before that of the province of Normandy in 1911.[13] France had only begun national anniversary holidays with the new Bastille Day in 1881.[14]

The festival was held September 10-12 and included a comprehensive academic conference on history and archeology (*the Congrès*) organized by the Academy of Mâcon, grand liturgical celebrations organized by the Church, and a lavish historical reenactment organized by the municipal council. Two volumes of documentation were published in the same year by Protat Frères in Mâcon.[15] They were divided into three parts. In volume one, part one consisted of a summary of the planning and events with supporting documents such as the invitation that was sent out to scholars, lists of committees, rules, programs, participants, remaining houses of the Benedictine order in 1910, newspaper coverage, poetry written by Academy members upon the occasion of the millennial anniversary, and descriptions of specific events. In part two, discussions, recommendations, toasts, and introductions occurring during the *Congrès* were all recorded in print. Part three completed volume one and filled most of volume two. This was the publication of the papers given at the conference. A small part four added two postscripts—reviews reflecting on events and Cluny's ongoing role in modern life.

A great deal can be learned from this material and it is a rare treat to have such a well-documented occasion. Clearly the administrators wanted to leave a record for posterity yet according to the first entry, the *compte rendu* (written by Armand Duréault, secretary of the Academy), the event had a slow start. The members of the Academy of Mâcon who thought the city would be on top of the upcoming occasion and happy for their proffered help were mistaken, as apparently nothing had yet been planned as of December 14, 1909. Pierre Goujon, writing in 1994, suggests that the municipal council dragged its feet because the occasion did not accord with Republican history; throughout the planning and implementation of events, the politicians tried to distance themselves from the religious aspects of commemoration.[16] The Academy thus decided to take the lead and plan a full-scale international congress of history and archeology. They had just purchased a Cluniac manuscript from 1325 and Jean Virey, president of the organization for 1910, had begun to contact members of the *Institut de France* in Paris to show it to them and to encourage them to participate in a local conference. With the help of the venerable Léopold Delisle, a committee was formed of individual members as well as official representatives from the Institute, including René Bazin for *l'Académie Française* and others who would contribute to the proceedings from *l'Académie des Inscriptions et Belles-Lettres, l'Académie des Beaux-Arts,* and *l'Académie des Sciences morales et politiques*. Local scholars and high-ranking prelates (including the archbishop of Reims) were also on the organizing committee.

The local bishop, Villard, wrote a little volume about the event published in 1911 much like the one that Auduc prepared on the jubilee (see chapter 3), including excerpts from the published proceedings.[17] He gives credit for the idea of a millennial celebration to the curate of Notre Dame de Cluny, Abbé Lauvernier. However, the responsibility for organizing such events about national patrimony, Iogna-Prat tells us, rightly fell upon the Academy of Mâcon, for that was considered the primary responsibility of these provincial societies.[18] Gerson's study of the cult of local history dates the high point for French reenactments much earlier in the century, at least in the North.[19] Cluny's medieval past was so tied up in that of the abbey and the huge church ruin that it was hard to shape a politically acceptable perspective. Yet without a specific focus for the pilgrimage cult and with a strong socialist electorate, its religious value was obsolete.

A number of alumni from the old école normale (by this date referred to as the École Duruy) attended the event as representatives for other organizations. Most importantly, the Academy of Mâcon invited exiled Benedictines to "a *millénaire* which is in fact their own".[20] One of three offered a place on the organizing committee declined returning to a country that had banished its monks. The other two, Ferdinand Michel Cabrol and Jean-Martial Besse, jumped at the opportunity for a public reception of their political activism on behalf of the Church.[21] The presence of Cabrol and Besse at this event was significant. In 1903, Cabrol was sent from Solesmes, where he had been prior, to found the abbey of St. Michael's Abbey in Farnsworth, England and become its first abbot. From 1890 on, Besse was a very active journalist, teacher and scholar. He worked as a writer, recruiter, and then teacher for the *Action française*. He founded the Revue Mabillon (1905) in honor of his great ambition to revive the type of Benedictine learning represented by Mabillon. Advisor to Huysmans and Paul Claudel, Besse advocated resistance and learning as part and parcel of the same movement to emulate great monastic leaders of the past and renew the spiritual life of France. In 1904, he described the indignities undergone by the monastery of Saint-Wandrille, mutilated for its lead, turned into factory and town hall, then repopulated by monks from 1894-1901. He wrote of the "soul" of the abbey waiting to rejoin its body on a resurrection day, which he hoped would also be that of a resurrected Christian France.[22] In 1910 he was at the height of his activism against the Republic and against all Catholic compromises and his name would have been familiar to participants in the Congrès, most certainly affecting the tenor of other contributions.

Congrès registrants were promised that their name would appear in the published proceedings. The fee was 6 francs for three days of papers, banquets, and entertainment in addition to a great number of excursions, demi-tarif on the national trains to get to Cluny, and free transportation for those lodging in Mâcon. The two volumes of proceedings, in contrast, would later cost 10 francs.

In February 1910, Virey gave a lecture at Mâcon about Cluny's history to begin to educate the public about the event. Like Duréault, Virey was a politically conservative local landowner, as well as a scholar of medieval art, and his interventions on behalf of an event celebrating local medieval history were unabashedly friendly toward Catholic designs. This was not true of all members of the Academy; it was after all a positivist, republican organization founded under the impetus of Guizot's reclamation of regional history. Duréault himself gave the position of secretary of the *Congrès* to departmental librarian and conservator Léonce Lex, a notoriously anti-clerical Freemason.[23]

While the organizing committee was drawing up plans for the conference program and sending out invitations to other scholarly organizations, the local Church began planning a *triduum*, or three-day liturgical event, and the municipal council, with help from the Academy, decided upon the reenactment of a key occurrence from the Middle Ages for the popular festival: the 1245 visit of Pope Innocent IV and King (Saint) Louis IX to Cluny. They thus opened the 1000th anniversary of the abbey to its entire medieval history in order to focus attention on the wider importance of the town. Every aspect of the 1910 *millénaire* reinforced Cluny's original relationship with the Church. Pope Pius X was still battling the effects of the 1905 law of separation and his French bishops deftly used this commemoration to highlight Roman Catholic pageantry within the republican taste for medieval history.

By choosing an event from the thirteenth century, the city made a choice not only to move beyond the exact anniversary year of 910 but also from the usual emphasis on Cluny's golden period of the eleventh and twelfth centuries for the more popular and visually elaborate reenactments of the Gothic period, as seen at "Le Vieux Paris" and "Paris en 1400" from the Paris 1900 Exhibition [fig. 4.1]. In a way, one could see the town choosing what Jacques Le Goff has called the "sauve, troubadour age" (imagined for 1245) over the "dark and obscure Middle Ages" (where lesser known 910 resided).[24] These spectacles were neither representations of the Middle Ages as the "Age of Faith" nor the noble, harsh period praised by Republican texts. Instead, Gothic recreations in Paris and Cluny spoke to a romantic and colorful fantasy world aimed towards popular consumerism and a type of ribald entertainment influenced by Victor Hugo's descriptions in *Notre-Dame de Paris*.[25] The 1900 Exposition stands as the first in a series of international fairs hosted by France as part of her careful self-image shaping that would be heightened during the interwar years.[26]

Other elements of this story also recommended it to Cluny's organizers; the meeting of the highest representatives of Church and State (a rapprochement in line with the aspirations of many participants), the public pageantry of a cortège (better than a static ceremony for accommodating crowds along multiple streets), and the opportunity for locals to play roles from the past (many of which allowed provincial notables to dress up in the regalia of their titled ancestors). Certainly there was more information about customs, costumes, and personages from the later medieval period, nevertheless it still seems awkward that an event commemorating the year 910, with multiple references by lecturers to Cluny's role in the *Trêve de Dieu* (Truce of God—the agreement proposed in 958 to limit private warfare by declaring certain Church feast days off limits) was at such odds visually and ceremonially. Perhaps that is only hindsight—at the time, popular distinctions between the appearance of the 10th and 13th centuries were minimal.

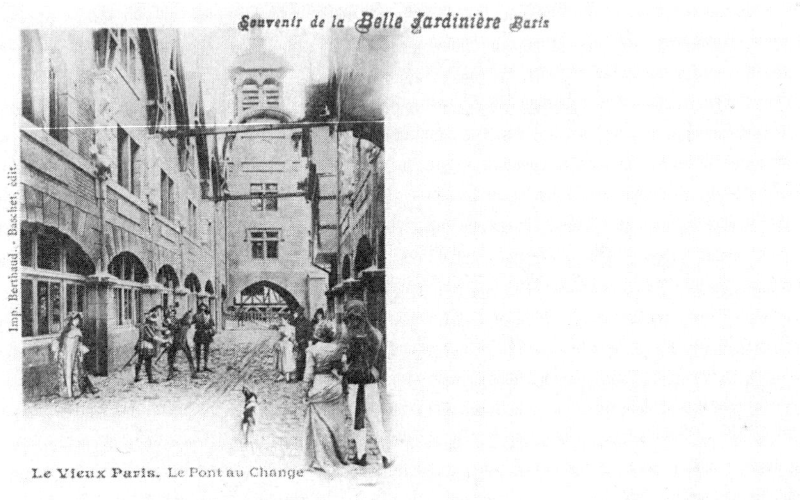

4.1 Postcard of Le Pont au Change from *Le Vieux Paris*, Paris 1900 exhibition (Elizabeth Emery)

The Academy of Mâcon had friends among the press who previewed and reported the millennial celebrations. At the end of March, *l'Echo de Paris* carried a story by literary figure, Léon de Tinseau, on Cluny's upcoming plans. In August, two more articles previewing the upcoming events were published in Paris by *Le Correspondant* and *La Liberté*. The Academy also added weight to requests for government funding toward repairs on the Tour Fabri, part of the old fortification wall of the monastery only recently classed by the Monuments historiques in 1902, in time for the arrival of interested scholars and scientists in the autumn. Protat, member and official printer of the Academy, published a volume of historical documents relative to Cluny in advance of the *millénaire*, under the direction of Francois-Louis Bruel, director of the Cabinet des Estampes of the Bibliothèque Nationale.

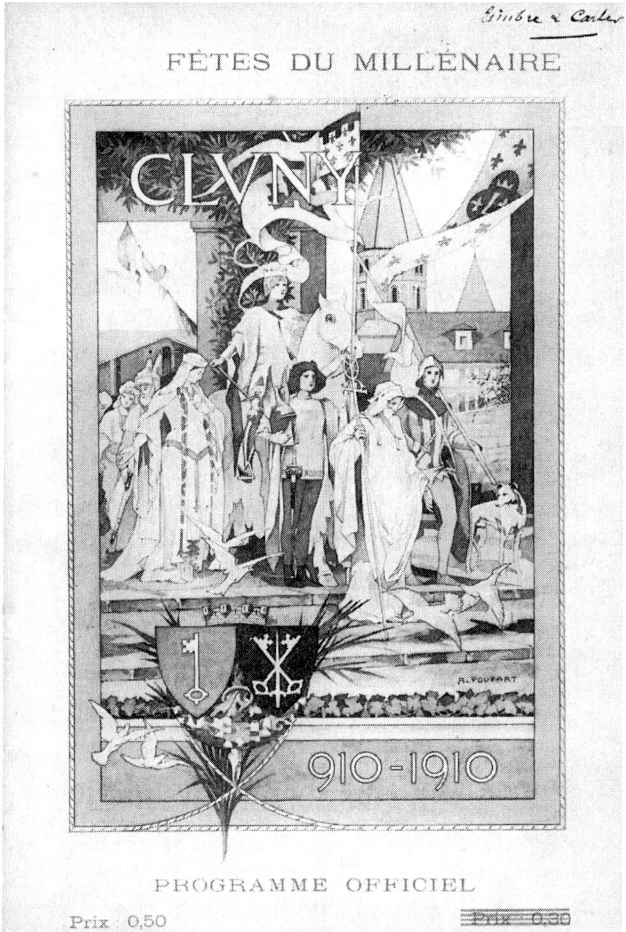

4.2 Program Cover, 1910 Millénaire de Cluny
(Cluny Collection: Loeb Library, Harvard University)

The event was planned for three days, probably in accordance with the ecclesiastical decision to hold a *triduum* although Duréault claimed the Academy first planned the conference for that time period. The cover of the program pamphlet showed a painted image of the *Trêve de Dieu* by the Mâconnaise artist Poupart, which was touted as attesting to the "peaceful and cordial harmony during the celebration of this grandiose occasion [fig. 4.2]."[27] This appears to have been an attempt to forestall Republicans who might attack the heavily religious character of the celebration; in fact it was merely a representation of figures from the pageant with some doves in the corners. Nevertheless, King Louis dominates the composition on horseback with his queen and attendants around him and though the abbot is shown as an old bearded man in a cowl leading the procession, the pope is not seen at all. Rather, the imperial couple from Constantinople appear behind the queen and even one of the royal dogs is pictured next to an odd figure carrying a flag who sports helmet and shield but is dressed in parti-color with tights. A removable four-page insert included all the religious festivities, showing approval by the diocesan bishop. On Saturday, September 10, the Academy planned a series of welcome speeches in the morning prefacing the first session of papers and then choice from three excursions for conference participants in the afternoon. These consisted of the first and most ambitious day tour in an automobile to Saint-Point via Tramayes, through the pass called "*la Mère Boitier*" and the Serrières valley, then through the *Grange-du-Bois* pass to Roche de Solutré. Return was by way of Milly-Lamartine and Berzé-la-Ville, in order to visit Abbot Hugh's chapel, and on to the chateau Berzé-le-Chatel. The second choice was by train to Monsols and on to Saint-Point. The last choice was also by train from Cluny to La Croix-Blanche-Sologny and on to Berzé-la-Ville and Berzé-le-Chatel. Those who visited Saint-Point were hosted by Lamartine's nephew. Poems read by participants extolling Lamartine and Saint-Point are recorded in the *Compte Rendu.* The author noted how these tours encouraged admiration of the Mâconnais region but of course they also underlined the two notables of Cluny: St. Hugh and Lamartine.

The program lays out the following days as well. After the excursions of day one, a second session of papers was held, followed by a grand banquet for 200 participants. The menu cover illustration, also by Poupart, incorporated Sagot's 1832 view of Cluny with the Hôtel Senecé of the Academy of Mâcon [fig. 4.3].[28] Very early Sunday morning there was a visit to the remaining medieval buildings, as well as the family homes of Lamartine and the painter Prud'hon, inside Cluny. Then the third session of papers began at 9 a.m., followed by a pontifical mass at 10 o'clock. A formal photograph of the nineteen bishops and Benedictine abbots who participated appears in volume one, plate V [fig. 4.4]. It must have been a moment charged with emotion when all these resident secular Church administrators lined up with their exiled monastic compatriots.

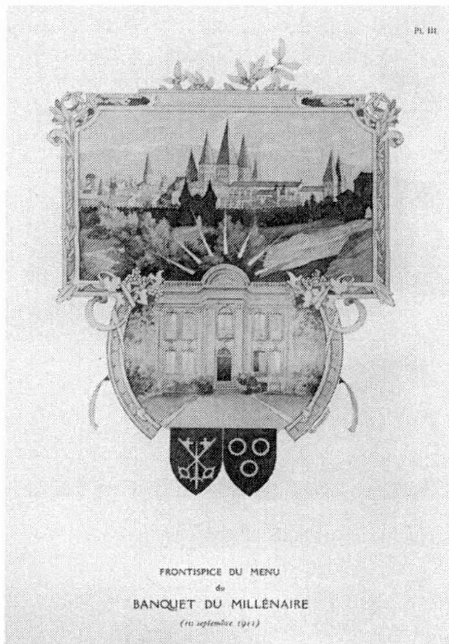

4.3 Menu cover, 1910 Millénaire de Cluny (Millénaire proceedings I, plate III)

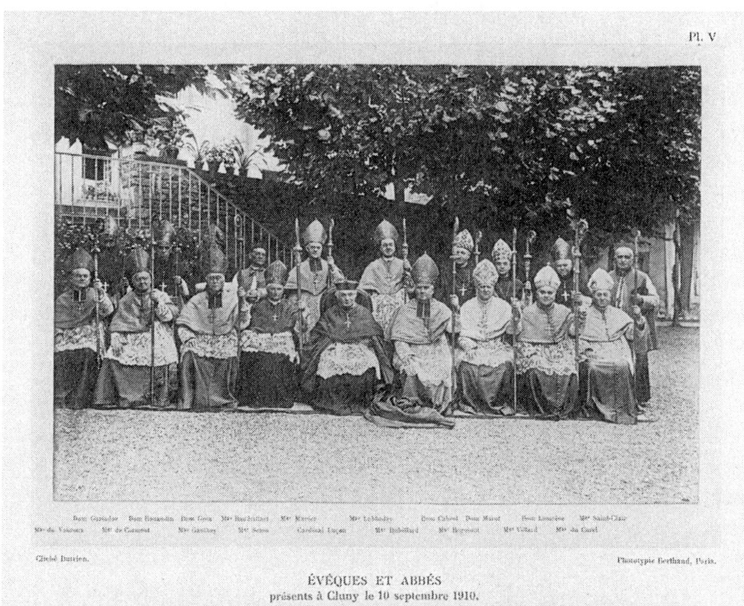

4.4 Ecclesiastics assembled for 1910 Millénaire de Cluny
(Millénaire proceedings I, plate V)

The afternoon was set aside for the historical reenactment of the royal cortege with local luminaries acting the parts of medieval aristocrats; a foldout diagram of the order is bound into volume I [fig. 4.5].

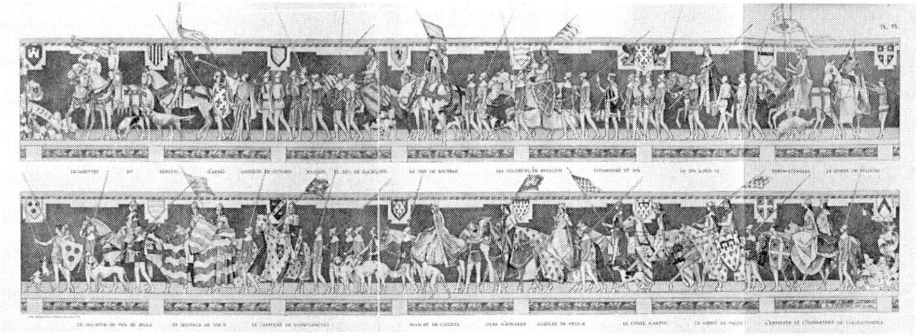

4.5 Diagram of cortege for 1910 Millénaire de Cluny (Millénaire proceedings I, plate VI)

Evening vespers completed the day with a grand procession of the clergy and a speech on Cluny and the papacy by Monsignor Baudrillart of the Catholic Institute in Paris (who, Iogna-Prat reminds us, would later become famous for his support of the Vichy).[29] On Monday, conference participants were taken to Charlieu and Paray-le-Monial, the latter significant not only for being architecturally comparable to the third abbey church at Cluny, but also because it was the center of the Ultramontane movement in France and a pilgrimage site of the recently popular Sacred Heart cult (see Chapter 3). The visit was not an archeological one; Dom Cabrol celebrated high mass with Cardinol Lucon and nearly all the other visiting prelates in attendance. The newspapers reported huge crowds of "pilgrims" from Cluny and the surrounding Charolais region.[30] In the evening were the final session and last words on the academic front as well as a public concert and fireworks display. Tuesday was dedicated to an exploration of Saint-Philibert at Tournus and a farewell banquet for the *conférenciers*; the working people would have surely already returned home to their jobs.

Amidst all these preparations, word came on July 21 of the death of Léopold Delisle in the museum at Chantilly where he was curator (along with being honorary head of the Bibliothèque Nationale), just after writing a letter to the secretary of the *Academy de Mâcon* asking that he be excused from presidency of the program committee due to ill health. He was 85 years of age and so revered that this letter was both transcribed into the *compte rendu* and a facsimile inserted into the publication (volume 1, plate II) as well as his photo separating parts I and II [figs. 4.6, 4.7]. He was not replaced as president of the *Congrès*, rather the committee continued under the auspices of his name. It was felt that there was simply no one else in France at the time who could serve as such a perfect political and academic link.

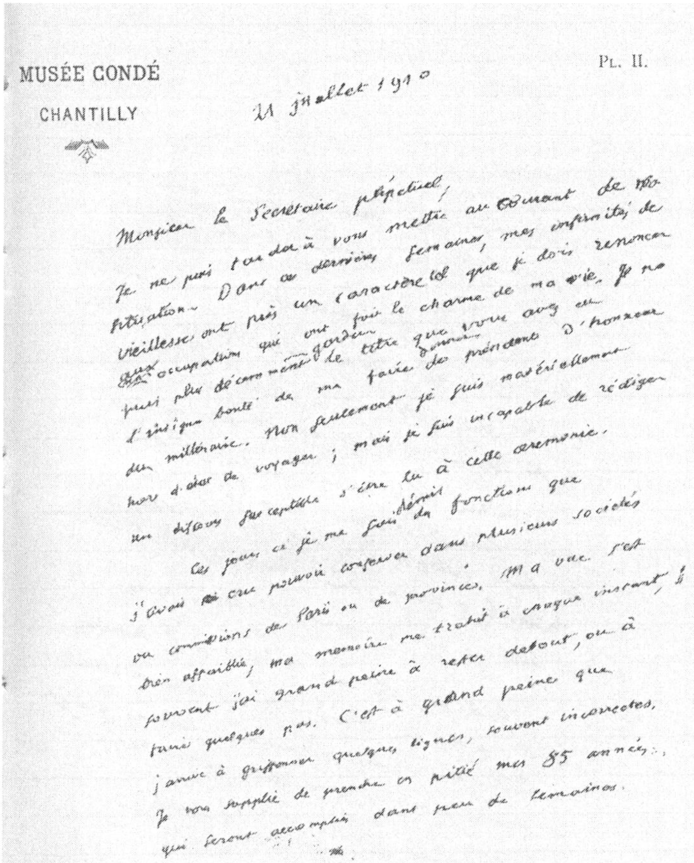

MUSÉE CONDÉ

CHANTILLY

PL. II.

21 juillet 1910

Monsieur le Secrétaire perpétuel,

Je ne puis tarder à vous mettre au courant de ma situation. Dans ces dernières semaines, mes infirmités de vieillesse ont pris un caractère tel que je dois renoncer aux occupations qui ont fait le charme de ma vie. Je ne puis plus décemment garder le titre que vous avez eu l'insigne bonté de me faire donner de président d'honneur du millénaire. Non seulement je suis matériellement hors d'état de voyager; mais je suis incapable de rédiger un discours susceptible d'être lu à cette cérémonie.

Ces jours ci je me suis démis des fonctions que j'avais cru pouvoir conserver dans plusieurs sociétés ou commissions de Paris ou de provinces. Ma vue s'est bien affaiblie, ma mémoire me trahit à chaque instant; souvent j'ai grand peine à rester debout, ou à faire quelques pas. C'est à grand peine que j'arrive à griffonner quelques lignes, souvent incorrectes. Je vous supplie de prendre en pitié mes 85 années, qui seront accomplies dans peu de semaines.

4.6 First page of Delisle's resignation letter from 1910 Cluny Millénaire (Millénaire proceedings I, plate II)

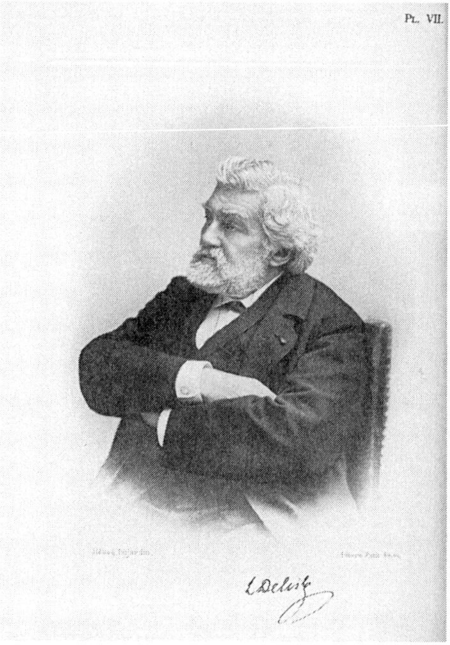

4.7 Portrait photo of Leopole Delisle (Millénaire proceedings, plate VII)

728 individuals registered for the *Congrès*. This exceeded expectations and complicated preparations, requiring additional lodging to be arranged in the dorms of the *École des arts et métiers* as well as in Mâcon hotels from where special trains ran to Cluny for these three days. It was also the director of the *École* who provided rooms for the conference sessions, an amphitheater for large addresses, and a bay of the cloister arcades for the banquet setting (the arches, hung with red velvet, were each illuminated by six electric lamps), thus allowing most of the conference to take place within the old abbey buildings. Though now eighteenth-century structures, these spaces were nonetheless the closest academics could get to retracing the steps of Cluny's medieval monks and many speakers referred to the special aura being there evoked. Three hundred chairs were added to the churches where services were held and 500 seats were reserved for *Congrès* participants to view the cortege. Unlike the commemoration of 1898, the press would show very active attendance in 1910; twenty-six newspapers sent special delegates whose names were published on a separate list in the proceedings (pages XL-XLI) and who were seated at their own table and thanked specially at the banquet.

The *Compte rendu* renders an interesting *Who's Who* of French scholars and clergy of the day, as well as local administrators and important families. The reenactment of Saint Louis's entry provided an opportunity to reestablish some hierarchical distinctions in the region that had been downplayed since 1789. Widely advertising the events at Cluny helped to bring the town back to the attention of both the academic world and the French government. Bringing distinguished scholars to the area was important for the status of the historical monument and reinforced Cluny as a subject for research studies.

The participants in the *Congrès* were all French, save one who was Swiss. All the papers were given in French and varied widely in their quality, length and focus. This is significant in the history of French scholarship on Cluny since in later years approaches became entrenched between national schools and the range of French studies narrowed.[31] It is also important to keep in mind that this commemoration was about the year 910 and thus, in spite of the foci for the tours and the cortège, offered some perspectives beyond standard assumptions that all developments at Cluny led to and away from the golden years under saints Odilon and Hugh. There was a mix between those who spoke directly to the role of Cluny in violent tenth-century Europe and those who generalized about her overall role in European culture. All were influenced by the nineteenth-century authors discussed previously, but they were also driven by their political affiliations.

Speakers reported on manuscripts once held in Cluny's library.[32] Jean de Valois reported details about the foundation of the abbey complete with the transcribed charter and Jean Virey showed a ground plan of the layout.[33] Others discussed comparable Benedictine Romanesque church architecture and decoration; most of these are the written records of tours and lectures given during the excursions.[34] Victor Terret gave a talk on Burgundian sculpture which initiated his monograph on the subject published four years later.[35] Various aspects of medieval life and monastic rule around Cluny were studied.[36] A few papers went further afield covering such diverse topics as the effects of the Revolution or even the *école normale* of the nineteenth century.[37]

Throughout the *Congrès,* various participants were called upon to render *"discours, allocutions, motions, toasts".*[38] From the beginning, the tone was set by Jean Virey who welcomed everyone, as president of the Academy of Mâcon, to the *vallée noir* where forests once covered the hills.[39] Cluny was enshrined by this event into a memory of a glorious lost patrimony, evidence of a better France when monks were cherished as pious, peaceful, academic, and artistic. Each subsequent speaker took the cue to laud bygone Cluny in a rosy light. The monks, as martyrs to the Revolution, were turned into saints much like Delisle. In fact, many of the toasts took on the character of eulogies; the mood was one of regret for the passing of Delisle, for the end of the Cluniac order, and for the destruction of historical architecture.[40] Virey referred to "*le mélancolique Cluny moderne*"[41]

> Pillaged, sacked ("*saccagé*"), by the Revolution, [the great abbey church] was left standing empty. The inhabitants did what they could to save it, but by an unbelievably fatal error, in the first years of the nineteenth century, public carelessness let it fall into the hands of a group of speculators who used it as a mine![42]

The word "saccagé" is the same one used by Besse in his 1904 description of Saint-Wandrille. Likewise Antoine Héron de Villefosse gave a "solemn homage to these monks who in the past dared to resist tyranny, who valiantly fought for liberty… " (by implication honoring those present such as Besse who continued the battle) and deplored the destruction of the abbey church:

> If, one foolish day, human hands destroyed this whole majestic basilica, which recalls the important place held by the monks of Cluny in the history of the world, we have the right to deplore it from all points of view. But that which remains still speaks with enough eloquence to our eyes and hearts of those who know how to understand the language of the ruins. Question, gentlemen, these admirable sculptures, listen to the voice which still sighs in these old stones! In the midst of a sacred silence you will receive from them the most fruitful instruction and the most profitable lessons.[43]

His sentiments were echoed in the quote at the top of this chapter from Le Comte de Lasteyrie who literally voiced the metaphorical notion of monuments as martyrs.

Other remarks framed the future of French patrimony, especially those by Édouard Aynard who called upon the academies throughout France to help conserve national treasures.[44] He heralded the rise of the photographic postcard as a popular yet effective way to spread knowledge of French art and history,[45] underlined the indissoluble relationship between France past, present and future and the need to keep national pride in the history of the country alive,[46] and made a specific jab at contemporary republicans when he asked the members "to foster national pride and deny the [ideas] of a certain element in France which persists in believing that the history of France only began in 1789".[47] Pierre Imbart de la Tour (representing *l'Academie des Sciences morales et politiques* and avoiding the religious associations as much as possible) called Cluny the birthplace of French culture: "France is there. A nation that knows how to remember, can venture far."[48]

Another theme, heavily dependent upon available literature, was woven through these men's addresses: the pious, intellectual abbey. Jean Virey called the abbots men of great virtue who quickly made Cluny a saintly center of the

Church and intellectual capital of Europe and he described the resident monks as delicate souls taking refuge against the abominable tenth century.[49] He acclaimed their accomplishments, giving them credit for the conservation of classical and patristic literature:

> What a brilliant spectacle thus offered the monastery! Full of pious souls, writers, thinkers, artists. The monks collected there what remained of Latin manuscripts, and, other than a few parchments which were erased for transformation into missals and song books, it is through them that we inherited the literary works of Antiquity and the writings of the Church Fathers. Their studies were important enough to allow curious minds to develop and thus form the scholars who brought about the intellectual renaissance of the 12th and 13th centuries.[50]

Ernest Babelon (delegate of the *Académie des Inscriptions* of the *Institut de France*), and Pierre Imbart de la Tour, speaking in the first session of the conference on Saturday morning, extolled the monks as agents of French morality and civility, assuaging the human misery of their age[51] and effecting the Truce of God.[52] Imbart de la Tour cast Cluny in particularly a romantic light: the monks who chanted while holding valuable books were administered under an ideal feudal equilibrium with perfect accord between authority and liberty, cooperation and rule, sensibility and reason; reconciling ideas and work, representing organization in the midst of anarchy.[53] Most of the early speeches were not academic presentations, but propaganda to rekindle interest, even sympathy, for Cluny as a worthy subject of study. As Héron de Villefosse said in his toast at the banquet: "The Congress of Cluny will have lasting results. The memory of these events will live on in the public eye, fixing there forever the role of these venerable monks and the great work that they accomplished."[54] Duréault's *compte-rendu* reinforced this plan. He expressed hope that the *millénaire* would give Cluny an archeological and historical apotheosis.

It is interesting that Émile Mâle did not participate in this event. Although he would not publish work on Romanesque art until 1922, he was already teaching medieval art at the Sorbonne since 1906 and certainly knew many of the participants. His critical skills in literary texts and his interest in ideas and iconography (see Chapter 5) would have added a level of analysis clearly missing. Perhaps he did not think there was enough artistic material left from the Middle Ages to warrant study at Cluny, with only the fragmentary choir capitals conserved from the Romanesque church and an empty Bourbon Chapel. This would also help explain why Cluny did not appear in surveys such as Édouard Corroyer's *L'Architecture Romane* from 1887, though here the entire region of Burgundy was ignored, or even later in the volume on Burgundy of 1954 from the Zodiaque series *La Nuit des Temps* directed by the nearby abbey of La-Pierre-qui-Vire (whose monks had attended Cluny's millénaire).[55]

Two reviews are published at the end of volume II in the proceedings. The second, *"Le Millénaire de Cluny,"* a long multi-part article by Ernest Babelon, began with the historical reenactment of the royal cortege of 1245 after quoting Michelet's definition of history as a resurrection.[56] He described a glorious event with colorful descriptions of the townspeople preparing for the procession, the general proclamations made the day before with trumpets in the manner of the Middle Ages, the garlands and heraldic motifs adorning the streets, and the huge crowds pouring into Cluny to see the 300 local participants in all their elaborate finery [fig. 4.8]. For Babelon, it created a "happy effect, harmonious, gay, medieval."[57] He echoes earlier authors on Cluny when he reinforces the immense size of the former abbey by recounting the story (via a traveler to the abbey in 1247, then Michelet and Lorain) that both the huge papal and royal parties were accommodated within the monastic living spaces without disturbing the routine of the regular residents.[58] He provides historical background on the reason Louis processed into Cluny and how the sumptuousness of his cortege was designed to compete with the visual authority of the Pope.

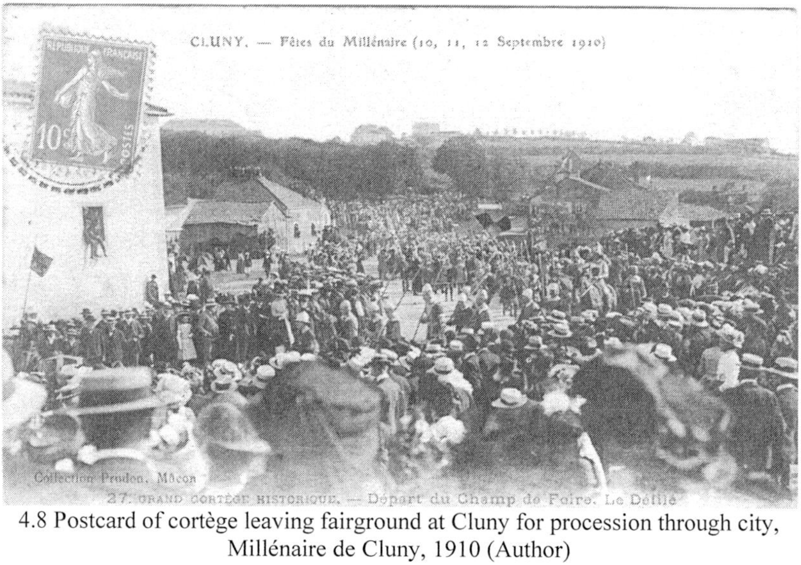

4.8 Postcard of cortège leaving fairground at Cluny for procession through city, Millénaire de Cluny, 1910 (Author)

For Babelon, the three groups that worked side-by-side in the town to bring about the modern events commemorating an "apogee of the medieval world"[59] were even more divergent in their views than those medieval visitors. He claimed this was one of the surprises of the affair; that clergy, the members of the Mâcon academy, and citizens "more or less radical and socialist who had to march in stride with the others even if feeling a bit out-of-sorts and pressured in the popular atmosphere" were in harmony during planning.[60] Listing the participants, Babelon stressed the fact that "authentic descendants" of the original knights, the "noblesse de Bourgogne", mixed with local people and that the church was packed with spectators for the religious celebrations (which, though also considered authentic, nevertheless included the sound of the "great organ", an anachronistic element no one seems to have noticed).[61] As a medievalist, like most other participants in the *Congrès*, Babelon was wholly enthusiastic about the inclusion of three days of Catholic liturgy in the program and hailed especially the return of the exiled monastic clergy. His vivid imagination brought the very art to life:

> A mysterious frisson ran through the onlookers; we had, for the moment, a veritable vision of the middle ages while watching the monks process, young and old, their faces imprinted with the indefinable combination of strength and sadness that comes from profound faith: we saw men of another time, figures from the very sculptures of the cathedrals walking through the crowd to bless it.[62]

In section two, Babelon recounted the foundation of the abbey, emphasizing Cluny's papal privilege and claiming the abbey became the right arm of the pope, many of whom had been Cluniac monks, in his battles against secular power (a nice image, since that is all that remains of the great church—the right transept arm.) He claims for Burgundy a designation as the crossroads of Christianity; describing the abbots as pilgrims crisscrossing Europe to administer their priories and reform monastic observance, setting an example of almsgiving and pursuing the intellectual arts.[63] "It is not enough to say that they marched with their time: they were at the head of their century in all branches of human activity….It is through Cluny and the Cluniac monks that the influence of the French spirit expanded and dominated the civilized world for so long."[64]

Babelon admitted that the "torch which guided the intellectual and moral world" passed into other hands with the corruption of Cluny's rule and the rise of the Cistercian and mendicant orders. He even went so far as to recognize that by the time of the famous royal entry of 1245 Cluny was already in decline, but he blamed the intervention of the kings for imposing their selection of abbots. In the abuses of power and money, he saw the justifiable seed of revolution yet condemned those who blindly destroyed monasticism without regard for its past service or its creations destined to become patrimony.

Finally, Babelon depicted the view of the visitor to Cluny in 1910 who, seeking the architecture of King Louis' time, was faced with eighteenth-century structures. He pointed out the medieval remains and described the abbey church at length, repeating most of the stories published in nineteenth-century histories about its destruction and attempts to save it. More interestingly, in the final two pages of this long collection of essays, speeches, and memorabilia for the *millénaire*, Babelon took a tone not yet seen.[65] Essentially, Babelon turned on the Clunysois who were just recently his hosts and asked how they could throw all the blame on the consular government when their abbey was only one of over a hundred wonders of architecture and it had simply been up to the local population, like others in France, to take the lead if they wanted to save it. He said they should have presented themselves to Napoléon when he came through on June 29, 1800 (interestingly enough, the abbey's feast day of SS Peter and Paul, though he does not mention this) to ask for help from the man who laid the first stone reconstructing Lyon, put up a monument at Valence to the memory of Pius VI, reopened the churches, and prepared the *Concordat.* And how could they condemn the Minister of Finance for not responding fast enough when the population, which held in private hands parts of the richest library in the world (burned and scattered in 1793), did nothing to try to reassemble the collection? He recalled hearing stories of the children in the schools, not more than fifty years earlier, making paper airplanes out of the vellum folios, choosing ones with the prettiest painted miniatures for their toys (Albert Thibaudet would also publish this story as oral history in 1928.)[66] And only twenty years before he wrote, when the remaining archives were rediscovered, if the townspeople had even suspected their importance would they have let them go without protest to the Bibliothèque Nationale? He admonished his readers not to cast blame upon one or another fanatic, but rather to take this lesson to heart and learn from it. It was an exceptionally curious way to end the collected materials of the *millénaire* and suggests some members of the Academy of Mâcon were not in complete disagreement with his views. Thus the laudatory remarks about Cluny's greatness and hopes that this *Congrès* would lead to new research seem to have been founded upon a defining sense of the participants' own academic superiority to the Clunysois. Whereas today we might look for a more evenhanded treatment of the realities of Cluny's role in medieval Europe, admitting their foibles along with their contributions, this is not where this first "modern" deconstruction lay. Rather, the distant past remained a romantic and sacred gem, waiting to be unburied and reclaimed. It was the recent past and the contemporary burghers who were villainized, justifying outside intervention and paving the way for the French government to grant permission for foreigners, such as Conant, to wield their picks in the town.

The photographic record is an important corollary to Babelon's essay, illustrating his descriptions of the events. There are 12 postcard images in a collection put together by Henri Gandrez and printed as part of an ongoing postcard series by Editions Saint-Seine-l'Abbaye in 1982, while others are available for sale and in local collections.[67] Gandrez's volume gives us a good sense of the town at this time and demonstrates that the elaborate constructions over the main streets for the celebrations had been previously realized. Already in August 1906, a regional musical gathering on the occasion of the dedication of a monument to Victor Duruy prompted elaborate festive preparations and we can see in one postcard photo (p. 48 of Gandrez's book) a view of a Cluny street covered with round arches decorated with leaves and flowers and connected by looped garlands hanging against the buildings. For the 1910 event, the shape of the arches was modified to a pointed form, apparently to conform to the Gothic style popular during the time period of Louis IX's visit (Gandrez pinpoints it as the "flamboyant" style) [fig. 4.9]. The streets were covered from side-to-side by simple ogive arches attached to tall single "columns" (metal or wood supports) some higher than the three-story buildings and in many cases complete with tracery in the spandrels evocative of Gothic windows. Both parts were covered with greenery and paper flowers. Garlands were draped against the buildings from columns also serving to support heraldic signs in shield shapes. Gandrez writes that "The effect was of an ivy-covered arcade of the cloister."[68]

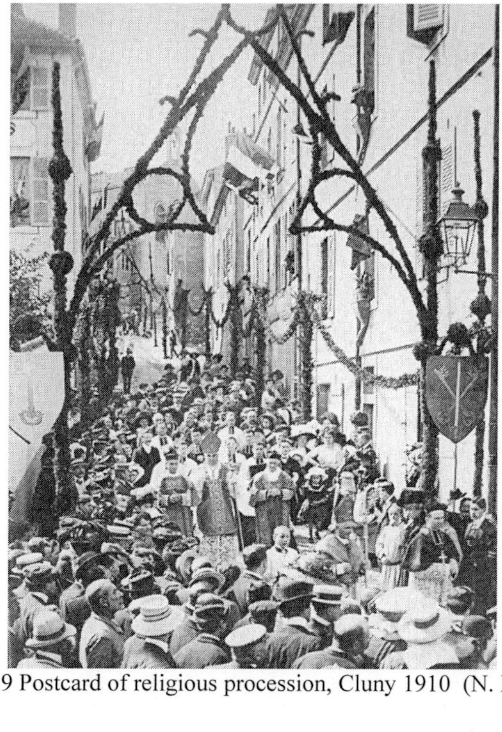

Fig. 4.9 Postcard of religious procession, Cluny 1910 (N. Roiné)

The processions of genuine clergy are hard to distinguish from images of the costumed participants in Louis's cortège. Mixing with the descendants of the medieval aristocracy, solemnly playing the role of the Church in a staged performance, decking themselves out in their finest and most elaborate liturgical garments—it seems incredible that barely a century before such events were ribald Jacobin parades, making festivals of anti-clerical propaganda with plundered vestments. Here there is barely a smile to be found, everyone seems to have been taking the occasion, and themselves, very seriously [figs. 4.9, 4.10]. Costumes and music were a mix of medieval references. In one view of the parade, we can see a four-bell instrument as found on the figurative capital for the fourth tone from the choir of the abbey church [figs. 4.11, 4.12] yet the ceremonies also included a performance by the Mâcon chorale singing the pilgrim's chorus from *Tannhaüser*, another anachronism.

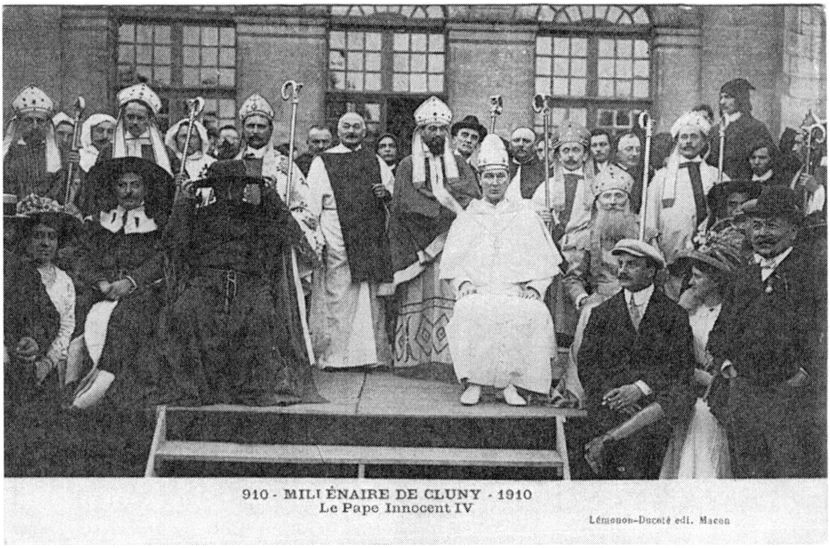

4.10 Postcard of pope and abbot awaiting arrival of king, Cluny millénaire, 1910 (Author)

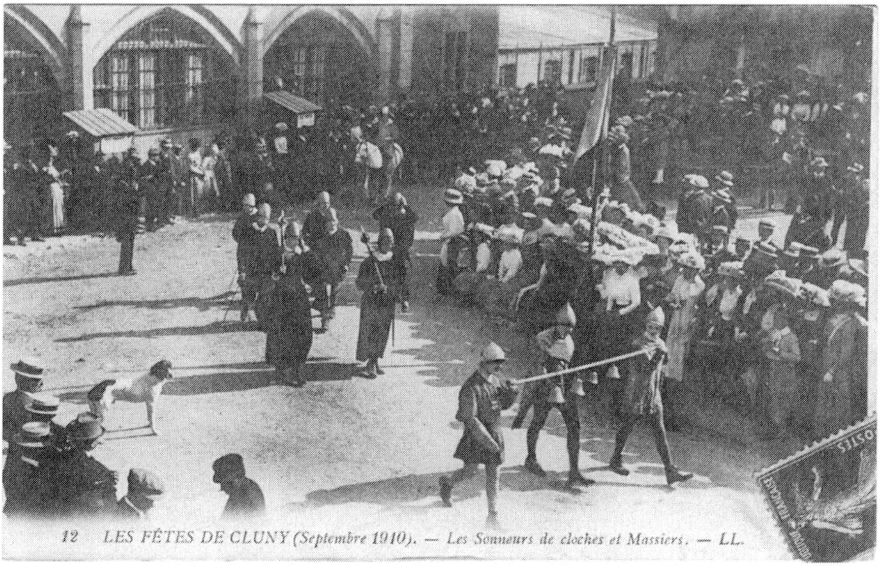

4.11 Postcard of crowd watching parade with medieval bells, Millénaire de Cluny, 1910 (Author)

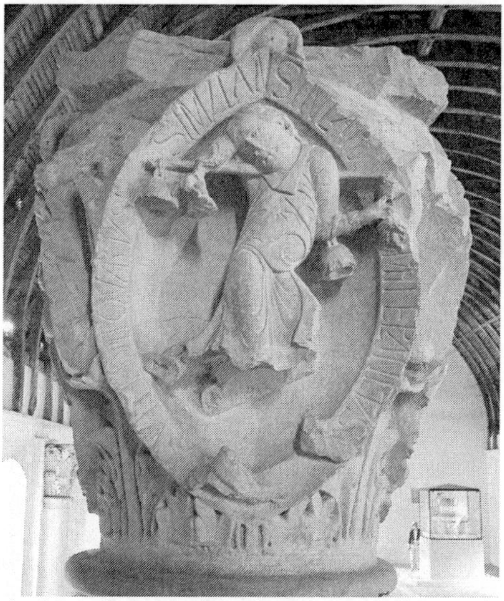

4.12 Sculpted capital of fourth tone originally from ambulatory choir, abbey church of Cluny, ca. 1100 (Andrew J Tallon 2002)

This latter view of the crowd shows the male onlookers in everyday suits with fashionable straw boaters, derbies, fedoras, or woolen *casquettes* [fig. 4.11]. Women sport wide-brimmed hats with flowers and feathers, long skirts and high-necked blouses, according to the fashion of the day. The dignitaries, on the contrary, wear formal dress with top hats and even some white ties [fig. 4.13].

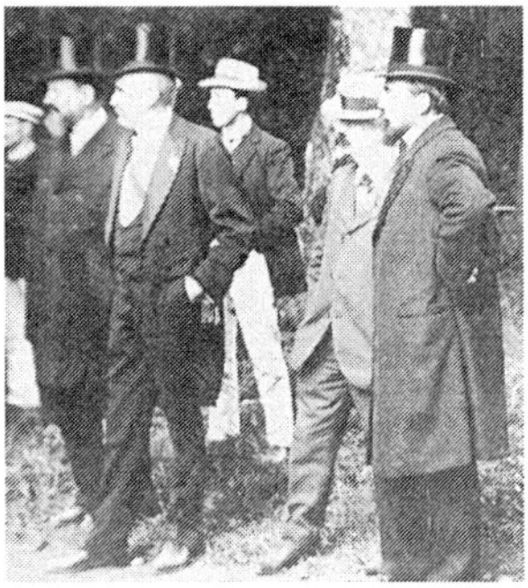

4.13 Postcard of Mayor Simyan and Minister Sarraut at Cluny for Millénaire events (N. Roiné)

The participants of the cortège had ornate costumes rented from a shop in Paris, credited in the program. The Byzantine emperor and empress appear twice in the postcards [fig. 4.14]. Their costumes appear to be a fusion of western notions of royal garb and fantasy about Eastern finery. The empress, for example, wears a pointed cap made of woven strands of pearls. The peaked shape at the top has a sort of triple-domed effect, unlike anything recorded in historical images.

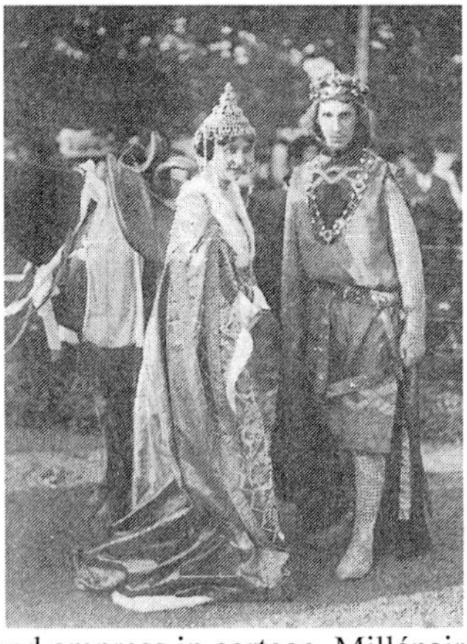

4.14 Byzantine emperor and empress in cortege, Millénaire de Cluny, 1910 (Illustré soleil du dimanche 39 [September 25, 1910], 11. N. Roiné)

Other figures seem to have a Hollywood quality about them as well. Women's eyes come across unnaturally dark in the photos and remind one of the makeup used by silent film stars such as Mary Pickford who was just becoming popular in D. W. Griffith's films (see empress and queen in 4.14 and 4.15). Attendants' costumes are as elaborate as the main characters; even horses are decked out in royal style. The two greyhounds appearing in the shot of Queens Isabelle and Blanche are a genuine medieval breed as seen in fifteenth century manuscripts like BNF, FR 616 (Gaston Phébus, *Livre de la Chasse,* folio 37v) [fig. 4.15].[69] A large number of the townspeople participated, with young girls serving as both handmaids and pages while most of the male members of the area apparently dressed as heralds and knights [fig. 4.16].

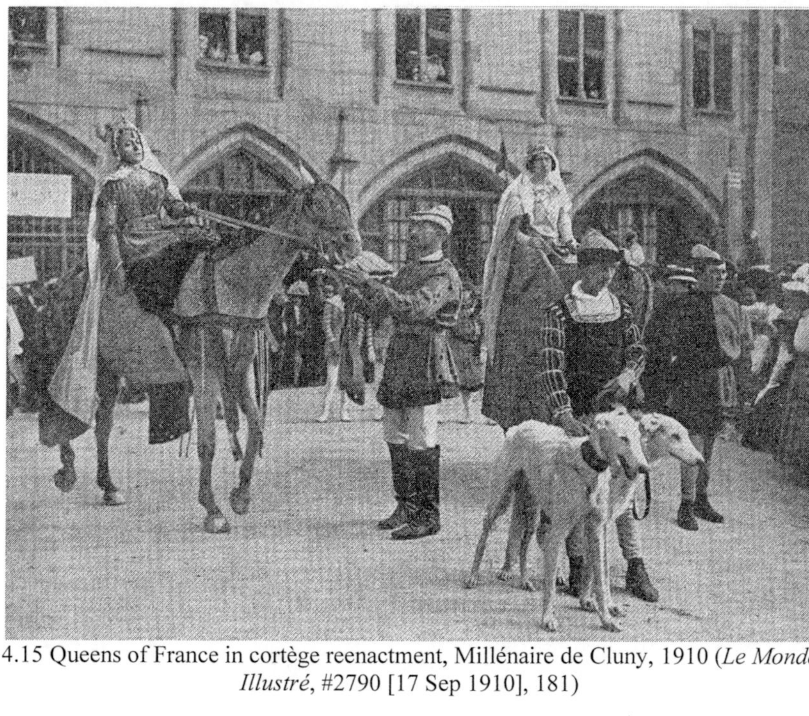

4.15 Queens of France in cortège reenactment, Millénaire de Cluny, 1910 (*Le Monde Illustré*, #2790 [17 Sep 1910], 181)

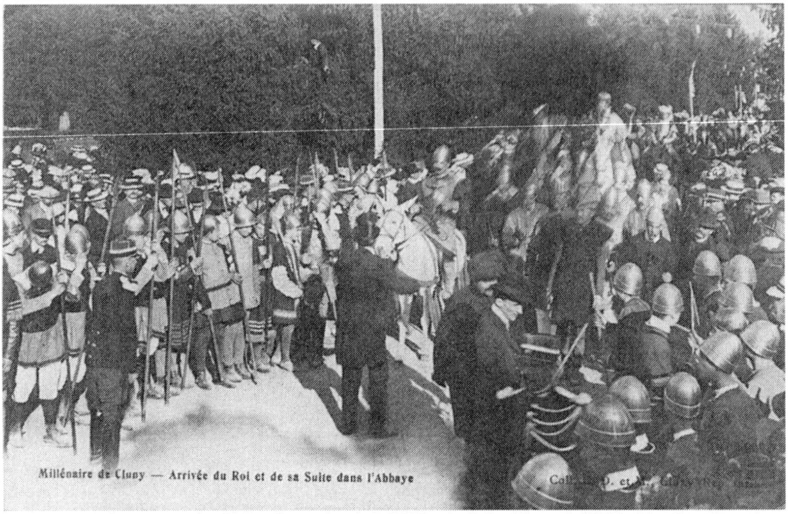

4.16 Postcard of king's arrival, Millénaire de Cluny, 1910 (Author)

Postcards were a new and growing industry around 1910 and the *millénaire* provided cause to print dozens of scenes. For instance, one shows the upper reaches of the choir of Notre-Dame with flags, shields naming the "Cluniac" popes, and inscription over the crossing arch that read: "910-1910 Science, Civilisation, Art & Religion" [fig. 4.17].

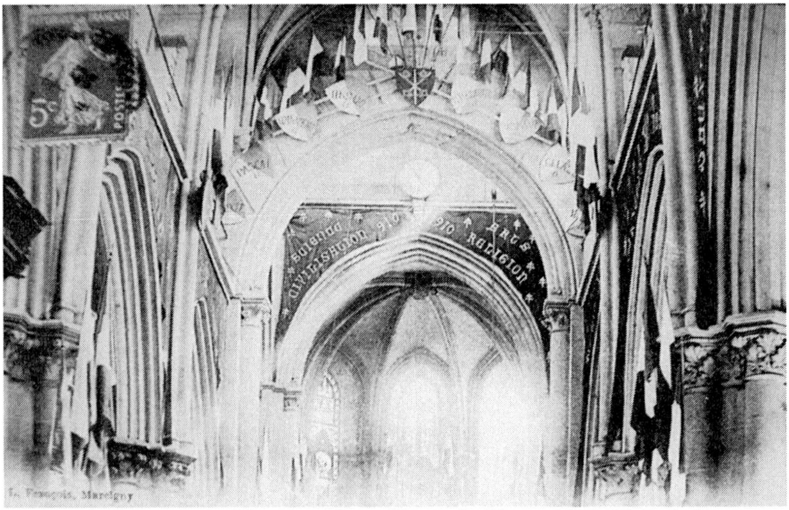

4.17 Postcard of interior, Notre-Dame de Cluny, 1910 (N. Roiné)

Another is just a snapshot of the large crowd exiting the church after the pontifical mass. The poster, program cover, and menu cover were also reproduced as souvenir postcards. There was even a special postal cancellation stamp established for the event.[70]

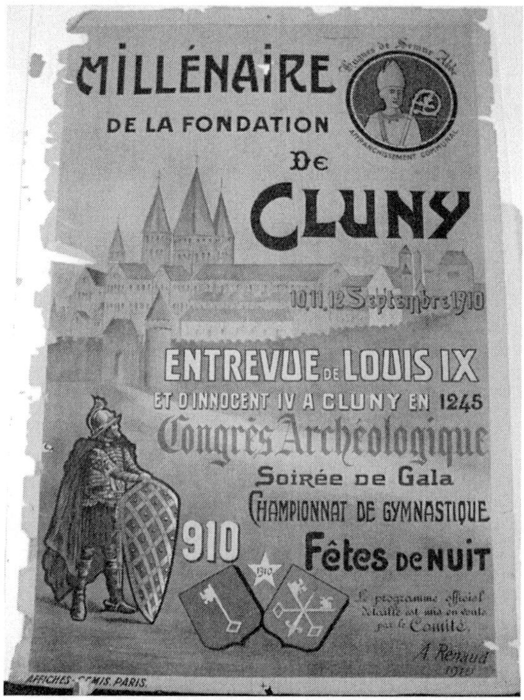

4.18 Poster advertising 1910 Cluny Millénaire
(Cluny Collection: Loeb Library, Harvard University)

Three images are important to examine: the poster advertising the fête (also reproduced on a postcard) [fig. 4.18], one of the official souvenir postcards [fig. 4.19], and a card showing both sides of the commemorative medal available [fig. 4.20]. On the poster, signed by A. Renaud, in an attempt to appeal to the widest possible audience, the main caption avoids specific mention of the abbey: “Millénaire de la fondation de Cluny 10, 11, 12 Septembre 1910”. Next to this in the upper right corner a little medallion with the bust of a man holding crook and wearing a miter is surrounded by the words “Hugues de Semur Abbé Affranchissement Communal”, thus giving credit for the town’s independence to the most famous abbot and limiting the religious connection to one corner. The main body shows a medieval knight outside the town walls with the familiar towers of the former church on the skyline comparable to those of any castle, Secondary text lists the "Entry of Louis IX and Innocent IV to Cluny in 1245", and the *Congrès Archéologique*. For an even more popular draw, also listed are the: grand finale, gymnastic championships, and evening festivities occurring on the same weekend.

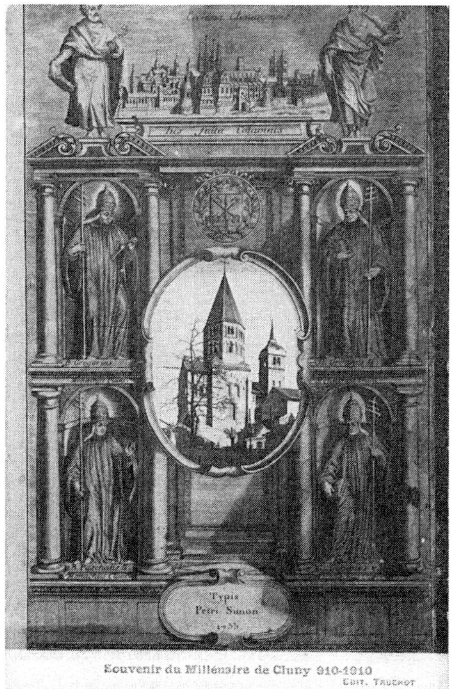

4.19 Souvenir postcard, Millénaire de Cluny, 1910
(Cluny Collection: Loeb Library, Harvard University)

A postcard captioned "Souvenir du Millénaire de Cluny 910-1910", published by Truchot, was modeled upon the frontispiece to the *Bibliotheca Cluniacensis* from 1664.[71] The abbey's historical connection is thereby emphasized with a monument to four of the Cluniac popes and an eighteenth-century print of the complete church along with a contemporary photograph of the remaining transept in a central cameo. This would appear to have little to do with the 910 commemoration and was simply providing more rich imagery of the former abbey for tourists.

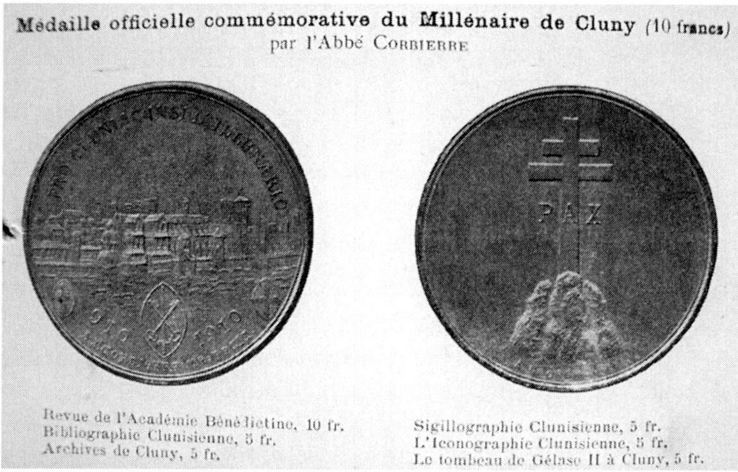

4.20 Postcard of commemorative medal for Millénaire de Cluny, 1910 (N. Roiné)

Finally, the card with the medal is the most religious item of all. Attributed to Abbé Corbièrre, the medal—available for 10 francs—shows an old view of the complete church over the dates 910-1910 on either side of the city arms and above in Latin: PRO CLUNIACINSI MILLUNARIO. The other side was a representation of the patriarchal cross with two arms (the shape of Cluny III with two transepts) on a hillock (thus forming the Calvary cross) crossed by the simple word "PAX". In this souvenir, the architectural accomplishment of the Romanesque church was not held to its republican value as a pure French engineering feat, rather the text and obverse image weighed it down with the political jargon of contemporary Catholic politics as practiced by the activist Dom Besse, enthusiastic participant from his exile in Belgium, who in his speech during the opening session of the *Congrès*, claimed Cluny was not a town but rather a monastic order and that its proper history had not yet been written.[72]

The local and regional press covered the *millénaire* better than they had the Centenaire.[73] Not only was it a grander occasion, it also appeared to include much more of interest to the general public than the purely religious events of 1898, During this period, there were many more newspapers available locally than today, running the gamut from Autun's conservative *l'Autunois* from the diocesan seat to Mâcon's radical-socialist L'*Union républicaine* published by former mayor and current deputy of the département, Jean Simyan, whom, with the prefect, was made an honorary president of the *Congrès* as representative of the State.

Since the organizing committee sent out lengthy press releases and the Academy of Mâcon published news notices, many of the papers reproduced the same material following the official viewpoints of these men. Pierre Goujon studied the subtle differences in emphases between articles hailing Cluny's historical importance for civilization in 1994.[74] The contrasting styles of reporting due to the newspapers' political orientations could also be striking. *L'Autunois* sent their own reporter, Jean Gallotti ahead of time on September 4th, to preview the site.[75] As might be expected, his front-page article is full of the standard regrets for the lost church and, in this romantically bitter mood, he classifies the museum as nothing more than an ossuary of sculpture. *Le Progrès de Saône-et-Loire's* reporter, André Lyonnais, gathered material from other newspapers in Paris and Lyon. He reported on September 10th at length on the return of the clergy, justifying the acceptance of the fête by republicans because of its historical value but warning the reader to separate the politics from the spectacle and writing "Remain quiet and attentive during the religious procession which should bring to mind the oppression of yesteryear…"[76]

The visit of the undersecretary for War, Sarraut [fig. 4.13], on the same day as the historical cortège, made big news in most of the papers. Radical deputy for the Aude, he made an appearance at various functions; arriving at Macon he was driven to Cluny to attend the opening of new rooms in the hospital and to preside at the *Congrès* next to Simyan, Ramonet (the prefect), Ballandras (the mayor), and officers of the Academy. He briefly saluted the French past and gave government approval of their work. After attending the *cortège*, he went on to present awards at the regional gymnastic finals. The winners of these prizes were listed in most papers along with the names of the actors in Louis and Innocent's retinues. According to *Le Progrès,* Sarraut actually presented a paper at the *Congrès* in his capacity as a member of the Academy of Carcassonne.[77] Lyonnais suggested that this distinction established him as a scholar, but then quoted the radical newspaper *Le Nouvelliste,* which complained that a member of the government had been sent to Cluny to pay homage to the pope and the Church. Pointing out the excesses of the clergy at the event, Lyonnais claimed that Sarraut was embarrassed by the heavy presentation of clerical pomp and the enthusiasm of the Clunysois who shouted "Vive le roi!" and "Vive le pape!", as well as the huge sums spent by individuals on their aristocratic costumes. Lyonnais compared it to Mardi Gras, asking what kind of influence these characters would have on viewers.

The *L'Union Républicaine* reported with glee that a small protest was held privately by some clerics and local squires under the direction of the comte du Murard, saying that everyone braced themselves for passionate words from Besse and when he did not deliver, were forced to accept a lame proposal by Mme la marquise de MacMahon protesting the expulsion of the clergy. In contrast *L'Indépendent de Saone-et-Loire* (Louhans) wrote nearly nothing at all on the entire event. On Sunday September 11th an article, seemingly in direct denial, appeared criticizing the pope's encyclical against modernism just above a note about Mme Curie and her important experiments with radiation.

After this grand celebration of Cluny's history, the town returned to daily life among her ruins. In *The French Nationalist Revival in France, 1905-1914*, Eugen Weber tells us that the shift from a Left-centered nationalist movement in the 1880s to a Right-supported revival of nationalism after the flight of General Boulanger caused growing cooperation between Right and center politicians around Raymond Poincaré about 1912, thus creating one of the first enduring government alliances since the Commune. At the same time, with the advent of the typewriter, more accurate records were kept in French archives as carbon copies became available. After the highly visible *millénaire,* efforts grew to rescue Cluny, which was increasingly seen as a threatened monument of historical value. Thus government archive materials on Cluny improve at the beginning of the twentieth century.

In June 1912, concern about Cluny from the Commission of Historic Monuments took the form of a plan to disengage the abbey buildings from those of the *Haras.* The chief architect, André Ventre, wrote a letter to the Fine Arts ministry, saying that it was absolutely essential that his administration take possession of some of the land around the existing south transept and Bourbon Chapel so that they could demolish old buildings of the *école normale* that were currently being used as storage sheds for the stables. He underlined the situation as "deplorable" because the latrines of the school and the muck piles of the stables were so close to the abbey buildings that they were creating a "cesspool" (*cloaque*) of unsanitary and unsavory conditions [fig. 4.21].[78]

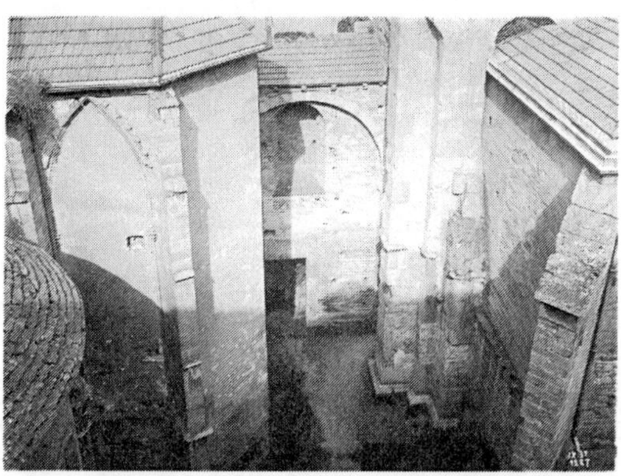

4.21 Area behind stables and between Bourbon Chapel and remaining abbey church ruins which Ventre called a "cesspool" in 1912, Loury photo from 1931 after Conant had dug excavation trenches here (Cluny Collection: Loeb Library, Harvard University)

A few days later, Ventre went on to ask for 500 francs to allow some excavation of the piers of the south side of the former abbey church, saying that if the amount were approved he would have to begin negotiations with the *Haras* administration. In October, the Commission of Historic Monuments ruled that no excavations were possible since the buildings touched so much public and private property. However, the plan to demolish the latrines and some other eighteenth-century structures, in order to free up the lower parts of the church, was acceptable as long as the Beaux-Arts administration could gain control of the remaining twelfth- and fifteenth-century buildings from the Ministry of Agriculture. The Agriculture minister refused to give up the structures, but agreed to excavations in the chapel area as long as the Beaux-arts ministry bore all costs and everything was returned to its original condition. This latter condition would become a regular feature of negotiations between the *Haras* and archeologists in the century ahead.

Only 1,916 out of 13,549 francs were approved from Ventre's request for both the excavations and ambitious renovations.[79] The assistant director of the stables agreed to temporarily move to an apartment elsewhere in town upon the decision to reimburse his rent.[80] In August 1913, Ventre and Malo began digging, photographing, and entering information on to a plan made by Malo. In May 1916 letters from the director complained about the danger of trenches that had been left open and Ventre agreed to recover the area.[81]

Very little else was accomplished on the site during the First World War. In 1922 the chapel again required urgent work (1300 francs) and it remained a focus for funding. Other little events demonstrate quixotic appreciation of the historical value of the ruins, such as in 1924 when the *école normale* alumni association requested permission to repair the inscription on the façade of the former school or in 1926 when letters and telegrams flew to affirm that the weathervane (*girouette*) on the top of the Tour des Fromages was part of the classed monument and could not be sold. Otherwise, the remains of the abbey slumbered, waiting for an American, armed with dollars and the vision of a great model Romanesque abbey, to arrive and request permission to take extensive measurements in order to fully reconstruct Cluny, in all her medieval glory, on paper.

Other Publications

Abbé Louis M. J. Chaumont published three books on Cluny between 1905 and 1911, expanding the *guide historique*.[82] Chaumont was a local resident and had done substantial reading before writing. He literally took readers on a tour of the town and surroundings, suggesting that they imagine themselves "profiting from the peace at the end of the Hundred Years War" to enter Cluny in the entourage of Jehan Germaine, "a humble carrier of holy water to the abbey" who is actually, we find out later, a bishop.[83] This conceit allowed Chaumont to describe the town as it appeared shortly after 1453, and include the towers, walls, streets, and buildings that had been removed by 1905. Although none of his sources were documented in the text, Chaumont repeated a great deal of information about Cluny's history already written by earlier authors (see chapters 2 and 3) and filled in some new material from later eyewitnesses.

Abbé Chaumont mourned the loss of the abbey buildings (the term 'hélas!' appears often) and echoed later nineteenth-century authors when he referred to the third church as the "*chef d'oeuvre de l'architecture romane,*" which, after being "sacked" (*saccagé*) by the revolutionary army in 1793, was "shamefully torn down" (*honteusement renversé)* from August 1798 to May 1810.[84] Claiming "*ce magnifique édifice a fait l'admiration de l'Europe pendant 700 ans,*" he uses adjectives like prodigious and majestic or descriptions similar to: "Around the main altar, a cupola resting on eight columns appears to be part of the celestial vault".[85] Old terminology from the abbey is recorded in his text, such as referring to the outer ambulatory aisle as the "walkway of the angels."[86] Chaumont was more liberal than his predecessors in his praise of all the styles of architecture at the abbey.

Chaumont echoed Lorain and the literary tradition as he credited the monks with complete piety and selflessness; claiming that their almsgiving, superior agricultural and trade knowledge, artistic advice, and other kinds of support made the townspeople more prosperous and cultured than other comparable towns in France. He underlined the memory of their generosity, which would survive any revolution, with statements based upon Ulrich's eleventh-century chronicle.[87]

The little book proceeds into structures and history which occurred after the date of the reader's imaginary visit, yet Chaumont seems to have forgotten his device and simply moves on. As the chaplain of the Sisters of Saint-Joseph of Cluny, he includes an entire chapter on the Récollets and the hospital. Chapter VIII follows the use of the conventual buildings from *collège* to *école normale spéciale* to *école des arts et métiers.* Finally, like authors before him, interesting sites to visit in the area of Cluny are mentioned. And, like Penjon, he ends with a chronological list of abbots.

A new edition of this guide appeared in 1909 in anticipation of the *millénaire* set to occur the next year. It was probably the most accessible source for most of the speakers at the Congrès. However, there was a flurry of such publications. A pamphlet by the formerly socialist cynic, Alfred Forest (see chapter 3), entitled *Cluny-Guide et ses environs* was also designed for visitors to the town during the 1910 *millénaire*.[88] Rather than writing in anticipation of another "arlequinade" in the upcoming *millénaire*, Forest's sober title page promised information on: Cluny ancien et modern; l'abbaye—les écoles; excursions; renseignements administratifs et commerciaux. Key texts are lifted from previous authors and it was illustrated with "numerous photographic views and reproductions of the oldest engravings". In a two-page introduction, Forest underlined previous claims to Cluny's civilizing force in Europe and listed both the great names and powerful administration coming out of the abbey in her heyday. He then enthusiastically invited the reader to tour the town and environs with him, giving a number of details that reveal the conditions of surviving buildings in 1909 and organizing the initial section of his guide as a series of four tours, starting at the Gelasius entrance and thus simultaneously introducing the school and the abbey. When referring to the elegant eighteenth-century structures, Forest felt compelled to remark to the sightseeing reader: "but [they are] devoid of art…ornament, sculptures, absolutely blank and without the least historical reference to the glorious centuries of the former abbey."[89]

Many times Forest listed objects or decoration lost since the Revolution but did not lay the regret on as thick as his predecessors. After all, he was the one in 1899 who wrote to lift the blame from the Clunysois in order to credit liberty and progress. In all, though Forest's facts were derivative, his characteristically quirky comments kept things fresh. No other author enjoyed recounting Prud'hon's letters about what a *bon vivant* Frère Placide was or commented that Abélard's Linden tree, though old, could hardly be the same one since it would have been there 800 years, or admitted that at the Récollets, the chapel of the nuns of the Order of St. Joseph, served in 1793 as the meeting place of the Jacobin club. Likewise, his cynical side returned when he mentioned the violin conserved in the museum, saying that rumor had it the instrument belonged to Charles IX who "preferred the melodies of the rebec and violin to the tocsin of St. Germain l'Auxerrois, prelude to the St. Barthlomew's Day massacres!"[90] And he returned to the story from his earlier book about the rue Fouettin being named for the punishment of adulteresses, again remarking that in his day the world was changed and anyone could walk there without fear. In mentioning the *École pratique de Commerce et d'Industrie*, he stressed that for all her old souvenirs, Cluny's leaders were forward-thinking and the city was now completely modern, hygienic, and well-supplied with water for the dry months. In fact, Forest never missed a chance to remark upon any evidence of progress in Cluny's architecture or industry.

Forest included other cultural aspects of the town, mentioning the traditional lace-making industry, the "caractère amiable et accueillant" of the inhabitants[91] and listing famous men from the area. One of the latter appears to have been a relative, Barthélemy Forest, a deputy in Paris on the far left of the Chamber. He also made a rather silly plea for a better statue of Prud'hon.[92] In later sections, Forest left Cluny for excursions to the outlying areas, regaling readers with the beauty of the routes. He ended with an apology for anything the locals might have felt he missed but begged the limited space and expressed his happiness while writing these entries. It is true that one gains a much more positive sentiment from Forest in this guide, over those authors who harangued the reader with countless expressions of tragedy and regret for Cluny's lost past.

Being a tourist guide, Forest's little book was filled with photographs of key sites. It was bound in lightweight cardboard and filled front and back with ads from sponsors who offered services in the area. These included more than the just the cities of Mâcon and Cluny—there are also hotels, restaurants, beauty shops, blacksmiths, bookstores, candy shops, riding instructors, delicatessens, wine shops, pharmacies, tailors and dress shops, among others, from vendors in surrounding communities such as Blanot, Tramayes, Saint Genoux, or Cormatin. The most interesting ad is a full-page image created for the Cluny dressmaking firm of Patouillard and Moreau [fig. 4.22]. Here we find the elaborate architectural frame designed by Sagot for the frontispiece in Lorain's 1839 history (see fig. 2.5) reused. The view of the church and statues has been removed to make room for the advertising text: "CONFECTIONS pour DAMES / Vêtements sur Mesures en tous genres / TISSUS NOUVEAUTÉS / Spécialité de Dentelles D'IRELANDE. Where the Latin inscription appeared in the original, the proprietors' names have been awkwardly inserted. The cover sported a reproduction of Sagot's view of Cluny from the south from Taylor's *Voyage Pittoresque* (see fig. 2.2).

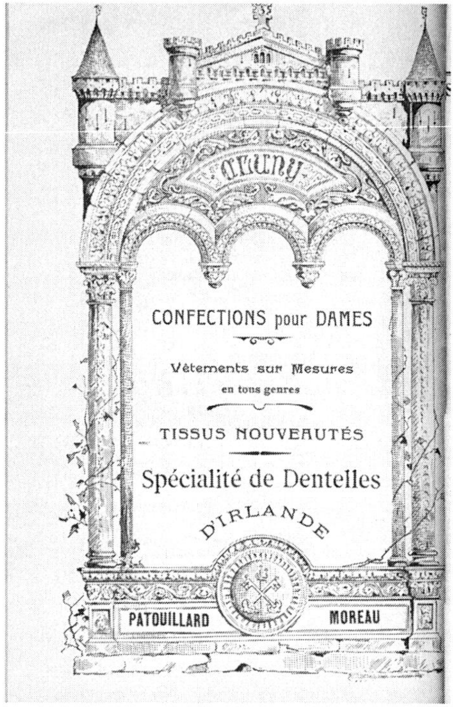

4.22 Advertisement from Alfred Forest, *Cluny-Guide*, 1909

Forest also wrote the romantic and florid introductory text for the official public program available during the *millénaire*. It is nearly a complete turnaround from his 1898 publication on the jubilee. After stating that "all French and foreign historians, philosophers, thinkers, writers about our people proclaim the civilizing influence exercised over the entire world by the Abbey of Cluny", Forest gives a very brief history of the abbey filled with unmitigated recrimination for nearly everything that happened after Peter the Venerable.[93] He ends with the names of the abbots, the Cluniac popes, and a great number of exclamations such as "Cluny! Admirable precursor to the Sorbonne!"[94] Finally, he exhorts the visitor: "Love the past, honor it, celebrate it! The past is advice for the future! It is but a stage in the constant evolution which must take man to the ideal goal: the cult of the Good and the Beautiful! The love of Humanity!"[95]

Another publication in 1910 by Francois-Louis Bruel titled *Cluni: Album historique et archéologique* was as serious as Forest was playful. [96] Bruel began his history with a summary and emphasized the points made by earlier authors like Cucherat about the reasons for Cluny's greatness: the papal privilege of independence and the creation of a "monastic monarchy"[97] through her reformation of other houses. Bruel attributed the downfall of the order to the jealousy of her rivals and the Wars of Religion which divided the Cluniac members in 1623. At least during this, Bruel remarked, the Rule was maintained, along with the most important art held by the order (here he was apparently disagreeing with Lorain). He blamed the Revolution for the removal of portable objects, but he saves the true blame for the municipality which allowed the demolition of the tombs and sale of the stones and marble, even before the troops came in 1793 to pillage and burn. Bruel also found it ironic that the consular government under Napoléon reclaimed a great number of buildings for the city only to have his imperial state destroy the rest of the abbey church in order to build the stallion depot. His remarks parallel those of Ernest Babelon in *"Le Millénaire de Cluny"*.

After this, Bruel's main account commences, clearly derivative of the previous scholars who wrote on Cluny in the nineteenth century and contemporary guides. He described the chateaux of Lourdon, Brancion, and Berzé, as well as the chapel at Berzé-la-ville, whose frescos had only been discovered in 1887, and then on to the buildings of Cluny proper beginning with the three parish churches. For the abbey itself, he wrote: "We can only imagine it and move on…"[98] The publication is most valuable for all the plans and views, both taken from previous publications or recent photographs, reproduced as his plates. Bruel included images previous authors did not such as portraits of later aristocratic abbots and the charter of Chevigne. Detailed notations on the plates comprise fifteen pages of Bruel's text.

Other publications, mostly in the form of reports to the scientific societies that sent them to the millénaire, appeared within a year or two of the event. Like one by Émile Monot, who came from the Jura, they are accounts of the activities undertaken by the delegate peppered with idiosyncratic perceptions.[99] Most maintain the flavor of the speeches and guidebooks, having little argument with overall ideological underpinnings.

A more literary and personal account of Cluny appeared in 1928 in a series called "*Portrait de la France*" ed. J.-L. Vaudoyer.[100] It appears to have ongoing appeal, since it was reproduced and republished in 2004 for a local bookstore.[101] The author, Albert Thibaudet (Tournus, 1874 – Geneva, 1936), was a prominent literary critic of the Third Republic and one of four regular contributors to the Nouvelle Revue Française (NRF). A liberal, in the early 20s he wrote in favor of the post-war pluralism and intellectual internationalism proposed by Andre Gide.[102] He was also another of Burgundy's romantic sons, waxing eloquent on the lost glory of his mother's native city, in which he spent much time. He wrote 87 lyrical pages about the experience, beginning with a story about Germans who assumed that, being French, he was from Paris but when corrected, recognized Cluny as another *'grande capitale'*[103] The little volume is an attempt to understand the character of Burgundian abbey towns, specifically Tournus and Cluny. The work is not history, but rather a literary piece and Cluny was essentially only a writing prompt. Nevertheless, his observations offer some insights to the local perceptions of the historical nature of the community.

A frontispiece of the remaining abbey church transept from a pencil sketch and a tiny, reversed woodcut scene of the original church and cloister established the nostalgic quality of Thibaudet's entry for this series. Taking as his starting point the quote at the top of this chapter about all Cluny inhabitants being born with the original sin of having destroyed the basilica of St. Hugh, Thibaudet had clearly absorbed this guilt and wrote that although the third abbey church was not the greatest monument ever built by mankind, it was the greatest and most venerable ever destroyed.[104] He had especially harsh words for the replacement of the church choir with the stables: "An enormous stupidity and ugliness has come, it seems, to directly mold itself on a grandeur both human and divine, substituting that presence for this one, bit by bit. In place of the basilica was built the anti-basilica."[105] He knew Tournus and Cluny before modernity, before the Great War. He is a middle-aged man, nostalgic for the things gone from his world. One repeating theme is the phylloxera crisis: "Life was divided into three nearly geological periods: before the phylloxera, during the replanting, and after the replanting."[106] He reminisced about the abbey charters having become the parchment seals for jam jars in three generations of women up to his grandmother [fig. 4.23]. And he retold the story of children using decorated manuscript folios for kites. In his book, Cluny becomes all these memories and more, a town imprinted with the remains of its famous past. "Ultimately, we have not destroyed Cluny, historical and monastic, because we have not replaced it….a heritage which no longer grows, a present which lives off the past, Cluny has been just this for centuries….The Cluny of today is not Cluny: it is the absence of Cluny…"[107]

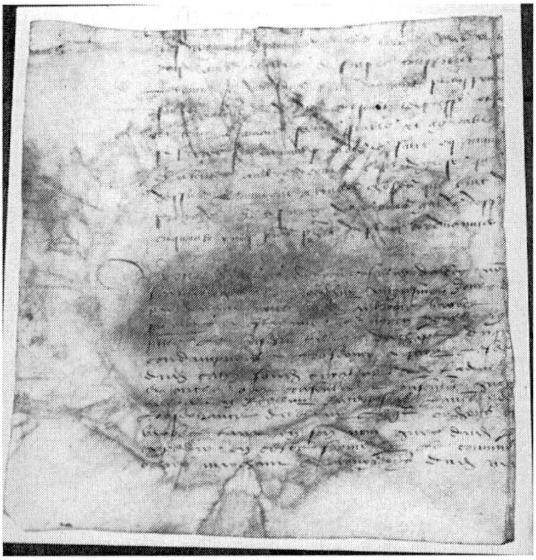

4.23 Kenneth Conant's photograph of abbey manuscript page once used to seal jam jar (Cluny Collection: Loeb Library, Harvard University)

Notes

[1] [...the story of our monuments is a long martyrdom, and there has never been a nation that squandered so foolishly its artistic patrimony.] Académie de Mâcon. Société des arts sciences belles-lettres et agriculture de Saône-et-Loire, "Millénaire de Cluny: congrès d'histoire et d'archéologie tenu à Cluny les 10, 11, 12 Septembre 1910" (Mâcon, France, 1910). vol. I, 67

[2] [All natives of Cluny are born with an original sin: that of having destroyed the basilica of St. Hugh...the Cluny of today is not Cluny: it is the absence of Cluny.] Albert Thibaudet, *Cluny*, ed. J.-L. Vaudoyer, *Portrait de la France* (Paris: Éditions Émile-Paul Frères, 1928). 4

[3] Avishai Margalit, *The ethics of memory* (Cambridge, Mass.: Harvard University Press, 2002). 25

[4] Jean Marie and Madeleine Rebérioux Mayeur, *The Third Republic from its origins to the Great War, 1871-1914*, trans. J.R. Foster, *The Cambridge history of modern France; 4* (Cambridge; New York/Paris: Cambridge University Press; Maison des sciences de l'homme, 1984). 161-169

[5] Ibid. 167

[6] Ibid. 167

[7] Ibid. 169

[8] Peter McPhee, *A social history of France, 1789-1914*, 2nd ed. (New York: Palgrave Macmillan, 2004). 257; Mayeur, *The Third Republic from its origins to the Great War, 1871-1914*. Chapter 7; Charles Sowerwine, *France since 1870: culture, politics and society* (New York: Palgrave, 2001). 69-73, 85.

[9] McPhee, *A social history of France, 1789-1914*. 257; Sowerwine, *France since 1870: culture, politics and society*. 85

[10] McPhee, *A social history of France, 1789-1914*.

[11] Michael Sutton, *Nationalism, positivism, and Catholicism: the politics of Charles Maurras and French Catholics, 1890-1914*, *Cambridge studies in the history and theory of politics* (Cambridge; New York: Cambridge University Press, 1982). 92

[12] Daniel J. Sherman, *The construction of memory in interwar France* (Chicago; London: University of Chicago press, 1999). 264

[13] Dominique Iogna-Prat, "Cluny, 910-1910 ou l'instrumentalisation de la mémoire des origines," *Revue Mabillon* 72 (2000). 164. Also collected in: Dominique Iogna-Prat, *Études clunisiennes*, *Les médiévistes français;* 2 (Paris: Picard, 2002).

[14] Sherman, *The construction of memory in interwar France*. 280; Paul Connerton, *How societies remember*, Themes in the social sciences (Cambridge; New York: Cambridge University Press, 1989). 51

[15] Saône-et-Loire, "Millénaire de Cluny: congrès d'histoire et d'archéologie tenu à Cluny les 10, 11, 12 Septembre 1910".

[16] Pierre Goujon, "Cluny, mille ans après," in *L'ouvrier, l'Espagne, la Bourgogne et la vie provinciale*, ed. François Robert et Françoise Bayard, *Collection de la casa de Velazquez* (Madrid: Presse Université de Lyon, 1994). 415-429

[17] Monsignor Villard, *Le Millénaire de Cluny (10-12 septembre 1910). Souvenirs religieux et littéraires* (Paris: Lethielleux, 1911).

[18] Iogna-Prat, "Cluny, 910-1910 ou l'instrumentalisation de la mémoire des origines." 167

[19] Stéphane Gerson, *The pride of place: local memories & political culture in nineteenth-century France* (Ithaca: Cornell University Press, 2003).

[20] "...un millénaire qui est en fait le leur". From a letter of Armand Duréault, perpetual secretary of the Academy, to Dom Besse on 1 February 1910 quoted in: Iogna-Prat, "Cluny, 910-1910 ou l'instrumentalisation de la mémoire des origines." 172

[21] Ibid. 171

[22] Quoted in Prévotat, "Dom Besse en son temps: sa vision du monde et de l'Église," 21

[23] Iogna-Prat, "Cluny, 910-1910 ou l'instrumentalisation de la mémoire des origines." 169

[24] "*...d'un côté le Moyen Age obscurantiste, lugubre, et par contraste le Moyen Age 'troubadour', suave*." Jacques Le Goff and Jean-Maurice de Montremy, *A la recherche du Moyen Age* (Paris: L. Audibert, 2003). 15

[25] See chapter 3. It is also interesting to note that the 1900 *Exposition Universelle* included arm reliquaries in presentation of national treasures, thus visualizing the venerable qualities of fragment relics (see Barbara Drake Boehm, "Body-Part Reliquaries: The State of Research," *Gesta* XXXVI, no. 1 (1997).)

[26] Romy Golan, *Modernity and nostalgia : art and politics in France between the wars* (New Haven: Yale University Press, 1995). ix and Chapter 5

[27] ...attestait l'accord pacifique et cordial de tous pour la célébration de cette solennité grandiose." Saône-et-Loire, "Millénaire de Cluny: congrès d'histoire et d'archéologie tenu à Cluny les 10, 11, 12 Septembre 1910". vol.1, viii

[28] Note that the menu includes a typographical error on the date "1911".

[29] Iogna-Prat, "Cluny, 910-1910 ou l'instrumentalisation de la mémoire des origines." 170. Baudrillart's paper was not included in published proceedings.

[30] *Le Courrier de Saône-et-Loire* (Chalon), #19.462, Wednesday 14 September 1910. 1
[31] See an excellent review of the secondary scholarship on Cluny in Chapter 1 ("The Lineage of Cluniac Studies") of Barbara H. Rosenwein, *Rhinoceros bound : Cluny in the tenth century* (Philadelphia: University of Pennsylvania Press, 1982). 3-29
[32] M. H. Omont, "Manuscrit de Raban Maur offert par saint Maïeul à l'abbaye de Cluny," Saône-et-Loire, "Millénaire de Cluny: congrès d'histoire et d'archéologie tenu à Cluny les 10, 11, 12 Septembre 1910"., vol. I, 127-129; Omont, "Deux nouveaux cartulatires de Cluny à la Bibliothèque nationale," Ibid. vol. I, 130-141; M. Victor Mortet, "Note sur la date de rédaction des coutumes de Cluny dites de Farfa," Ibid. vol. I, 142-145; Hildephonsus Schuster, "De Fastorum agiographico ordine imperialis monasterii pharphaensis," Ibid. vol. I, 146-176; Jean Virey, "Note sur un manuscrit du xive siècle sur parchemin, provenant de l'abbaye de Cluny," Ibid. vol. I, 264-290
[33] Jean de Valois, "Sur quelques points d'histoire relatifs à la fondation de Cluny," Ibid., vol. I, 177-219; Jean Virey, "Un ancien plan de l'abbaye de Cluny," Ibid. vol. II, 231-247
[34] Eugène Lefèvre-Pontalis, "Essai sur quelques particularités des églises romanes bénédictines," Ibid., vol. I, 220-230; Camille Enlart, "Le porche de Charlieu," Ibid. vol. I, 231-234; G.-Teresio Rivoira, "L'architecture des Bénédictines en Bourgogne au xie siècle," Ibid. vol. I, 389-392; Léonce Lex, "Le Christ en gloire de Saint-Amour-Bellevue," vol. II, 31-32; Léonce Raffin and Louis de Conteson, "L'église et le doyenné clunisien de Saint-Gengoux-le-National," Ibid. vol. II, 59-91; Léonce Lex, "Peintures murales de la Chapelle du Château des Moines de Cluny à Berzé-la-Ville," Ibid. vol. II, 248-256; Félix Sorgues, "L'ancienne église de Vitry-en-Charollais," Ibid. 206-308
[35] Victor Terret, *La sculpture bourguignonne aux XIIe et XIIIe siècles* (Autun/Paris: L'auteur; Librairie d'art catholique, 1914).
[36] Raymond Houdayer, "L'exploitation agricole des moines de Cluny," in: Saône-et-Loire, "Millénaire de Cluny: congrès d'histoire et d'archéologie tenu à Cluny les 10, 11, 12 Septembre 1910", vol. I, 235-246; Gaston Letonnelier, "L'abbaye de Cluny et le privilège de l'exemption," Ibid. vol. I, 247-263; Léon Guilloreau, "Les prieurés anglais de l'ordre de Cluny," Ibid. vol. I, 291-373; P.-Bonaventura Egger, "Die schweizerischen Cluniacenserkloester zur Zeit ihrer Bluete," Ibid. vol. I, 374-386; Léon Cornudet, "Les possessions de l'abbaye de Cluny à Jully-lès-Buxy," Ibid. vol. II, 300-305; J.-B. Martin, "Bibliographie liturgique de l'abbaye de Cluny," Ibid. vol. II, 147-163; August Penjon, "Abélard et Pierre le Vénérable," Ibid. vol. I, 393-403; Léonce Lex,"Un Office laïque de l'abbaye. Le prévôté et crierie de Cluny," Ibid. vol. I, 404-422; Maurice Bauchond, "Un sermon de Saint Odilon (962-1049), cinquième abbé de Cluny," Ibid. vol. II, 103-113; Léonce Raffin, "Une forteresse clunisienne. Le château de Lourdon," Ibid. vol. II, 164-210; Louis de Contenson and Léonce Raffin, "Description architecturale du château de Berzé-le-Châtel, Ibid. vol. II, 257-299; Gilbert Lafay, "Le Monnayage de Cluny," Ibid. vol. II, 325-330;
[37] Paul Denis, "Quelques notes sur les derniers moines de l'abbaye de Cluny," Ibid. vol. II 114-146; Barbat, "Dévastation du prieuré de Charlieu pendant la Révolution," Ibid. vol. II, 308-315; Célestin Roubaudi, "L'ancienne école normale spéciale de Cluny," Ibid. 316-324
[38] For a complete list, see the table of contents, Ibid. vol. 1, 424-425
[39] Ibid. 3

[40] Ernest Babelon even asked if this anniversary was not something of a funerary commemoration: "Au surplus, cette fête du Millénaire de Cluny n'a-t-elle pas, par elle-même, quelque chose d'une commémoration funèbre?". Ibid. 23
[41] Saône-et-Loire, "Millénaire de Cluny: congrès d'histoire et d'archéologie tenu à Cluny les 10, 11, 12 Septembre 1910". 4
[42] "Pillée, saccagée, par la Révolution, elle [la grande église abbatiale] était resté tout entière debout. Les habitants firent ce qu'ils purent pour la sauver, mais par une incroyable fatalité, dans les premières années du XIXe siecle, l'incurie des pouvoirs publics la laissa aller aux mains d'une bande de spéculateurs qui y firent jouer la mine!" Ibid. 7
[43] "...solennel hommage à ces moines qui ont osé jadis résister à la tyrannie, qui ont vaillamment combattus pour la liberté..." Ibid. 55. "Si, dans un jour de folie, la main des hommes a détruit l'ensemble majestueux de cette basilique, qui rappelait ici la grande place occupée par les moines de Cluny dans l'histoire du monde, nous avons le droit de le déplorer à tous les points de vue. Mais ce qui en reste parle encore avec assez d'éloquence aux yeux et aux coeurs de ceux qui savent comprendre le langage des ruines. Interrogez, Messieurs, ces sculptures admirables, écoutez la voix toujours frémissante de ces vieilles pierres! Au milieu d'un religieux silence vous recevrez d'elles l'enseignement le plus fécond et les leçons les plus profitables." Ibid. 57. Villefosse gave his notes away to a member of the press after speaking and thus had to reconstruct for the publication. Archives départmentales de Mâcon: 1 F 119.
[44] Goujon divides the remarks into local pride which declared Cluny an historic place to celebrate and more general interest in the work accomplished by the monks at Cluny. His analysis of the press coverage is most relevant. (Goujon, "Cluny, mille ans apres.")
[45] Ibid. 63
[46] "Nous, Messieurs, hommes de cette France nouvelle que nous aimons et que nous servons, nous relions et associons profondément l'époque où nous vivons à tout notre passé que nous aimons et respectons en son entier. Laissez-moi vous le redire :le jour où l'on aura pu faire pénétrer, dans l'intelligence de toute la démocratie française, cette notion que la France du passé forme un tout indissoluble avec la France du présent et la France de l'avenir et que tout citoyen doit sa vénération à toute l'histoire de son pays, notre esprit public, qui malheureusement a trop de tendances, de tous les côtés, à des partis pris absolus, sera infiniment amélioré." Ibid. 63
[47] "...de propager le sentiment national et de ne pas permettre qu'une certaine partie de la nation persiste à croire que l'histoire de France n'a commencé qu'en 1789." Ibid. 60-61
[48] "La France est là. Une nation qui sait se souvenir, peut beaucoup oser." Ibid. 38
[49] Ibid. 4
[50] "Quel brillant spectacle offrait alors le monastère! abri des âmes pieuses, des lettrés, des penseurs, des artistes. Les moines y avaient recueilli ce qui subsistait encore des anciens manuscrits latins, et, sauf quelques parchemins qu'on grattait pour les transformer en missels et en antiphonaires, c'est par eux que nous furent transmises les oeuvres des littératures antiques et les écrits des Pères. Les études y étaient assez larges pour permettre aux esprits curieux de se développer et former ainsi les savants qui préparèrent la renaissance intellectuelle des XIIe et XIIIe siècles." Ibid. 5-6
[51] Ibid. 25, 31

---

[52] Ibid. 30. The Truce of God grew out of the Peace of God from the 10th century and was attributed to Cluny, it appears, simply because Pope Urban II, a former Cluniac monk, extended it at the Council of Clermont that he convened in 1095 to continue the reform program begun by his predecessor, Gregory VII, also a Cluniac and to muster an army to aid the Byzantine emperor, Alexius I, against the Seljuk Turks. At the time of Cluny's *millénaire*, Urban II had been beatified by Leo XIII less than thirty years earlier, in 1881. Ernest de Babelon specifically claimed authorship of the Truce of God for Odilon at Bourges in 1031 in his review of the events, Académie de Mâcon. Société des arts sciences belles-lettres et agriculture de Saône-et-Loire., *Millénaire de Cluny : congrès d'histoire et d'archéologie tenu à Cluny les 10, 11, 12 Septembre 1910*, 2 vols. (Mâcon, France: Protat Frères, 1910). 341-363

[53] Ibid. 34-35

[54] "Le Congrès de Cluny aura des résultats durables. Le souvenir de ces fêtes vivra dans l'esprit public pour y fixer à jamais le rôle véritable des moines de Cluny, pour faire connaître à tous la grande oeuvre qu'ils ont accomplie." Ibid. 58

[55] Édouard Corroyer, *L'Architecture romane*, 1900 ed., *Société Française d'Édition d'Art* (Paris: Picard et Kaan, 1887). Also, for the twentieth century : Jean Baudry, *Bourgogne romane*, 1ere ed. (La Pierre-qui-Vire (Yonne): Zodiaque, 1954).

[56] Ibid. vol. II, 341-363

[57] Ibid. vol. II, 343

[58] Prosper Lorain, *Histoire de l'Abbaye de Cluny depuis sa fondation jusqu'à sa destruction à l'époque de la Révolution française* (Paris: Sagnier et Bray, 1845).156; Jules Michelet, *Histoire de France.* 1869. vol. 1. 213. For the original source, see Jean Virey, *L'abbaye de Cluny*, 4 ed. (Paris,: H. Laurens, 1957). 12, n. 1

[59] Ibid. vol. II, 346

[60] Ibid. vol. II, 346

[61] Church organs made their appearance in the Western churches during the tenth-century monastic revival, but only as small instruments and most likely not by 910. See Stanley Sadie and Alison Latham, *The Norton/Grove concise encyclopedia of music*, 1st American ed. (New York: W.W. Norton, 1988). 544

[62] "Un frisson mystérieux parcourut la foule recueillie des assistants; nous eûmes, pour un instant, véritablement une vision du moyen âge en regardant passer ces moines surtout, jeunes et vieux, au visage empreint de ce mélange indéfinissable d'énergie et de douceur que donne la foi profonde: nous vîmes des hommes d'un autre âge, des figures détaches des sculptures des cathédrals et marchant à travers la foule pour la bénir." Ibid. vol. II, 347-8

[63] Ibid. 351

[64] "Ce n'est pas assez de dire qu'ils marchaient avec leur temps: ils étaient à la tête de leur siècle dans toutes les branches de l'activité humaine....C'est par Cluny et les moines clunisiens que l'influence de l'esprit français se répandit et prédomina longtemps dans tout le monde civilisé." Ibid. 354

[65] Ibid. 362-363

[66] Thibaudet, *Cluny*. 6

[67] Henri Gandrez, *Le canton de Cluny en 1900—à travers les cartes postales* ([Saint-Seine-l'Abbaye]: Éditions de Saint-Seine-l'Abbaye, 1982). 50-55. In addition, Nadine

Roiné of Cluny generously allowed me to take digital snapshots of her papers relating to the fêtes.

[68] "On croit voir une ossature de cloître sertis dans un réseau de lierre." Ibid. 50

[69] Identified by Stephen Canfield.

[70] Notice in numerous local newspapers: "Rappelons que l'administration des postes timbrera pendant les journées des 10, 11 et 12 septembre, à l'aide d'un cachet spécial d'oblitération, les cartes postales officielles émise par le comité et déposées dans les boîtes aux lettres comprises dans l'enceinte des fêtes (abbaye)."

[71] Noticed by Giles Constable.

[72] Archives départementales de Mâcon: 1 F 119

[73] In addition, a small academic journal, *Revue des questions historiques,* carried a paper on the Cluny 1910 event by H. Rubat de Mérac within a section titled "Mélanges" in vol. 88 which appeared October 1, 1910. Although a timely subject, the article was merely derivative history from other authors covered here with nothing new.

[74] Goujon, "Cluny, mille ans apres."

[75] Jean Gallotti, "Le Millénaire de Cluny," *l'Autunois*, 4 September 1910. 1

[76] "Soyez calmes et attentifs devant le cortège religieux qui rappellera à votre mémoire l'oppression d'autrefois…" André Lyonnais, "Le Millénaire de Cluny" *Le Progrès de Saône-et-Loire* 10 Septembre 1910. 1

[77] André Lyonnais, "Le Millénaire de Cluny" *Le Progrès de Saône-et-Loire* 14 Septembre 1910. 3

[78] 26 June, 1912: "L'ensemble de ce bâtiment est englobé à gauche par les Haras, et à droite par les annexes de l'École des Arts & Métiers de CLUNY. Celle-ci a installé, dans la cour de la chapelle de Bourbon des latrines à fosse perdue qui font de cette cour un véritable cloaque." Paris, Bibliothèque du Patrimoine: 81/71, 181/1, 17

[79] See details of the series of plans in Neil Stratford, Brigitte Chabard and David Walsh, *Corpus de la sculpture de Cluny*, vol. I (Paris: Picard, forthcoming). I.3 (c)

[80] This money was not immediately forthcoming and we find a letter in March, 1915 (Paris, Bibliothèque du Patrimoine: Cote 81/71, 181/1, Box 17) from the Minister of Commerce demanding payment of 520.25 francs from the minister of Beaux-Arts and in April and May 1915 there are more letters indicating the assistant director was still trying to get those funds.

[81] For more details of what exactly was demolished and a photo of the exterior conditions before Ventre and Malo began, see Stratford, Chabard and Walsh, *Corpus de la sculpture de Cluny*. I.3. (c)

[82] Louis M. J. Chaumont, *Nouveau guide de Cluny, ou Explications historiques des cartes postales et vues de la ville et de l'ancienne abbaye* (Domois-Dijon: Impr. de l'Union typographique, 1905).

[83] Ibid. 14

[84] Ibid. Page 1 of unpaginated Introduction

[85] "Au delà du maître autel, une coupole reposant sur huit colonnes de marbre donne l'illusion d'une section de la voûte céleste..." Ibid. 23

[86] "promenoir des anges." Ibid.

[87] Ibid. 18

[88] Alfred Forest, *Cluny-guide et ses environs ... Cluny ancien et moderne -L'abbaye - Les écoles - Excursions - Renseignements administratifs et commerciaux* (Cluny: Truchot, n.d. [1909]).
[89] "...mais sans oeuvres d'art...sans ornements, sans sculptures, absolument nus et sans les moindres souvenirs historiques des siècles de gloire de l'ancienne l'abbaye." Ibid. 4
[90] "...préféra aux mélodies du rebec et du violon le tocsin de St-Germain l'Auxerrois, préludant aux massacres de la St-Barthélemy!" Alfred Forest, *Cluny-guide et ses environs.* 9-10
[91] Ibid. 15
[92] "Il nous semble qu'un Comité intelligent arriverait vite à Paris, à l'aide des artistes et du grand Public qui les entoure, à réaliser le projet d'une statue à Prud'hon. À Cluny la place semble tout indiquée sur la pelouse du jardin abbatial, face à l'Hôtel-de-Ville." Ibid. 16
[93] "Tous les Historiens Français et Étrangers, Philosophes, Penseurs, Écrivains de race ont proclamé l'influence civilisatrice exercée sur le Monde entier par l'Abbaye de Cluny." Alfred Forest, "Cluny à travers les siècles," *in Programme du Congrès d'Histoire et d'Archéologie du Millénaire de Cluny* (Académie de Mâcon, 1910).
[94] "Cluny !...C'est l'admirable préface de la Sorbonne!"
[95] "Aimons les Passé, honorons-le, fêtons-le ! Le Passé, c'est l'enseignement de l'Avenir ! C'est l'étape de l'incessante évolution qui doit conduire l'homme au but idéal : Le culte de Bien et du Beau ! L'amour de l'Humanité !"
[96] François-Louis Bruel, *Cluni : album historique et archéologique, précède d'une étude résumée et d'une notice des planches* (Matiscone: Fratrum Protat, 1910).
[97] Ibid. 6
[98] "Il faut nous figurer par l'imagination, en continuant tout droit notre chemin..." Ibid. 33
[99] Emile Monot, *Millénaire de Cluny* (Lons-le-Saunier: Lucien Declume, 1911).
[100] Thibaudet, *Cluny.*
[101] Reprinted by A Contrario, Cluny, 2004 with an Afterword but no indication of the original publication date.
[102] Klaus-Peter Sick, "A New Idea of Europe: the Liberal Internationalism of the Nouvelle Revue Française (1919-1925)," *European Political Economy Review* 1, no. 1 (Spring 2003).
[103] Thibaudet, *Cluny.* 2
[104] Ibid. 4
[105] "Une énormité de bêtise et de laideur est venue, semble-t-il, se mouler exactement sur une grandeur humaine et divine, substituer sa présence à cette présence, parcelle par parcelle. Opposée à la basilique, cela fait une anti-basilique." Ibid. 34
[106] "...la vie divisait en trois périodes presque géologiques: avant le phylloxera, pendant la replantation, après la replantation." Ibid. 13
[107] "Le Cluny, enfin, historique et monacal, que nous n'avons pas détruit parce que nous ne l'avons pas remplacé....un héritage qui ne s'accroît plus, un présent qui vit du passé, Cluny l'était depuis des siècles....Le Cluny d'aujourd'hui n'est pas Cluny; c'est l'absence de Cluny..." Ibid. 7-8, 33

CHAPTER FIVE

AMERICAN INTERVENTION: KENNETH CONANT'S VISION I[1]

Tout le monde sait que ce monument magnifique est presque entièrement détruit : il ne subsiste que…précieux restes qui nous donnent l'échelle de l'édifice, et qui permettent à l'imagination de se représenter l'ensemble.
—Jean Virey, 1892[2]

Toute l'histoire de l'architecture romane de Bourgogne est dominée par le nom de Cluny.
—Charles Oursel, 1928[3]

We have little logic here, and simple faith, but we have energy.
—Henry Adams, 1904[4]

Forerunners of Conant who shaped American perceptions of Cluny

Henry Adams

Henry Adams' perennial bestseller, *Mont Saint Michel and Chartres,* which came out in 1904 but began with his interest in Gothic architecture from 1895, was as much a study in philosophy as art history. Adams took the reader on an imaginative journey, suggesting the freedom of Romantic visualization and the ability to impute historical intention. He spoke directly to the need to develop appreciation in the reader:

> Here is your first eleventh-century church! how does it affect you?
> Serious and simple to excess! is it not? Young people rarely enjoy it. They prefer the gothic, even as you see it here, looking at us from the choir, through the great Norman arch. No doubt, they are right, since they are young: but men and women who have lived long and are tired,—who want rest,—who have done with aspirations and ambition,—whose life has been a broken arch—feel this repose and self-restraint as they feel nothing else. The quiet strength of these curved lines, the solid support of these heavy columns, the moderate proportions,

even the modified lights, the absence of display, of effort, of self-consciousness, satisfy them as no other art does.[5]

Themes of faith, creativity, and beauty pervade the text. It is meant to uplift our mundane responses to dirty, old, stone buildings with stories about when they were new. Reality intervenes, however, when Adams laments about lost monuments:

Civilization made almost a clean sweep of art.[6]
The English wars and the wars of religion brought new dangers, sieges and miseries; the revolution of 1792 brought actual rapine and waste; boys have flung stones at the saints, architects have wreaked their taste within and without, fire after fire has calcined the church vaults; the worst wrecker of all, the restaurer of the nineteenth century, has prowled about it; yet the Porch [of Chartres] still stands, mutilated but not restored, burned but not consumed, as eloquent a witness to the power and perfections of Our Lady as it was seven hundred years ago, and perhaps more impressive.[7]

Adams's interest in Mont Saint Michel was not strictly in the Gothic style of nineteenth-century preference, but it is an easily romantic site nonetheless, complete with spire and enveloping sea. Chartres represented the beginning of the Gothic and allowed Adams to treat the cult of the Virgin and medieval schools of thought better than any other church.

Adams would not have considered the contrast I have distinguished between Christian and Republican heritage at Cluny. He preferred the experience of imagining a better past over the reality of old things. As Raymond Carney says of Adams's approach in comparison to that of Wallace Stevens in his introduction to *Mont St. Michel and Chartres,* "the modernist insight is not necessarily a sad one. It can also be excitingly liberating." For instance, if one imagines the state of Cluny in the 18th century before the Revolution, it is highly unlikely that the Romantic notions of serene monks, Gregorian chant, and pristine white walls would have been accessible. Whereas, once the actual 900-year-old institution had been nearly completely eradicated, one could pose the remaining ruins in a panoply of tranquil visions of medieval life. However, unlike his friend and contemporary Henry James, Adams was equally pessimistic about anyone's power to imagine him/herself into a world that he believed was tightly controlled by factors outside the individual's direction. In which case, the 'fun' he takes in imagining historical medieval sites can only be understood next to his premise that reality would not have allowed either the guilt or the pride of the modern individual contemplating Cluny's destruction to make any difference in the larger scheme of events.

The next generation was surely less affected by Adams' final chapters on Abelard, the mystics, and Aquinas, than with the initial idea of evoking an historical milieu:

> Like all great churches, that are not mere store-houses of theology, Chartres expressed, besides whatever else it meant, an emotion, the deepest man ever felt, - the struggle of his own littleness to grasp the infinite."(103) "…when one sits here, in the central axis of this complicated apse, one sees, in mere light alone, the reaction of hundreds of energies, although time has left only a wreck of what the artist put here.[8]

Thus two stimuli for further study are thrown out to the 20th-century scholar of medieval architecture by Adams in 1904—to experience that charged atmosphere and to recover as much of the lost evidence as possible. To both Conant would respond.

Émile Mâle

Two years before Conant first visited Cluny, Émile Mâle's second monograph on the art of the Middle Ages appeared (*Religious Art in France: The Twelfth Century, A Study of the Origins of Medieval Iconography*, 1922). This was the second in a series of three studies, coming twenty-four years after his published dissertation on the thirteenth century (1898). Mâle thus followed a summary of the period most beloved by the nineteenth century with one that would encapsulate the new aesthetic judgments of the twentieth. His work was well known among American art historians and Conant would have certainly read and absorbed the lessons of Mâle's study.

Mâle was adamant about two points which were not lost on Conant: that Cluny was the center of twelfth-century art and that the irreparable losses due to the Wars of Religion and the Revolution were a severe challenge to the progress of art history:

> The traveler searching throughout France for twelfth-century art comes repeatedly upon Cluny…. We owe these great men our profound gratitude. They believed in the virtue of art. At the time when St. Bernard was stripping his churches of all their ornaments, Peter the Venerable was having capitals and tympanums carved. He was not convinced by the eloquence of the ardent apostle of austerity that beauty was dangerous; on the contrary, as St. Odo said, he saw in beauty a presage of heaven. Love of art was one of Cluny's claims to greatness, and it had many. The magnificent and melancholy name of Cluny will be repeated throughout this book. It is a name that now evokes only ruins but seems still to retain the sense of majesty of the great ruins of Rome[9]…Our revolutions, indifferent to art and to glory alike, swept away our past".[10]

Although more scientific than Henry Adams, Mâle too wanted to restore the Middle Ages to a dignified place in history, repopulate it in people's imaginations, and bring the art alive by refreshing the stories behind the imagery. He returned to a deeply religious practice of his Catholic faith once turning his studies to medieval art, a pattern Conant would repeat in converting to Greek Orthodoxy.[11] He threw down the gauntlet to archeologists when, in a book focusing on decorative arts, he wrote:

> If a single figure had been preserved from the portal of Cluny, it might immediately change our hypothesis into certainty. Unfortunately, the portal was totally demolished and no comparison between the work at Moissac and Cluny is possible…No loss is more regretted by art historians today, for this portal would have solved the problem of the origins of Burgundian sculpture.[12]

Mâle's work summarized and codified the scholarship begun by German and French art historians in the nineteenth century and brought it to a new level of analysis. His iconographic investigations renewed interest in the meaning of the medieval decorative arts and his evocative descriptions of patrons and designers reestablished the academic integrity of religious artistic thought. As Mâle acquired an encyclopedic knowledge of church sculpture and manuscript miniatures for his iconographic studies, bringing in his training in classical literature and his amateur love of drawing and painting, so Conant traveled all over Romanesque France with his eye as a trained architect to learn the various components of church buildings from ca. 1000. However, besides a passing concern for the west portal imagery when fragments from Cluny were found—a puzzle he passed on to his students to untangle, Conant had no interest in Mâle's iconographic contributions to art history. He was only interested in the buildings, not their decoration. Yet he would try to do for Early Christian and medieval church architecture what Mâle had done for decorative religious art of the Middle Ages. He surely also believed Mâle's evaluation of Cluny as the "greatest creation of the Middle Ages."[13]

Arthur Kingsley Porter

Mâle shared his belief in Cluny with Arthur Kingsley Porter who confirmed the evidence one year later in his ten-volume publication *Romanesque Sculpture of the Pilgrimage Roads* (Boston, 1923). Mâle and Porter had developed a similar thesis: Romanesque sculpture centered at Cluny and spread via the pilgrimage roads throughout France and Spain. Mâle went so far as to say that Cluny was responsible for the pilgrimage to Compostela, as well as being the greatest sponsor and initiator of artwork and artistic thought throughout Europe, thus making France the center of Western art. He differed with Porter when he championed the artists of Langedoc over Spain as the earliest Western conductors of Eastern models.

Porter did not agree with Mâle's assessment of French aesthetic invention and his meticulous stylistic analyses proved that an American could acquire familiarity with European art equal to European nationals. With his unlimited budget, Porter traveled around by chauffeured car, seeking out remote locations and taking detailed photographs. As such, he presented a strong challenge to Mâle's nationalism because he was willing to consider cross-cultural origins and developments. "Before the XIII century the mountains formed no barrier.... This fundamental fact has nevertheless been ignored by archaeologists and historians of art. All students of Romanesque sculpture have followed one another in establishing a rigid division following the modern frontier."[14]

Although Mâle reclaimed the East's primary importance as genitor of iconographic scenes, he attributed the rise of twelfth-century sculpture, the form of the tympanum, and the historiated capital to France. His attempt to distinguish the regional origins of twelfth-century from thirteenth-century art (the South versus the Ile-de-France) nevertheless retained its most basic premise—that France was the cradle of medieval art and that her greatness was paramount. Porter retained the centrality of Cluny to the development of the sculpted tympanum after 1095, but used his concept of the "pilgrimage school" to account for the diffusion of Romanesque art across Europe. He took Mâle's initial idea of the role of the Spanish Beatus manuscript in developing the *Majestas Domini* tympanum scene and expanded it to include Spanish sculpture, metalwork, and ivory carving. He was also intensely aware of the importance of contemporary Italian artists, especially in the North, whereas Mâle tended to think of Italian and Byzantine influences in their Early Christian form.

However, in spite of his pointed criticism of such an approach, Porter was still wedded to the notion of progress from "archaic' or "primitive" styles to more naturalistic and he made complex stylistic stemmas which give no allowance for differences in training, access, experience, funding, materials, or patron preferences.[15] He categorically claimed autonomy for medieval artists: "Paradoxical as the statement may seem, it is probably true that mediaeval sculptors were more individualized, freer, less trammeled by convention than artists of the present time."[16]

The significance of the pilgrimage to Compostela and the role of Spain in the development of Romanesque art was key to Porter's creed. This he passed on to Conant, whose dissertation was on the medieval church of Santiago de Compostela. Porter did a thorough study of sculpture; he left architecture to his architect-student.[17] When Kenneth took an extended trip in 1924, Porter recommended that he visit and measure at Cluny.[18] It would be his great legacy to Conant.

Conant also consulted the current literature on Cluny, while researching plans and descriptions of the pre-Revolutionary abbey such as the important art-historical work of Jean Virey and Charles Oursel as well as the conservative 19th-century histories of the order which emphasized the great disservice its dissolution did to France (see chapter 3).

Conant's background and training

Kenneth John Conant was the eldest son of a Wisconsin basket factory owner and an art teacher. He studied for a fine arts degree at Harvard from 1911-1915, taking classes in the history of architecture from the dean who founded the graduate school of architecture, Herbert Langford Warren, and was successful in his studies as a result of which he graduated Magna Cum Laude. Among various awards received, Conant was sent, in 1916, on a traveling fellowship to become acquainted with the monuments of Italy, France, and Spain. He was received as an Associate Fellow at the American Academy in Rome and was in Europe when the United States entered the First World War. Conant rushed home to enlist and was placed in a camouflage unit, thus both avoiding conscription into the infantry and fulfilling his desire to help defend the countries of his favorite artistic sites. During the years of travel, including his military duty, Conant made a large body of pencil sketches of architectural sites that were featured in an exhibition at the Fogg from which a large number were purchased.

Wounded in France, Conant nonetheless seemed to find the entire experience to be a privilege: "I have a very interesting job that is very much in my own line and important too….I can't help remarking how fortunate I am in being in this service – It is all I ever hoped for and I am correspondingly delighted."[19] He preserved his battlefield impressions in carefully crafted letters written in the articulate and eloquent style of the day, demonstrating his Romantic receptivity:

> …While I was trying rather crossly to get to sleep again the fracas all at once magnified itself astonishingly, and we forgot all about going to bed, for we could not help realizing that here was something really extraordinary. We stepped out of the tent, and the full sweep and grandeur of it broke on us. The thing was being done on an immense scale. We stood amazed as fury after fury was released, telling each other how wonderful it was. It had the glory of a storm, not a whit less impressive, and more sustained and terrible. Cannon shots followed one another like the beat of the knives of a planer, —it doesn't seem possible to you but it is true without exaggeration. Think of shells being sent on that fast for

> hours, smashing trenches into nothing, and raking the back area for miles and miles; think of making a hurricane like that, and putting to shame God's best thunder. Lights of all kinds were in the sky, which was strangely streaked with low-hanging clouds, lights made by the bright flashes of the gun near us replying to the Germans, and great illuminations, like a curiously dislocated dawn, where enemy shells fell. It was magical and creepy, unearthly darkness, unearthly lights, and that unearthly roar engulfing it all—the sound of unimagined power, which we felt in the grinding and trembling of it, just as one standing by the drive of a great engine feels its power; and there was the sound a of unimaginably great iron things thundering their way across the brazen roof of the sky, —oh, a huge and marvelous roar that put awe into our hearts. And now they began to come nearer to us, but we were too interested to heed them very much…[20]

He also made friends while stationed in France who would help focus his later visits. Grateful for American aid, French civilians were generous toward most US soldiers, but he seems to believe it was due to his own personality:

> …Mme. Goll and Mlle Hérold are having me to dinner again I'm happy to say. Wherever I go somebody tries to be nice to me and help make me happy. I wonder what the reason is for it?—perhaps because I won't unfold myself except to those who attract me greatly. Then, content with a few such, I have time to make real friends of them, and can take the trouble to really care for them—I find it a very good substitute for some of the more ordinary army pleasures, such as drinking and trotting about with more or less attractive girls picked up on the street…[21]

It was only after being sent home to recover from being wounded that Conant was able to continue his studies and take an advanced degree in architecture. The continued influence of Warren was seminal. Warren had worked with H. H. Richardson, the great Romanesque revivalist whose design for Trinity Church in Boston in 1872 would change the course of medieval revival architecture in America.[22] Conant's thesis for the architecture degree in 1919 was also clearly influenced by the Early Christian art history course taught at Harvard. The plans for a monastery included a basilica derived from Italian models such as Old St. Peter's in Rome and completed by a Lombard-Romanesque campanile [fig. 5.1]. Conant made a second European tour as a Sachs Research Fellow in 1919, and another exhibit of nearly one hundred drawings of France and Spain was held at the Fogg Art Museum in fall 1920 [fig. 5.2]. The Boston Transcript noted that the architectural monuments of "old Spain" had "cast their spell upon the artist's fancy" who revealed with "tireless ardor the marvels of Gothic art in all their affluence, romantic and elegant, or noble and substantial, picturesque and strange, a world of artistic achievement, with a complete sense of appreciation in the interpretation…Every last line and dot is informed with a fine architectural imagination and a sensitive appreciation of beauty and dignity."[23] Some of these works were published for sale by Foster Bros., Boston in 1923.

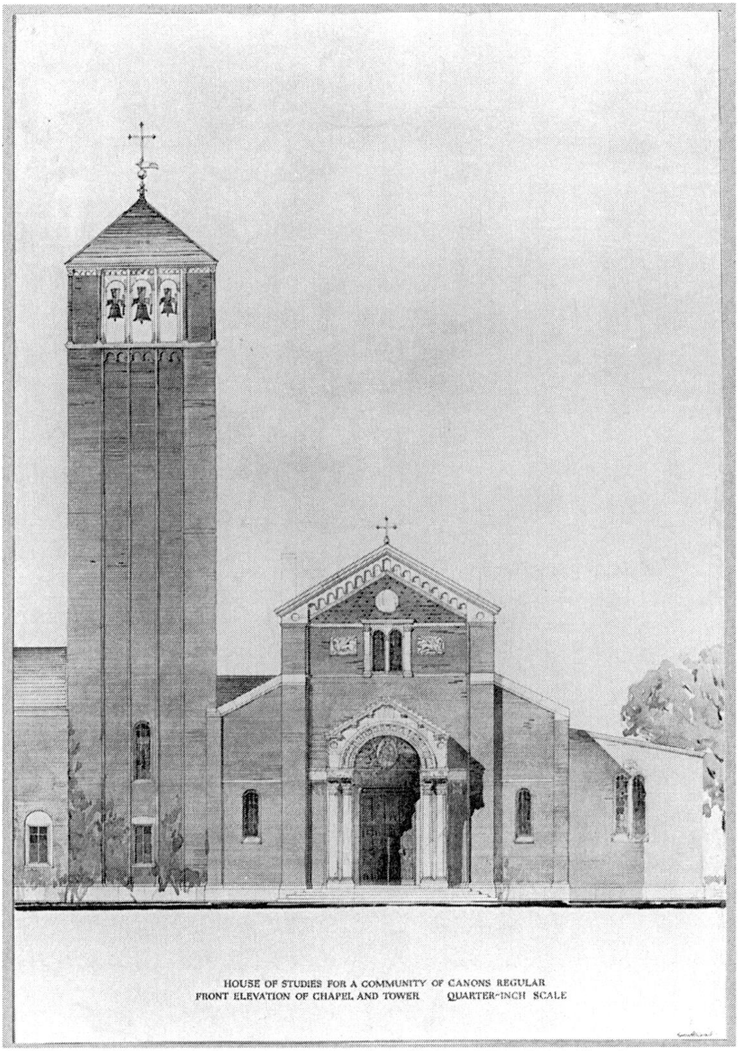

5.1 Kenneth Conant's thesis plan for "House of Studies for a Community of Canons Regular", front elevation of chapel and tower. 1919 (Cluny Collection: Loeb Library, Harvard University)

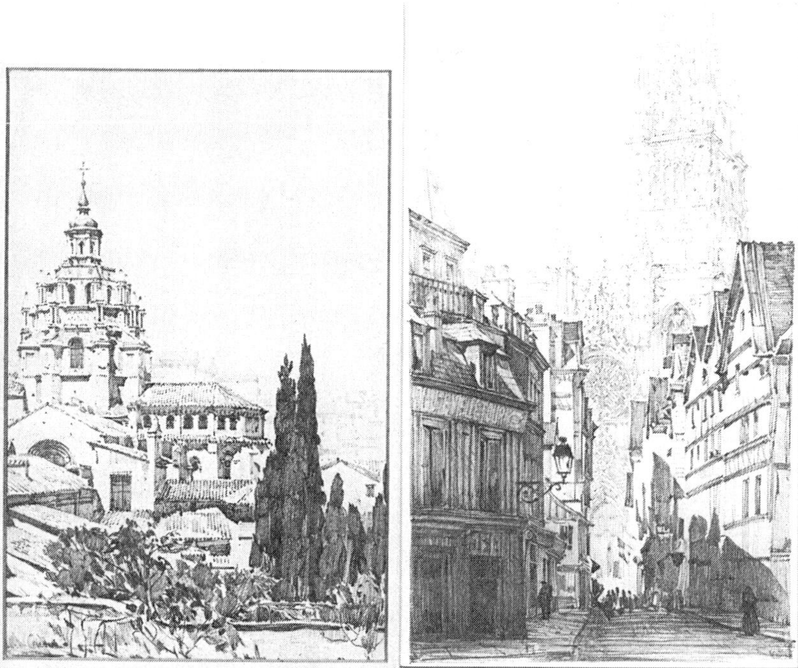

5.2 K.J. Conant, Sketches from European travels
(Cluny Collection: Loeb Library, Harvard University)
These are pencil sketches, which is why the tower is barely visible in the sketch on the right.

Architects, such as Ralph Adams Cram, were impressed with his ability and, upon seeing his drawings, had offered to hire him after the war.[24] However, as art, the results were dry and draughtsman-like, revealing his architectural focus. For this he was roundly criticized, for instance in another 1920 exhibition, presumably of the same works mounted at the Fogg, held at the Harlow gallery in New York City.[25] A portion of this review is worth quoting, for it previews what would become Conant's strength in his restoration drawing work (unknown author):

> ...Rejoicing in him architecturally, we are nevertheless a little disappointed in him as an artist. We alluded just now to his "impressions." The term is not, perhaps, altogether exact. It connotes, ordinarily, a certain tincture of personality, and there it must be confessed that Mr. Conant's drawings are not noticeably rich. He has the defect of his quality. That firm sharp line of his is accurate, as we have said, but it is also somewhat colorless, somewhat akin to a mechanical process. He has an extremely self-possessed and even authoritative manner. He

> hasn't, on the other hand, a style. Or, if we must call this a style, this stamp that he places upon all his drawings, it is an extremely conventional style. He gives us, indeed, records, and though they are better than the records made by the camera they come perilously near to falling into the same category. We are familiar with many of the monuments he has drawn and we are struck by the fact that he has not enveloped any of them in the French, Spanish or Italian atmosphere in which they respectively belong. He draws everything in the same dry light. It is partly a matter of method and partly, we suppose, matter of temperament.[26]

This type of draughtsmanship had a very important place, just not in the gallery. Going through an architectural training program, Conant learned the type of exact rendering necessary to that discipline. Also, as the reviewer said, at this time, precise pen-and-ink work was often preferred to cumbersome photography for utilitarian purposes. The American government employed thousands of people during World War II, for example, to make intricate pen-and-ink records of mechanical and electrical systems. Likewise in art history, the work of highly accurate lithographers had often showed details missed by other viewers. Porter himself depended upon the work of F. de Dartein, whose extraordinary prints of Lombard architectural sites were published in a large-format volume from 1865-1882.[27] The kind of visual analysis which Dartein brought to this task along with his detailed plans and elevation, copies of which Conant could have seen at Harvard, must have set high standards for similar work. Conant's first published restoration studies would be made of the cathedral of Avila (*Art Bulletin* 8 [June 1926], pp. 191-193) and the southwest tower of Chartres (*Speculum* 2/1 [January 1927], p. 66).

After taking the professional degree in 1919, Conant left again to study in Europe, having been awarded another Sachs fellowship of 2000 dollars. In fall of 1920 he was recalled to teach part-time in Architectural Design at Harvard in the Graduate School of Architecture and he joined the office of the Boston architects Perry, Shaw and Hepburn. He also did some design work beginning in January 1921 for a monastery outside Boston, Portsmouth Priory, for which his father secretly donated seventy-five dollars a month to the organization through a mutual friend, La Rose, who was also selling Kenneth's drawings.[28] This was clearly to help establish Conant's name as well as pay his bills and would represent the first time that he was exposed to planning conventual and church architecture, as well as the lifestyle it supported. Popularity of Richardson's Romanesque revival style grew into the academic study of the European sources and at Harvard, Conant was in the thick of this process. In 1923 he decided to quit Perry, Shaw, and Hepburn to pursue a second degree in Art History under Harold Edgell, with thesis direction from Arthur Kingsley Porter whom he had met in Europe in 1920. He also married

Marie Schneider on September 1 of this year, a girl from Wisconsin like himself. Although they would have two sons and Marie would help with the work at Cluny, the marriage was not successful and they would later divorce under bitter circumstances.

In 1924 Conant made another solo tour of Europe in preparation for his architectural history courses. Upon Porter's suggestion, he visited Cluny and made some measurements, staying in the Hotel de Bourgogne whose proprietor was then Marconnet, later to prove so obliging with the excavations. On that trip, while in residence at the American School in Rome, Conant took two tours of Greece. He also visited Hagia Sophia, in Istanbul, where he began to think about making more reconstructive drawings. He completed his dissertation, on the medieval structure of the cathedral of Santiago in Compostela, Spain, the following year (published in 1926). In 1926 he was made Assistant Professor of Architecture at Harvard and his first son, Kenneth, Jr., was born.

By following Porter and choosing to specialize in medieval art, Conant was entering the most established field of art history in America at the time. Although Bernard Berenson (1865-1959) had introduced connoisseurship and the Italian Renaissance with his works published beginning in 1894 that followed the earliest studies in the field in Europe,[29] the cutting edge of art history was being forged at Harvard and Princeton by those who were bringing the ideas of German scholars, especially Wilhelm Vöge and Adolph Goldschmidt, from Germany.[30] Porter was a direct link in this process for Conant since he followed Vöge's theories of stylistic change as being driven by the artists, rather than patrons with abstract notions. Vöge linked the similarities between sculptural forms in disparate locations to the interactions between real people who shared ideas and techniques.[31] Mâle, writing shortly after, did not concur. Instead, he followed French predecessors and believed in the passive adherence of the medieval artist to dogmatic Church designs and, for this reason, emphasized iconography over style.[32] Porter would apply Vöge's approach to his study of Romanesque sculpture in order to chart the development of the forms across the pilgrimage roads of Western Europe.

Conant's dissertation on the cathedral of Compostela is an architectural study of the building process. The work primarily involved an analysis of the existing church in order to produce detailed reconstructive drawings of its medieval forms. He was only able to measure above ground, being allowed very few opportunities to obtain soundings for foundations below the surface. Yet he was skilled at reading the history of the masonry, he knew the necessary building principles, and that was enough by the accepted methods of medieval archeology for his day.[33] He was also thinking along the lines of Porter's "pilgrimage route" and this plan would be later developed in his work as part of a pilgrimage plan series.

Porter's theories about the pilgrimage roads and the dissemination of Romanesque art in southern Europe were developed at the same time as those of the Catalan scholar, Joseph Puig i Cadafalch (1869-1957), whose first international publication appeared only in 1928 but whom Porter brought to Harvard in 1926.[34] Puig i Cadafalch was a Catalan architect who led the modernist revival of regional medieval forms in lieu of Beaux-Arts neoclassical standard training. As such, he was defining a politically charged architecture that recalled a period of self-determination of the Catalan people. Already in 1889 Puig i Cadafalch was student president of the *Lliga de Catalunya*, following his mentor Lluis Domènech i Montaner. Both published articles on national architecture and regional styles in the magazine *La Renaixensa.* Artistic patrimony was a hot political issue for the *Lliga* members during the years around 1900 when the Catalan language was being revived, as Puig wrote in 1896: "by mapping our architecture and studying our homeland we hope to build a new art and a new Catalonia."[35] In this sense, Puig set himself and his movement apart from the *modernista* movement which he saw as sterile and superficial.

Puig i Cadafalch would have been at Harvard the year after Conant completed his dissertation on Compostela. Through their mutual connection to Porter, as well as Conant's language skills in Spanish and French, one can only imagine that Conant actively engaged with him during that visit. At this point, Puig had fled the political climate in Spain and was already deeply involved in the travel and research for a lecture series in Paris 1924-25 which developed into his 1928 book, *Le premier art roman,* which related buildings of the tenth and eleventh centuries from Catalonia to those of northern Italy and southern France. He would be politically exiled during the 1930s and have the opportunity to continue this research and publish many more studies. His prestige as an expert on the history of Catalan architecture was established along with a reputation for serious contributions to theories on the origins of European Romanesque.[36]

Unlike Conant, who learned to draw as an undergraduate but turned that wholly into his professional skills as a trained architect, Puig applied his artistic eye to the decoration and restoration of buildings. He saw these latter as integral to the expression of the Catalan aesthetic. He also analyzed the ornamental elements in buildings along with their structural imprints when making his art historical studies. And he was accepted by Parisian scholars as an academic in a way that Conant never was. For all these reasons, Puig's career and publications followed a richer path than Conant's. Love of his homeland and original ideas about the broad application of the Romanesque style which he shared with Porter gave Puig i Cadafalch a wider intellectual experience from which to draw conclusions. In spite of his contact with Puig and probable discussion of the political and social implications of architectural form, Conant would eschew many of the same questions in his own work. Instead, Conant would remain a specialist in the history of architecture that, though international in scope and perceptive in comprehension, was more suited to the world of the practicing architect than art-historical discourse. Even his most successful work, his highly acclaimed volume for the Pelican series on the history of art under the direction of Nikolaus Pevsner, *Carolingian and Romanesque Architecture 800-1200* (1959), centers on a comparative technical development of church architecture (see chapter 6). Reading it today, one marvels at the number of times Conant invented explanations for building forms or made authoritative statements backed only by personal opinion. Conant's devotion to his reconstruction drawings of Cluny would also eventually pit him against anyone whose theories might undermine their accuracy and in his later years he became entrenched in defensive positions.

However, at the beginning, Conant's drafting skills were recognized as valuable tools and older scholars thought that he had great potential to expand his applications. After his success reconstructing the original form of the church at Santiago, Porter suggested he continue this study method at three locations in France: St. Martin, Tours; St. Martial, Limoges; and the abbey church at Cluny. Because these monuments had been heavily damaged, mostly destroyed, after the Revolution, someone with archaeological skills would be necessary in order to determine the measurements necessary to complete drawing restoration work, similar to that which Conant had done at Compostela. Seeking to refine the archeological digging techniques he had encountered in his work in Spain, Conant was awarded a grant from the Carnegie Institute of Washington D.C. to join an expedition to the Yucatan in order to make drawings of Chichen Itzá. He was also sent to excavations at Pueblo Bonita in New Mexico's Chaco Canyon through the National Geographic Society for the same purpose. He used both opportunities to observe the archeologists at work. A *bon voyage* letter upon his departure for the Yucatan from his Radcliffe students, written in May of 1926, demonstrates that he was meanwhile becoming a popular lecturer who could recruit adherents to his interest in the history of architecture.[37]

It is clear from letters that Conant read both French and Spanish, and possibly German. However, we see little evidence that he consulted the work of other scholars in a more than cursory fashion, believing as he did that he was breaking new ground with his excavations. The academic rigor of German art historical study was one of Porter's strengths and his books draw upon a wide range of European scholarship. Seeing himself primarily as architect and now archaeologist, Conant preferred to work directly with primary source documents. Even in his dissertation the footnotes are concerned with available images of earlier plans, medieval descriptions of the buildings, or a few scholars who had opinions about the forms earlier structures took. Conant did not treat the imagery on the church and was not influenced by Vöge/Porter towards what would later become "social art history," à la Arnold Hauser (1951) to consider builders, patrons, or audience (other than a nineteenth-century romantic view of sainted abbot builders and pious monk residents). Thus we cannot look to Conant to extend the emphasis of the German school of art history in the United States toward the meaning of artworks. Instead, it would be done by other students of Porter and, more importantly, through the lecture-visits of Goldschmidt as well as German émigrés in Britain and America.[38] Conant's contribution to art history in the United States would be more pragmatic; his sketches grew into formal elevations, cutaways, and plans that showed with crystal precision the state of medieval buildings throughout their development. The authority of such representations is not to be underestimated. Compared to confusing photographs of contemporary conditions at these sites, or lengthy written arguments and descriptions, Conant's images provided golden material for the classroom. This process culminated in the Pelican volume and in the Foreword to that book, Conant names his sources—mostly scholars known to him personally. He also calls himself the "heir of Herbert Langford Warren and his teachers Henry Hobson Richardson and Charles Eliot Norton" thus implying that he was carrying on the torch of medieval revivalist design.[39]

First Seasons at Cluny

In 1926, Conant wrote a proposal for 950 dollars to the Guggenheim Foundation to work on the three churches identified by him and Porter during the summers of 1927 and 1928 and was funded the sum of 1000 dollars for each year. (By 1929 the Foundation had spent 3100 dollars on the project, which, already at the end of the first summer, Conant had narrowed to include only Cluny.)[40] His proposal details the techniques he used at Compostela as well as the value of such labors, showing an awareness of the classroom needs of American professors in teaching medieval architecture:

> Restorations of this kind are very welcome material for magazines like the Art Bulletin, Art Studies, the Speculum, or the American Journal of Archaeology. Once the plates are made for such a publication, it becomes possible to republish in book form at a minimum of expense....Of course it goes without saying that each of the restorations would be accompanied by an essay explaining and justifying it, and these essays could be designed for later gathering into a book. From the magazines or the books these restorations would be copied on lantern slides, in other books dealing with the same material, and in works of vulgarization. In this way they would contribute to the need, increasingly felt, of sufficient illustration in the history of art.[41]

Kingsley Porter wrote Conant an introduction letter to his close colleague, Charles Oursel in Dijon, angling to get him invited as to represent Harvard at the Congress of the Burgundian Learned Societies held at Dijon June 12-18, 1927 [fig. 5.3]. He emphasized his work at Compostela and while stating that Conant was above all an architect, and still quite young, affirmed that he was also a good archeologist. The invitation followed and while at the Congress, Conant joined a tour of Burgundian monuments and made important contacts for his future endeavors, including such influential men as Oursel and Jean Virey. From Dijon, Conant proceeded to the libraries in Paris in order to consult original documents on the Cluny abbey church, his first planned subject of study. While in Paris, he met with officials at the Beaux-Arts ministry, showing them his preliminary drawings of the ruins made in 1924. He was authorized to pursue his plans and he went on to Cluny. While there, Conant filled 86 pages of what he terms a "field book" with "measurements of the abbey establishment."[42] He visited the government architect at Chalons-sur-Saône, Edmond Malo, and was invited to attend a meeting of the Academy of Mâcon, which he subsequently joined. He also went to measure some of the choir stalls from the abbey church which had ended up at the Cathedral of Lyons.

During this first summer, Conant worked in the remaining transept, analyzing the tower with its Gabriel Chapel and publishing the results in 1928 in the *Bulletin monumental*.[43] In the same year, *Speculum*, the scholarly journal of the Mediaeval Academy of America, brought out a short piece from Conant's research entitled "Five old prints of the abbey church of Cluny" demonstrating the Academy's interest in his results.[44]

Anticipating that he would need additional funding beyond the Guggenheim, already before he left in 1927 Conant had turned to the recently formed Mediaeval Academy to propose a publication project.[45] In line with the avowed goals of this organization, Conant outlined the potential for an important monograph complete with a "complete and accurate restoration of the great abbey church as it was before the lamentable demolition of a century ago." In addition, he promised data on the pre-Romanesque churches and partial restoration of the medieval conventual buildings. He clearly stated that no comprehensive study of the buildings had ever been undertaken and that the site represented "one of the greatest masterpieces of mediaeval building." He attached drawings from work he had done since 1924 and listed an impressive retinue of friends he had made in high places who could help pave the way for permissions to dig. He also mentions that he had been received as a member of the Academy of Mâcon.

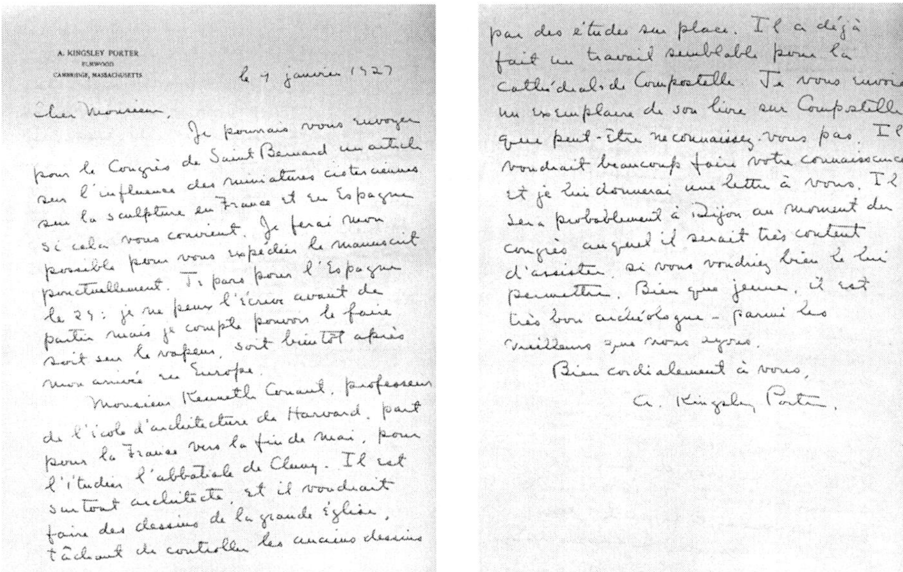

A. KINGSLEY PORTER
ELMWOOD
CAMBRIDGE, MASSACHUSETTS

le 7 janvier 1927

Cher Monsieur,

Je pourrais vous envoyer pour le Congrès de Saint Bernard un article sur l'influence des miniatures cisterciennes sur la sculpture en France et en Espagne si cela vous convient. Je ferai mon possible pour vous expédier le manuscrit ponctuellement. Je pars pour l'Espagne le 29 : je ne peux l'écrire avant de partir mais je compte pouvoir le faire soit sur le vapeur, soit bientôt après mon arrivée en Europe.

Monsieur Kenneth Conant, professeur de l'école d'architecture de Harvard, part pour la France vers la fin de mai, pour l'étudier l'abbatiale de Cluny. Il est surtout architecte, et il voudrait faire des dessins de la grande église, tâchant de contrôler les anciens dessins par des études sur place. Il a déjà fait un travail semblable pour la cathédrale de Compostelle. Je vous envoie un exemplaire de son livre sur Compostelle que peut-être ne connaissez-vous pas. Il voudrait beaucoup faire votre connaissance, et je lui donnerai une lettre à vous. Il sera probablement à Dijon au moment du congrès auquel il serait très content d'assister, si vous voudriez bien le lui permettre. Bien que jeune, il est très bon archéologue – parmi les meilleurs que nous ayons.

Bien cordialement à vous,

A. Kingsley Porter.

5.3 Letter from Kinglsey Porter to Oursel introducing Conant in 1927
(Cluny Collection: Loeb Library, Harvard University)

In this outline, Conant proposed four summers of excavations and study including the second one funded by the Guggenheim. He promised an efficient plan of attack as old plans existed which indicated where to dig first. He did not guarantee any finds aside from foundation walls that would yield measurements for his drawings, though he admitted sculpted stones would surely be found in the process. Finally, Conant anticipated the expense of campaigns from 1928 to 1931 to run about 5,000 dollars plus an additional 1500 dollars for his own expenses with the following closing caveat: "Events may prove this estimate wide of the mark, but it allows for the uncovering of about half a mile of foundation at the rate of two dollars a cubic yard for removing and replacing earth. Interesting and unexpected discoveries might call for further digging, but the program of excavation could doubtless be adjusted to the appropriation."

In October, copies of the proposal were sent to the members of the executive committee for review. Only one, Charles Rufus Morey, gave unconditional approval.[46] The others suggested various responses such as only promising funds for two years at a time or finding another scholar to review extant documents and coordinate with excavation findings. Overall, however, Rockwell's comments from his position at the Union Theological Seminary sum up their interest in the work: "…I feel that the significance of Cluny is very great indeed. When I made a flying visit to it in 1922, I was distressed to see how little of the mediaeval Abbey remains....It would be worthy of the Academy to arrange for the publication of an adequate volume at a price between five and ten dollars, publishing not merely the results of excavations to be made under its oversight, but also reproductions of old prints and miniatures which show Cluny as it was in the days of its leadership." He felt that the Academy should only pay for excavations if "friends of Harvard" provide the money. Otherwise he felt it was "putting money into a bottomless pit". Publication was his first interest in all things. "How interesting it would be to have an American scholar publish under our auspices a worthy volume illustrating the evolution of those monastic buildings whence went forth during the middle ages so many noble impulses for the reform of art and of religion."

This proposal came at a crucial point in the Mediaeval Academy's history. Having just made the decision in December of 1925 to incorporate as a national organization, the first members stated as their purpose: "To conduct, encourage, promote and support research, publication, and instruction in Mediaeval records, literature, languages, arts, archaeology, history, philosophy, science, life, and all other aspects of Mediaeval civilizations, by instigating and maintaining research, and by such other means as may be desirable, and to hold property for such purpose." They applied for membership in the American Council of Learned Societies and solicited dues for individual membership as well as seeking important academics to serve as various administrative advisors. Already one year later, in December of 1926, the Mediaeval Academy had 746 paying members as well as one "patron", one "benefactor", 3 "sustaining members", 25 "life members" and 91 "contributing members", these terms representing the level of donations from generous individuals. One of the "life members" (representing a one-time payment of 100 dollars) was Arthur Kingsley Porter, who sat on the first Board of Councilors. In 1928 the Committee on Research was founded, to free up the editors of their journal, *Speculum,* on whose behalf the Executive Committee applied to the Carnegie Corporation and was granted a revolving publication fund of 25,000 dollars. The Committee on Research included Porter and John Nicholas Brown, a college friend of Conant's who had also been deeply influenced by Porter's courses at Harvard. Both these men encouraged Conant's study and Brown became Treasurer of the Academy, funneling his own wealth into Academy projects, especially the work at Cluny.

The Cambridge architect, Ralph Adams Cram, was elected Clerk of the Academy. According to a story told by Conant's son John, Cram introduced Conant to Isabella Stewart Gardner who became aware that, though married to a Roman Catholic, Conant had never been formally baptized and she insisted standing as his sponsor for the Episcopal Church before he work with Cram on plans for the monastery she was donating to monks in Cambridge.[47] The ceremony was held, appropriately enough, in H. H. Richardson's Romanesque Trinity Church in Boston. Conant claimed that Cram's design for the Cambridge establishment was influenced by Conant's knowledge of the simple Burgundian Romanesque style. Work on the site occurred in two stages: The current guesthouse was the original monastery built by Cram 1924-28 and then in the mid 30s he designed the chapel and an additional monastery wing.[48] Certainly Cram's belief in monasticism as, in the words of Peter Fergusson, "both the agent of civilization and patron of the arts" was a strong influence on Conant's own ideals about Cluny's role in medieval Europe.[49]

Cram, working at the American Church in Paris during 1928, gave a copy of Conant's Compostela text to Marcel Aubert who was then the head of the Commission of Historic Monuments in France. Aubert was impressed and began helping the American Ambassador to France, Myron T. Herrick, obtain permissions to undertake digging at Cluny. Herrick was contacted by John Nicholas Brown and an opportunity was arranged for Conant to meet with the Ambassador before his departure for France. Copies of a letter from the executive committee of the Mediaeval Academy introduced Conant to both the Minister of Public Instruction and the Director of Fine Arts and Herrick wrote a cover letter from Paris underlining his accord wth the project. On March 23, 1928 the cable came from Cram to the Mediaeval Academy: "CLUNY CONCESSION GRANTED HURRAH LETTER FOLLOWS."

Conant's relationship with France and with Aubert and Herrick should also be considered in light of Robert Young's recent book on French propaganda in America from 1900-1940.[50] Although uneven, dispersed, and marked by continual changes of office and personnel, France's attempt to curry a positive image in America was primarily directed at the elite and educated of the East Coast. In particular, academic exchanges were some of the first methods the French employed to convey information about French political and economic policies as well as emphasize France's cultural and intellectual prowess among nations. By offering medals to students studying French, donating French books to American libraries, forming associations for French teachers and cultural administrators, and subsidizing travel between the two countries, French directors of propaganda efforts never stopped hoping that "educated Americans saw France as part of their own cultural patrimony."[51] Conant was one of those elite who had studied French and whose Beaux-Arts architectural training had predisposed him towards sympathy with France. Although he also traveled in most other European countries, and wrote his dissertation on a Spanish monument, the climate both in his childhood home and later at Harvard shaped an appreciation of France as the most desirable cultural model.[52] He applied for support of his undertaking at a lucky time:

Marcel Aubert had lectured at Yale and was solidly behind Franco-American exchange in the interest of better diplomatic relations; Herrick was a particularly sympathetic ambassador who had received the Legion d'honneur's *grande croix* in 1914.[53] It is significant that Conant was stationed in France in 1918 as well. He had sketched French historical architecture and had seen some of it harmed. He was welcomed into the homes of civilians who became lifelong friends. He was wounded there and later claimed that personal sacrifice showed his commitment to the country.

On March 4th, 1928 the pro-French New York Times Magazine ran a story on the upcoming expedition. Calling Cluny "the greatest center of learning in the Middle Ages", the author, Thomas S. Bosworth, underlined how ruined the site had become. "The town of Cluny, which is quite off the beaten track, set in its 'black valley,' is a town of comparatively little interest to travelers. By automobile it is not far from its vastly more interesting neighbor, Autun, with its roman gate and fine church; nor from Lyons." Making reference to the remaining transept with its "orphaned tower", Bosworth told American readers about the abbey's glorious past and powerful abbots, ending with its demise: "In the violence of the French Revolution all the monastic buildings disappeared, save the abbot's lodging, a small bit of the abbey walls and that part of the transept that was saved for a parish church—now gloomy, silent and bare under its covering of whitewash. The walls of Cluny no longer echo to the music of psalms, and the old abbots lie in nameless graves." Bosworth apparently had done a bit of research, finding some of the more romantic nineteenth-century accounts to paraphrase.

On May 25, 1928, the Mediaeval Academy served Conant with "A Letter of Instruction."[54] Acceptable expenses were specified as well as requirements for recordkeeping. He was to send short monthly reports to the Mediaeval Academy office "from the field" and a full report of the season was due October 30, 1928. The letter also claimed all publication rights for the Mediaeval Academy. Conant wrote to acknowledge receipt and acceptance of terms on Mediaeval Academy letterhead, so probably while in the office under Marshall's guiding eye. Meanwhile, on May 25, John Nicholas Brown also confirmed his verbal offer to donate 12,000 dollars to the Academy, payable in three annual installments, for excavating and publishing Cluny.[55] A letter of credit was issued through the Harvard Trust Company for Conant to use in France. Apparently on the same day a press release was delivered to the Boston Evening Transcript because on the 26th, W. A Macdonald wrote an article entitled: "From Harvard to Recompose the Lines of a Ruined Abbey: Kenneth J. Conant, Assistant Professor of Architecture, going to France for His Second Summer at Cluny, Over Whose Structure the Records Disagree". Five illustrations took up the greatest proportion of copy space, two of which represented an engraving done before the demolition and a model constructed shortly after but which are labeled "inaccurate". The focus of the story was not only on Conant's purpose to prepare restoration drawings for publication, but to reconcile extant materials which did not agree as to the exact form of the former buildings. "Last summer Mr. Conant measured things remaining above ground; this summer he hopes to dig below. The testimony of the past disagrees on measurements, on vaults, niches, ornaments. The task is to patiently make a new record of labor impatiently erased." Macdonald drew out the human-interest angle for his story, and he gave us a sense of Conant's own trepidation before departure.

> Then it will be possible for architecture to know again all the problems of the men who built at Cluny. It may be that there was pioneering there: that difficulties were solved in a manner never devised before. The history of architecture has paid scant attention to the place....The work in which Professor Conant will engage himself...involves problems sometimes forgotten by laymen: the human problems of social relations with those who may by their attitude help or hinder the investigator. The activities of the technical school, of the [horse] breeding establishment of the Government [*Haras*], of the people of the town must be considered, their convenience consulted. "They may not want us digging around year after year," says Mr. Conant. He is a young man and he has enthusiasm. He must be seen and questioned by the authorities before the permission he seeks is finally granted. They will want to know, he is aware, what his attitude will be toward the work he desires to do. They will want to be assured what kind of person he is. That he will pass this test cannot be doubted by anyone who has talked with him. A scholar who is a likeable and attractive human being is not too often found...

Letters were also prepared to present Conant to the appropriate authorities, in particular Marcel Aubert, director of the French Archaeological Society, to whom he was to present himself directly upon arrival in Paris.[56] Caution had been recommended by Cram in March 24: "It appears from what I have learned from Mr. Lafond and Mr. Aubert that Professor Conant, was not altogether wise in some of his actions at Cluny in the past, that is he did not, so I am told, act always with official authority and did one or two other things in the way of investigations which slightly prejudiced his case for the future."[57] A three-person commission was formed in Paris to advise Conant, consisting of Mr. Herriot (Minster of Education and Beaux-Arts), Aubert, and the chief architect of the Commission of Historic Monuments, Paul Gélis. The architect appointed for Burgundy by the Commission, Edmond Malo, had begun excavations at Cluny in 1913, before the war intervened, so he was assigned as the local liaison.

Conant's written French seems to have been quite good since there is no indication that he procured help with his letters. According to current residents of Cluny who knew him well in later years, his spoken French was passable but he never lost a strong American accent.[58] One has to imagine that his assured style and widely-attested charming personality carried Conant through more of the early meetings and negotiations than fluent language skills.

Obtaining permission to work on the site from the government and town was not all that was at stake. The former abbey grounds, including portions of the church, were, as has been outlined in chapters one through three, being utilized by the *École Nationale des Arts et Métiers* as well as the National *Haras.* Thus the ministries of Education and Agriculture became involved in the proceedings, as well as small shopkeepers and the proprietors of the *Hotel de Bourgogne,* where Conant was lodged.

Conant left for France on June 1 1928, sailing from New York and arriving at Le Havre on June 8. He met with Aubert on June 11 and with Gélis on June 13. He was given the title "Director of Excavations at Cluny." Before heading to Cluny, however, he participated in another archaeological conference at Dijon where excursions to relevant sites were planned. He was able to again meet several important French archaeologists and interest them in his project. He was particularly pleased with scholars who were rethinking the development of the Romanesque, as he clearly hoped to influence their assessment of Cluny's role.

Arriving at Cluny on June 24, the director of the école had been briefed on the situation and offered his unconditional consent as long as Conant waited until after school closed on July 15 to begin work. Thus Conant had time to set up his bank account, present his letters to the city authorities and gain their cooperation, as well as query Malo about recommendations for a contractor. Malo showed up with the man who, with his son, would be the contractor for all the excavation work throughout Conant's years at Cluny—*Cartier et fils.* Cartier had extensive knowledge of restoration as ordered by the Commission of Historic Monuments and was able immediately to draw up estimates of the costs to submit to both Conant and Malo and then send on to the Mediaeval Academy. Since they had arrived on June 29, the feast of SS. Peter and Paul who were the patrons of the old abbey and the date on which rents had always been collected, Conant thought it nicely symbolic to make a ceremonial beginning to work on that day. The president of the tourist office found a pick and Conant appropriately offered Malo "the first stroke, because it was he who was in charge of the excavations begun in 1913 and interrupted by the war. He is resigning into my hands, with the utmost good will, a project which he held very dear."[59] They began at the west portal, and photographed the occasion [fig. 5.4].

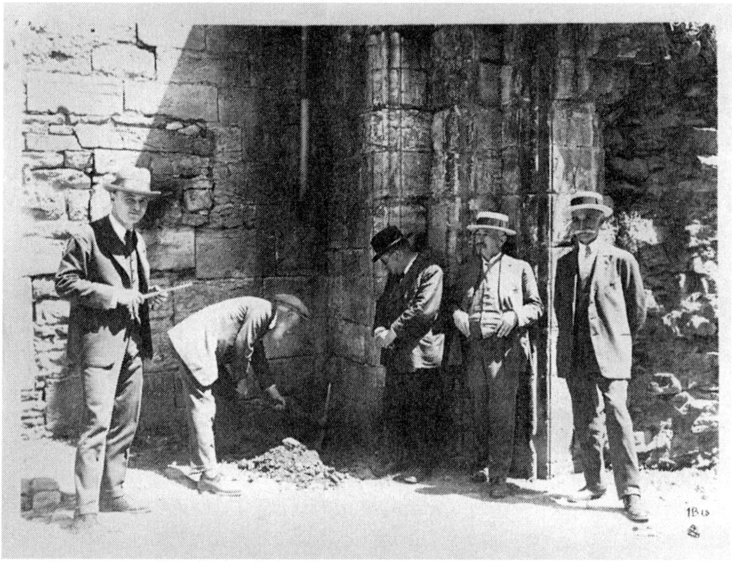

5.4 Ground breaking, Mediaeval Academy excavations Cluny, July 29,1928. Conant is on the far left, Malo is wielding the pick. (Musée d'art et d'archéologie, Cluny)

On July 4, Conant dutifully wrote personal letters on behalf of the Mediaeval Academy thanking Verdier, head of the *Monuments historiques*; Paul Léon, Director of Fine Arts, and a third to Edouard Herriot, Minister of Public Instruction whose copy is marked with an underline "…remerciements pour l'autorisation que vous avez bien *voulu donner aux fouilles de Cluny*" and an exclamation at the top: "rien à l'Enseignement Superière!"[60]

Unfortunately, permission was not as forthcoming from the *Haras* director since he had not been notified in advance and was unwilling to proceed until he received the requisite signed papers from his Ministry. Since the planned excavation work would have upset the daily routine of the stables, Conant recognized that for the meantime, he would "have to be content with soundings in this area." In the first monthly report to the Mediaeval Academy, however, Conant addressed the *Haras* issue at length. He nurtured great hopes for a few years that it would be relocated so that he could raze the entire area and open extensive excavations. This was never feasible, even though Malo drew up a plan with estimates of the cost and Conant specified a deficit of about 20,000 dollars, which no agency in France at the time could bear. He felt that the opportunity was one not to be missed both for clear access to the outline of the foundations and "the likelihood of finding sculptured fragments." It must have been a shock to those back in Cambridge to find that already, in his first report home, Conant was serving to engender notions of American gold. "…I have been asked particularly not to approach Mr. Rockefeller, who has been so generous at Reims and Versailles. I hope that something might be done through the Academy."

It would seem that both Conant and Brown took Rockefeller's altruism as a model for their own project. Rockefeller claimed through his donations towards repair of the roof, and later more, of the damaged cathedral at Reims, to have made that monument a part of the world's patrimony, rather than merely a symbol of France's medieval heritage.[61] Certainly such a noble notion of democratic sponsorship would have rung true to Conant's vision for Cluny; democratic in the sense that Conant believed the French should share access to their great art but ironic in the face of his simultaneous possessiveness about his beloved project. Likewise, John Nicholas Brown was young and rich and looked to the older members of his class who had been active during the crisis of the last war. Too late to make a difference for such popular causes as the "martyrdom" of Reims, Brown must have hoped that his direct subvention of the Academy sponsorship would result in a major contribution to scholarship on medieval architecture. The publicity which the Academy sought and their publications of the excavations' progress indicates that this hope was shared among the directors.

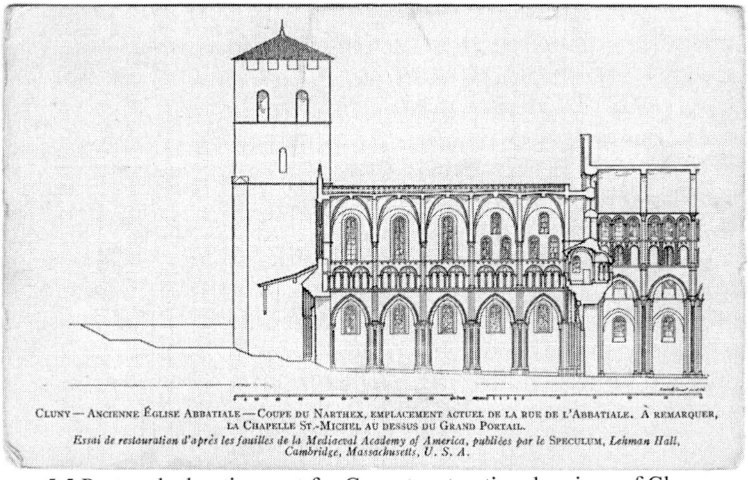

5.5 Postcard advertisement for Conant restoration drawings of Cluny (Cluny Collection: Loeb Library, Harvard)

John Marshall, as executive secretary of the Mediaeval Academy, wrote in to Conant response to his first monthly report that they were using the photographs he sent together with short write-ups on his commencement of the work to begin a press coverage of the project. Although the traditional word on Conant among the next generation was that he never missed an opportunity to toot his own horn about Cluny, reading through the materials of the Mediaeval Academy interventions suggests, at least at the outset, it was rather John Marshall and perhaps Cram, who should be credited with the intention to keep the project before the public eye. In the report of the executive secretary for the Council meeting of April 26, 1929, plans to reproduce Conant's restoration drawings on postcards was recorded [fig. 5.5]. They were to be available at the meeting of the Corporation and at Cluny. In addition, a prospectus was sent to members of the Archaeological Institute announcing a series of articles on the Cluny work to appear in Speculum [fig. 5.6].[62]

SPECULUM

A JOURNAL OF MEDIAEVAL STUDIES

Announces a series of articles on

EXCAVATIONS ON THE SITE OF
THE ABBEY CHURCH AT CLUNY

BY

KENNETH JOHN CONANT
RESEARCH ASSOCIATE IN ARCHAEOLOGY
OF THE MEDIAEVAL ACADEMY OF AMERICA

PUBLISHED BY

THE MEDIAEVAL ACADEMY OF AMERICA
CAMBRIDGE, MASSACHUSETTS

5.6 Advertisement for Conant's *Speculum* articles on Cluny, 1929
(Mediaeval Academy of America)

Ralph Adams Cram may also account for some of the rhetoric Conant employed in support of excavations necessary to make reconstructive drawings of the ruined abbey church at Cluny. Cram had published a book in 1915, with a 1918 reprint, called *Heart of Europe.* It was a passionate plea on behalf of European artistic monuments threatened with violent destruction during World War I. Comparable to the language of nineteenth-century authors we saw writing with regret on the demolition of Cluny due to the architectural vandalism fostered during the French Revolution, Cram captures the attitude being fostered by the contemporary American press which condemned the Germans for their shelling of Reims and other French monuments. He thus contributed to the efforts by partisans who wished the United States to enter the war on behalf of France's allies. Letters home in the Loeb collection at Harvard show that Conant was traveling around Europe during the years of the war, impatiently waiting for the United States to enter so that he could enlist. He wrote of his concern for the French cathedrals in particular. Conant had first met Cram in 1911, worked with him during the 1920s, and owned his books.[63]

During the first excavation in 1928, Conant kept in close touch with Cambridge. On the fifth of July, he cabled the Mediaeval Academy office: "DIGGING PORTALS SMALL FRAGMENTS IMMEDIATELY" and followed that on the 23rd of the same month with: "IMPRESSIVE NARTHEX EXCAVATION MERITS PRESERVATION PLEASE INDECATE [sic] LIMIT FROM SEASON SURPLUS OF TWO THOUSAND".[64] Involving a question of money, the matter was turned over to John Nicholas Brown as Mediaeval Academy Treasurer and he replied: "IS PRESERVATION NECESSARY TO YOUR WORK STOP CABLED INFORMATION INSUFFICIENT STOP ON RECEIPT OF DETAILED REPORT WILL CABLE DECISION STOP SEND MORE PHOTOGRAPHS". Conant wrote a detailed letter the same day as his original cable. He referred to photographs previously mailed and two drawings he attached (elevation and section of exposed fabric) as well as a postcard showing the state of the portal before current excavations [fig. 5.7]. "Now we have a hole from twelve to fifteen feet deep embracing it. No one who has gone down into the excavation has failed to remark how fine it would be to preserve it. It gives an entirely new idea of the portal." He doubted the Commission of Historic Monuments could assist with the expenses but promised to ask.

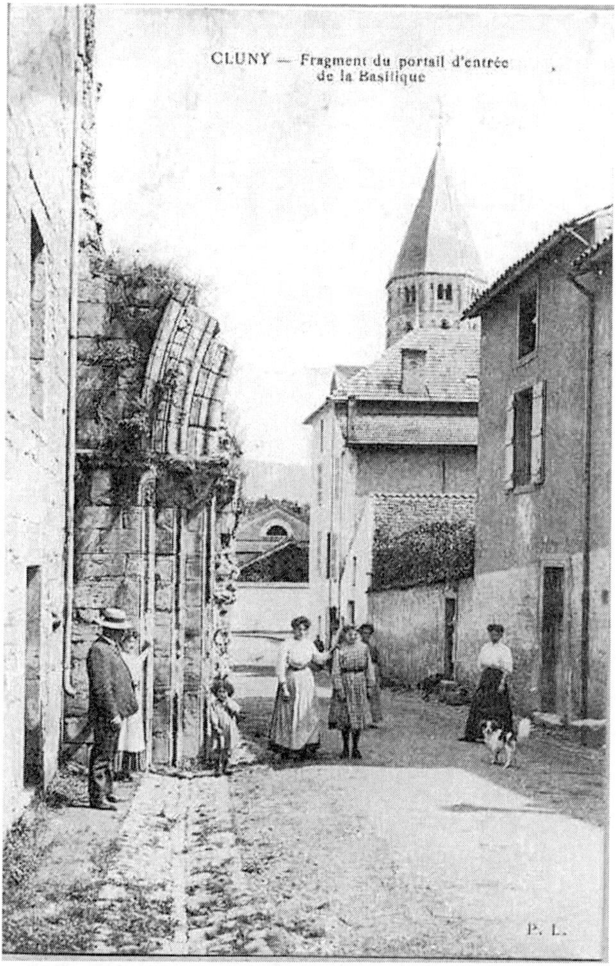

5.7 View of west portal of abbey church of Cluny before 1928
(Cluny Collection: Loeb Library, Harvard University)

The cables from the United States are undated and therefore it is unclear how much time passed until Brown replied saying: "AUTHORIZE EIGHT HUNDRED DOLLAR LIMIT FOR UNDERPINNING WITHOUT SETTING PRECEDENT". A photograph of 1929 shows town dignitaries peering into this preserved opening: the pit around the base of the narthex portal, protected by iron fence work [fig. 5.8]. The town was beginning to take notice of their monument.

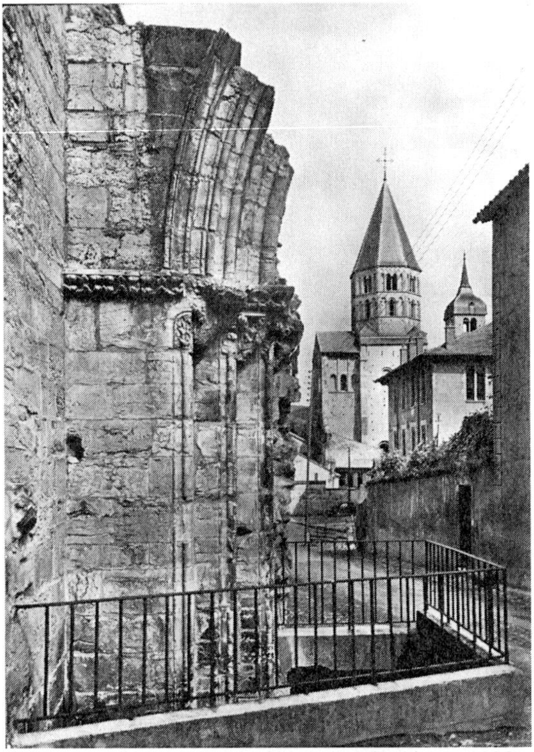

5.8 Pit 1 at West portal, abbey church, Cluny, 1929
(Cluny Collection: Loeb Library, Harvard University)

In Conant's report for the excavations during July 1928, he records that real work began on July 5th with a crew of "four good men". He began with the two west portals (the later narthex and the original entrance). Conant also employed a student, René Folcher, as his assistant for 1000 francs for the summer. The men immediately encountered difficulties in their working relationship. "…M. Cartier had not made it clear that I was in command and that he would back my orders financially. The men were not used to sifting their earth, and took my archaeological vigilance as a personal matter. They disliked the constant changing of orders, necessary of course when trial trenches are being run and unexpected conditions met. Neglect to observe my order (conflicting with orders left by M. Cartier) led to a thoroughgoing explanation on July 9. At this time I decided that, on account of the exceptional character of the work, each man should, during good behavior, receive in addition to his pay a half-bottle of wine daily (price six cents). The results of this interview have been extremely happy; I have a contented and satisfactory crew, and the personal relations and esprit de corps are all that could be desired. I have given the men photographs of themselves, of the excavations, and of the interesting finds, believing that it would help to give the men an indispensable interest in their work [figs. 5.9 and 5.10]."

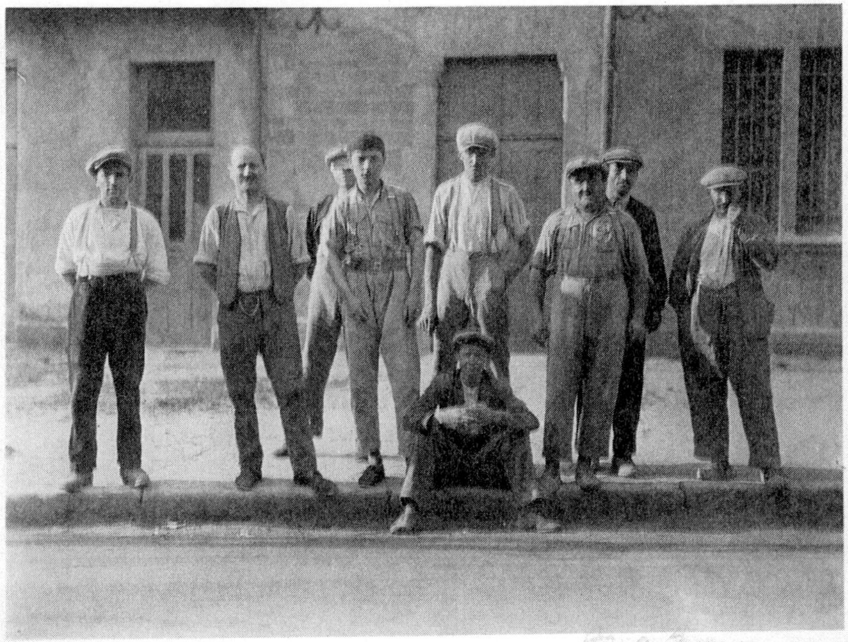

5.9 Workers posing for photograph during Cluny excavations around 1928

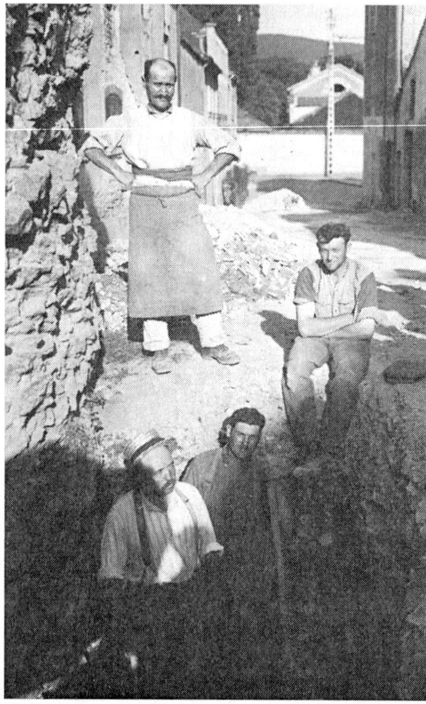

5.10 Men posing in excavation pit at Cluny, 1928

The dichotomous notions of "good behavior" and "esprit de corps" show Conant's awkwardness with his elite status as privileged overseer among *ouvriers*. Photographs taken in 1931 portray the same striking contrasts; in one Conant in his three-piece suit complete with fedora, stands stiffly to the side of the men who are in two rows, seated and standing at the edge of a "pit" (his word for the French term "*sondages*" or "trial trenches") in the court of the *Haras* [fig. 5.11]. In another, he perches uncomfortably on a pile of dirt while workers pose around him [fig. 5.12], and in a third, he stands next to a crew that has just unearthed a fragment of architectural stone [fig. 5.13]. In all, the men's rough clothes, suspenders, *casquettes,* and wooden clogs remind us of the extraordinary cultural and class differences inherent in a project conducted in rural Burgundy by a Harvard professor at this time.

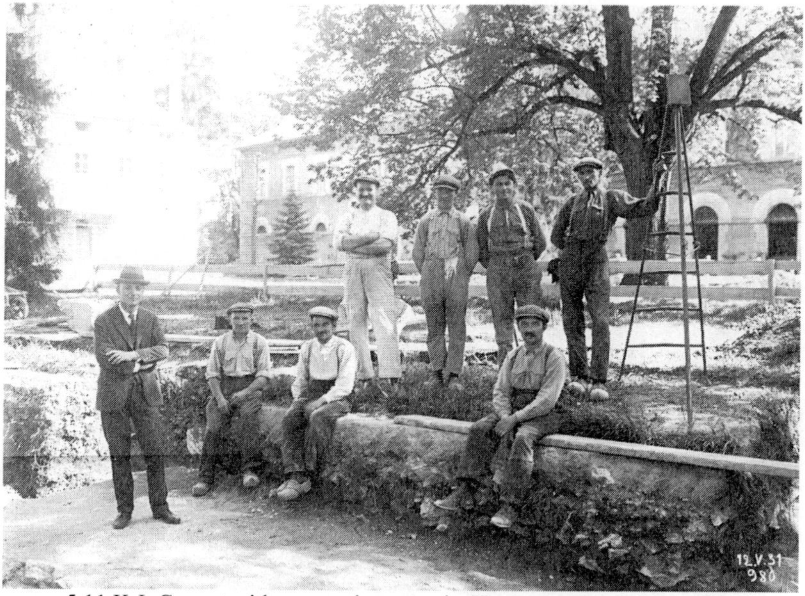

5.11 K.J. Conant with excavation crew in *Haras* courtyard, May 1931
(Mediaeval Academy of America)

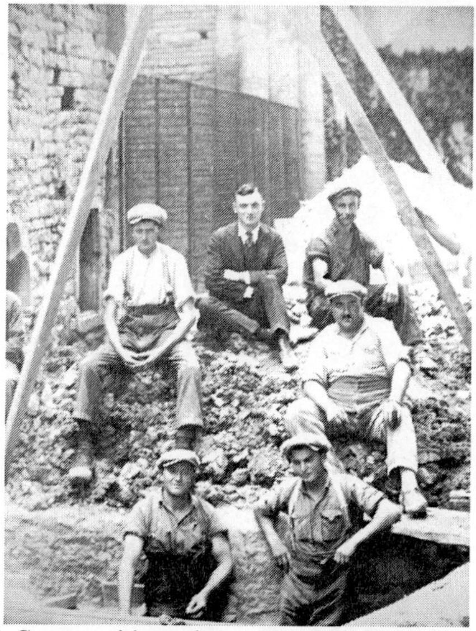

5.12 K.J. Conant with workers around pit IV in 1929 (detail)
(Musée d'art et d'archéologie, Cluny)

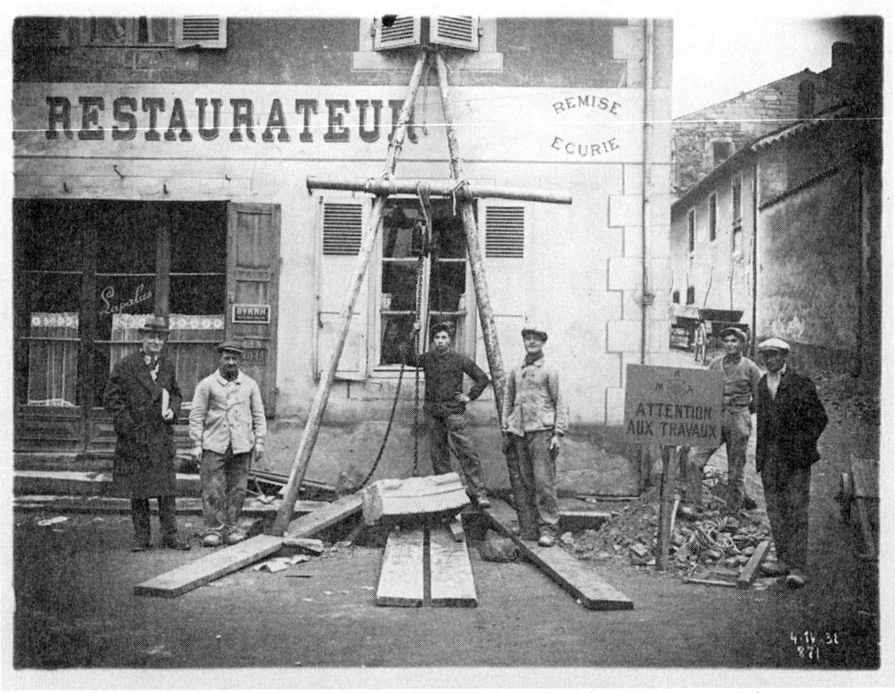

5.13 K.J. Canant posing with team of workers after unearthing architectural fragment, 1931 (Cluny Collection: Loeb Library, Harvard)

Conant arranged with the local photographer, Loury, to document the excavations, including all the sculptural finds, on uniform heavy photographic paper of 7 1/4 by 9 5/8 inches [fig. 5.14]. He designated one set to serve as an "archive", later placed in Paris with the Commission of Historic Monuments, and retained another for his own study purposes. (The former is now in the archives of the Musée d'art et d'archéologie at Cluny and the latter in the Cluny Collection of the Loeb Library at Harvard.)

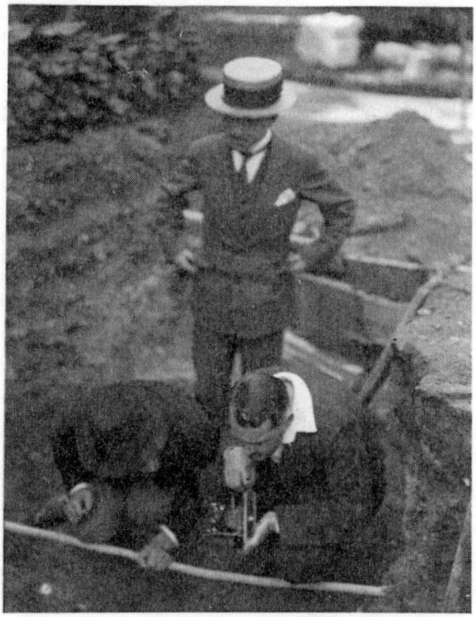

5.14 Loury photographing pit during Cluny excavations
(Cluny Collection: Loeb Library, Harvard University)

The two first pits yielded rewarding finds. In later articles on his method, Conant remarked that the locals thought he was a magician to know exactly where to dig.[65] But he was using diagrams made in the eighteenth century when the monks were planning to replace major portions of the conventual buildings. Their accuracy allowed him to chart dimensions in such a way that his excavations were at first really only confirmed measurements. The first pit exposed the foundation of the northern narthex portal including the column bases. This is the one he requested to make a permanent exhibit. The other, pit II, was less interesting to look at but turned up more exciting fragments such as, on July 9, a polychrome head which was the subject of an emotional letter to Verdier describing the circumstances of discovery, the remarkably fresh colored paint on the piece when first unearthed, and the heart-wrenching experience of watching that color fade—literally in the moments that Conant took to record what he saw [fig. 5.15].[66]

The best sculptural finds and most complete blocks of stone were numbered, photographed and then placed into a holding area for the municipal museum, still the former abbot's palace. This would soon prove to be too small for all that Conant was unearthing. The smaller bits and pieces were boxed into wooden cases labeled with the appropriate pit number. The archeological daybooks now on file at Cluny show how carefully Conant kept track of the exact section of earth excavated each day, coordinated with the numbered box. These cases were stored in the basement of the museum. Already after one month of work, 42 cases were thus lodged [figs. 5.15 and 5.16].

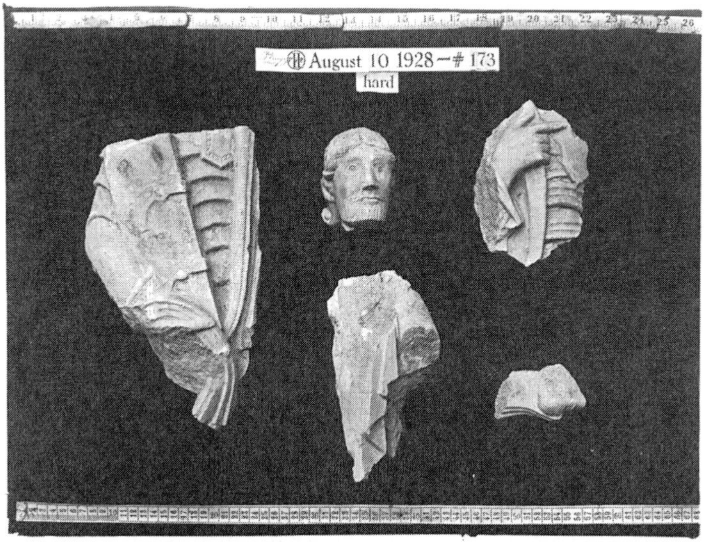

5.15 Typical documentation photograph of sculptural fragments including polychrome head, 1928 (Cluny Collection: Loeb Library, Harvard University)

Conant's approach to the actual digging of each pit was less careful. As David Walsh explained during the 1988 Colloquium at Cluny, few excavations of the day included understanding of vertical stratification.[67] Conant neither kept records on the relative depth of fragments he found nor described the surfaces his workers dug through. He also did not pursue levels below the eleventh- and twelfth-century construction. All the openings he made were designed to expose the foundations of the last abbey church. Their purpose was simply to "feel" down below later surface levels and thus were made narrow or wide as necessary to hit their target. Sometimes more than one "pit" connected or the workers tunneled to a nearby point that Conant wished to confirm.

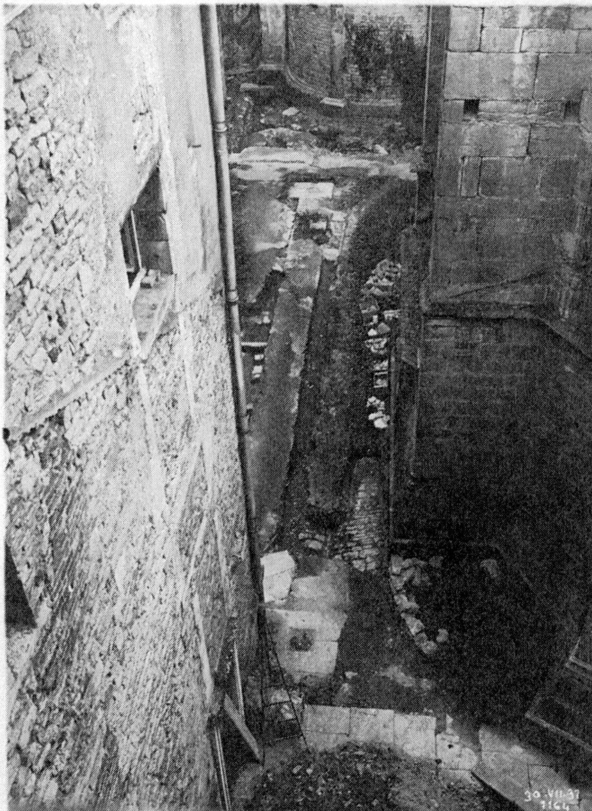

5.16 View from transept tower of excavation area around Bourbon chapel with boxes of fragments, 1937 (Cluny Collection: Loeb Library, Harvard University)

It has generally been assumed that his daybooks, now in the archives of the Musée d'art et d'archéologie at Cluny, are firsthand entries of his archeological process [fig. 5.17].[68] On closer examination, however, it becomes clear that these, like so many other records Conant left us, were carefully shaped for the historical record. He was convinced that his intervention in the site would be memorable and it appears that from the very beginning he determined to leave a careful account of his place among the names associated with Cluny's architectural record. In the nineteenth-century tradition, his records were meant to be professional daily records of work undertaken. Although he occasionally notes the arrival of visitors and keeps a careful expense record for his Mediaeval

Academy account, none of the emotional or logistical ups and downs which must have engulfed him during his studies are evident.

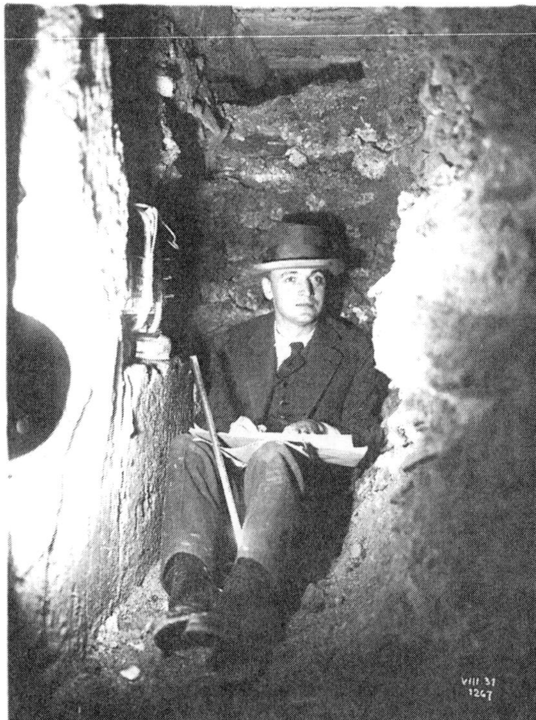

5.17 K. J. Conant in excavation pit at Cluny, August, 1931 (Mediaeval Academy of America)

Nonetheless, the daybooks are interesting material. Although all identically bound and numbered, one can yet tell that Conant worked from perforated lined paper pads, recopied his notes on the same type of paper, and then took the pages he wanted to keep and had them bound. The early journal entries began too high up on the page to allow binding directly as were later books, so they are glued onto plain paper headers. There is also a surviving example of a little sketch book filled with lists of measurements or workers' hours per day, as well as scribbles apparently made to pass the time such as loose versions of Byzantine church plans and elevations.

Proof of Conant's editing method exists in occasional loose pages inserted into the bound journals. Very loose sketches—made without a straight edge—and scribbled notes, entered at different times, cover these papers. In the finished daybooks, Conant copied the notes on a separate page for each day with more carefully drawn plans and clearly legible fragment numbers and measurements [fig. 5.18]. He also made a careful record of the weather, visitors, hours worked, expenses and photographs either taken or still necessary. These loose sheets, mostly kept in envelopes labeled "NOTES ON FRAGMENTS", show that daily notes were recopied right away, most likely each night in Conant's room at the Hotel de Bourgogne when he could still remember all the details and clean up the sketches. The original papers are often crossed out, written around the edges, erased, smudged, even partly in other hands. In contrast, the final versions in the copied daybooks have been carefully organized and bound. They are in pristine condition, even though the paper is very cheap newsprint quality. None of the expected wear and tear of pages carried into the field during wind or rain or dirty conditions is apparent.

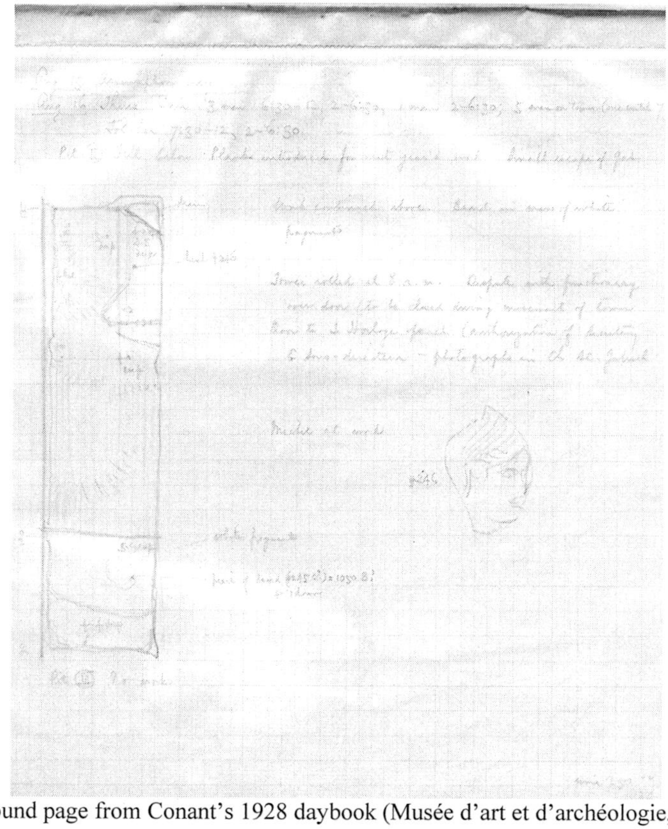

5.18 Bound page from Conant's 1928 daybook (Musée d'art et d'archéologie, Cluny)

At the Musée Ochier there are also manila envelopes of single unlined pages of Japan paper with drawings, organized by year and titled by pit and day. Here are larger, more exact records of the excavations, including multiple section views that Conant rarely included in his daybooks. Sometimes Conant has a marginal notation that he has copied *from* the daybook, yet in most cases it seems clear these were the original sketches from which he extrapolated small plans for the daybook entries. Conant was more specific about the location in which the pit occurs and indicated more information about such things as the soil, mortar, or condition of fragments than in the journal. His assistant, Frederic Palmer made some of the drawings, or gave Conant information. In turn, Conant made notes on his sketches to Palmer to recheck certain points or compare measurements. He also postulated about what he has found or could have found with deeper digging (latter notes may have been entered years afterward.) The dates of these drawings do not necessarily correspond to daybook entries, often they were made on a Sunday or another day when there was no progress made in the excavation. Sometimes there are pit entries in the daybooks for which the only visual records appear in these Japan paper pages.

The men stopped work at 7:30 in the evening and it is light until after 10:00 p.m. in Burgundy in the summer. (Daylight-saving time was initiated in France in 1916). There was little pressing on Conant after he had dined. Between the oft-repeated claims of those who knew him that he spent most evenings in his room drawing and walking around the site and the fact that there was little to do in the town after hours, we can easily imagine that Conant made nearly all his detailed drawings as well as his final daybook entries in the manner of professional records after the bustle of the day when he could carefully number the finds, check his measurements, list his expenses and visitors, and leave room to add photo numbers or even later corrections.

Conant was very aware of the importance of the historical record and edited his own for posterity. He later prefaced lectures on his work by saying that he had left his archeological materials to the Ochier so that others could check his process.[69] Many of the daybook pages are neat lists of numbered finds and expenses that imply the historic importance of this undertaking as he assiduously assembled them in the quiet of his hotel room from his notes. Dated notations about revisions of thinking or better access to fragments or later removal of slabs show that he went back to the books as well as the loose drawings over the years to make sure the record stayed accurate. (This is typical of Conant's lifelong precision; letters he sent to his parents during the war in which place names were erased by the army censors show Kenneth's neat replacement of the words in parentheses after he returned home.) Questions, assumptions, predictions, hopes, worries, or frustrations that he must have felt never crept into his dry daybook reporting and only rarely onto the larger drawings. He was careful that the formal record maintained a professional face on it.

The "archeological" method of excavation was not so careful, however proud Conant was of the project [fig. 5.19]. Rough, local workmen were hired to use picks and shovels to move earth and stones. Since Conant knew that Cluny III was not built over Cluny II, he did not worry about multiple layers when excavating the churches. We read over and over of water lines punctured, gas pipes pierced, drains broken, fragments damaged in place. Conant lists many instances of paying from his Academy funds to have such municipal and private services restored. It is a credit to his personality that he was still able to endear himself to so many of the townspeople when he effected such interruptions in their daily lives.

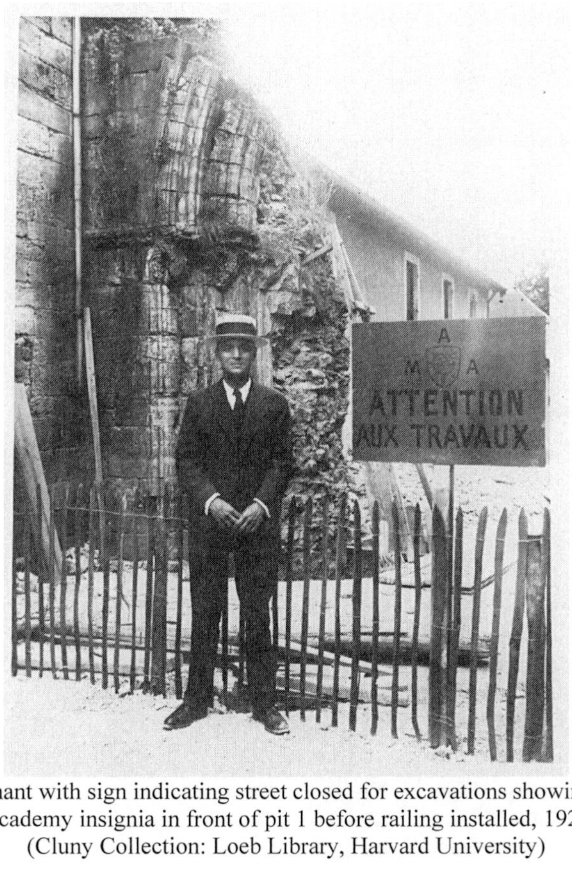

5.19 K.J. Conant with sign indicating street closed for excavations showing Mediaeval Academy insignia in front of pit 1 before railing installed, 1928 (Cluny Collection: Loeb Library, Harvard University)

Many of the pits tended to follow foundation wall lines without concern for adjacent areas. Unlike later archeological methods, which would open an entire area and keep careful track of the vertical layers, in this process any fragments that did not fall right next to the walls during the demolition, or which were not built back into later walls, would have been missed. Yet, although the excavation approach was far from those of modern archeologists, Conant did occasionally stop, clean up the areas, take measurements (usually by a hired local assistant) and have them photographed. The fragments found were photographed off site with their cataloging numbers and a process of checking them in and out of storage with receipts. He also received receipts for every piece that went into the museum or other storage. It is nevertheless surprising that his method changed very little over the years from 1928 to 1950. The same style of entries appears in the daybooks; the same method of digging was apparently followed by the workers. By 1950, certainly more scientific and less invasive methods of excavation had been developed. Yet we must keep in mind that Conant was primarily looking straight down for foundation evidence to support his reconstructive plans of the third church. Fragments of architectural material or decorative sculpture were simply applied to theories about their elevation. He never became interested in studying the horizontal layers of evidence below ca. 1100 remains or in learning how to excavate larger, generalized areas for more widely varying finds.[70]

Malo visited during the first month and seemed satisfied. The press picked up on the event and local coverage occurred. Conant himself claimed to have sent information only to the European edition of the New York Herald Tribune, which ran a story on July 26 headlined: "Americans Excavate Site of Mediaeval Abbey at Cluny -- Townspeople Believe Golden Treasure Is Being Shipped to U.S. — PORTALS LAID BARE — Harvard Professor Directs Work on Largest Romanesque Ruin in France". The first two paragraphs of the story apparently represent the material Conant would have supplied, explaining the method and purpose of the excavations, beginning with the visits of Malo and Jean Virey, "observers for the Ministry of Public Instruction and Fine Arts". But then the story seems to take off with the journalist's flair for the dramatic, and accounts for the mixed headline. "The excavators have been much entertained by the local excitement over their work: the popular imagination has credited them with finds in solid gold and wrought iron, and the objects found (actually deposited in the local museum) are said to have been shipped to America. The children of the town believe that the enterprise has been undertaken in order to unearth a mummy like the one in the museum." We would know from Conant's accounts if a journalist had actually visited Cluny, otherwise it is tempting to imagine the latter comments also coming from Conant during a interview where he chuckled over his effect on the provincial townspeople.

In the report for August, Conant continued his account of the activity according to the numbered pits. Pit 1, at the western entrance of the narthex, continued on into the garage of the Hotel de Bourgogne, whose owner authorized an open pit so that the workers would not have to tunnel. Based upon Brown's authorization of up to 800 dollars for this project, Conant offered 5000 francs toward the retaining wall for preserving the excavation. Marcel Aubert was grateful and found Commission of Historic Monuments funds for the remainder.[71]

Pit II yielded the most interesting fragments after refilling the area around the portal jambs and digging to either side. Although his official report is rather dry, mentioning eight heads with three in good condition plus many small figures in fragments and architectural pieces, Conant's cables home suggest he was reading more into the material:

> 4 August 1928 "GREAT PORTAL NON [sic = now] SOLVED BY FRAGMENTS AND TRACES NARTHEX PORTAL PRESERVATION NEGOTIATED"
>
> 15 August 1928: "BEAUTIFUL FRAGMENTS OF PAINTED HEAD OF CHRIST FROM GREAT TYMPANUM"

In his final, detailed report for the 1928 season, Conant identified each object and discussed size, material, and possible subject matter.[72] He also did not mention in the monthly reports any finds related to dating the east end of the church, the issue which would become hotly debated between Parisian scholars and those who followed Porter's suggestion. Yet a cable sent to the Mediaeval Academy August 22 must have made the folks back home smile: "PROVE AMBULATORY CAPITALS ELEVENTH CENTURY." In the final report, this claim, which was developed in his article on the St. Gabriel chapel also appearing in 1928, is explained.

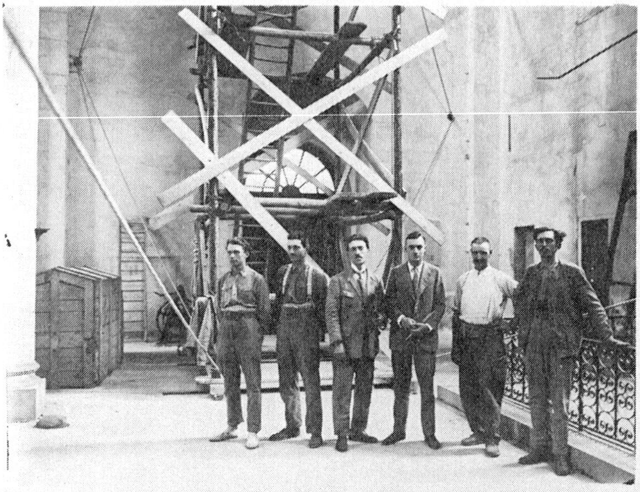

5.20 K.J. Conant with workmen in front of scaffolding used to photograph upper transept and towers, probably 1928 (Cluny Collection: Loeb Library, Harvard University)

He derived the conclusion from photographs taken by Monsieur Loury who was busy on scaffolds in the remaining transept, documenting both general views and architectural details [fig. 5.20]. It is worth quoting in full. Conant describes the capitals and mentions that similar ones exist in the smaller tower then goes on to say:

> …It suffices here to say that an inscription, painted in red upon a coat of stucco overlying the original stucco finish of the interior, certifies in characters of the first quarter of the twelfth century that the chapel was dedicated and relics were deposited in the altar by Peter, Bishop of Pamplona (†1115). The date is given as the II Ides of March; the year has been lost, but 1100 plausibly fills the lacuna, and it seems certain that the construction is to be dated within a few months or years of that time. This necessarily means that the transept was built at that time also. There is indubitable evidence that the capitals in the chapel and transept were carved when they were set.
>
> Thus we may say that seventy-one fine pieces of sculpture surely dated close to the year 1100 have been introduced on the field of a hotly contested archeological battle. It is the coup de grâce to the system of certain French and German scholars who would have us believe that Cluny was largely the work of the twelfth century well advanced….
>
> More interesting still, the ivy on the east wall of the great transept yielded a capital which, so far as I am aware, was unnoticed and unpublished [fig. 5.21]. It formerly supported the west end of the arch between the westernmost bays of the south choir aisles; it is in situ in a portion of the building surely ascribed to the

end of the eleventh century. The undercutting of the capital is so disposed as to constitute preremptory [sic] proof that it was sculptured at the time of setting. In style it is as advanced as any of the rest, and in design and execution it is patently related to the ambulatory capital devoted to the fifth, sixth, seventh, and eighth tones—so patently related that it is probably a work of the same artist. A similar capital, executed at some time after 1104, exists at Vézelay. But the important thing is that this eleventh-century Cluny capital, taken in conjunction with the other evidence presented above, makes it infinitely probable that the ambulatory capitals were carved at the same period—that they were quite possibly completed at the time of the dedication of 1095, and are to be counted as masterpieces of the eleventh, not of the twelfth, century.

This conclusion has implications which run counter to the conceptions of many as to early history of Romanesque sculpture. It corroborates the doctrine of those—notably M. l'Abbé Terret, M. Oursel, and Mr. Porter, who have done battle to prove the priority of the great Burgundian abbey and the significance of the work which was done there…

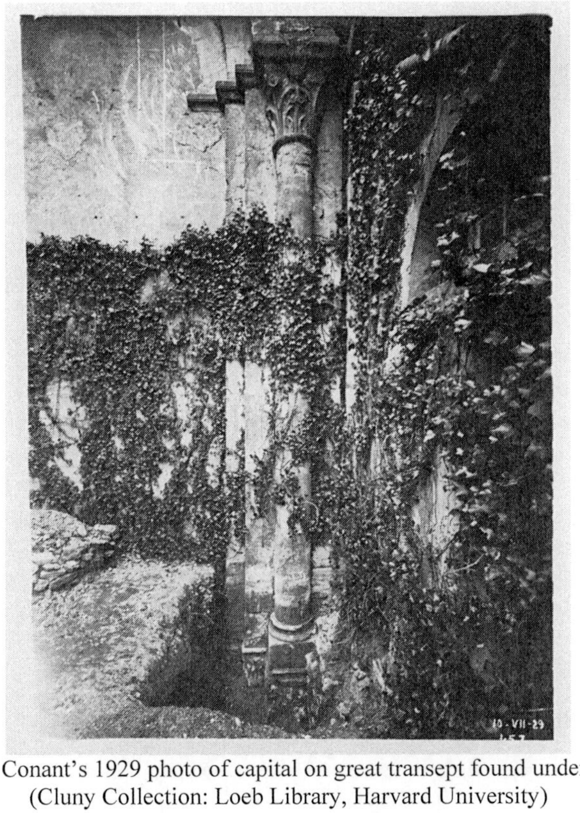

5.21 Conant's 1929 photo of capital on great transept found under ivy (Cluny Collection: Loeb Library, Harvard University)

The "battles" to which Conant refers in this passage have been reviewed by David Walsh in his paper given at the 2004 International Mediaeval Congress in Leeds, "Medieval Art Wars: French-American Academic Conflict in the 20th Century". The positions of the Parisian scholars, supporting the dating of the choir capitals given by Paul Deschamps around 1125, later became entrenched against those who supported the early Porter/Conant dating of the east end of the church, based on the belief that it was finished when the pope came to consecrate the altar in 1095.[73] Eventually these supporters included the Burgundians, Americans, and, through such friends as Joan Evans and later followers as Neil Stratford, the English. The first to support Porter's suggestion was Charles Oursel in 1928, and his friendship with Conant clearly influenced much of the latter's presentation of Cluny as the center of Romanesque art, an idea originally found in Viollet-le-Duc.[74] There are numerous references to the dating argument among the proceedings for conferences at Cluny, in articles written by Conant and Francis Salet (from Paris), and in letters between Conant and colleagues.[75] It extended to other parts of the building as well. For instance, Conant felt it necessary to emphasize, in his progress report to the Mediaeval Academy in November 1936, the following statement:

> Incidentally, those Frenchmen who still deny Mr. Porter's date for the great capitals have agreed with our dating of the portal (ca. 1109-115) which is early enough to place it before the other great monuments of French Romanesque sculpture. They therefore admit Mr Porter's theory and teach, as Mr. Porter did, that the French style of the great age of Romanesque sculpture was inaugurated by Cluny and at Cluny. [his underlines]

The reports for July and August, as well as the overall season, were translated into French and sent to the head of the Commission of Historic Monuments, along with an offprint of his Gabriel Chapel article.[76] The same material appeared in volume LXXXVIII (1929) of the *Bulletin Monumental*. Conant's final paragraph for his season report was picked up by those who wished the French government to support the project with funding from the *Monuments historiques*. It is wildly acclamatory and dismissive, in the best Prosper Lorain style, but it was apparently effective at the time:

> ...The renaissant art of monumental sculpture is seen to have received a wonderful impulse at the very start from the great genius who carved Cluny ambulatory capitals, just as the art of architecture did from the designer of the giant church. Both rose fully to a stupendous opportunity in producing this splendid witness to the grandeur of the order and the greatness of the builder abbot. Cluny was then a focus like the Constantinople of Justinian or the Florence and Rome of the Renaissance. We should no more be asked to explain

> the achievements of the artisans of Cluny by mechanically regular steps in development (as some writers propose) than we are in the case of Isidoros and Anthemios, Donatello, or Michelangelo. Once the inspiration of Cluny is recognized, and its activity between 1088 and 1109 admitted, the flowering of Burgundian art and architecture which followed the closing of its chantier early in the twelfth century needs no further explanation.

In Conant's report letter to the Guggenheim for the 1928 season, he included his articles and excavation reports sent to the Mediaeval Academy and then asked for continued funding by appealing to the Secretary of the foundation, Mr. Moe, for advice: "I realize that the Foundation has been generous to me, but if indeed it wishes to continue its support to the Cluny research, it will greatly relieve me by giving me, for study, the time which I should have to spend in pot-boiling in order to earn the expenses. If you advise it, I shall apply for a renewal; advise me frankly." Further application was evidently encouraged and he writes eloquently in December of 1928 asking for 300 dollars expense money and 400 dollars toward "the work of restoring the sculptures" of the Great Portal, a part of the structure "obscured by additions in the thirteenth century…and…not…seen as represented in my drawing since the year 1128 or thereabouts—eight hundred years ago." [fig. 5.22]

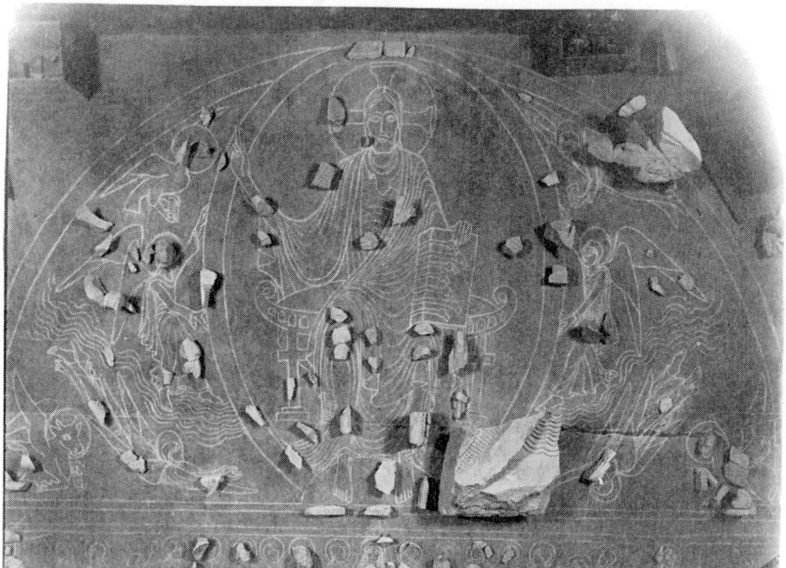

5.22 Photograph of an early phase of Conant's chalk layout drawn on floor for reconstructing fragments from the tympanum of west portal

Conant continually underlines the value of the abbey church building in these proposals, echoing the kind of affirmations found in earlier letters to the French ministry requesting repair funding. He places himself into a position of history-making and repeats the genius associations seen in the 1929 report: "I have, as a result of my studies, a profound conviction that the great structure which I am making available to the workers in architectural history was as important in Romanesque architecture as St. Sophia in Byzantine, or Chartres in Gothic architecture. And I have besides, as a result of my work, a profound appreciation for the majestic beauty of the building, which will be in a way re-created by my restoration drawings." His Guggenheim funding was continued in the amount of 750 dollars for each of two years, the second being a time when the Mediaeval Academy did not fund excavations and Conant traveled to study other churches in Europe related to Cluny.

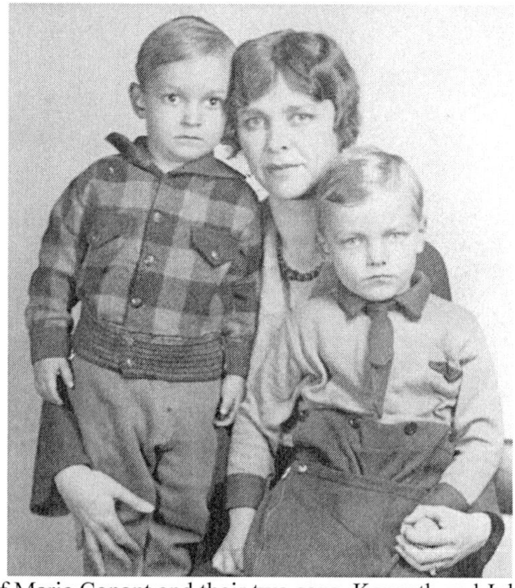

5.23 Photograph of Marie Conant and their two sons, Kenneth and John in January, 1931 (Cluny Collection: Loeb Library, Harvard University)

In January of 1929, the Mediaeval Academy published an article with Conant's first technical report of the excavations in *Speculum* (IV, 1, 2-26). Like his daybooks, these reports are professional, dry, and informative. They evidence none of the personal turmoil or enthusiasm that clearly accompanied his efforts. Although visitors' arrivals are recorded, their impact on his sense of self-esteem or accomplishment is not. His first son, Kenneth, Jr., was joined by another, John, born in 1927 [fig. 5.23]. The family stayed at home the first year.

Finances must have been tight. Conant was young, not yet well established at Harvard, with doting parents who expected great things. It is from extant letters home that one can begin to get a glimpse of the more personal side of this effort. Letters to his parents were often done on a series of postcards (often as many as 45-50 at a time) recording excursions he took to other monuments. Every year he complains about being eaten alive by mosquitoes, regales them with stories of wild tours around the area in cars with local luminaries, and reviews every fragment of architecture he visits. He also brags a bit and expresses hopes and fears and financial plans, as one would expect. Excerpts make him real for us and bring the entire project alive:

> …on the return, M. Oursel, my special friend in Dijon at the Library, gave a talk on the Cistercian manuscripts there, and after dinner a talk on the school of Cluny in monastic and cathedral architecture. It revolved around the chapel I discovered a year ago. It is fun to hear oneself referred to on the lecture platform. It must happen often! I must be a good archeologist!
>
> … (you amuse me, by the way, by adding 'archaeologist—Cluny abbey" to my address.-I am as well known here now as the mayor or the town drunkard)
>
> … The 19th century lithograph on this card is the one which has been used to give me an idea of this portal. It is all wrong, and I can prove it
>
> …. My work on this portal will really add to my reputation—I have had requests for information from England, France, Germany, Switzerland, Spain, and the United States. So I got started first on the portals—awaiting the departure of the students and the arrival of the official paper for the other areas. I had enough to do—I get up at 6—work begins at 6:30 and keeps on until 6:30 p.m. with two hours for lunch. That really means a 12 or 13 hour day for me, for I have to watch the excavations, make no end of arrangements and explanations, and do my paper work besides. Among my visitors was the chief of the Archives Service of the League of Nations.
>
> Back to work the next day of course—I work six days a week, I tell you, and I shall really have to come home to get a rest but I am thriving on it. Ten hours a day in the sun does me no harm, and the work is of course endlessly interesting. Think of my *beginning* my career as an excavator with one of the greatest mediaeval sites in France—but their 'prentice hand will make a good job I think, don't you?

In 1929 Conant was accepted as a member of the French National Archeological Society in Dijon and in 1930 made the level of Associate Professor at Harvard. He was also officially named Research Fellow of the Mediaeval Academy as this organization continued funding the Cluny project through the anonymous donations of John Nicholas Brown. Invitations began to come fast and furious now. He lectured at Boston, Yale, Princeton, the Metropolitan Museum in New York City under the auspices of the Archeological Society of America and the Courtauld Institute in London. In the summer of 1930 he was invited to lecture, in French, at Orléans and Dijon. From 1930-1933 he was given a leave of absence for every second semester in order to begin the excavation season at Cluny in spring weather.

Local papers chronicled the work at Cluny. A *L'Union Républicaine* article on July 16, 1928 announcing the inauguration of the excavations is typical of the tone taken:

> Archeological Digs: They were inaugurated this past June 29th in the presence of Mr. Kennelh, John Conact [sic], professor at the University of Harward [sic], in Cambridge (Massachussetts), and Mr. E. Malo, government architect. Monsieur Conant, director of the excavations, noted author of a scholarly work on the medieval Spanish city of Saint Jacques de Compostela, has already consecrated three months of the summer of 1927 to record, in the most minute details, the plan of our old abbey and her vast dependencies.
> This year, he returns to us to realize a mandate from the Mediaeval Academy of America [in order to] practice excavation methods on the same ground where he hopes to recover the vestiges interred there of the monastery.
> Authorized by our Beaux-Arts administration and empowered by the municipality of our city, Mr. Conant has had the good fortune to uncover, at more than two meters of depth, the bases of the marble jambs at the level of the church floor tiles. He now undertakes the study of the foundations of the basilica portal while following the directions indicated by each discovery[77].

As the work continued over the years, big finds, such as when abbots' tombs were discovered, continued to appear on inside pages of regional newspapers. In 1931 *Le Figaro*, out of Paris, carried a long feature on the project that included a short history of the abbey, apparently garnered from the guidebooks now easily available. This was reprinted, in shortened form, in local papers. American newspapers in Boston and New York continued coverage as well, apparently generated from press releases written at the Mediaeval Academy. As the years progressed, Conant's reputation heightened and the names of his student assistants such as Frederic Palmer and Helen Kleinschmidt, were included in the stories [figs. 5.24, 5.25]. Among those assistants, these two became essential to his work. Palmer had an architecture degree from Harvard and he worked on detailed plans of the excavations for Conant beginning in 1929 (for a salary of 30 dollars a week). Kleinschmidt was the art historian who did the lion's share of study to reconstruct the original west portal of the abbey church.

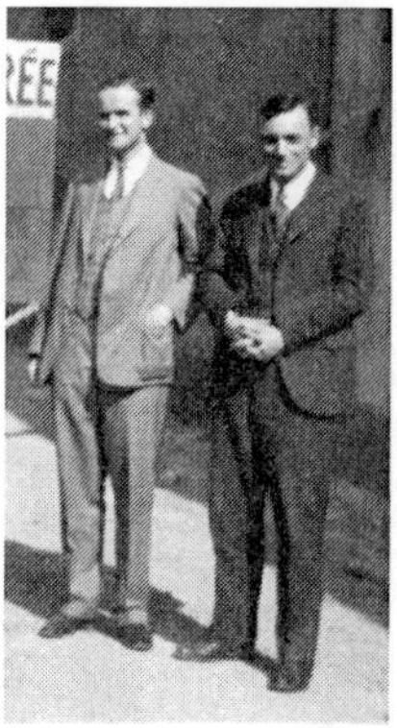

5.24 Frederic Palmer and K.J. Conant in 1929

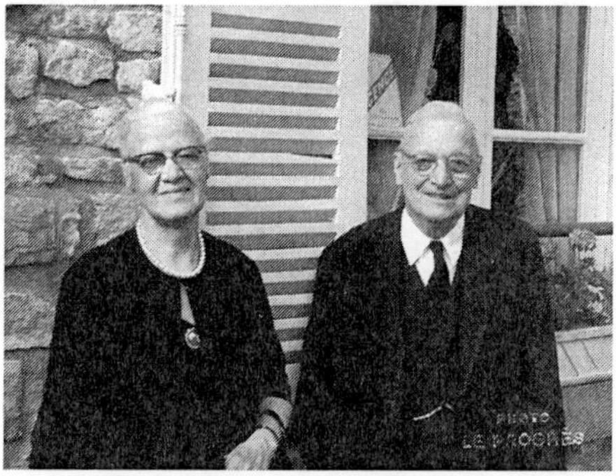

5.25 K. J. Conant and Helen Kleinschmidt visiting Cluny in their later years

(Cluny Collection: Loeb Library, Harvard University)

During the 1929 season, Conant was kept busy at Cluny. In a letter of 25 August to John Marshall, he listed twelve open pits and countless visitors, including John Nicholas Brown, as an excuse for his poor correspondence. He also managed to negotiate the donation of some narthex portal column shafts unearthed by a resident to the town of Cluny and effect their restoration on the uncovered northern base. His wife, Marie, was listed in the first monthly report as working for several weeks measuring and numbering fragments; she would do the same in 1931. Conant clearly stated that she received no salary. Specifications for Palmer's drawings were also given and Conant mentioned that Palmer would replace him in his absence. He underlined the friendly reception he received and the willingness of the local administrators to cooperate fully in the ongoing enterprise, although the *Haras* kept him on a tight schedule and he admitted in his report for July that "The officers do not conceal their dismay at seeing the pick and shovel attack the beautifully leveled drive, the flower bed, and the lawn of their handsome court of honor…" [fig. 5.26]. He ended rather soberly compared to the previous year. "No great difficulties are anticipated, nor any sensational finds; the expedition has entered a work-a-day phase which will produce essential data for the restoration drawings of the church."[78]

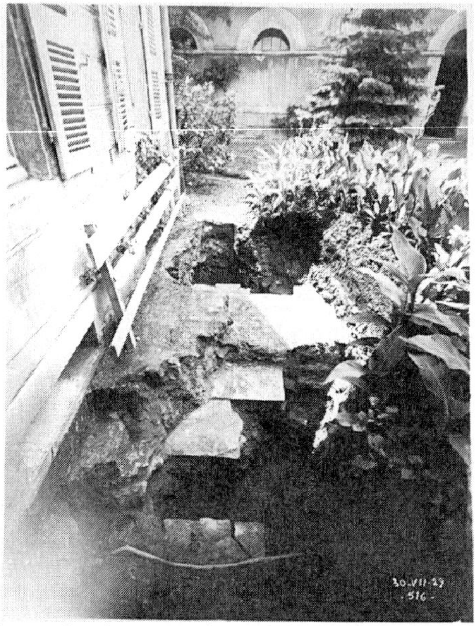

5.26 Photo of early excavation work in the *Haras* yard, 1929
(Cluny Collection: Loeb Library, Harvard University)

Conclusion

Kenneth Conant's authoritative style is evident from his first proposals regarding the need for measurements at Cluny to his assured conclusions about the importance of abbey church in architectural history. Reading his excavation reports published in *Speculum,* his Pelican volume on Carolingian and Romanesque architecture, or his letters to family and colleagues, one is struck today by the lack of documentary proof cited in support of his theories. He was quick to engage in ideas about the function of medieval buildings and specialized in making comparative reconstructions between extant structures and those replaced or damaged. But most of his favorite work was hypothetical in nature and the only time he really used source material was when he was searching for drawings of Cluny made before its destruction. As such, Conant was first and foremost an architect. The criticisms of his "dry" drawing style actually highlight a carefully nurtured skill to present commanding architectural views. He was known to be generous to colleagues and there is plentiful evidence of this in extant letters. However, the generosity was bound up in opportunities to propagate his theories and to distribute copies of his drawings. It rarely extended to serious analysis and adoption of others' academic ideas.

From all accounts, his teaching consisted of an entertaining lecture style that was also fired by his excitement over sharing his personal travel experiences of historical buildings and his trained eye's analysis of their architectural properties.[79] His energy in the classroom was fueled by the kinds of comparisons and reconstructions of buildings across the world that characterized his work on Cluny.[80]

What supported such assurance? One can only admire the single-minded conviction, the nearly religious belief, of Conant's vision for Cluny. It could have come straight off Henry Adam's page—the imaginative journey back in time, peopled with reassuringly pious and ingenious medieval figures whose buildings Conant could draw in minute detail as if he had seen them firsthand. He loved being in France, but he seemed to have an idea of France that was closer to that of the nineteenth century than the France after World War I. This would not have been hard, staying most of his time away from Paris in a small Burgundian city like Cluny, surrounded by vineyards, farms, and the petty heirs of Lamartine's provincial aristocracy. As such, Conant promulgated notions of the abbey that he would have found in those written histories and guidebooks discussed in chapters two and three of this study. He made the respect and the awe and the regret of these authors his own, then turned around and codified that into masterful presentations of hypothetical reconstructions as scientific data. With the weight of Harvard behind him, both in his degrees and teaching position, authority came easy to Conant. If he had not had it before, he certainly would have acquired it along with his elite peers while in attendance. We will see in the next chapter how this style continued to play out for the duration of the Cluny project.

Notes

[1] Portions of this chapter previously appeared in an article entitled "Un Romantique à la recherche du passé: K. J. Conant à Cluny" in *Cahiers de Civilisation médiévale* 48:3 (2005), 327-340 and as an on-line feature article for the Mediaeval Academy of America.

[2] [Everyone knows that this magnificent monument is nearly entirely destroyed: all that remains are precious fragments which give us the scale of the edifice and allow the imagination to reconstruct the whole.] Jean Virey, *Les églises romanes de l'ancien diocèse de Mâcon* (Paris: Picard, 1892). 31

[3] [The entire history of Romanesque architecture in Burgundy is dominated by the name of Cluny.] Charles Oursel, *L'Art roman de Bourgogne* (Dijon: Librairie L. Venot, 1928). 57

[4] Henry Adams, *Mont Saint Michel and Chartres* (New York: Penguin Books, 1986). 13

[5] Ibid. 13

[6] Ibid. 44

[7] Ibid. 69

[8] Ibid. 152

[9] Émile Mâle, *Religious Art in France: The Twelfth Century. A Study of the Origins of Medieval Iconography*, trans. Marthiel Mathews from 1953 corrected edition (by Mâle himself), vol. XC 1, *Bollingen Series* (Princeton, New Jersey: Princeton University Press, 1978). xxx
[10] Ibid. 343
[11] Joseph F. Byrnes, *Catholic and French forever: religious and national identity in modern France* (University Park, PA: Pennsylvania State University Press, 2005). 128
[12] Mâle, *Religious Art in France: The Twelfth Century. A Study of the Origins of Medieval Iconography*. 388, 386
[13] Quoted in Wolfgang Braunfels, *Monasteries of Western Europe: The Architecture of the Orders* (London/Princeton, New Jersey: Thames and Hudson Ltd./Princeton University Press, 1972). 51
[14] A. Kingsley Porter, *Romanesque Sculpture of the Pilgrimage Roads*, 10 vols. (New York: Hacker Art Books, 1966). vol.1, 197
[15] "The history of art has been viewed as a gradual and continuous unfolding from crude beginnings towards ultimate perfection. Periods of decline have of course been recognized, but have not been allowed to disturb belief in evolutionary principles." Ibid. vol. 1, page 14.
[16] Ibid., vol. 1, page 159
[17] Conant made it clear, during his years of work on Cluny, that he was not interested in making a study of the sculptural fragments and would leave that to others. In fact, he tried to leave the problem of reconstructing the sculptural program of the monumental west portal to Helen Kleinschmidt but ended up becoming heavily involved himself.
[18] Letter from Conant to Porter, April 18, 1924 in the Harvard University archives, Arthur Kingsley Porter correspondence HUG 1706.102. (My thanks to Janice Mann for sharing this reference.)
[19] April 13, 1918 letter home, Cluny Collection, Loeb Library, Harvard University
[20] July 25, 1918 letter home, Cluny Collection, Loeb Library, Harvard University
[21] Undated letter home, Cluny Collection, Loeb Library, Harvard University
[22] Kathleen Curran, *The Romanesque Revival: Religion, Politics, and Transnational Exchange, Buildings, landscapes, and societies series 2* (University Park, Pa.: Pennsylvania State University Press, 2003).280
[23] W. H. Downer, "Drawings by Mr. Conant," *Boston Evening Transcript*, October 30, 1920.
[24] See letter to Conant's father from LaRose, dated June 9, 1918:
"The other night I had Mr. R. A. Cram, the distinguished architect, to dinner. After dinner I was showing him Kenneth's drawings. "If, after the war, there's any work for architects to do—there is none now—I want that fellow in my office." "But, Cram," I answered, "in a great office like yours, draughtsman are so keen to get in that they come for nothing a week, or at best a paltry $5. Conant, unfortunately, can't afford to do that." "Great Scott, man," answered Cram, "they're not fellows like this—I'd start Conant at $25 a week."
[25] Paul Sachs, Director of the Fogg Museum at Harvard, wrote the catalog copy for this exhibition but asked that his name not be attached to it since he did not consider it a "serious contribution." The text reveals the mentoring concern Sachs had for Kenneth

and explains some of the fireworks that occurred later in their relationship when Conant did not continue to consult him:

"Kenneth John Conant was born in Wisconsin in 1894, and received his early training in drawing from his father and in Milwaukee schools. Entering Harvard in 1911, he took the degree of Bachelor of Arts with high distinction in the fine arts in 1915, and that of Master in Architecture in 1919, receiving the American Institute of Architects' medal for general excellence in his work. His teachers were Robert Edmund Jones, Martin Mower, and Herman Dudley Murphy.

It was while in Italy in 1916-1917 as the holder of a Traveling Fellowship from Harvard, and Associate Fellow at the American Academy in Rome, that Mr. Conant "found himself" as an artist. He brought back a series of architectural drawings which the Fogg Art Museum, not ordinarily open to student work, offered to the public in a short special exhibition.

After an interruption, caused by a year in military service and the completion of his technical studies, Mr. Conant returned to Europe for an extended tour as holder of "The Sachs Research Fellowship in Fine Arts of Harvard University." The ninety-six drawings of France and Spain which form the bulk of this exhibition are a portion of the work done on this trip.

The drawings show the author's great love for the fine and the picturesque in old architecture, particularly old ecclesiastical architecture. They are done with a sensitiveness which tells of an authentic understanding not only from a pictorial but from historical, aarchaeological [sic], and constructive points of view. Those who have seen the venerable stones which are portrayed will, it is hoped, feel the sympathy and reverence of the artist in his interpretation, the care with which the work was done, and the constant effort to present a spirited or poetic composition without the sacrifice of literalness and truthfulness even in detail; and it is hoped that lovers of good drawing will find in these examples the artist's deep appreciation of beautiful form.

The drawings were all done out of doors, and the small ones completed, in general, in two or three sittings, and with the use of one or occasionally two grades of pencil. To this, and to the sureness due to a thorough knowledge of the architectural subject itself, comes the cleanness and certainty of the draughtsmanship; but something of their freshness is due to the fact that they were drawn without preliminary studies, or layout by means of guide lines. They owe their atmosphere of light and sun to the artist's manner of presenting his building in the terms of its own shadows, using local tones and color value where it is to the advantage of the composition or texture of the picture. The simplicity thus attained leaves room, without overloading the drawing, for much intricate and exquisite detail, which is, after all, the characteristic feature of Mr. Conant's work."

[26] Unattributed clipping in the Cluny Collection, Loeb Library, Harvard University.

[27] F. de Dartein, *Étude sur l'Architecture Lombarde et sur les origins de l'Architecture Romano-Byzantine.* (Paris: Dunod, 1865-82), My thanks to Marie-Thérèse Camus for bringing this work to my notice.

[28] Letters between Mr. Conant, Sr. and LaRose in the Cluny Collection, Loeb Library, Harvard University

[29] Mary Ann Calo, *Bernard Berenson and the twentieth century* (Philadelphia: Temple University Press, 1994).

[30] Kathryn Brush, *The Shaping of Art History: Wilhelm Vöge, Adolph Goldschmidt, and the Study of Medieval Art* (Cambridge: Cambridge University Press, 1996). 144-145.
[31] Ibid.68
[32] Ibid.72
[33] Peter Fergusson, "Necrology—Kenneth John Conant (1895[sic]-1984)," GESTA XXIV (1985), 87-88
[34] Xavier Barral i Altet, "Josep Puig i Cadafalch, historiador del arte medieval" In: *Josep Puig i Cadafalch: L'arquitectura entre la casa i la ciutat = Architecture between the House and the City : 4 de Desembre de 1989-11 de Febrer 1990*, ed. Centre Cultural de la Fundació Caixa de Pensions (Barcelona: La Fundacío, 1989). 76-79. I am grateful to Eric Palazzo for suggesting that I consider Puig i Cadafalch in relation to Conant.
[35] "…no pretendemos resucitar artes muertas; pero con el estudio de nuestra arquitectura y de nuestra tierra esperamos construir un arte nuevo y una nueva Cataluña". Quoted in Judith Rohrer, "Puig i Cadafalch: The Early Work" Josep Puig i Cadafalch and Fundació Caixa de Pensions (Barcelona Spain). Centre Cultural, *Josep Puig i Cadafalch: l'arquitectura entre la casa i la ciutat = architecture between the house and the city : 4 de desembre de 1989-11 de febrer 1990, Centre Cultural de la Fundació Caixa de Pensions*, 1. ed. (Barcelona: La Fundació, 1989). 22-23 (her translation)
[36] Xavier Barral i Altet, "Josep Puig i Cadafalch, historiador del arte medieval" In: Ibid. 64-65
[37] Cluny Collection, Loeb Library, Harvard University
[38] Brush, *The Shaping of Art History: Wilhelm Vöge, Adolph Goldschmidt, and the Study of Medieval Art*. 148-149
[39] Kenneth John Conant, *Carolingian and Romanesque Architecture 800-1200*, ed. Nikolaus Pevsner and Judy Nairn, Second ed., *The Pelican History of Art* (Harmondsworth: Penguin, 1959; reprint, 1974). 11
[40] Information gleaned from Conant's proposals and reports to the Guggenheim Foundation, kindly photocopied from their files by G. Thomas Tanselle, Senior Vice President.
[41] Guggenheim proposal essay from 1926 entitled: "Advanced work and research."
[42] Quotes are from letter to Henry Allen Moe, Secretary of the Guggenheim Foundation, as a report on the summer of 1927, written February 29, 1928.
[43] *Bulletin monumental* 87, 1/2, pp. 55-64
[44] *Speculum* vol. 3, 3, pp. 401-404
[45] Copy on file with the Mediaeval Academy of America in their Cambridge MA offices. All of the following quotes are taken from this document.
[46] These letters are on file at the Mediaeval Academy offices in Cambridge MA.
[47] Interview with John Conant (Brother Gregory) at Stillwater Monastery, Harvard, Massachusetts, January 2002.
[48] See Peter Fergusson, "Medieval Architectural Scholarship in America 1900-1940: Ralph Adams Cram and Kenneth John Conant", in *The Architectural historian in America : a symposium in celebration of the fiftieth anniversary of the founding of the Society of Architectural Historians*, ed. Elisabeth B. MacDougall (Washington; Hanover: National Gallery of Art; Distributed by the University Press of New England, 1990).

127-142. Information on the website for Society of St. John the Evangelist Community in Cambridge MA 2005: http://www.ssje.org/retreats.html
[49] Ibid. 132
[50] Robert J. Young, *Marketing Marianne: French propaganda in America, 1900-1940* (New Brunswick, N.J.: Rutgers University Press, 2004).
[51] This remark refers to Girardous's *Amica America* from 1917, reprinted in 1938. See: Ibid. 144 and note 10.
[52] Lucy Ell Conant, Kenneth's mother, even wrote letters in French to Conant's children to encourage them to study the language (Cluny Collection, Loeb Library, Harvard University). Harvard's president, James B. Conant, was listed in a directory of pro-French individuals and organizations by the French embassy. See R. Young, 132.
[53] Young, *Marketing Marianne: French propaganda in America, 1900-1940*. 42
[54] Appendix A of Council minutes for May 27, 1928 (not bound in with minutes, rather kept in loose Cluny file folders). All this information on the Mediaeval Academy is from files in their offices, Cambridge MA.
[55] Mediaeval Academy files, Cluny 1927-1931. A summary prepared in 1933 by John Marshall also clearly lists Brown's contributions from 1928-1932 along with tentative budgets for 1934 and 1935. It is interesting to note that the Academy planned on a reserve toward publication (of 2,500 dollars) and that budget concerns were such that a final paragraph reads: "Mr. Conant is quite willing to postpone for a year the work now planned for 1934 and 1935, if financial considerations make postponement desirable."
[56] Copies of both the English versions on Mediaeval Academy letterhead and a handwritten translation into French by John Nicolas Brown are kept in the files of the Culture Ministry in Paris (Paris, Bibliothèque du Patrimoine: Cote 81/71, 181/1, Box 17).
[57] Letter of March 24, 1928 from Ralph Adams Cram on American Church of Paris letterhead to John Marshall, executive secretary of the Mediaeval Academy of America.
[58] Michelle and Jean Claude Gosse, interview June 2003; Mme. Melin, interview April, 2005
[59] First monthly report to the Mediaeval Academy, dated July 3, 1928, on file in the Mediaeval Academy offices, Cambridge MA. Subsequent quotes from this period come from same document.
[60] [Thank you for the your voluntary support of the excavations at Cluny…Nothing to the training school!]
[61] See Elizabeth Emery's article "The Martyred Cathedral: American Attitudes toward Notre-Dame de Reims during the First World War" in: *Art and Architecture after the Middle Ages* ed. Janet Marquardt and Alyce Jordan, Cambridge Scholar's Press, 2008 (forthcoming). She presented her paper at the March 31 2006 annual meeting of the Mediaeval Academy of America in Boston during a session with the same title as the anthology and chaired by its editors.
[62] Minutes of the Meeting of the Council of the Mediaeval Academy of America, Appendix 2: Report of the Executive Secretary, page 4.
[63] For instance, the copy of Cram's *Ruined Abbeys of Great Britain* held by the Cluny Collection, Loeb Library, Harvard University was donated by Conant. Also see JSAH 36, 1 (1977), 57

[64] Provincial French telegraph operators are apparent in numerous misspellings, including his name which in this instance is recorded as "CONAY".
[65] Kenneth John Conant, "Excavations at the Monastery of Cluny," *The American Society Legion of Honor Magazine* IX, No. 2 (1940). 171
[66] 9 juillet 1928: Paris, Bibliothèque du Patrimoine: Cote 81/71, 181/1, Box 17.
[67] David Walsh, "The Excavations of Cluny III by K.J. Conant." *Actes du Colloque scientifique international "Gouvernement d'Hugues de Semur à Cluny", Musée Ochier, Cluny 1988*. (Mâcon: Buguet-Comptour, 1990). 317-325
[68] Ibid. 320-322
[69] Remembered by both Edwin Rae (phone conversation January, 2002) and David Walsh (email December, 2003).
[70] Discussions with David Walsh on this subject enhanced my understanding.
[71] Postcard from Aubert to Conant in Mediaeval Academy files for 1928, Cambridge MA
[72] This report and those of following years are available both in the Cluny Collection, Loeb Library, Harvard University (uncatalogued) and Paris, Bibliothèque du Patrimoine: Cote 81/71, 181/1, Box 17
[73] Paul Deschamps, *French sculpture of the Romanesque period* (Firenze: Pantheon, 1930). Aside from this dating disagreement, Conant admired Deschamps as a fine scholar as can be seen in his review of Deschamp's book on the Crak des Chevaliers from 1934 in the *American Journal of Archaeology* 41/1 (Jan., 1937), 170-171
[74] Charles Oursel, *L'art roman de Bourgogne* (Dijon: L. Venot, 1928). See also Meyer Schapiro's incisive review from *The Art Bulletin* 11, 2 (June 1929), 225-231
[75] For instance, see "Le problème de Cluny," *La Revue de l'art* LX (1942), 141-154 and 189-204
[76] Paris, Bibliothèque du Patrimoine: Cote 81/71, 181/1, Box 17
[77] "Fouilles archéologiques: Elles ont inaugurées le 29 juin dernier, en présence de M. Kennelh, John Conact, professeur de l'Université Harward, à Cambridge (Massachussetts) [sic], et de M. E. Malo, architecte du Gouvernement. M. Conant, directeur des fouilles, auteur remarqué d'un savant ouvrage sur la ville médiévale espagnole de Saint-Jacques-de-Compostelle, a déjà consacré trois mois de l'été de 1927, à relever dans les plus minutieux détails les plans de notre ancienne abbaye et de ses vaste dépendances.

Cette année, il nous revient en réalisateur mandaté par l'Académie médiévale d'Amérique pour pratiquer les affouillements utiles à même le sol qui recouvre les vestiges enterrés du monastère.

Autorisé par notre Administration des Beaux-Arts et habilité par la municipalité de notre ville, M. Conant a eu la bonne fortune de dégager, à plus de deux mètres de profondeur, les bases du jambages restant du marbre, au niveau des dalles de l'église. Il entreprend actuellement la recherche des fondations du portail de la basilique en attendant de poursuivre sa prospection dans le sens qu'indiqueront les prochaines découvertes."
[78] Conant's report to the Mediaeval Academy for the month of June, 1929. On file in the Cambridge MA office.
[79] Per former student Edwin Rae (phone conversation January, 2002)

[80] See, for example, his wide-ranging choice of images in the published University Print compilation for his Modern Architecture course from 1930 (University Prints Boston and Kenneth John Conant, *University prints. Series G. M. Modern architecture* (Boston, MA: The University prints, 1930).

CHAPTER SIX

THE "RESURRECTION" OF CLUNY: KENNETH CONANT'S VISION II

> You have, I think, cheated time a little...by making something that time has destroyed come to authentic life again.
> —Joan Evans, 1960s(?)[1]

> ...M. Kenneth John Conant...me disait, en août 1929, que l'on trouve, à Cluny, plus de deux cent cinquante photographies ou cartes postales illustrées des anciens monuments, et il se propose d'en faire encore beaucoup d'autres.
> —René Champly, 1930[2]

In 1929, Conant published his first in the series of *Speculum* articles on the excavations at Cluny. They would eventually run to seven installments. With other articles on related topics, a total of eleven *Speculum* issues would contain something about Cluny by Conant. The 1929 publication was a summary of the detailed report that Conant had submitted to the Mediaeval Academy for the 1928 season's work. However, Conant added introductory remarks that set out his Romantic viewpoint, squarely landing him in the tradition of lamentation for the lost church. He took the stand that Cluny was the most influential monastic institution in the history of Europe as well as an architectural example of unsurpassed grandeur. He regreted that, as of 1928, it was rarely visited: "...the tourist confuses it with the Cluny Museum...and many a student and teacher, having heard that the abbey was destroyed in the Revolution, passes it by."[3]

He emphasizes the senseless destruction as well as modern adaptations: "...except for a magnificent fragment and some lesser ruins, it is only a memory...This practical age has spoiled the stately layout of the Benedictines of the time of Louis XV." The cause which he took up with the government regarding both the growth of the *Haras* and his desire to save some of the excavations are also addressed to the American reader: "Now it is proposed to extend still further the unhappy stable for which the church had to be destroyed, and thus to damage many of the old pier bases of the nave still standing under the peaceful sward." [4] This is an exaggeration, as the *Haras* was, as we have seen, certainly not the direct cause of the church's demise. Likewise, the picture he paints of a "peaceful sward" is purely Romantic; all areas of the former nave not covered by buildings were under the pavement of the street and central marketplace. He even uses the article as a platform to call for funding to help the French ministry implement a plan to arrange for the building of a larger stable in another location and "for the demolition of those which already dishonor this ground." The missing word that we should read here before 'ground' would most certainly be 'sacred', for Conant still considered the area where the church sanctuary had been to be consecrated ground. "The funds necessary to cover the additional cost, some twenty thousand dollars, are not available, so that the plan, if it is to be put into effect at all, must appeal to the generosity of some benefactor who thinks that the fabric of Cluny has suffered enough, who would like to see the venerable place in a more suitable condition, and who would like to see the old foundations left accessible to archeological research. It seems hard that a site so august, so rich in great memories, should be given over to horses, grooms, and their gear."[5] This anthropomorphic treatment of the abbey, in an attempt to grandstand a sympathetic response, was clearly aimed at Americans' need for historical connection. We might even assume he was thinking specifically of John Nicholas Brown, since we know that Conant wrote him when he wanted something bankrolled, such as the narthex portal pit preservation.

This first article on the excavations also contains Conant's romantic evocation of an imaginary ideal medieval atmosphere "…a glimpse of [Cluny's] all but vanished grandeur has greatly moved many a visitor, giving in a flash a vision of the ampler lost horizon, and penetrating sense of what perished by the stupidity of a century ago. Such was the case with the author, who visited Cluny in 1924 and received, while walking among the eloquent remains of the martyred abbey, an unforgettable impression of Cluny's greatness"[6] Here we find Conant even using the same term Cram had employed regarding Reims cathedral during World War I (see chapter 5) and that Le Comte de Lasteyrie had employed about Cluny in 1910 (see chapter 4). Characterizing the remains into the relics of a "martyred abbey," Conant implied that visitors engaged in a holy pilgrimage when traveling to the site. His prose embodies Malraux's characterization of the post-WWI generation longing for faith in something, moved by "a better world than it is living in"[7] by turning back to the previous generation's yearning for, as Conant wrote, "the ampler lost horizon" of an ideal Middle Ages.

In 1929, Conant put together funds from his Guggenheim grant, "an anonymous donor", and 1000 dollars from Harvard to order a set of the casts from the Trocadero Museum (comparative sculpture study center) of the ambulatory capitals to send to Cambridge. Over the next few years, with the help of students, he worked out the original order in which they appeared and then mounted them in the court of the Fogg Museum at Harvard on temporary shafts "where the lighting conditions are similar to those in the destroyed sanctuary of the abbey church." [figs. 6.1, 6.2][8] A photo of the installation appeared on the cover of the Fogg's *Bulletin* in 1933, but this was also the issue containing Porter's obituary, which eclipsed Conant's project.[9] Over time, this work and the presence of the casts caused friction with the Fogg director, Paul Sachs, and Conant finally took the casts to Mt. Holyoke College where he occasionally taught.[10] They have since been lost; word that they were returned to Harvard at the end of the twentieth century has led to a dead end.

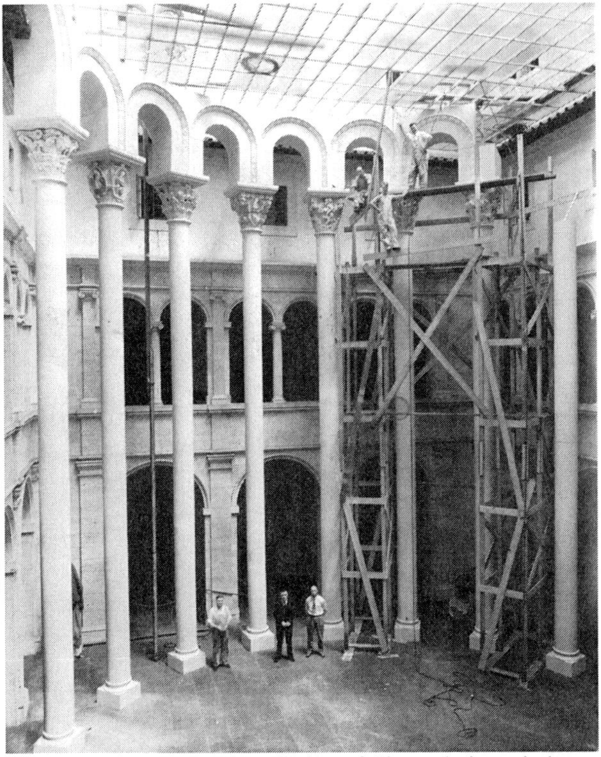

6.1 Conant with workers during installation of Cluny choir capital casts in Fogg Museum, Harvard University, June, 1933. (Cluny Collection: Loeb Library, Harvard University)

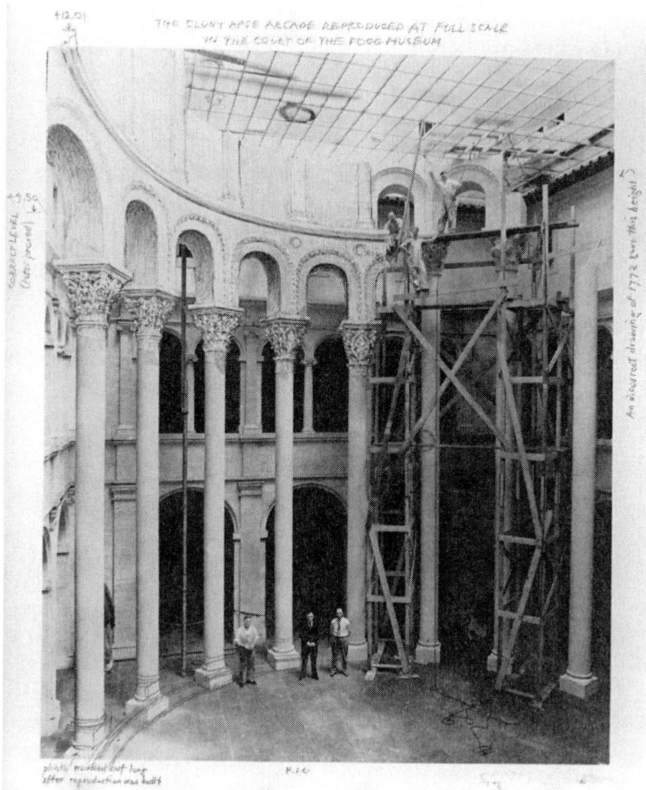

6.2 Modified photo of Cluny choir capital casts in Fogg Museum, 1933.
Conant made a note on the right margin that the Fogg installation height was wrong, based upon a drawing of 1772. He has drawn over the photograph to lower the arcades and indicate the next higher wall level in the original church
(Cluny Collection: Loeb Library, Harvard University)

In 1930 there were no formal excavations at Cluny but Conant had his final year of Guggenheim allowance and some remaining Mediaeval Academy funds previously allocated so he hired Palmer and another architect, John Bolles, to work there on drawing plans for the existing abbey buildings. Conant himself only spent three weeks in Cluny, looking at archival material, checking on the progress of photographic work and the installation of a permanent railing around the pit in the *Haras* courtyard for which he had petitioned the government at length. Then he left for the rest of the summer to travel around Europe studying related monuments and networking with other scholars. He gave lectures on the work at Cluny in London, Orléans, and Dijon. He planned to re-erect the Baroque portal of the Pape Gelasius entry, sketch restorations of the church over photographs taken by Loury that year, and piece together fragments from the west portal using the restoration drawings he and Helen Kleinschmidt had begun. None of this would be terribly useful in the future.

Cordial and supportive relationships with other scholars were very important to Conant; in 1931 he lobbied the Mediaeval Academy to supply financial aid to Victor Terret, who was trying to get his monumental work on the sculpture at Vézélay published, by agreeing to purchase 50 sets of the two-volume work. During early 1931, Conant worked on an article for the *Revue de l'Art* that would counter the first strong resistance from Paris, in the form of an earlier article in the same journal, to his (and Porter's) thesis about the dating of the church by the ambulatory capitals. In May, he reported back to the Academy that, in discussions on this subject, he felt he had convinced Jean Virey to support his point of few in his upcoming publications. Not publishing substantial scholarship himself, Conant did not have an established reputation behind his claims about Cluny so he was forced to rely upon personal explanation, professional precision, and the warmth of his charm to gain supporters.

Conant's report for June 1931 projects completion of all excavation work on the church by the next spring and then in 1932 pushes it to the end of July (when the stallions returned from their regular annual absence of February through July.) Twenty-two pits were open by this time, all in and around the third abbey church, giving him all the data he needed for measurements of that building.[11] He thus suggested a season not be planned for 1933, rather that he stay in Cambridge and work on the restoration drawings, leaving the few details to be cleaned up in two further midsummer campaigns. This in spite of the fact that Harvard had approved half-year appointments from 1931-1933 and he had planned to leave Marie and the boys in France while he went back to teach fall semesters while living in one of the dormitory rooms where he was an Associate. ("Mme. Conant" was actually named Kenneth's official collaborator on the archaeological excavations in the letter of permission issued by Paul Léon of the Beaux-Arts for 1931, though he never acknowledged her help in publications.)[12] It would also be another thirty-five years before he would finish writing the book with the results he had promised. What happened in the meantime?

For one thing, he had already warned his sponsors not to rush him:

> The publication will certainly be a long time in preparation. The material at hand from the excavations is so voluminous, and any study of this site has so many ramifications, that years must elapse before it can all be synthesized and presented in proper form. The site is so important that a hasty publication with insufficient drawings and an undigested text cannot be thought of. The

> commanding position of the building in the art of its time is not yet well realized, and this means that a careful analysis of the genesis and influence of the church will be necessary if our monograph is to restore this great monument to its rightful place.[13]

Reading reports and letters from the following years, one also receives the impression that Conant was not ready to leave Cluny and sequester himself at Harvard, teaching and writing a book. In spite of his plan simply to determine the measurements of the abbey church for a ground plan, he became caught up in finding other remains that might help him prepare detailed elevations, plans for the earlier churches, reconstruct sculptural elements, or prepare a comprehensive layout of the entire monastic complex. These concerns would necessarily move him into much deeper waters, involving structural analysis, dating proposals, sculptural decoration, and even questions of usage. Without more than the fragmentary transept arm and foundation soundings to go on, a great deal of conjecture would be involved. In his French role as "Director of Excavations" and Mediaeval Academy role as "Research Associate", Conant must have felt most qualified to take them on. They were roles he was clearly loath to relinquish.

Conant wrote to Marcel Aubert on May 16, 1931 announcing that they had found two sarcophagi while digging in the *Haras*.[14] Although there was no proof, based on the locations, Conant and his French colleagues, Malo and Gélis (architects for the Monuments historiques), decided that they could be those of (Saint) Hugh of Semur (d. 1109) and Peter the Venerable (d. 1156). From this supposition, Conant moved to identifying them as such and proposed two lead plaques – a small one for the inside of Hugh's empty base and a large one to cover Peter's [fig. 6.3]. He wrote Latin inscriptions, although Aubert suggested simpler French texts, marking the graves as those of the saints and the year at which they were exposed (1931). Of course, there were other burials in this area. Even Conant admits that in 1791, when the tombs were broken during Revolutionary anti-clerical actions, the one he calls Hugh's was already empty and in his June report to the Mediaeval Academy he records that they took a small fragment of the sarcophagus stone to test since he felt that the quality of the stone cutting made it unlikely to date so early. In the one he calls Peter's, only bones and a bit of fine sand from the decomposed body remained. Nothing distinguished these abbots from any others buried in the church. If, in fact, the previous abbey church was not built over but had been located to the north and slightly west of the larger one as Conant claimed, the cemetery which had always followed monastic custom (for instance at St. Gall or Farfa) and been situated to the east and south of the earlier apse could have accounted for numerous burials covered by the new construction. On the photograph documenting the lead plaque, Conant wrote that the remains were attributed by the local "pharmacy inspector", Léon Daclin [fig. 6.4].[15] The next year they found another in the same area that again was identified by locations on old plans but also by contents in the tomb as belonging to Ponce de Melgueil.[16] Ponce was a disgraced abbot who had been excommunicated so the presence of a broken crozier seemed to the scholars present a sign of his burial. At least it quickly became that in the press all over Europe, though in his report for April to the Mediaeval Academy, Conant relates confusion over the size of the body, let alone the fact that there WAS a body (Ponce died in Rome and was originally buried there), and reports that another abbot had supposedly been buried under this of which he could find no evidence. In any case, these finds were generating interest and support for his work, even if he could not always support the tentative attributions picked up by the press. And he was under time pressure at every discovery while working in the Depôt, especially in horse stalls (where Peter the Venerable's supposed tomb was found) that could not be left uninhabitable for the high-strung and valuable government stallions.

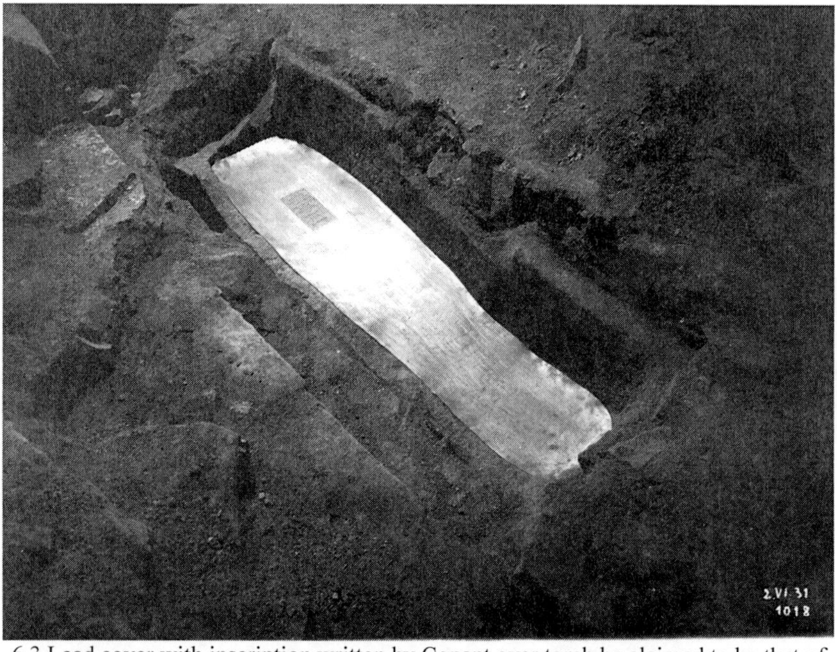

6.3 Lead cover with inscription written by Conant over tomb he claimed to be that of Peter the Venerable, 1931 (Cluny Collection: Loeb Library, Harvard University)

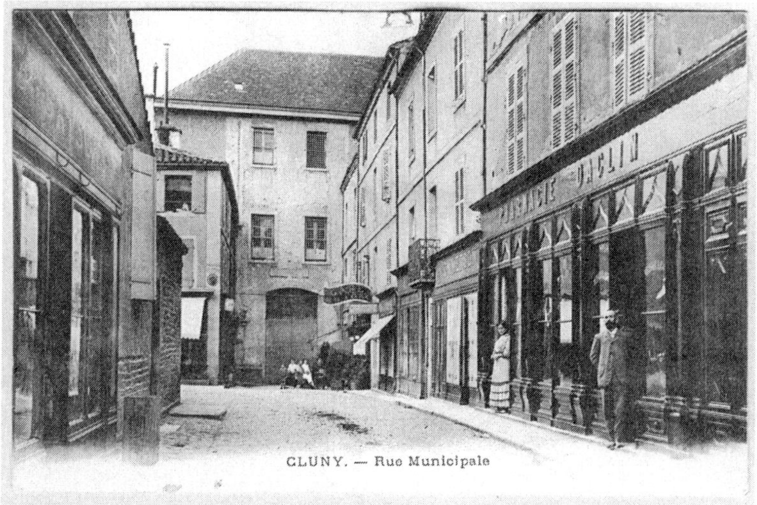

6.4 Postcard of M. et Mme. Daclin in front of their pharmacy in Cluny around 1910 (Cluny Collection: Loeb Library, Harvard University)

Conant’s presence was also adding weight to requests from various functionaries who were located in the area. On February 11, 1931, the Director of the *Haras* wrote to the Monuments historiques at the Beaux-Arts Ministry via his own minister (Agriculture) that stones from one of the chapels used by the stables had that morning begun to fall.[17] This was a space he claimed to be indispensable to running the facility since it was used to store fodder for twenty horses and a place where people constantly came and went all day long. Since his depot was then holding the maximum number of horses manageable, he had no other space for these essential things and thus underlined the urgency of repairs which, being of a classed building, were not the financial responsibility of the *Dépôt d’Etalons de Cluny.* This letter is in unusually strong language that the Director will not make any concessions toward adapting other spaces and that his ministry was not responsible for payment. It is doubtful he could have been so intransigent before Conant’s interventions brought the historical monument such prestige.

In 1931, Conant gave a lecture at the Fogg Museum for the Mediaeval Academy on the excavation finds from that year. He was still publishing annual reports in *Speculum* and he was still riding a good wave at Harvard. In 1930 he had been made associate professor with a permanent, joint appointment at Harvard and Radcliffe. Porter withdrew from teaching that year and Conant was able to take over his architecture courses. He was also still taking small design commissions, such as gates for the Gardner Museum. In 1935 he would be made full professor and he received constant requests for lectures and expert advice from around the country. As Paul Sachs, director of the Fogg Art Museum, wrote regarding his promotion, they were proud of him (as their alumnus) with his "international reputation" and his successful teaching.[18] Conant continued to research Cluny sources (his Bibliothèque Nationale reader's card was validated every year from 1931 to 1935) and he had the opportunity to live in Paris when he was made exchange professor with the Sorbonne for fall, 1935. That summer he had studied at Montecassino with Henry Willard, in charge of those excavations, and he went to Istanbul and Kiev to analyze Byzantine monuments. (Conant also harbored the idea for some years that he needed to get access to Caucasian architecture in order to understand Cluny's sources.) He returned to Istanbul, along with Jerusalem and other cities containing important early monuments, while on sabbatical in 1938.[19] This would lead to his participation in excavations in Kiev and the preparation of restoration drawings for Hagia Sophia. It was also on the 1935 trip that Conant became enamored with the liturgical spectacle of Greek orthodox Christianity. He felt that chant performances in these churches were the closest he could come to a medieval monastic experience.[20] He converted, wholly, and upon his return to Boston presented himself to the metropolitan (Greek orthodox bishop) there. He was a devoted member of that church for the rest of his life.

In the end, Conant did not return to the excavations during the springs of 1933 or 1934; only short summer campaigns were undertaken. He reported that the excavation of the third abbey church was complete and he needed time to work up his notes. He had also run a deficit in 1932 and had extended personal credit that he held against pledges for later years. Likewise, he had to take into account fluctuations in the exchange rate; during 1933 the dollar fell a great deal, making it lucky that the new director of the Ecole had demanded everything be returned to perfect condition before the commencement of the school year in fall 1932. Thus the deficit Conant had paid in 1932, he carried in dollars during 1933/34. Unfortunately, some of the fill shrank and further expenditures were necessary to return to ground level. On the other hand, the French franc was devalued in 1936, resulting in a small gain.

During these years, Conant was hiring Frederic Palmer on a regular basis to draw up detailed plans for the third abbey church with the data provided by the excavations. From Palmer's large scale layout of the church Conant planned to begin geometric restoration drawings in 1936-37. Similarly, Helen Kleinschmidt, with grants from Radcliffe and Harvard but formally considered by Conant as "an experienced volunteer",[21] was very active in cleaning and identification of the sculptural fragments. She worked in Cluny during the summer of 1934 while Conant stayed in Cambridge teaching summer school and moving into a new house. There she tried to "solve" the problem of the

Great Portal, by careful study of the fragments, pre-demolition images of the abbey, medieval manuscripts, and comparably-dated Burgundian churches. She also discovered, and reported, thefts of some of the fragments. By 1936 she was able to make a colored drawing based upon her observance of polychrome residue. That year she was in charge of a one-month excavation, carried out while Conant was in residence but under her direction as "Research Assistant" with Mediaeval Academy funds. By the end of this year, a total 25,000 dollars had been pledged toward the Cluny project from the Mediaeval Academy (Brown) with 22,500 spent. Conant listed the remaining 2500 in reserve for publication. It was used in 1938 for the preliminary survey of his results in Koehler's memorial volume to Porter.

In 1936 he wrote to his parents, full of accomplishment:

> This trip really marks an epoch for me, for it finishes a twenty-year campaign of travel, begun in the fall of 1916, when I still thought that I should be an architect. It was really my drawing, my love of architectural history, and my detective sense which turned me toward archaeology. Without these journeys of study, my contacts with specialists in archaeology, and my luck in arranging the Cluny excavations, my history would be a very different one; my advancement is entirely due to this very special work: just what the new Harvard administration most desires.
>
> I began a very long job in 1916. Only in 1922, 1923, 1925, and 1934 did I stay at home, and only in 1921 and 1924 did I pay for the trip myself. Fifteen trips involving 100,000 miles of land travel. My journeyman trips. Now I go back to my full professorship with that big long job done. The Cluny excavating is also finished; now I can stay at home and work up my results. I am content to have this active part of my job behind me. The excavations came out well: I solved my last big problem in Cluny a few days ago…[22]

Conant wanted to continue with the excavation of other abbey buildings. However, throughout the rest of the 1930s, he only made short stays in Cluny to oversee small digs involving Cluny II (1935 and 1938) or to see the progress made by his assistants and volunteers. Numerous students became interested and traveled to Cluny, most likely at their own expense, and Conant dutifully reported to the Mediaeval Academy their work on cataloging the photographs, drawing up models for acoustics and casts of the tympanum, or even commencing study on other Cluniac churches in the area for degrees at Harvard. Small pits were opened in the hopes of determining measurements for Odilo's eleventh-century monastery. Yet ultimately, for this phase of Cluny's history, Conant relied almost exclusively upon the description of an ideal Cluniac monastery from the Farfa customary and only made occasional checks into real remains. He proclaimed the excavations concluded in September 1938.

In March 1939 Conant sent a bristling memo to the Mediaeval Academy Executive Committee about a book dated 1936, published by a commercial firm in Mâcon in 1938, by Joseph and A. Talobre entitled "La construction de l'abbaye de Cluny". Having eschewed cooperation with Conant, the Talobres then used his incomplete plan of Cluny II that he claimed they must have copied from a casual drawing he made on a stone for some tourists. What really rankled him, however, was that Marcel Aubert liked the book for its attempt to disprove Porter's dating of the ambulatory capitals and published a review to that effect in the *Bulletin Monumental.* Conant promised the executive committee members that he would respond to it in *Speculum* with a note correcting the church plan and with mention of the advantages Joan Evans had experienced by her genial arrangements with Conant for her *Romanesque Architecture of the Order of Cluny* (1938, Cambridge University Press). He concluded by writing: "The less said about the ethics of archaeological opponents, the better. The Talobre book will drop out of sight when our results are published."[23] By January 1940, he was singing a different tune, claiming that the Talobres' interpretation of the evidence had allowed him to refine his version of Odilo's church and monastic buildings.[24]

After making contact for the 1938 book, Evans and Conant corresponded for the rest of their lives. Joan, one year older than Conant and very aware of her position as half-sister to Sir Arthur, became both an art historian and the family historian [fig. 6.5]. She also never married, living with a housekeeper at her family home, "Thousand Acres", in Wotton-under-Edge Gloucestershire, and at a flat in London. Already published on Cluny with her 1931 book "Monastic Life at Cluny", Dame Evans also wrote on Ruskin and other subjects such as medieval jewelry. She enjoyed great success as President of both the Royal Archaeological Society and the Society of Antiquaries, receiving numerous honorary degrees as well as the French Légion d'Honneur. Her independent wealth not only gave her the leisure to pursue full-time research, it also allowed her to rescue Abbot Hugh's chapel at Berzé-la-Ville by purchasing it and donating it to the Academy of Mâcon. The letters she wrote to Conant, now in the university archives at Harvard, show a strong hand, friendly humor, and insightful judgment of academic character. His to her have been lost, along with her other papers which were destroyed after her death. But it is clear that they shared a mutual affection and in their later years, treasured the length of their acquaintance.

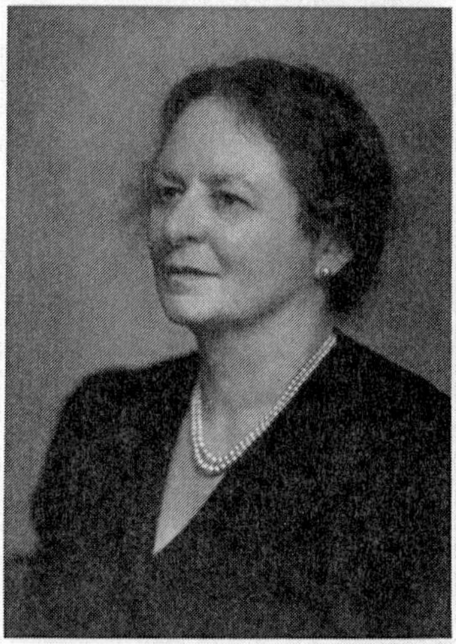

6.5 Joan Evans (Cluny Collection: Loeb Library, Harvard University)

In her autobiography, *Time and Chance,* published in 1964, Evans reminisces about her travels in France exploring Cluniac dependencies. Remarking on a visit to Cluny in 1928, she writes:

> It was an unforgettable visit, for I found that Kenneth Conant was there, excavating in the abbey ruins on behalf of the Mediaeval Academy in America. At first I feared that he might consider all Cluniac art his field, and that there would be no room for my work; but as soon as we had met I realized that he was an antiquary of the old generous sort, who sought not the promotion of his own career but the increase of knowledge. He showed us the fragments of the portal that he had found, laid out in a touching disarray on his bed; and drew conjectural plans of all the abbey's three churches on the marble-topped table of the estaminet of the Hotel de Burgogne. Never have I enjoyed a more generous unfolding of discovery.[25]

By 1940, they were corresponding regularly. Their mutual love of France and Cluny focused the war years' letters, but always there was discussion of their Cluny projects. In the early 1940s, Conant sent Evans photos of some of his reconstructive drawings of the interior of the third abbey church. She responded: "You have, I think, cheated time a little rather as my brother used to do, by making something that time has destroyed come to authentic life again."[26] Evans' background made her sympathetic to Conant's inventive point of view, being from a family where father, mother, and older half-brother all studied archeology in the "collector" style of the pre-modern era. She wrote in her autobiography: "I have lived to find a home and a life I have known in ruins;

and by virtue of this experience I have lost my faith in any kind of archaeology that does not attempt imaginative reconstruction."[27] In May 1944 she asked Conant if after sixteen years of friendship they could use each other's first names "in France it would be forward but not in England or the USA".[28] Through these letters we begin to see the break-up of Conant's marriage at the same time that Kenneth, Jr. was in an English hospital. 17 June 1945 Evans wrote: "I am very sorry that fate has been cruel lately. I remember so well Mrs. Conant's cheerful courage in undertaking the adventure of living at Cluny; it is hard to realize that it is overclouded. It must be an acute tragedy for you." They recommended each other for memberships and honors; they defended each other's work from critics.

The French were not inactive about Cluny during the 1930s. Charles Oursel, conservator at the Dijon library who taught the history of Burgundian art at the university there and a great supporter of Conant, lobbied the Monuments historiques in 1932 to have the Cluny engineering school prepare some sort of line marking the ground where the important abbey buildings had stood. His letter suggests that this would be good both for students of medieval architecture as well as for the tourist trade. It was supported with a cover letter from Robert Jardillier, *deputé* of the Côte d'Or. However, Malo and Gélis felt that it was a complicated notion, particularly since much of the outline would be either in the *Haras* or inside the school boundaries. The public was not allowed in either place. They also thought that the variety of surfaces on the ground made it difficult to imagine a material that would always be readable, as well as durable, and the amount of material and work involved would be expensive. The matter apparently went no further. However, an aerial photograph was taken before the excavations of 1988 showing the outline of the abbey church made by a student at the *école*, using white cloths to form thick lines on the ground and roof tops.[29] Recent articles in both the local newsletter and *Le Monde* project a similar project in the works as part of preparations for the anniversary year 2010.[30]

Paul Gélis served another report to the Monuments historiques in December 1937 on the "deplorable" condition of the extant south transept arm of the former abbey church, which, he emphasized, was visited by numerous tourists and archeologists.[31] After listing the work on the walls and floor that needed to be undertaken, he ended by saying that during the process the interior would be arranged to show the plans of the abbey in order to "bring the ruins to life".[32] In the event, though work continued to maintain the building, the only reference for tourists that appeared was a print of Conant's drawing of the rest of the interior of the basilica hung on the wall that closed the former passage into the main crossing [fig. 6.6]. The view did not conform to what would have been seen from this vantage; rather it showed the nave opening out from the west entrance.

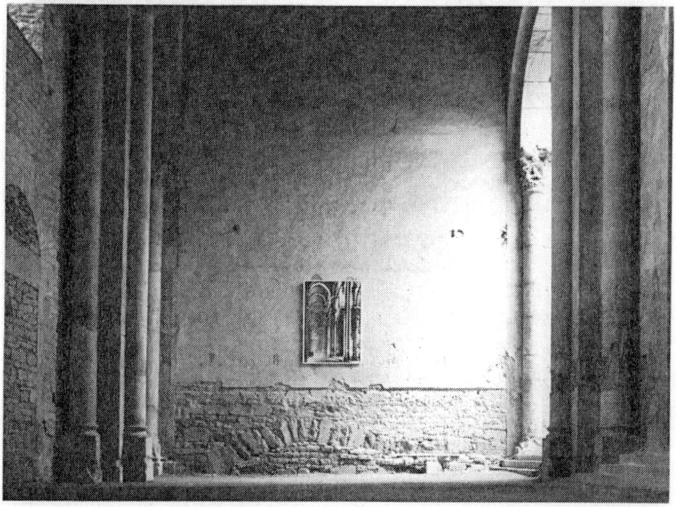

6.6 Interior view of remaining transept, Cluny abbey church, showing photograph of Conant drawing on closure wall where rest of church once stood (Cluny collection: Loeb Library, Harvard University)

In the final paragraph of Conant's 1 January 1941 report to the Mediaeval Academy, he briefly remarked on the war. "As far as we know the fall of Paris did not affect our photographic archives, which are deposited there. A great section of the German army passed through Cluny on its way to Lyon just before the French collapse, and the town was occupied by Bavarians for twenty days. Since all of our measurements and photographic prints are in Cambridge, the events in France have not caused us any difficulty."[33] It was a dry statement about another major upheaval in Europe which again threatened the medieval monuments Conant treasured. This time, however, it was up to the next generation to volunteer their services and when the United States entered the war, Kenneth Jr. went to Europe and was wounded there in fighting. (The younger son, John, would join the Coast Guard for the Korean war.) In the next year's report, Conant even seems to use the war as an excuse to extend his publishing timeframe, although it had little to do with his apparent procrastinations:

> Understandably enough the activity of the past year has been limited to a study of our collected data, and the exploration of collateral problems. There is no temptation for us to rush into print; the hiatus caused by the war is likely to bring a number of interesting studies to fruition, definitely to the advantage of the

> Cluny study. It is a good thing to allow our various archaeological solutions to mellow, so that when they are published they will represent mature results.[34]

At the end of the report, he again offered news about the town:

> Word has come through from our friends in Cluny and Dijon of the sombre conditions existing there. Cluny is in the unoccupied area. The school continues to operate, but the remains of the church are 'open only to members of' the German Armistice Commission'(!) except by permission of the director. The strain on the French in both regions is obviously very severe. But M. Oursel of Dijon, our friend, mentor, and collaborator, while he speaks of oppression, still hopes that a diminished France may succeed in reconstituting its traditional Christian civilization.

Oursel was writing to Conant from the Vichy-controlled area. He was also conveying the party line—that the German occupation would rid France of recent radical and corruptive influences for the better. Like the adherents of the Sacred Heart movement during World War I,[35] Oursel and those like him thought that if the country would rededicate itself to Catholicism, it would have been worth the price of the war. Others were not so passive. Cluny was the home of an active force of the *maquis* or French resistance movement. Members of the Cluny regiment were part of 1500 *maquisards* who marched in the Liberation parade through Mâcon on September 4, 1944. Conant's wrote to his son in the hospital in June 1945 with news of their French friends:

> The Auberts, the Oursels and the Vireys are safe, but Mademoiselle Zimberlin was the one who organized the Underground in Cluny. The Gestapo caught her; she spent nearly a year in the Buchenwald concentration camp, and died on her way home. She liked you very much as our little Kenny and you should be proud to have known a real heroine.[36]

Once the French were liberated, they began the task of evaluating the effects of the war on sites classed as *monuments historiques*. Near the end of the war in August 1944, the Germans had dropped bombs in Cluny's main market square, renamed the *Place du 11 août*, formed from the cloister area of the eleventh-century abbey. (The date, August 11, refers to the day the Germans were pushed back from Cluny by the F.F.I.—*Forces françaises de l'intérieur*). The bomb damage proved less important to the authorities than the advantage of disengaging buildings that had obscured old abbey structures. Although the Tour des Fromages was damaged at the top, plans had already been made in the previous year to repair that area. It belonged to a private citizen, Monsieur Laguette, who had offered it to the city in 1943 since he could not afford the appropriate repairs [fig. 6.7].

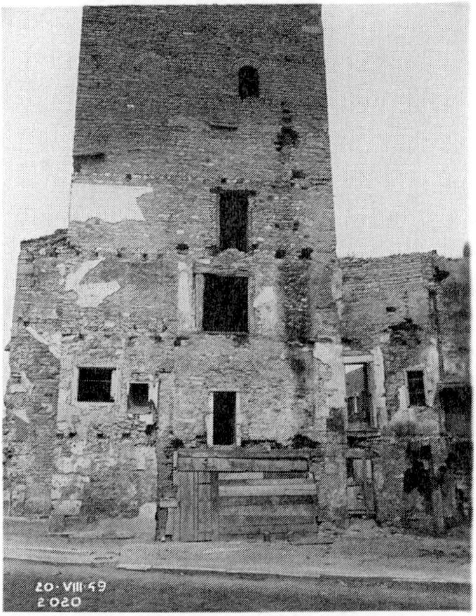

6.7 La Tour des Fromages in 1949 before restoration
(Cluny collection: Loeb Library, Harvard University)

It was the area just to the north of the *tour* that was revealed in the bombing [fig. 6.8]. There was a two-story structure running north/south with a large ground floor that had been incorporated into a more recent layer of houses. The disengagement of some of the later walls revealed large arched openings in the ground floor with bays allowing passage between the tower and the *place* suggesting medieval commercial shops.[37] A large barrel-vaulted room, enlarged in the eighteenth century, joined this building to the tower. Other buildings were also revealed, including further north near the *Justice de Paix* where piers with engaged columns from the church were found below modern ground level.

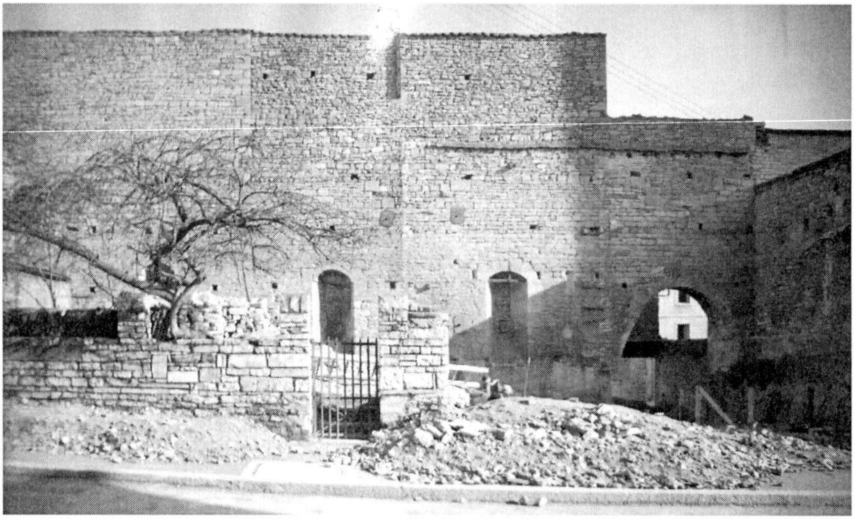

6.8 Site of a 1944 bomb, Cluny (Cluny collection: Loeb Library, Harvard University)

The city planner, Berry, proposed that they continue to pierce through newer construction, enlarging the *Place du 11 août* and constructing a street between it and the rue Mercière to allow a view of the Romanesque building called the *Écuries* (stables) of St. Hugh. It was to this building that the town's cinema had been moved in 1945 since the previous location had been destroyed in the bombing.[38] It remains there to this day. The Tour des Fromages, now at a key corner between the main commercial street and access to the abbey buildings, was made into the local tourism office.[39] This project continued through 1947 with some new construction and much repair. The so-called façade of Pope Gelasius was severely damaged by a bomb that landed right in front of it (see fig. 2.3). The second-story windows had been an ongoing problem of glare for visitors and interior heat for students of the *École des arts et métiers* and by 1950 were replaced with tinted glass.[40] A project was also briefly floated to the Monuments historiques in 1949 that the baroque portal be restored. A consensus could not be reached and the idea never materialized. It was also during this time that restoration of the abbey's *Farinier* (granary) began with a view to installing a sculpture museum there [figs. 6.9, 6.10]. Excavations were opened in some areas, notably in the middle of the *place* directly in front of the present day tourist entrance to the abbey. These were under the direction of the Monuments historiques.

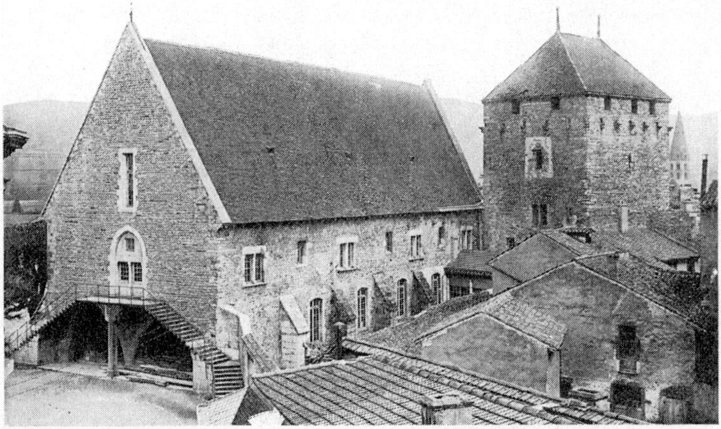

6.9 Former granary and mill tower at abbey of Cluny, exterior
(Ricard, *Cluny et les Environs,* plate VII)

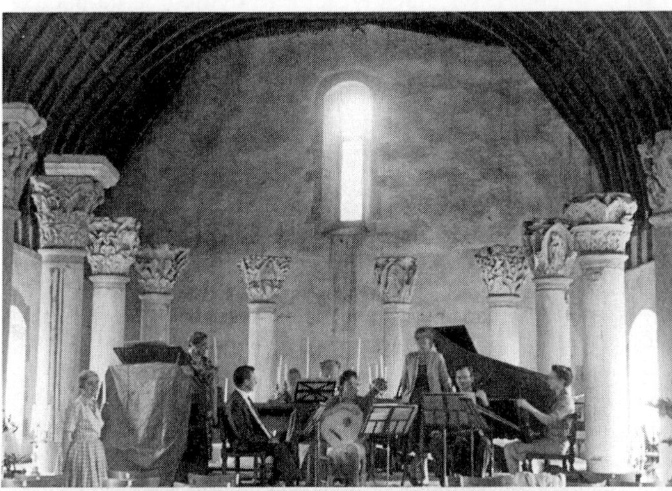

6.10 Museum installed in former granary of Cluny abbey, here seen in 1960 hosting a small concert under the direction of Conant's second wife, Isabel Pope (far left) (Cluny Collection: Loeb Library, Harvard University)

Joan Evans visited Cluny shortly after the war ended and upon her return home wrote to Conant:

> You really *must* go to Cluny and work soon. The bombardment of nearly all the houses on the abbey site has made possible all sorts of fresh investigations and if you don't come I fear they may well be carried out less skillfully by others. There is also talk of removing the Haras. There are some interesting new sculptured fragments that turned up in the bombed ruins. The old lady who keeps the Musée Ochier sent you loving messages. No one has ever spent so much time in her Museum as you, she says. The Hôtel de Bourgogne has been done up and has a new proprietor but I think the old drains! However its lunch—complete with escargots, was excellent. Dr. Pleindoux, the mayor, is all that is kind and friendly. There is great talk of reorganizing the Museum. So for goodness sake hurry up![41]

Dr. Pleindoux was very supportive of Conant's work and as mayor, became proactive in raising awareness of the site's importance. He decided to organize another major celebration at Cluny, held June 9-11, 1949.

The Celebrations of 1949

The events of 1910 (see Chapter 4) were repeated and even outdone by those of 1949; it became the largest celebration relating to the history of the abbey at Cluny. In both cases, three types of festivities, based upon a medieval theme, were directed toward all segments of the population: administrators and academics, those in religious orders, and the general populace. 1949 was a particularly interesting year; Pleindoux justified the commemoration as being the anniversaries of the deaths of abbots Odo (927-942) and Odilon (994-1049), suggesting that the millennial commemoration for Odo was delayed by the war. More importantly, this was the time of recovery for France. Not quite a full five years after the occupation ended, the French had been through the divisive trials of collaboration, the misery of a ruined economy and industry, starvation, cold deprivation, and a staggering need to replace lost buildings. Their role as world cultural leader was finished and they were still struggling to find political stability amongst bitter, splintered opposition parties. The effects of economic recovery were just becoming apparent and people could begin to conceive of a celebration of national patrimony once again. For Cluny, this meant pulling the entire region of Burgundy back into its realm, re-inscribing the historical monument as important to art, as central to the development of both European political and Church history, and as—once again since the Occupation—French.

By 1949, Cluny had evidence of its medieval glory to show with the work done by Conant. He had revived interest in the abbey and it was appropriate that the abbey became the center of this thanksgiving ceremony, for Church faith had revived during the desperate years of the Occupation. The publications of Simone Weil, a philosopher who converted from Judaism to Catholicism, had come out posthumously in 1948 to an avid public. By the end of that year, a bill was introduced in the Chamber of Deputies to grant amnesty to the remaining approximately 8000 alleged collaborators in prison. There was a mood of gaiety too, for this was the first year that most products became available again since the war—especially important in regards to food for which Janet Flanner wrote that the greater percentage of the population would spend their Christmas funds.[42] She also recounts that the 1949 season was astonishingly good for travel. Europeans who had either been unable to move about or, conversely, had been forced into undesired emigrations found that there were finally enough trains, food, and money to support tourism. Thus the leaders of Cluny could imagine drawing visitors not only from Burgundy, but even from outside the region.

Newspaper accounts of the events were uniformly upbeat. *Le Progrès* reported that the skies over Cluny were heavy with clouds on Friday night but that by Saturday morning, July 10th, the sun shone and lit the garlands and shop-windows decorating the town[43]. At 10 a.m., the *Congrès* convened with over 100 academics in attendance. The plenary addresses were evocative and full of recognitions for scholars who had helped reclaim Cluny's greatness. The participants then separated into three parts: History, Administration, and Art/Archeology. The day was filled with rich exchanges between experts. The paper noted with special merit the remarks given by Joan Evans on Cluniac iconography and the lecture tour led by Conant at 5 p.m., "long applauded" and thanked by Marcel Aubert (as president of the Mâcon Academy) for his contributions. An article dedicated to Conant's arrival at Cluny in preparation for the colloquium had already appeared in *Le Progrès* on June 20, 1949.[44]

On July 11th, the final day of the festivities, *L'Écho* of Lyon ran a story entitled "Les Fêtes de Cluny" as caption to a large photograph of a liturgical procession coming down the steps from the Musée Ochier through the marketplace [fig. 6.12].[45] *Le Petit Mâconnais* headed their story on the same day "Les fêtes abbatiales de Cluny."[46] The liberal paper *Le Progrès* ran two articles.[47] Neither was headline news, but the use of large and varying fonts made the coverage stand out. The text of the large banner on page one sets a definite mood of festivity: "CLUNY A CÉLÉBRÉ DANS L'ALLÉGRESSE saint Odon et saint Odilon qui firent de l'abbaye un foyer de civilisation" [fig. 6.11]. Roughly translated this would read: "Cluny cheerfully celebrated Saint Odo and Saint Odilo who made the abbey a hearth of civilization." The opening two paragraphs are in bold face and bring together wide appeals to nationalistic values associated with the site:

> Cluny! Center of worldwide radiance! Few cities in Europe have held equal place in the intellectual, artistic, and religious concerns of the previous six centuries.
>
> For us, from lower Burgundy, its name evokes a quiet little town crossed by the idyllic Grosne [river], set within a belt of gentle hills where woods crown the surrounding fields, but also [it evokes] one of the most dramatic and glorious episodes of the Résistance.[48]

The article continues with Cluny's claim to "one of the most enduringly rich spirits of the Middle Ages."[49] Reference to current work on the site was centered on the French authorities in this article. A shorter piece, further back in the paper, gave the report on Congrès and mentioned Conant.

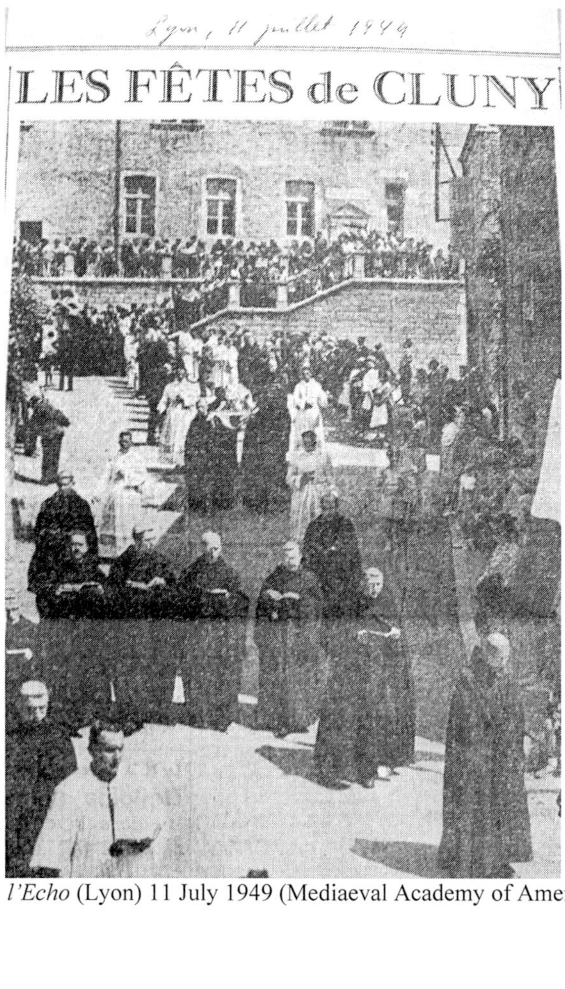

6.11 *l'Echo* (Lyon) 11 July 1949 (Mediaeval Academy of America)

The festivities had a broad appeal and reminded *Le Progrès*'s journalist of those held in 1910 for the millennial commemorations. On Sunday (the 10th), the town was lit, emphasizing key historical locations: the façade of Pope Gelasius fronting the eighteenth-century conventual buildings on the marketplace damaged in the bombardments of 1944; the Farinier tower, the abbey gardens, and the old parochial church of Notre-Dame "whose octagonal towers were set against the sky like [manuscript] miniatures of past times."[50] Large numbers of cars evidenced visitors from all the nearby departments. The journalist identified costumes donned by townspeople for this celebration as fifteenth-century. Tumblers and jugglers performed, spicing up their acts with jokes about anachronistic elements like the microphone on stage [fig. 6.12].

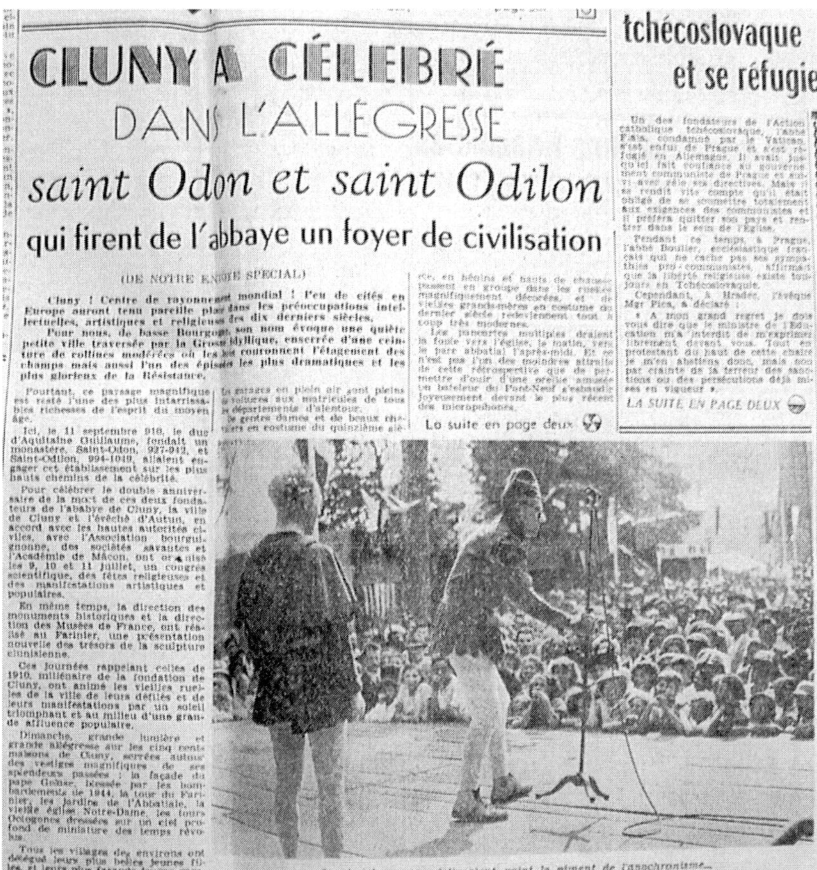

CLUNY A CÉLÉBRÉ DANS L'ALLÉGRESSE

saint Odon et saint Odilon

qui firent de l'abbaye un foyer de civilisation

(DE NOTRE ENVOYÉ SPÉCIAL)

Cluny ! Centre de rayonnement mondial ! Peu de cités en Europe auront tenu pareille place dans les préoccupations intellectuelles, artistiques et religieuses des dix derniers siècles.

Pour nous, de basse Bourgogne, son nom évoque une quiète petite ville traversée par la Grosne idyllique, enserrée d'une ceinture de collines modérées où les bois couronnent l'étagement des champs mais aussi l'un des épisodes les plus dramatiques et les plus glorieux de la Résistance.

Pourtant, ce paysage magnifique est resté l'une des plus intarrissables richesses de l'esprit du moyen âge.

Ici, le 11 septembre 910, le duc d'Aquitaine Guillaume, fondait un monastère. Saint-Odon, 927-942, et Saint-Odilon, 994-1049, allaient engager cet établissement sur les plus hauts chemins de la célébrité.

Pour célébrer le double anniversaire de la mort de ces deux fondateurs de l'ababye de Cluny, la ville de Cluny et l'évêché d'Autun, en accord avec les hautes autorités civiles, avec l'Association bourguignonne, des sociétés savantes et l'Académie de Mâcon, ont organisé les 9, 10 et 11 juillet, un congrès scientifique, des fêtes religieuses et des manifestations artistiques et populaires.

En même temps, la direction des monuments historiques et la direction des Musées de France, ont réalisé au Farinier, une présentation nouvelle des trésors de la sculpture clunisienne.

Ces journées rappelant celles de 1910, millénaire de la fondation de Cluny, ont animé les vieilles ruelles de la ville de leurs défilés et de leurs manifestations par un soleil triomphant et au milieu d'une grande affluence populaire.

Dimanche, grande lumière et grande allégresse sur les cinq cents maisons de Cluny, serrées autour des vestiges magnifiques de ses splendeurs passées : la façade du pape Gélase, blessée par les bombardements de 1944, la tour du Farinier, les jardins de l'Abbatiale, la vieille église Notre-Dame, les tours octogones dressées sur un ciel profond de miniature des temps révolus.

Tous les villages des environs ont délégué leurs plus belles jeunes filles, et leurs plus farauds jeunes gars.

Les garages en plein air sont pleins de voitures aux matricules de tous les départements d'alentour.

De gentes dames et de beaux chevaliers en costume du quinzième siècle, en hennins et hauts de chausses passent en groupe dans les rues magnifiquement décorées, et de vieilles grands-mères en costume du dernier siècle redeviennent tout à coup très modernes.

Les [illegible] multiples drainent la foule vers l'église, le matin, vers le parc abbatial l'après-midi. Et ce n'est pas l'un des moindres attraits de cette rétrospective que de permettre d'ouïr d'une oreille amusée un bateleur du Pont-Neuf s'esclaffer joyeusement devant le plus récent des microphones.

La suite en page deux

Les bateleurs ne négligeaient point le piment de l'anachronisme...

tchécoslovaque [illegible]

et se réfugie

Un des fondateurs de l'Action catholique tchécoslovaque, l'abbé [illegible], condamné par le Vatican, s'est enfui de Prague et s'est réfugié en Allemagne. Il avait jusqu'ici fait confiance au gouvernement communiste de Prague et suivi avec zèle ses directives. Mais il se rendit vite compte qu'il était obligé de se soumettre totalement aux exigences des communistes et il préféra quitter son pays et rester dans le sein de l'Église.

Pendant ce temps, à Prague, l'abbé Boulier, ecclésiastique français qui ne cache pas ses sympathies pro-communistes, affirmait que la liberté religieuse existe toujours en Tchécoslovaquie.

Cependant, à Hradec, l'évêque Mgr Pics, a déclaré :

« A mon grand regret je dois vous dire que le ministre de l'Education m'a interdit de m'exprimer librement devant vous. Tout en protestant du haut de cette chaire je m'en abstiens donc, mais non par crainte de la terreur des sanctions ou des persécutions déjà mises en vigueur ».

LA SUITE EN PAGE DEUX

6.12 *Le Progrès* (Mâcon) 11 July 1949 (Mediaeval Academy of America)

At 9 a.m., the bells of all the churches of Cluny pealed out, announcing the arrival of a procession of the bishop of Autun, priests, and monks from the Burgundian monastery of La-Pierre-qui-Vire (Yonne) for a high mass. The church of Notre-Dame, where this took place, was filled to overflowing. The visiting Benedictine monks chanted the liturgy and the bishop's secretary general gave a sermon about the two saints being honored that day: Odo and Odilo, "grand abbés de Cluny parmi les grands abbés". Following the services, a solemn procession led through the streets of Cluny "taking on a special character due to the setting"[51] where ten centuries earlier the very saints whose relics were being followed had themselves trod the same route. By 1949, nevertheless, one must imagine that this reenactment was becoming commonplace at such commemorations.

After the religious celebrations, it was time to inaugurate the new museum installed in the Farinier. In the upper room were set up some of the ambulatory capitals on column pieces, just as they remain today. The museum director gave a talk about the project while Paul Deschamps, director of the *Musée des monuments francais* in Paris, spoke on the altar exhibited there, identified as the one consecrated by Pope Urban II in 1095 when he had come to France to preach the first crusade [fig. 6.34]. A block of white marble veined in black, he said that it came from the Midi and was most probably made at Saint-Pons.

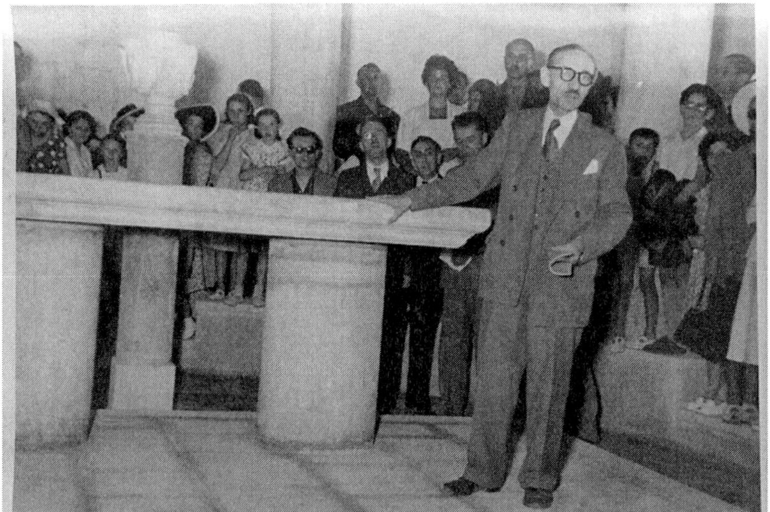

6.13 Deschamps lecturing in Farinier museum at Cluny, July 1949 (Cluny collection: Loeb Library, Harvard University)

Still on Sunday, at one in the afternoon, an official banquet was held inside the Farinier [fig. 6.14]. Francois Mitterrand, state secretary for information, appeared at the table of honor along with the mayor, the bishop, the inspector general of the Monuments historiques, a representative of the prefect's office, and assorted academics—including members of the French Academy and the Institute of France. Dr. Pleindoux welcomed the guests and gave thanks that the war had spared the "riches of Cluny" at the same time as it allowed new access to the framework of the site (referring to the bomb which exposed parts of the abbey that had been integrated into modern buildings). After thanking appropriate people, he stepped down and the president of the Académie de Mâcon spoke of the 1910 events and thanked "those who had helped bring Cluny out of her ruins,"[52] especially Jean Virey (organizer of the 1910 commemoration) and Joan Evans who had since saved the frescoed 11th-century chapel at Berzé-la-Ville for Cluny. The bishop got up and talked about the spiritual import of the observances. Finally, Monsieur Mitterrand spoke. He recalled the monks who had come to Cluny "to conquer the black country", a traditional reference to this forested valley of the Saône. "More of Cluny remains," he went on, "than the stones and a bell-tower, but also a civilization. Cluny knew the splendor, the distress, the state of being forgotten and soon her resurrection as people from all countries met to honor her; for [Cluny] did not belong to any one person but to all the world."[53]

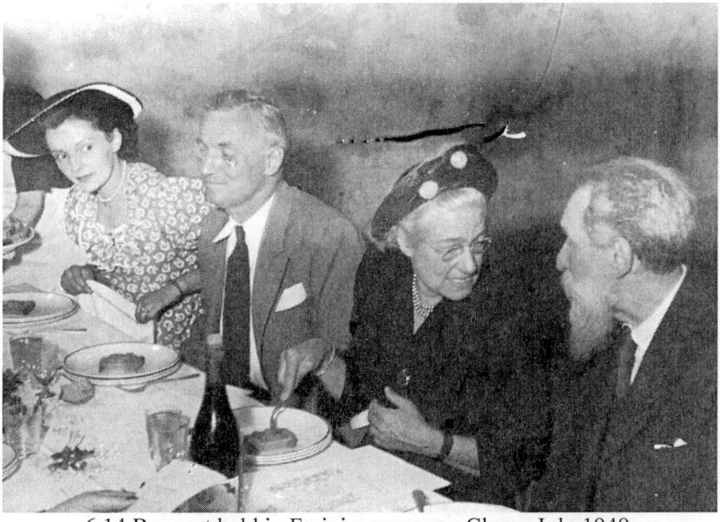

6.14 Banquet held in Farinier museum, Cluny, July 1949.
Conant is between the two women; Marcel Aubert is far right
(Cluny collection: Loeb Library, Harvard University)

The popular entertainment began at 2:00 p.m. in the gardens of the *mairie*, former abbatial palace of Jacques d'Amboise. Artisanal stands, decorated on a medieval theme, were set in a circle offering games, crafts, and refreshments [fig. 6.15]. The bazaar also offered a stage with medieval Parisian scenes enacted by costumed players. Five women demonstrated authentic Clunysois lacemaking techniques. The poetic journalist of *Le Progrès* remarked that during these events, a little airplane flew overhead, reminding participants of their own time.

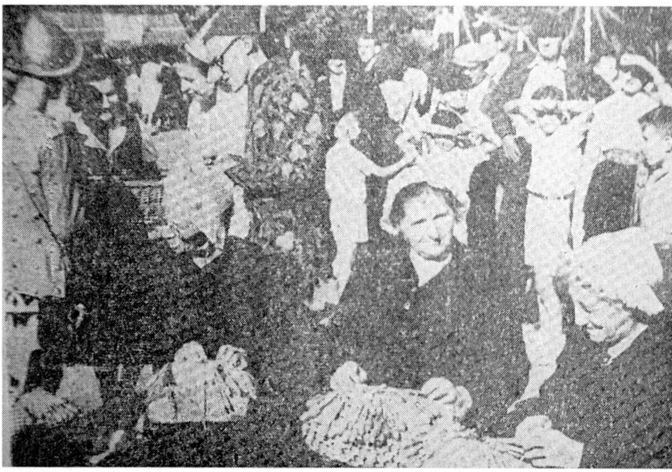

6.15 Women demonstrating Cluny lacemaking techniques, Cluny, July 1949 (*Le Progrès*, Mâcon)

The ubiquitous presence of the national *Haras* was not forgotten in this salute to Cluny's importance. Beginning at 6 p.m., a huge crowd gathered to watch a colorful parade of the most magnificent horses in France. The day ended with a show beginning at 9:00 p.m. in the open-air theatre at the foot of the Fabri Tower. A group from Paris presented two medieval street comedies "well placed in this setting rich with great memories."[54]

The fuller coverage of Cluny's event by *Le Progrès* is significant at a time when the government was again on the point of collapse. Ongoing struggles between the Communist and Socialist factions for control of the government after the Liberation were related to their role in the Resistance and their attitude toward the collaborationist Vichy. Cluny was a site that, as stated in the opening paragraph of the newspaper story cited above, stood for both a nineteenth-century version of national historical pride and the recent movements of the resistance.[55] Right on the line between the occupied and free zones, it had also been under the Vichy government until Germans moved in during 1942. *Le*

Progrès was a liberal, republican voice, highlighting Cluny's attempt to reclaim her place in French patrimony beyond standard regrets for destruction of religious sites toward recognition of the region's contemporary role in France.

As reported in the press, the 1949 festivities at Cluny thus incorporated the three elements of medieval society as understood during the eleventh century when Cluny was at its height, those who fight, pray, and work, into a modern setting.[56] The ruling class of the mid-twentieth century, politicians and academics, met at the Farinier and told each other about their work on the history of the site and the monastic order. With them were the clerics, hand in hand as in the Middle Ages, sharing their pride at administrative accomplishments. A Lyon radio station broadcast key speeches from the weekend on the following Monday. The religious celebrations reincorporated clerics into the life of the town—a theme since the re-Christianization of France under Napoléon. And the fair, open-air entertainers, and artisanal demonstrations were aimed at the general public. Of the newspaper coverage, it is interesting to note that the paper from Lyon chose to illustrate the events with two large photos of the liturgical procession and a detail of two academics while *Le Progrès*, a "journal république quotidien" showed two photos of the popular entertainment.

This uneasy alliance between the secular and religious spheres, similar to that of 1910 but with the added baggage of the recent Vichy behavior, was present from the very beginning. The *Comité d'honneur* for the event listed state functionaries, religious authorities, and scholars. Two presidents were named: the president of the Assemblée Nationale (Edouard Herriot) and the Archbishop of Lyon (Cardinal Gerlier). Only two members were from outside France: Conant and Evans (whose title awkwardly appeared as "Le Docteur Miss Joan Evans.")

Proceedings for the *Congrès* were again published, edited by Charles Oursel. Marcel Aubert presided and his introductory speech was printed in full. Overall, the presentations were of higher academic quality than those of 1910. Conant had brought much to light for study, and his theories had also presented a challenge to French scholars. Yet at this date, he was still surrounded by friends and supporters and his work was highlighted at the event [fig. 6.16]. No further sparks flew when A. Talobre read Joseph Talobre's submission on Odilon's sepulcher at Souvigny. That paper was part of the Art/Archeology section of the Congrès, which was introduced by Joan Evans speaking on Cluniac iconography.[57] Among others who contributed was the Benedictine scholar from Solesmes, Dom Hesbert, who reviewed the Cluniac liturgy relating to Odo. Raymond Oursel (son of Charles) sent a paper, read by Paul Deschamps, which claimed a date for Anzy-le-Duc before Vézelay, an idea to which Marcel Aubert objected. Louis Grodecki discussed the form of the transept of Cluny II, a talk that apparently generated a great deal of discussion among other participants. This section was planned to end well after the other two tracks of the Congress in order for everyone attending to hear the final presentation by Conant. He began by leading a tour around the site, explaining his plan of Cluny II based upon his excavations some twenty years earlier (relying heavily on the Farfa customary as well as on propositions by Alfred Clapham and acknowledging the Talobres' research). This was followed by an elaborate presentation in the auditorium of the engineering school where Conant chronicled his work at Cluny from 1927 to 1938, as well as the more recent interventions made from 1939 to 1949. Marcel Aubert graciously thanked Conant and paid tribute to his contributions to French archeology.[58]

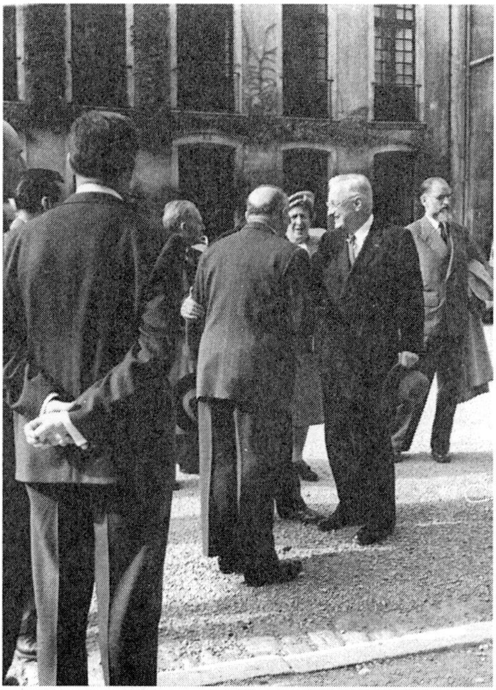

6.16 Kenneth Conant in Cluny during 1949 Congrès
(Cluny collection: Loeb Library, Harvard University)

Interesting work appears in the proceedings of the Congrès from the other two sections as well. Georges Duby, 30 years of age and at the beginning of his career, took from his thesis on the Mâconnais region during the eleventh and twelfth centuries for a paper on the city of Cluny in Odilon's time.

Although he must have presented in Section I, History, his participation is not recorded in the *Compte-Rendu* yet his paper is published in the proceedings. Others in this section, all either clergy or archivists, commented upon primary sources. Section II, Discipline and Administration, also included some important scholars such as Jean Leclercq who spoke on Odilo's ideal monastery. The introductory speech by Marcel Nicolle, secretary of the Academy of Mâcon, listed every time Cluny had been addressed by that society since 1818 and saluted the importance of the lost past of the abbey, much in the same manner as those eulogies given in 1910. These are not the papers that interested Conant in his review of the published volume for *Speculum* in 1954.[59] Rather, he praised Lemarignier's work on monastic exemption, Thomas on Odo and music, and those on the town's development where he highlighted the contribution of Jean Virey, who was honored for his long career as a scholar of Burgundian archeology.

Conant recorded work in nine pits during 1949, exploring evidence for structures other than the churches. He would open one more in the remaining south transept in 1950; it would be the last excavation work Conant would oversee at Cluny. His life was changing, moving beyond the narrow associations of the excavations at Cluny [fig. 6.17]. He had traveled in the eastern Mediterranean during 1938 and with a Rockefeller grant to South America in 1945. He served as exchange professor at the National University of Mexico in 1942, the University of Buenos Aires in 1947 and was renewed for another French exchange in 1950. In a tiny photograph of thirty-eight archeologists who visited Iran in 1955, Conant appears front and center, the only member seemingly fully aware of and posing for the camera.[60] He gave a series of lectures on architectural history at Johns Hopkins University in 1939, at the Archeological Institute of America in 1948-49, at Columbia in 1949-50 and at the University of Illinois in 1955. One lecture from 1947, on Benedictine contributions to church architecture given at St. Vincent College in Latrobe, Pennsylvania was published as a small book in 1949.[61] Of the thirty-eight pages, 14 concerned Cluny. This lecture was classic Conant and shows us how confident he was of his architectural history even as it was shaped around a personal vision. Likewise, the Foreword which introduced him as "an acknowledged authority", is representative of his effect on non-academics:

> Ripe scholarship and creative imagination enable Professor Conant to reconstruct edifices once glorious, now gone or existing only in ruins and traces. About the lofty vaults of these imaginary but authentic reconstructions he guides one with a graceful agility and surefootedness matched only by the charm with which he presents his discoveries.

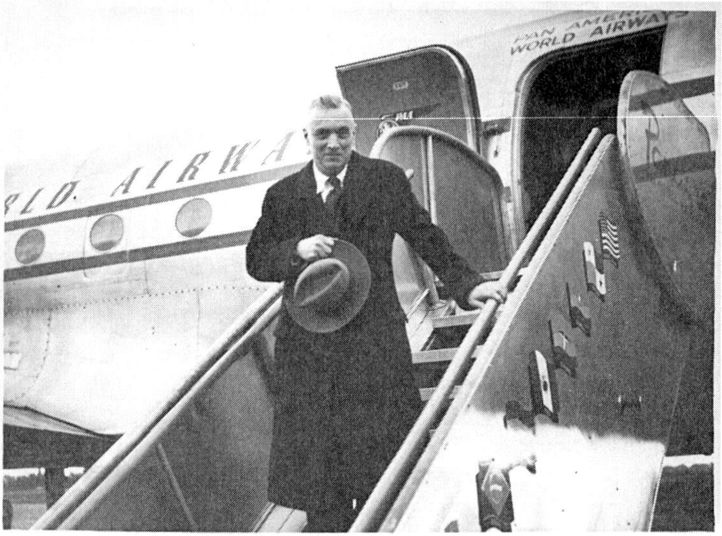

6.17 Kenneth Conant posing in front of Pan Am flight to South America, 1940s (Cluny collection: Loeb Library, Harvard University)

Conant also published more articles on Cluny including one in the Porter Memorial volume in 1939,[62] in the *Annales* of the Instituto de Arte Americano from 1952,[63] and in journals for both the French and American branches of the Society of Architectural Historians in 1957, as well as a note on medieval vaulting in the Gazette des Beaux-Arts of 1944[64] and two entries in the Encyclopedia Britannica on Byzantine and Romanesque architectures in 1957. Other interests bore fruit with publications on Early Christian churches in Jerusalem.[65] He wrote the important Pelican volume on Carolingian and Romanesque architecture 1951-1952 but complications with the plates delayed publication until 1959. It was a great success, earning Conant a medal from the Society for Architectural Historians, and finally gave him a solid reputation in art and architecture history.

In *Carolingian and Romanesque Architecture*, Conant treated Cluny as a central organizing element. It first appears in Chapter 7: France 900-1050 where he established the plan of Cluny II as a model. He then went on to treat Cluniac architecture in an independent chapter as a central source for the Romanesque style (Chapter 10: The Role of Cluny in the History of Romanesque Architecture). Conant wrote in an authoritative fashion, incorporating historical information from his research with proposed structural reconstructions of the monastery and presenting all as accepted fact. Influence from the nineteenth-century histories of Cluny and Jean Virey's art-historical publications (reviewed here in chapters 2 and 3) is apparent in his emphasis on Cluny’s papal privileges and hagiographic treatment of the most famous abbots. Underlying his discussion is the familiar regret for loss—loss of the main abbey, loss of the art of the dependencies, dilution of Cluniac architectural contributions by time and distance. He credited Joan Evans for her identification of all the extant Cluniac architecture and then, while denying the notion of a Cluniac “school” (as did Virey), went on to categorize the building types into five groups appearing across Europe. These types appeared to Conant as the culmination of Carolingian trends as well as the transition between “early Romanesque” and “mature Romanesque”, even as the model for later Cistercian building. He listed the proportions, structural details, sculpture, and innovations of the third abbey church with constant references to their preview of French Gothic accomplishments. Both before and after this point in the book, Conant’s discussions of the Romanesque style of architecture throughout Europe is constantly colored by its comparative basis of definition in Cluny.

Reviews of *Carolingian and Romanesque Architecture* were favorable. It was clear that Conant had first-hand knowledge of an enormous number of sites as well as excellent organization and consistent treatment of the plethora of examples. Authors acknowledged Conant’s focus on the monastic origins of the Romanesque, and bias towards Cluny, but most did not fault the book for it. While Peter Kidson, writing for the *Art News & Review* of London, was harsh overall about the premature conclusions in the text as well as “inordinate stress on Cluny,”[66] other reviewers were happy to reinforce Conant’s position. Moholy-Nagy, reviewing for *Progressive Architecture* December 1959, was grateful for the “[Romanesque’s] historic function as the mother lode of all subsequent architectural styles.”[67] The most telling review, however, is whether other scholars will incorporate the conclusions into their own work. For this, Wolfgang Braunfels’ *Abendländische Klosterbaukunst,* published in 1969 (and translated into English in 1972 as *Monasteries of Western Europe)* serves as the greatest compliment.

The Pelican volume should have given Conant confidence to complete the Cluny monograph, promised to the Mediaeval Academy so many years before. Another boost to Conant’s academic writing may have been when he married again in January 1956, this time to Isabel Pope, a scholar of medieval Spanish music. Her academic orientation seems to have encouraged Conant and he updates her on his writing progress in their correspondence. Pope brought more than an intellectual discipline to Conant, she also came from a wealthy family of lawyers in Chicago, Illinois, had taken her degrees at Radcliffe, and knew how to move among the elite circles at Harvard. They shared love of Spanish medieval culture, travel, and academic circles. She was producing her own academic studies during the years Conant was supposed to be working on the Cluny book and her letters encourage him to persevere. However, Conant also spent a year living in Washington DC while working at Dumbarton Oaks on Byzantine architecture and he visited the Middle East with a group of archeologists in 1955, going to Isfahan and Teheran, so he was most definitely not entirely focused on the task at hand with his Cluny *opus*.

Conant continued to visit France, giving lectures and visiting colleagues, helping with brochures and exhibition decisions about the finds at Cluny. At the end of the decade he worked with the fabricators of an elaborate 1/25th-scale model of the east end of the third abbey church, the Latapies of Paris, by preparing detailed drawings for them. He reported to the Mediaeval Academy in 1958 that his analysis of the modular system of the basilica was complete.[68] Reading these reports, one begins to sense a stalling tactic on Conant's part; he clearly preferred drawing to writing and networking with other scholars to working alone.

The town of Cluny petitioned the Beaux-Arts ministry to allow them some of the profits from entry fees to the sculpture exhibited from the abbey, arguing that as caretaker of the work, the city deserved recompense.[69] A favorable decision on this request awarded them forty percent of the income. Dr. Pleindoux went further as well, outlining the steps taken to develop tourism and hiring a conservator to reorganize the museum. For this he asked that the city be given fifty percent of the museum admissions for five years. This too was granted, reduced only in 1956 to forty percent.

André Sallez, Maurice Berry, and the mayors of Cluny kept estimates for repairs and exhibitions in front of the Monuments historiques throughout the 1950s and 1960s, reminding them in inspection reports of the importance of the site and the dangers of negligence. Conant's finds, drawings, and conclusions were often used to bolster arguments. The city pursued acquisition of buildings that had been built over the old nave and which, since the 1944 bombing had opened up this area, stood in the way of renovating the area around the remaining portions of the church.[70] To purchase these properties, the city utilized some demolition funds from the Interior Ministry and received additional support from the receipts of the entry fees taken by the *Caisse Nationale des Monuments historiques*. Even Conant put some Mediaeval Academy funds at the disposal of the project in 1956. In 1957, after giving permission for a widow, Mme. Dutrion, to rebuild her home on the bombed site near the Tour des Fromages, Maurice Berry, *architecte en chef* of the Monuments Historiques, was surprised to find that the wall adjoining her property was not the enclosure wall but rather the façade of a medieval building, complete with windows embrasures. He wrote to Sallez for assistance in finding an alternative site in Cluny for Mme. Dutrion's architect from Macon to build her house, believing that the archeological value of the exposed building was too important to miss. The affair was not easily resolved and dragged on until 1960 before the city succeeded in buying out Mme. Dutrion.

It was during the 1960s that Conant finally finished the monograph on the former Abbey of Cluny that he had proposed to the Mediaeval Academy of America in 1927. In French and published by the firm Protat Frères used by the Academy of Mâcon, it was in an impressive large format, filled with his drawings and reproductions of pre-Revolutionary images. Many grants underwrote the job since the Mediaeval Academy had secured publication assistance from the Carnegie Corporation, the Simon Guggenheim Memorial Foundation, and the American Council of Learned Societies. John Nicolas Brown was also still deeply involved as donor to the Cluny fund of the Mediaeval Academy and he corresponded with Conant about special copies for his family and friends.

Conant reviewed the primary sources at his disposal that gave information on the original form of the abbey. He reproduced old drawings and transcribed appropriate descriptive passages from Bouché de la Bertelière, Mabillon, the Farfa customary, and other private sources and charters. He then went on to recount the history of construction, dividing it according to abbacies much as he had done in English for the Pelican volume with added detail but in the same authoritative voice. The influence from Virey's model is again wholly evident. This section comprised less than ninety pages, though the text was set in two columns on tall pages thus equaling somewhat more than the standard. Appendices included dimensions and systems of measurement as well as a list of abbots—something easily available in most of the nineteenth-century publications. The remaining half of the book was taken up by the plates divided into eight groups: various abbey plans, views from 1617 to 1819, restoration studies by Conant of the monastery and final church, photos of extant parts, sculpture, and later buildings from the twelfth to nineteenth centuries. Throughout Conant's drawings analyze, enhance and reconstruct the evidence.

Reviews of this monumental project were mixed, at best. Robert Branner, then at Johns Hopkins, wrote for the *Art Bulletin* in 1973 (volume 53). Although grateful for and impressed by the quality of the drawings, he was critical of the act of faith involved—both by Conant in his deep devotion to Cluny and by the reader in following his conclusions. Branner found Conant's romanticizing long and his proof short, his elevations merely "conjectural" yet their presentation "vigorous" without clear warnings in the captions of their tentativeness.[71] He went so far as to call Conant's hypotheses about the modular construction of the basilica "unsupportable clairvoyance", following Francis Salet's concerns that no such huge medieval building was ever built in a single campaign over a single design. In the end, Branner felt that though Conant saw this work as the final word on Cluny it was really only a beginning and that the questions it raised would offer future generations many research problems. In this he was certainly correct.

Francis Salet had already posed even more difficult questions in the *Bulletin Monumentale* in 1969.[72] If, as the excavation plan on plate II shows, Conant did not open a pit in the Saint-Martial chapel area of the south transept, how could he know for sure that his reconstruction of its shape like the others, and unlike its fourteenth-century form that remains, was more than a desire for symmetry? In fact, regarding these excavations, Salet wished for more information than the three articles in Speculum from 1929, 1931, and 1954 offered. Instead he found that the great monograph still sent him back to Conant's original daybooks, deposited at the Musée Ochier, if he wanted to make a detailed analysis. Salet was also disappointed to find that the famous plan of Cluny III drawn by Frederic Palmer, so long awaited, was not reproduced on a large scale within this publication, otherwise so richly realized. On dating, Salet reached to his primary arguments with Conant. However, his concerns were justified by inconsistencies in Conant's own work, not just a stalemate on differences of opinion. He found that over the years, Conant had changed his dating of many parts of the great church and not just once but numerous times. And yet, similar to measurements that also varied, his presentation of the figures in this volume were treated definitively. Although some of Salet's points seem a bit petty, Conant's language, using terms like *sans doute* or *non...contesté*, certainly drew notice. Although Salet thanked Conant for providing transcriptions of inaccessible documents, such as the Dumolin description, he also asks for the presentation of other texts that served to support dating arguments (considered flimsy by Salet) such as those relating to the papal visit of 1095. Likewise, Salet questioned Conant's claims for the purpose of major donations based again upon dating discrepancies. He saw no basis anywhere for the reconstructions of the west façade and he would have liked to find more facts in the book. For instance, he thought that simple tests could have provided proof in lieu of suggestions for some of the building materials. His concerns over the lack of new information on the choir capitals and the lack of photographs of all their sides presented Conant as entrenched and impeding new scholarship. Ultimately, like Branner, Salet saw the work as fantasy mixed in with some archeological suggestions. At the end of his remarks on Cluny III he wrote: "As for Cluny III, archeologists should take care not to let too perfect an image of this vanished masterpiece impose itself and not to confuse reconstructions and reality, hypothesis and truth."[73]

What these authors were pointing out, and what Conant failed to accept, was that since he began his study in 1927 the academic world had changed. No longer could he live in the days of Berenson and Porter's peripatetic connoisseurship. The disciplines of art and architectural history had matured. Scholars wanted evidence, proof, accuracy, dry objectivity. The dedication and enthusiasm, which had kept Conant at his task and brought Cluny back to international notice, was valuable in the late 1920s, even in the early 1930s. But his excavation methods, his documentation, and his analyses were outdated by the 1960s. Thus the monograph, which would have been such a welcome contribution to study if it had appeared when he finished the excavations in 1938, was too late to offer more than a point from which to mine the controversies calling for further study.

Nevertheless, Conant continued to publish on Cluny throughout the 1970s, though making no major changes to any of his arguments (see complete bibliography of Conant's published works, as compiled by Minott Kerr, in Appendix A). In fact, most of his contributions seem to have been written in the defensive mode. A direct response to Salet appeared in *Monumentum* 75 (1971) where the title, "The History of Romanesque Cluny as Clarified by Excavations and Comparisons" could as easily substitute "justified" for the word "clarified". As is usual for his publications, the text is not long; Conant preferred to make his case through drawings. However, here he reproduced many already quite familiar and supported his reasoning for their appearance primarily through the "careful study of analogous buildings", many of which were already themselves the product of Conant's reconstructive conjecture. The dating for the east end of Cluny III returned to rely upon his personal sense that Abbot Hugh would have needed a larger space sooner rather than later for the increased size of the monastic congregation. In other ways his very defense suggested the weakness of his facts—much is made of the Mediaeval Academy "team" from Harvard, of the professional training in archeology, architecture, and engineering necessary to fully understand the conclusions (implying, of course, that Salet had none of these). He repeated excuses for the late appearance of the monograph with reference to the long period of technical study necessary after the excavations were completed. His excavation notes, donated to the Musée Ochier and referred to in this article as "our Day Books" are recommended for use by "learned visitors" who will "instantly see" why it was inconvenient to reproduce something on a scale of 1:100, thus implying that Salet was either not learned or had refused to consult such a rich resource, donated to France. In fact, in this article, Conant employed the royal "we" for all references to his work—even the monograph, linking himself to the greater authoritative body of the Mediaeval Academy "team", mostly Conant's own students from Harvard and Radcliffe.

An earlier publication of this old argument appeared in a review Conant had written in 1957 for *Speculum* on Raymond and A.-M. Oursel's work, *Les Eglises romanes de l'Autunois et du Brionnais.*[74] There he was still fresh in the fray and turned nearly the entire book review into a tirade on his position. It is a telling little article. He introduced the debate by claiming that

Jean Virey was forced by his professors in 1888 to ascribe later dates for churches in the region of Cluny, labeling it "post-dating documentary evidence…the besetting sin of the Parisian school." He went on:

> When in 1920 Arthur Kingsley Porter proposed an earlier system of dates, and with the support of documentary evidence proposed to recognize Cluny as the key to artistic problems of the High Romanesque style, his ideas were rejected, and the oldsters persuaded one of the younger art historians (so I am told on unimpeachable authority) to publish a refutation on conventional lines. Another refutation was published when my articles began to appear, strengthening Mr. Porter's thesis. The accepted system was based unimaginatively on the idea of small and regular increments of capability as the key to progress in the arts. It had little or no place for the wonderful, unpredictable surges of aesthetic power and inspiration which really do bring about the great achievements in the fine arts, producing monuments which are far superior—of course!—to their exact contemporaries.

Charles Oursel's *L'Art roman de Bourgogne* (1928) is included in Conant's comment that "those who understood Cluny, and believed in the culmination that occurred there at the end of the eleventh century, failed to persuade the Parisians, and were obliged to retire from the battlefield and sharpen their weapons." The review thus offers Conant the opportunity to show how thirty years down the road "a new generation in Romanesque studies" was coming around with Oursel's son and daughter-in-law carrying the torch for Burgundy.[75]

As well, two book reviews written in 1976 and 1977 show that whether Conant liked someone's work or not had a lot to do with how they had treated Cluny. In 1976 he reviewed the translation of Wolfgang Braunfels' *Abendlândische Klosterbaukunst* for the *Art Bulletin*.[76] As mentioned above, Braunfels drew heavily on Conant's work, though he published before the Cluny monograph was available. For this reason, among others carefully cited in the review, Conant liked Braunfels' book. Nevertheless, he could not resist the opportunity to correct Braunfels' mistaken caution about restoration drawings and took issue with the line "all the efforts of Conant do not suffice to reduce [Cluny] to artistic reality." This was certainly an innocent enough remark, in the light of a fragmentary ruin and reasonable academic standards. However, it went to the heart of Conant's identity with Cluny. He believed that his mission, and the best use of his talents, was to do exactly that—bring it back to artistic reality. Saying that any limitations Braunfels encountered in Conant's preliminary publications were "dissipated in the Cluny monograph," Conant pointed out that some of his newer reconstructions, based upon "the canons of classical archeology" studied at Cluny over fifty years, were borrowed for the English translation in 1972. He also included another of his drawings, this of

Montecassino, as an illustration of the improvement a restoration drawing makes over one from nineteenth century sources.[77]

The next year, Conant wrote a review of Hans Erich Kubach’s *Romanesque Architecture.*[78] This work did not fare so well in Conant’s account. Less than two columns long, still half of Conant’s review was about Cluny. Conant admired Kubach’s ability to treat the German Romanesque and he appreciated the high quality illustrations, however he feels that Speyer is championed at the cost of Cluny. Kubach is cited for failing to mention the four abbot-saints of Cluny and their great work, as well as for the lack of any illustrations of this abbey. He justifies this stance in absolute terms: “[Cluny] introduced the pointed arch into monumental church architecture…the apse had the first extensive medieval sculptural allegory, and the great portal—the first on a grand scale…actually triggered the fabulous series of portals at Moissac, Vézelay, Autun and the rest.” Ultimately, Kubach’s book could not stand as a valid study of Romanesque architecture because, Conant wrote, “it is impossible to know the full potentialities of the study without understanding [Cluny’s] great design.”

Conant was showered with honors and recognition for his efforts at Cluny. In 1948, the street covering the nave of the former abbey church at Cluny, running alongside the Hotel de Bourgogne and toward the transept ruin, was named “Rue Kenneth John Conant” by the town [figs. 6.18]. He was presented with the *Légion d’honneur* in 1966 [fig. 6.19]. The French Academy of Architecture gave him their silver medal in archeology in 1972 and he received the Haskins Medal in the same year from the Mediaeval Academy of America. In 1974, he presented a program on Cluny for French television, taking viewers on an imaginary visit with the help of a maquette of the abbey church.[79] Conant spent happy visits at Cluny for his 70th, 75th, and 80th birthdays, fêted by his friends and supporters and still the subject of local newspaper articles.[80] The love the Burgundians felt for him was real and is best summed up in the dedication written by Roland Martin for a volume of essays offered to his honor in 1977:

> This volume in honor of K.J. Conant constitutes a gesture of esteem and admiration towards the passionate master of the Cluniac resurrection. It is also the evidence of a brilliant and rich renewal of regional scholarship and an act of faith [in this fresh topic] on the part of its contributors.[81]

Conant died in 1984 at the age of 89 with, according to a conversation recorded by Peter Fergusson, Cluny still figuring large in his imagination.[82]

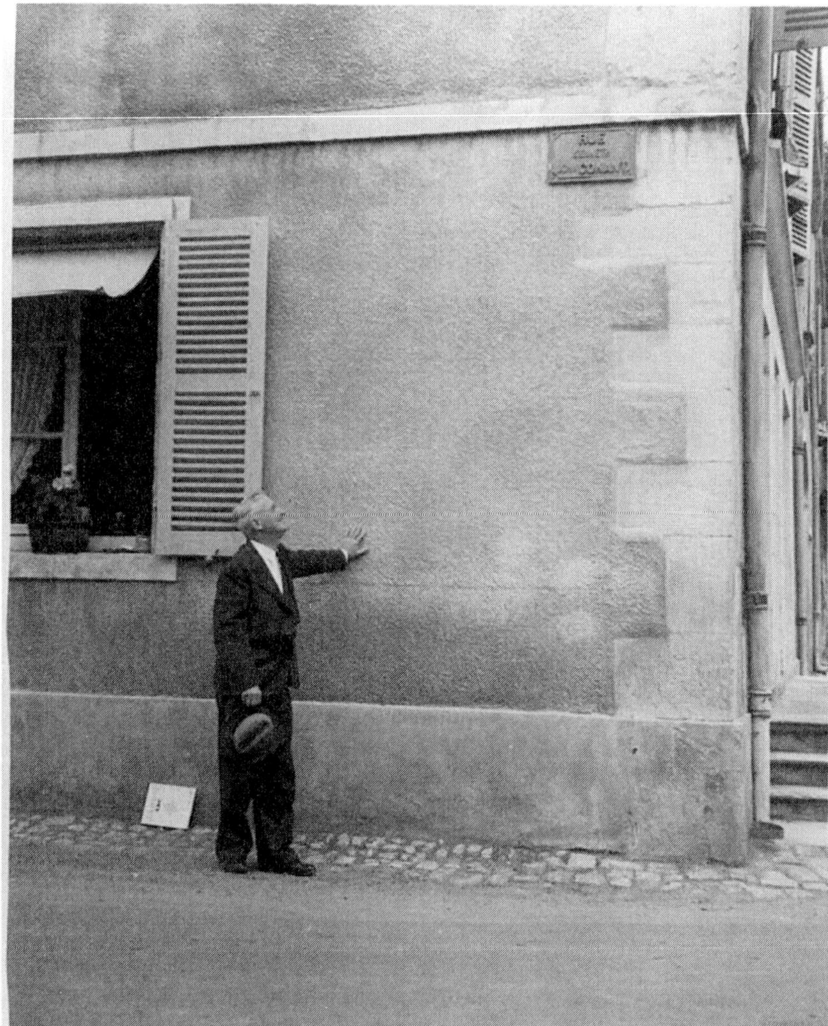

6.18 Conant looking at the sign of street named after him in Cluny, 1948 (Cluny collection: Loeb Library, Harvard University)

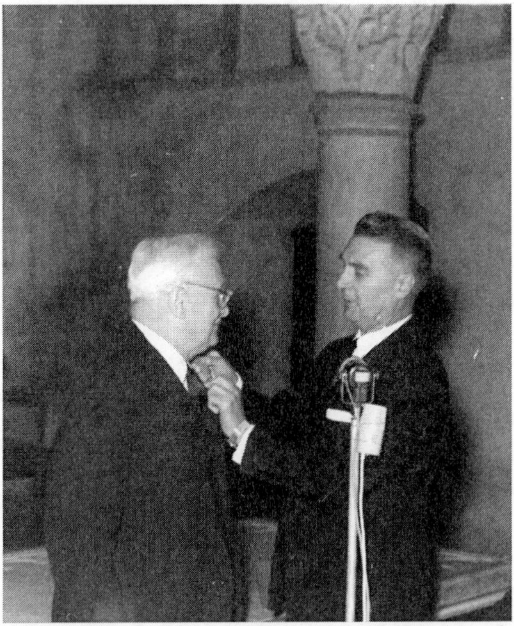

6.19 Conant receiving the French Legion of Honor from the prefect of the Saône-et-Loire in the Farinier museum, 1966 (Cluny collection: Loeb Library, Harvard University)

Many of Conant's plans of the monastery and elevations of the churches are now being rethought in the light of continuing excavations by French archeological teams. They have published reports on their finds and recently (2003) Anne Baud's book, *Cluny: Un grand chantier médiéval au coeur de l'Europe,* has collected all this material and appeared as part of the series *Espaces Mediévaux* (Picard). In her work, she carefully retraces the building history of the abbey and, along the way, shows where Conant was mistaken.[83] With the distance of time, she is able to sift through the written and drawn materials, finding the true contributions made by the Mediaeval Academy project and making kinder treatment of Conant.

Conclusions

Kenneth Conant was working at a time when the monographic presentation of data, "one building at a time", to quote Michael Davis, was *de rigueur* for an architectural historian.[84] He was expected to report on his inspection of the site and, using comparative buildings, make suggestions for chronology. We know that Conant spent a great deal of time traveling to and studying other monuments, this much is clear from his letters to his parents as well as the theories and drawings published in his *Carolingian and Romanesque Architecture.* He also made a review of the available documents when he began by visiting the Bibliothèque Nationale for old plans and reading the two journals of Bertelière written during the revolutionary period held in the museum at Cluny. In this way, a circular method determining Cluny's centrality was pursued. On the one hand, Conant traveled all around France to both small and large Romanesque churches, particularly Cluniac dependencies, in search of models for all the elements missing from the basilica he was attempting to reconstruct at Cluny [fig. 6.20]. He took a tower from here, the ambulatory from there, and, justifying their use as coming from architectural directives of the motherhouse, compiled them pastiche fashion to fit the measurements and archaeological evidence at Cluny. Then, in turn, he extrapolated Porter and Mâle's notion of Romanesque sculpture's indebtedness to Cluny by saying that Romanesque church architecture shows a dependence upon Cluny as an *ur*-model and innovator. Since his drawings of Cluny II and III were made up of references to most existing Cluniac ecclesiastical buildings, this was easy to prove![85]

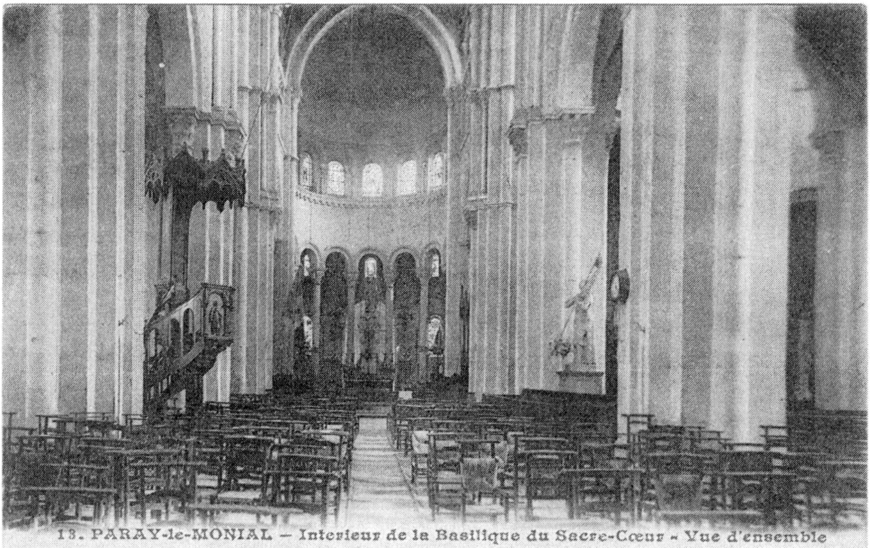

6.20 Postcard showing choir of Paray-le-Monial abbey church which Conant used as a model to help recreate the larger east end of Cluny III (Author)

Travel also made possible comparative analyses that allowed Conant to project reconstructions of the earlier stages of other buildings in the detailed drawings he published in the successful Pelican volume. These drawings, as well as the photographs he took of the original buildings and the postcards he collected, were the core material of his masterful history of architecture courses at Harvard. The writing style in the Pelican text surely reflects his lecture style—assured, wide-ranging, and filled with architectural terms. In fact, Conant published the first catalog of modern architecture for classroom use in a collection of *University Prints* in 1930. The collection offered a clear presentation of the seventeenth- and eighteenth-century origins of American architecture in European models and the importance of recognizing the role of revivals in shaping architectural forms since the end of the Gothic period. He picked structures in an eclectic and innovative fashion, including designers whose work would be considered outside the narrow "canon of modernism" that developed around the concept of functionalism in the 1940s. Conant also pioneered the first course on Native American architecture that covered cultures from South and Central America as well as the southwestern United States. In all, his efforts brought American work to American students in a way that had never been done previously.

During the 1930s, Joseph Hudnut, who was dean of the newly named Graduate School of Design, restructured the architectural training program to place more emphasis on modern innovations free from references to past styles.[86] Conant's courses on the history of architecture were cut back and then moved to the Department of Fine Arts and Fogg Museum in 1936. In 1937, Hudnut brought Walter Gropius to Harvard, making Conant's comprehensive presentation of historical models seem even more outdated.

Nevertheless, the art history classroom since Conant has owed much to his lead. He stressed showing the original building whenever possible, for instance in examples of American references to European models. But more importantly, he used his architectural drafting skills to produce original plans and elevations for buildings that no longer existed or had been obscured by changes. He made dozens of these drawings for his Pelican volume, often adapting those made by others with corrections, and took on larger studies for major works such as St. Peter's in Rome or Hagia Sophia in Kiev. Compared to the lantern slide projections of contemporary photographic records of these monuments being used in other classrooms in his day, Conant's analytical studies—even if sometimes based upon questionable data—were clear and engaging for student viewers.

By the time Conant's monograph on Cluny came out in 1968 he was retired from teaching, most of the conclusions were passé, and the controversies he stimulated had given higher marks to other scholars such as Francis Salet.

Conant's strength was never along the lines of the intellectual investigations that Mâle and Porter undertook nor the consideration of scientific versus aesthetic approaches. For Conant was an enthusiast, taking Porter's dictate to see the beauty in medieval art to heart, and adopting any method—scientific or otherwise—that would help him reconstruct his Romantic vision of historical religious structures. He equated the creative genius of the medieval master-builder with that of modern architects and was so charismatic in his presentations that his students still tell me how fully entertained they were during lectures.[87] Many of these students were invited to work at Cluny [fig. 6.21] or help with drawings and maquettes back in Cambridge and the interest their participation generated, along with those others who were the recipients of Conant's generous sharing of his material, helped develop methods of teaching art history in the United States which are still employed today.

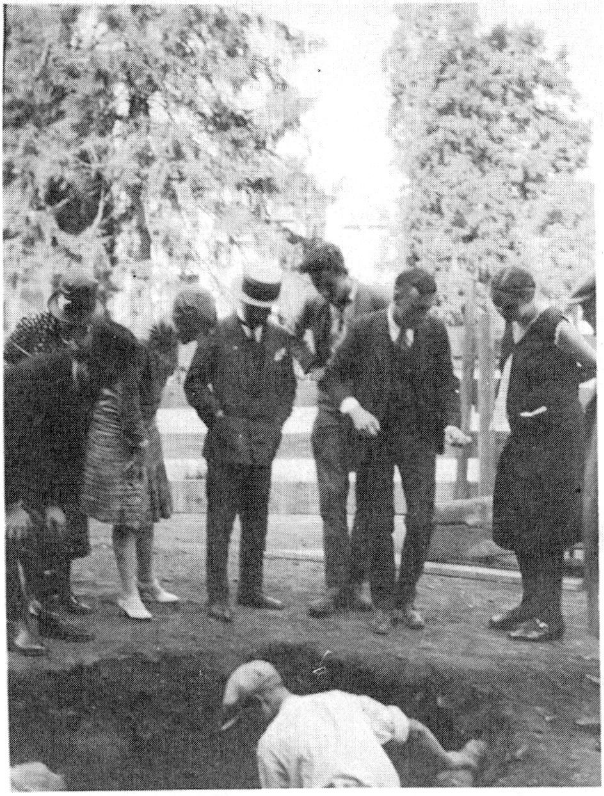

6.21 Radcliffe and Harvard students at Cluny with Conant during the early 1930s (Cluny collection: Loeb Library, Harvard University)

What Conant did not do, and which could have made all the difference by the time his monograph came out, is keep up with contemporary scholarship in his field. Although he certainly knew about publications, and even reviewed a few, he does not seem to have been interested in newer trends in architectural investigation that were moving away from the mere physical analysis and toward broader readings of the cultural setting.[88] When "social art history" and Marxist analyses of contextual factors strengthened in academic popularity during the 1970s, Conant's dry and laborious comparative reconstructions were of little interest and his methods passé for the moment. Yet the value of Conant's drawings remained because they were repeatedly used in the classroom and reproduced in publications by both admirers and detractors. Whether or not his reconstructions were always correct, they were certainly always impressive. Seducing the viewer into a world he treasured, the serene and erudite monastic Middle Ages imagined by Conant and his teachers, these drawings came to enrich the teaching of Mediaeval art in the United States precisely as Salet had both predicted and feared. Their ubiquity, in the absence of viable alternatives and with the enthusiastic reception by so many of his students teaching art history to the next generation, formed a popular vision of Cluny that entered the canon. As Eliseo Vernon remarked in 1979 about televised information, they were "images that will remain in the memory and will ensure the homogenization of the social imagination."[89]

Notes

[1] Undated letter. Pusey Library, Harvard University: HUG (FP) 21.5 Box 1, Conant file

[2] […Mr. Kenneth John Conant…told me, in August 1929, that one could find, at Cluny, more than 250 photographs or illustrated postcards of the old monuments, and he planned to make many more.] Louis Henri Champly and René Champly, Histoire de l'abbaye de Cluny, 3. éd. (Paris: Librairie centrale des sciences, 1930). "Avertissement pour cette troisième edition" n.p.

[3] Kenneth John Conant, "Medieval Academy Excavations at Cluny: The Season of 1928," *Speculum* 4 (1929).

[4] Ibid. 3-4.

[5] Ibid. 4.

[6] Ibid. 4.

[7] Quoted in Janet Flanner, *Men and monuments* (New York: Harper, 1957).13

[8] Quoted from Conant's report to Mediaeval Academy for July 1929. Mediaeval Academy office, Cambridge MA.

[9] Kingsley Porter disappeared in mysterious circumstances off the coast of Ireland in 1933. It was assumed that he accidentally drowned, but alternative theories have since been proposed. See: Hilary Richardson, "The Fate of Kingsley Porter," *Donegal Annual* 45 (1993).

[10] Letter from KJC dated August 29, 1970: "The casts were made as my study material, and have so served in Cambridge and in South Hadley [at Mt. Holyhoke]. Since they have now served their purpose, they are, from the point of view of the grants, surplus items of which I may dispose as I wish, for good purposes. I offer these casts to Mount Holyhoke College as a gift. If the College cannot use them, I bespeak the aid of the College in finding a place where they will be useful, and I will concur in any reasonable situation." (KJC underline). Letters from May, 1937 between Conant and Sachs. Fogg Museum archives, Harvard University.
[11] David Walsh, "The Excavations of Cluny III by K.J. Conant." *Actes du Colloque scientifique international "Gouvernement d'Hugues de Semur à Cluny", Musée Ochier, Cluny 1988*. (Mâcon: Buguet-Comptour, 1990). 319
[12] Paris, Bibliothèque du Patrimoine: Cote 81/71, 181/1, Box 17
[13] Report to the Mediaeval Academy Council for April, 1932, p 2. Mediaeval Academy office, Cambridge MA.
[14] 16 mai 1931. Paris, Bibliothèque du Patrimoine: Cote 81/71, 181/1, Box 17
[15] "...une placque [sic] en plomb inscrite avec le nom de l'illustre abbé épouse la forme du fond du sarcophage et protège un dépôt azoté, gras de cadavre présumé selon l'analyse du pharmacien inspecteur et de première classe M. Léon Daclin de Cluny." Daclin wrote a series of articles entitled "Double Tentative de Sauvegard de la cy-devant Abbaye de Cluny et de son Église," in *Le Petit Clunysois* during 1932 (2 February to 9 April) bringing to light the early nineteenth century documents that showed the process of destruction and preservation at Cluny in order to follow up on Chavot's criticism of Lorain and vindicate the townspeople against accusations that they destroyed their great monument.
[16] Report to the Mediaeval Academy Council for April, 1932. Mediaeval Academy office, Cambridge MA.
[17] Letter of 11 February, 1931. Paris, Bibliothèque du Patrimoine: Cote 81/71, 181/1, Box 17
[18] Letter from Paul Sachs, 1935. Cluny Collection, Francis Loeb Library, Harvard University: Box 4
[19] Cluny Collection, Loeb Special Collections, Harvard University: Box 31
[20] According to his son, John (Brother Gregory) in interviews January, 2003 and May, 2004 at St. Benedict Abbey, Still River, Massachusetts.
[21] November 11, 1933 report to Mediaeval Academy. Held in Mediaeval Academy office, Cambridge MA.
[22] Letter on series of postcards. Cluny Collection, Francis Loeb Library, Harvard University: Box 10
[23] 8 March, 1939 memo to the Executive Committee. Mediaeval Academy office, Cambridge MA.
[24] January 1, 1940 report to Mediaeval Academy. Mediaeval Academy office, Cambridge MA.
[25] Joan Evans, *Prelude and Fugue: An Autobiography* (London: Museum Press Limited, 1964). 134-135
[26] Letter without date. Pusey Library, Harvard University: HUG (FP) 21.5 Box 1, Joan Evans file. [All the letters in these files have lost their envelopes. Since Evans did not put

the year in her heading dates, without the postmarked envelopes one can only date them by context.]

[27] Evans, *Prelude and Fugue: An Autobiography*. 51

[28] Letter dated 7 May "and looks like Eve of VE Day". Pusey Library, Harvard University: HUG (FP) 21.5 Box 1, Joan Evans file.

[29] The photograph was made in 1988 by Gérard Regnier of the former abbey church outline. It is reproduced in M. Koob, *Cluny: Architektur als Vision,* Editions Braus, 1994, plate 25, page 62. No one seems to know who owns the copyright.

[30] "L'abbaye de Cluny cherche à se rendre visible" *Le Monde*, 1 July 2006, page 25; "Abbaye de Cluny: Bientôt 1100 ans!" *La Gazette de Cluny* 88 (December 2005).

[31] "Le croisillon sud du transept, visité annuellement par de nombreux touristes et archéologues, attirés par la renommée mondiale d [sic] l'ancienne abbaye, présent un aspect déplorable qui soulève des réflexions regrettables, un badigeon jaunâtre recouvre les maçonneries et les pierres de taille, les enduits tombent partiellement. »

Le sol est recouvert d'une chape en béton de ciment défoncée par endroits." Report of Gélis to Monuments historique, project outline with photo, 2 Decembre 1937. Paris, Bibliothèque du Patrimoine: Cote 81/71, 181/1, Box 17

[32] "Dans la suite, l'intérieur devrait être aménagé pour recevoir les plans de l'abbaye, pour rendre plus vivants aux yeix [sic] des visiteurs les restes encore visibles de l'ancienne abbaye." Ibid.

[33] January 1, 1941 report to Mediaeval Academy. Mediaeval Academy office, Cambridge MA.

[34] January 1, 1942 report to Mediaeval Academy. Mediaeval Academy office, Cambridge MA.

[35] Raymond Anthony Jonas, *France and the cult of the Sacred Heart: an epic tale for modern times*, Studies on the history of society and culture 39 (Berkeley: University of California Press, 2000). Raymond Anthony Jonas, *The tragic tale of Claire Ferchaud and the Great War* (Berkeley: University of California Press, 2005). 158-159

[36] June 26, 1945 letter from KJC Sr. to KJC Jr. (apparently undelivered). Cluny Collection, Francis Loeb Library, Harvard Design School, Box 3

[37] These descriptions come from a report with accompanying photographs and a plan by André Sallez, the chief architect for the Monuments historique sent to the Education Minister 20 December 1944. Paris, Bibliothèque du Patrimoine: Cote 81/71, 181/2, Box 18

[38] Sallez sent a letter to a Monsieur Martineau on January 16, 1947 that since the new street had been pierced, it was apparent that his chimney was blackening stones on this beautiful twelfth-century building and would not be tolerated. He was ordered to revamp his system immediately or the Monuments historiques would intervene. Sallez also got the Service des Ponts et Chaussées to move a large transformer that had been adjacent to the *Écuries.* Paris, Bibliothèque du Patrimoine: Cote 81/71, 181/2, Box 18

[39] In 1959 the interior staircase was replaced to allow visitors access to the view from its summit.

[40] 24 Oct 1949—31 Oct 1950. Paris, Bibliothèque du Patrimoine: Cote 81/71, 181/2, Box 18

[41] Letter dated 18 June. Harvard University archives, HUG (FP) 21.5 Box 1, Joan Evans file.
[42] Janet Flanner and William Shawn, *Paris journal*. [1st] ed. (New York,: Atheneum, 1965). 98-122
[43] "Cluny a célébré," *Le Progrès*: *Journal Républicain Quotidien*, Lundi, 11 Juillet 1949.
[44] "M. Conant, illustre archéologue américain est arrivé à Cluny," *Le Progrès*, Jeudi, 30 Juin 1949.
[45] "Les Fêtes de Cluny," *l'Écho*: *La Liberté*, Lundi, 11 Juillet 1949.
[46] "Les fêtes abbatiales de Cluny," *Le Petit Mâconnais*, Lundi 11 Juillet 1949.
[47] "Cluny a célébré." "Les fêtes du Millénaire," *Le Progrès* 1949.
[48] "Cluny! Centre de rayonnement mondial! Peu de cités en Europe auront tenu pareille place dans les préoccupations intellectuelles, artistiques et religieuses des dix derniers siècles.

"Pour nous, de basse Bourgogne, son nom évoque une quiète petite ville traversée par la Grosne idyllique, enserrée d'une denture de collines modérées où les bois couronnent l'étagement des champs mais aussi l'un des épisodes les plus dramatiques et les plus glorieux de la Résistance."
[49] "Pourtant, ce paysage magnifique est resté l'une des plus intarissables richesses de l'esprit du moyen âge."
[50] …les tour Octogones dressées sur un ciel profond de miniature des temps révolus."
[51] "…une procession solennelle qui revêtit un caractère tout particulier du fait du cadre dans lequel il se déroulait."
[52] "…et a fait l'apologie de ceux qui sortirent Cluny de ses ruines…"
[53] "Enfin, M. Mitterrand, secrétaire d'État à l'Information, rappela que les moines sont venus à Cluny pour conquérir le Pays Noir."
"Il reste Cluny, dit-il, plus que des pierres, un clocher, mais une civilisation. Cluny a connu la splendeur, la détresse, l'oubli et bientôt la résurrection, car des hommes de tous les pays se réunissent pour le célébrer car il n'appartient à personne, mais à tout le monde.
[54] "…bien à leur place dans ce cadre riche des plus grands souvenirs."
[55] On the reverse of the page recounting Cluny's festival in *Le Progrès* (page 3) is an article on the bestowal of the *croix de guerre* on the nearby town of Montceau-les-Mines for bravery and sacrifice in the Resistance from 1940-1945.
[56] It appears the first reference to these three divisions was by Aelfric, an English monk, in the tenth century. It was picked up and formalized 1023-1025 in response to the Truce of God by Adalbero of Laon and Gerard of Cambrai. See: *Georges Duby, The three orders : feudal society imagined* (Chicago: University of Chicago Press, 1980).
[57] Societe des Amis de Cluny, ed., *A Cluny: Congrès Scientifique. Fêtes et cérémonies en l'honneur des saints Abbés Odon et Odilon 9-11 Juillet 1949* (Dijon: Imprimerie Bernigaud & Privat, 1950).
[58] Ibid. 22
[59] Kenneth John Conant, "Société des Amis de Cluny, ed., *A Cluny: Congrès Scientifique. Fêtes et cérémonies en l'honneur des saints Abbés Odon et Odilon 9-11 Juillet 1949*," *Speculum* 29, no. 1 (January, 1954).
[60] "U.S. Archeologists Arrive In Iran," *The Tehran Journal* 1, #246 (March 17, 1955)

[61] Kenneth John Conant, *Benedictine Contributions to Church Architecture*, Wimmer Lecture, 1947 (Latrobe, Pennsylvania: The Archabbey Press, 1949).
[62] K. J. Conant, "The Third Church at Cluny," *Mediaeval Studies in Memory of A. Kingsley Porter*, ed. W. Koehler, Harvard University Press, 1939. 327-338
[63] K.J. Conant, "El monasterio de Cluny en Borgoña," *Annales del Instituto de Arte Americano e Investigaciones Esteticas* 5 (1952). 11-20
[64] "Observations on the vaulting problems of the period 1088-1211," *Gazette des Beaux-Arts* juillet-decembre,1944. 127-134
[65] "Holy sites at Jerusalem in the first and fourth centuries AD," *American Philosophical Society Proceedings* 102, 1 (1958). 14-24; with Glanville Downey, "The Original Buildings at the Holy Sepulcher in Jerusalem," *Speculum* XXXI, 1 (1956)
[66] Peter Kidson, "Advancing Backwards in Time," *Art News & Review* (London), 12 September 1959. Cluny Collection, Loeb Library, Harvard University: Box 23
[67] Sibyl Moholy-Nagy, "The Mother Lode of Western Styles," *Progressive Architecture,* December 1959. Typewritten copy. Cluny Collection, Loeb Library, Harvard University: Box 23.
[68] April 18, 1958 report to Mediaeval Academy. Mediaeval Academy office, Cambridge MA. Conant continued to submit reports as long as his position as Research Associate in Archeology was renewed.
[69] Letters from R. Perchet, Director of Architecture at the Secrétariat d'Etat aux Beaux-Arts, Bureau des Travaux et Classements, 20 November 1951 and 10 April 1952. Paris, Bibliothèque du Patrimoine: Cote 81/71, 181/2, Box 18
[70] Maurice Berry, architecte en chef, in his letter to Perchet 5 July 1956 refers to these later buildings as "constructions parasites".
[71] Robert Branner, "K. J. Conant, Cluny, Les églises et la maison du chef d'ordre," *Art Bulletin* 53 (1973). 248
[72] Francis Salet, "Kenneth John Conant, Cluny, Les églises et la maison du chef d'ordre," *Bulletin Monumentale* 127, no. 2 (1969). 183-186
[73] "Comme pour Cluny II, les archéologues devront prendre garde de ne pas se laisser imposer une image trop précise du chef-d'oeuvre disparu et de ne pas confondre restitutions et réalité, hypothèse et vérité." Ibid. 185
[74] Kenneth John Conant, "Raymond and A.-M. Oursel, Les Églises romanes de l'Autunois et du Brionnais (ancien grand archidiaconé d'Autun)," *Speculum* 32, no. 4 (Oct., 1957).
[75] Oursel, referring to this argument, places Porter, Conant, and himself on one side with Paul Deschamps and Francis Salet on the other, in Raymond Oursel, *Invention de l'architecture romane* ([La Pierre-qui-Vire]: Zodiaque, 1970). 112
[76] Kenneth John Conant, "Wolfgang Braunfels, Monasteries of Western Europe," *Art Bulletin* LVIII, no. 2 (1976). 287-88
[77] Ibid. fig. 1, page 288
[78] Kenneth John Conant, "Hans Erich Kubach, Romanesque Architecture," *Journal of the Society of Architectural Historians* 36 (1977). 44
[79] Sunday, 10 February, 1974 at 1:30 p.m. on Channel 2. The maquette was made to Conant's order by the Latapies in Paris and kept in the Farinier museum.

[80] For instance, on the occasion of Conant's seventieth birthday, both *L'Echo* (22 June 1964) and *Le Progrès* (5 June 1964) ran stories on the homage Cluny paid him. My thanks to Guy Lobrichon for sharing these articles.

[81] "Le volume d'hommage à K.-J. Conant est certes un geste d'estime et d'admiration adressé à un artisan passionné de la résurrection clunisienne, mais il est aussi la marque évidente et brillante d'un renouveau fécond de la recherche régionale et un acte de fois de la part des ses animateurs." Association Splendide Bourgogne, ed., *Mélanges d'histoire et d'archéologie offerts au professeur Kenneth John Conant* (Macon: Éditions Bourgogne Rhone-Alpes, 1977). 8

[82] The story concerns a visit to the nursing home, shortly before Conant's death when, asked if the rainy weather reminded him of Cluny, Conant replied "Ah, Cluny…how wonderful…only paradise is more beautiful." Peter Fergusson, "Necrology—Kenneth John Conant (1895 [sic]-1984)," *Gesta* XXIV (1985).

[83] Anne Baud, *Cluny, Un grand chantier médiéval au coeur de l'Europe*, Espaces Médiévaux (Paris: Picard, 2003). For example, he believed that the foundation walls he found below those of the second abbey church were from the original sanctuary of Berno's day. In fact, as Christian Sapin has shown, the lower level was simply the crypt of that church (page 49.)

[84] Michael Davis, "Sic et Non: Recent Trends in the Study of Gothic Ecclesiastical Architecture," *Journal of the Society of Architectural Historians* 58, no. 3 (1999). 418

[85] According to Peter Fergusson, Conant's interest in other lost monuments (Old St. Peter's, S. Benigne in Dijon, St. Martin at Tours) had initially led him to propose these sorts of reconstructions as the basis for his Pelican volume but Pevsner would not allow it. See: Peter Fergusson, "Medieval Architectural Scholarship in America 1900-1940: Ralph Adams Cram and Kenneth John Conant," in *The Architectural historian in America : a symposium in celebration of the fiftieth anniversary of the founding of the Society of Architectural Historians*, ed. Elisabeth B. MacDougall (Washington; Hanover: National Gallery of Art; Distributed by the University Press of New England, 1990). 137 and note 41

[86] For a complete study of the Graduate School of Design at Harvard during these years see: Anthony Alofsin, *The Struggle for Modernism: Architecture, Landscape Architecture, and City Planning at Harvard* (New York: Norton, 2002).

[87] Peter Fergusson mentions the same testimonials and suggests that his influence was greatest in his role as a teacher. See: Fergusson, "Medieval Architectural Scholarship in America 1900-1940: Ralph Adams Cram and Kenneth John Conant." 137-138

[88] Again, I am indebted to Michael Davis's article (Davis, "Sic et Non: Recent Trends in the Study of Gothic Ecclesiastical Architecture") for his review of these trends.

[89] Eliseo Verón, Jorge Dana, and Antoinette Franc de Ferrière, *Construire l'événement : les médias et l'accident de Three Mile Island* (Paris: Éditions de Minuit, 1981). Quoted in Jacques Le Goff, *History and memory*, European perspectives (New York: Columbia University Press, 1992). 212

CHAPTER SEVEN

CONCLUSIONS: FROM MARTYR TO MONUMENT

> Of all nations, is not France the only one thus to doubly define itself, finding its collective identity as much in Reason as in Catholicism?
> —Pierre Birnbaum, 1998 (2001)[1]

> By itself culture is never an 'asset': in order to transform it into one it had to be classified as part of 'heritage', and then enhanced by discourse.
> —Claude-Marie Bazin, 1995[2]

> When we contemplate ruins, we contemplate our own future.
> —Christopher Woodward, 2001[3]

In the Middle Ages, following Classical tradition, illustrations often served to stimulate memory.[4] Whether painted figures on the page or described physical destinations, they were conjured as meditation devices to remember texts and organizations of ideas. The form of an architectural location thus could function as a "memory site", a mnemonic conceit, to conjure associative memories, stimulating the viewer's imagination from meditating upon the physical object to a greater vision. In the modern period, as Pierre Nora has shown, there are also "memory sites" (lieux de mémoires). These are repositories of collective memories and cultural histories. They can be physical locations or books, songs, even recipes. Roland Mortier wrote "[the ruin] is a sign, an indicator which allows the spirit to momentarily forget the irreversibility of history and to allow itself to be carried away by time's flow."[5]

The ruins of the abbey of Cluny have come to serve as both medieval and modern memory sites. In Nora's terms, the former mother house of the largest abbey in medieval Europe recalls a period in France's history when monastic power and monastic ways of life were pervasive and the Church was implicitly linked with the Crown in governing peoples lives and shaping their knowledge. It also records an architectural style claimed by the French as their invention and advertised by the Burgundians as a regional attraction. Yet like a medieval memory site, Cluny has likewise been used to conjure an historical myth and rebuild a lost structure. Meditating upon its ruins, beginning with Lamartine's 1813 poem, became a source for imagining the medieval past.

Cleansed and elevated, Cluny's role in history grew to become the very source of European civilization. The small fragment of her prodigious church served as a stimulant for reconstructed visions of her former glory, imagined as sublimely cohesive and inventive solutions to medieval architectural challenges.

Cluny was an early example of French heritage offered to the world. We saw François Mitterrand in 1949 (Chapter 6) lauding the monument in these terms long before late twentieth-century trends universalized patrimony in order to attract national admiration.[6] One could argue that a revived interest in French cultural heritage grew out of the Third Republic's response to World War I and the greatest loss of life among all combatant nations.[7] It grew during World War II with Pétain's emphasis on historical tradition forming a France better than the one conceived by recent governments. Cluny fit both the idea of the "petite patrie" or regional pride (for Burgundian Romanesque) as well as the "grande patrie" of French medieval (and Catholic) architectural achievement.[8]

Nostalgia for a lost time had begun in France after the French Revolution to create what Svetlana Boym terms "collective frameworks of memory…rediscovered in mourning", offering safe havens from the rapid changes of modernity.[9] To Boym, nostalgia can take two forms: restorative and reflective. Reflective nostalgia accesses collective memory to gain distance from the lost subject and comment on the signs and stories it invokes. Restorative nostalgia, on the other hand, is the one responsible for the creation of new histories of nations and cultural myths about tradition, turning the past into "heritage" or what Avishai Margalit calls "event-stories".[10] Boym claims that the more rapid and sweeping the pace and scale of modernization, the more conservative and unchangeable the new traditions tend to be."[11] Sentimental nostalgia accounts for the type of regret that engendered the accounts of Cluny's golden medieval past as a contrast to the horrors of the Revolution and the shabby modernity of growing industrialism, and encouraged the kind of physical conservation of the abbey remains that pandered to imaginative tourism. It also set up the ongoing wishful consumption of restored spaces, whether in the flesh or visualized through creative media.

Kenneth Conant inherited a utopian nostalgia of the Middle Ages from Mâle and Porter, for whom this distant past represented a time of invention and social order. As Janice Mann has shown in her article on the two men's romantic identities, their anti-modernism was also steeped in "one of modernity's most potent myths…avant-garde originality".[12] For people at the beginning of the twentieth century, the Middle Ages were known through the romantic associations of the nineteenth century. Conant was as enamored as Mâle and Porter of the perfect imagined past and he crusaded for Cluny's place as the originator of the mature Romanesque style. The medieval abbey took on a veneer of modernism in his hands; the Cluniacs became avant-garde innovators of an architectural style. As a trained architect, Conant was able to realize his personal conception of Cluny's physical form in drawings and three-dimensional maquettes.[13] He thus stopped one process of imagining while stimulating another; viewers now had a prescribed form already conjured but they could go on to populate those spaces with their own notions of medieval life. Cluny was also able to fully reenter architectural debate since the reconstructed building allowed comparison with other extant structures. Conant's measurements and choices stimulated discussion, even dispute, while further studies, even when disproving some of his theories, remain indebted to his stimulus.

In fact, it is tempting to compare Conant's meticulous reconstruction of the plans of Cluny III to the medieval genre of schematic *pictura* which Mary Carruthers describes when complex structures were visualized in order to guide readers through an encyclopedic organization of information.[14] The same might be said for Conant while reconstructing the detailed minutiae of the third abbey church. Though he was actually inventing many details, Conant believed he could describe the building as it was at the beginning of the twelfth century. There is even an article from 1970, "Sur le pas de Lallemand à Cluny," where Conant both admires and takes Lallemand to task for his faulty understanding of Cluny in his 1784 *Voyage* as if Conant could see the building better than the man who was alive before it was demolished. The first sentence gives us a sense of Conant's projection into the past: "Jean-Baptiste Lallemand a été l'un de mes bons compagnons depuis un demi-siècle."[15]

Conant lived within his vision of the abbey church and the conception of medieval monasticism that he held dear. That Romantic idea, of a distant past when monks were truly pious intellectuals living quiet and contemplative lives, certainly came to Conant from the previous generation of Boston's arts and architecture crowd such as represented by Bernard Berenson and Ralph Adams Cram. Followers of a medieval revival formed on Pre-Raphaelite aestheticism, these men (and a few women) championed an idealizing religiosity in all the arts.[16] For Conant, however, in the next generation after its popularity, medieval idealism became an architectural style. When he left the East Coast and took his notions back to the source, as it were, in France, he found a receptive audience in the small provincial town. The administrators at Cluny were ready for a new way to focus attention on their monument in order to get funds for repairs and revitalization. They too had been affected by the histories and guidebooks written in the eighty-plus years before Conant arrived by clerics painting sympathetic pictures of earnest monks. Conant and Cluny were a good match in the first half of the twentieth century and they served each other well.

Collective memory and history are not, as we well know after Halbwachs and Koselleck,[17] the same thing. One must separate collective memories of the past from the notion of history in any given time and place. Yet both were employed to create the ideals we have of national heritage and patrimony. And both have fluctuated according to times, temperaments, and needs. Tracing the perception and reception of medieval art and architecture after the Middle Ages involves the ever pervasive and fluctuating notions of conceptualized memory. One must disentangle the constructed memories of the Middle Ages that are found in charters and wade through the various layers of cultural memory that have been formed over the intervening centuries. By "cultural memory" I am referring to the work of Jan and Aleida Assmann, who have taken Halbwach's "collective memory" and extended it to show how, once original witnesses are gone, memorialization continues to occur in mediated ways.[18] This latter process is a social and secondary act of communication that reproduces and transforms local traditions, varying according to the needs of time and place. It follows Jacques Le Goff's contention that the past is never over, that it is "constantly being constructed and reinterpreted."[19] Likewise, David Harvey has defined heritage as a "cultural process" and a "contemporary product shaped from history."[20] This is not far from Dean MacCannell's definition of tourism, "…an ideological framing of history, nature and tradition; a framing that has the power to reshape culture and nature to its own needs."[21] Certainly heritage and tourism have become inextricably linked and the presentation of historical sites as visitor attractions is a major component of governmental concerns over national patrimony. Again one can apply the distinction between the terms that I introduced in chapter 1—where heritage is the unfiltered past that can never be fully recovered but patrimony is the cultural past as it has been framed for posterity. Jan Assmann further makes a distinction between memory and a "culture of recollection".[22] His term relates to Halbwachs's social and group identity, with the central issue being not only what is remembered by individuals in the group, but also what is *not allowed to be forgotten*.

Forgetting is an important element in cultural memory. Paul Ricoeur reminds us that the past was shaped by forgetting unwanted parts or what he calls "narrative configuration".[23] By this he is not referring to the involuntary human mental act of forgetting, but the orchestrated exclusion of people, things, and events that do not fit a particular viewpoint or version of accounts. Forgetting is here also not associated with the moral act of forgiving, which Margalit shows us are quite different anyway (see his comparison in chapter 6 of *The Ethics of Memory*, 2002.) The creation of commemorative ceremonies at Cluny negotiated such a configured narrative, similar to the memorial rituals for the dead of the Great War of which Daniel Sherman has written: "The dynamic of any commemorative ritual involves a constant tension between creating, preserving, and destroying memories…"[24] Less universally or personally tragic, the loss of the monastery after the Revolution had helped shape the town's modern identity but its impact was known via an ongoing ideological process that eventually formed the official positivist history of the abbey, or what can be called its "dominant memory".[25] The parts of Cluny's history which the clerics and local historians who first wrote accounts wanted to safeguard in memory concerned recent violent change that destroyed the powerful abbey and its artistic monuments. Less obvious losses or everyday traditions did not seem such noteworthy subjects. It was a type of "death", a radical end, which Halbwachs and Jan Assmann suggest drives commemoration.[26] In this case, the written form of commemoration came first as a type of call for posterity, later it appeared in the physical preservation of the ruins. The unremarkable events of the past, including those performed by women, would be forgotten since they did not fit into these historians' contemporary frames of significance. As they began to record a formal history of the site, collective memory was halted in favor of a formula, much as oral traditions are narrowed into one version once written down.[27]

Cluny's history is of men: monks, abbots, kings, popes, counts and mayors. It is of an exclusive world of medieval power where women seem not even to exist. Commemoration of Cluny has stripped the town of half its population and made the abbey's inhabitants the only historical residents of the community. In this history, Greek and Christian emphases on men's superiority has been immortalized in the collective and written memories of one French town. From the first medieval chroniclers to the first nineteenth-century historians and on through twentieth-century academics, every one has built upon the same sources. Brief glimpses of reality come through in sources—widows owning houses the town wants to buy, women who organized Resistance fighting during World War II, even queens who accompanied kings in the famous visit of 1245—but these appearances are so faint they do not interrupt the accepted profile of a male-dominated history. Is this important? Perhaps it helps demonstrate the extent to which Cluny's history has been pruned and shaped into something that is slightly bigger but much less than it really was. Perhaps it should remind us that "patrimony" is a gendered term, originally relating to the transfer of property between male heirs, and that many stories about cultural inheritance follow the traditional model of the history of great men. Perhaps it helps us understand how much the cultural memory of the area around Cluny has homed in on the abbey as its only historical contribution to the "True France", as Herman Lebovics terms it, or Pierre Birnbaum's "La France imaginée".[28]

In fact, cultural memory-making for the medieval abbey occurred in three historical periods: while the abbey was writing its own chronicle, nineteenth-century writers, and Conant's work in the twentieth century.

The first shaping was made during the centuries after the central Middle Ages while the abbey was still functioning. Both the lack of historical accuracy in the charters and then the increasing distance from those who knew the stories forced the community to form an institutional self-image which heightened the importance and mythologized the image of some medieval members and events at the cost of others. There was also the need to justify the organization's principles and practices, beginning already in the twelfth-century with the rise of the Cistercian counter-order. The pervasive view of the medieval period as tied to the lives of "abbot saints" grew out of this process.

The second time an idea of Cluny's medieval past was crafted occurred after the congregation was dissolved in 1792. During the nineteenth century, politicians and historians struggled to reconcile the French religious past with republican nationalism. At this point, not only were no longer any medieval monks or townspeople alive to tell the "true" memories (as Pierre Nora worried in 1997 would always be the modern condition), but most of the physical evidence of the monastic site had been demolished, thus changing altogether perceptions of what Cluny had once been. Dominique Poulot has written that the "historical, that is, scientific, value of monuments came to supersede their intended original significance, whether it was merely forgotten or challenged."[29] This was problematic at Cluny since the ruinous state of the great church left no room for completely forgetting its implications for the Republic, inevitable once attempts to retool the building as a secular factory had failed.

To write a history of Cluny, early modern authors were forced to rely upon old records and recollections, piecing them together in an attractive and coherent package. The "glue" that initially held these accounts together was regret and righteous anger at the loss, so the fact that many of their sources had been created by and for the abbey with its peculiar panegyric and self-serving slant was useful. Although records certainly existed for the centuries after Cluny's success, the abbey had been compromised by its attachment to other congregations and its association with abbots appointed by the crown. Therefore the entire story after the twelfth century was most often relegated to one or two single chapters in long books about Cluny and seemed nearly to fade away within the cultural memory of the town. Thus the ruined abbey began its new life as a memorial site and Burgundian tourist destination within the context of its "glorious" medieval past. The Romanesque church began to stand for the entire Cluniac order as well as ideals of medieval monasticism. Early Renaissance style buildings that survived were incorporated within a Gothic appreciation of the site, beginning with the fourteenth-century Bourbon chapel to the south of the surviving transept. Twelfth-century houses suddenly acquired new life and became a source of physical heritage culture for the town, in spite of a brief period of economic desperation after the First World War which caused many shop owners on the main commercial streets to sell their Romanesque facades to collectors and replace them with large plate-glass store windows.

These first histories written in the mid nineteenth century formed the core material for the subsequent 'working memory' at Cluny (the term is Aleida Assmann's *Funktions-gedächtnis*).[30] Multiple layers converged as townspeople and clerics interested in Cluny's history began by "remembering" what they considered special about the golden period of Cluny in the Middle Ages and sought confirmation in primary source documents. This was a variation of what Halbwachs had described as "collective" memory. These histories then formed the seed of Cluny's past identity that became the basis for the organization of commemorative events, which in turn included papers by scholars who used the early publications as source material. Administrators also pulled from these recently compiled works extolling the abbey's original worth when writing funding solicitations to the government designed to move Cluny up a notch within the hierarchy of 'classed' historical monuments in France, and thus warrant appropriations for repairs and renovations. Such proposals then served as models for the verbal and textual presentation of the ruins to visitors. Each publication, ceremony, and presentation of the physical ruins built upon the ones before as slowly a composite "cultural memory" of the site was formed.

This new "memory" was acted out in major commemorative events held at Cluny beginning in the years 1898, 1910 and 1949 and then at regular intervals throughout the twentieth century. These public demonstrations of the town's identification with the past exhibit consciously constructed yet shifting cultural memories about medieval Cluny. They stemmed from the French government's post-Revolutionary development of public ceremonies to stabilize identity in the State[31] as well as the growing movement after 1870 to reinvigorate Catholic participation in public life. Cluny was within an Ultramontane orbit through her place in the diocese of Autun and her nearly exclusively monastic past, in spite of the rural population's tendency to vote on the left. This movement sought to revitalize ties to Rome and monarchical government with the medieval notion of imaginary pilgrimage, also called "memory sites", occurring through the vehicle of prayers and using French religious locations metaphorically. At the same time, the Middle Ages had been secularized through celebration of early urban independence in popular festivals at both the local level and for international expositions in Paris.

Commemorative ritual gives communities "connective" memories (here Jan Assmann's term) and allows individuals to belong to a past that will shape their future.[32] "They remember their history in order to have a history and to make history."[33] Passive monuments that serve as memory sites are activated by human participation in the past they suggest. It may not be the accurate past, or even the same time period, but it defines the community's sense of tradition and stimulates the transition from heritage to patrimony.

Once visitors had increased at Cluny at the end of the nineteenth century, mostly due to the rise of the railroad, the site's identity became an open question. It could return to a strict ecclesiastical focus and try to again embody visual symbols of Church power as it had in the eleventh and twelfth centuries, but this would be very hard to do without a monastic organization or a complete church building. There was an attempt by the dioceses to reestablish monasticism at Cluny with the foundation of the priory of St. Mayeul in 1894, however this organization only lasted about a decade. A compromise was reached with the few remaining twelfth-century houses that allowed the non-monastic city to celebrate its roots from the historical period of the abbey's strength. As we saw on the poster for the 1910 Millénaire, the foundation of the abbey was merged with that of the city.

The metonymic association of the town of Cluny, standing as well for the former abbey of Cluny, could work both for and against the contemporary community. On the one hand the leaders wanted outsiders to associate the word "Cluny" with the famous abbey and its medieval ruins by which they were learning they could connect to other lucrative Burgundian Romanesque tourist attractions in the region. On the other hand, the city had a modern life of its own aside from that past, and tried to remember being a civic entity even while the abbey was flourishing. It was significant that the thousand-year anniversary of the abbey's founding in 910 was celebrated with an event from 1245. This demonstrates an extraordinarily generalized notion of the Middle Ages. Apparently the tenth century had few visual associations and seemed back in a "darker" age whereas the pomp and luxury of France's Capetian period, with all the romantic notions of Gothic that it entailed, were currently fashionable and could promise livelier entertainment for spectators. Besides, the abbot saints were useful touch points for abbey history but Saint Louis was a far greater connection to advertise.

Kenneth Conant orchestrated the third period of imagining Cluny's history with his extensive reconstructive drawings. Conant was dependent upon the two previous layers of the abbey's cultural memories, but he also brought fresh architectural skills and a great energetic curiosity. Unlike most of the nineteenth-century authors who were clerics writing out of bitter regret for the abbey's destruction, Conant had a positive goal. Although he too bemoaned the physical loss, it nevertheless challenged him to excavate in order to determine the original location, plans, and elevations of the abbey buildings. If the church had yet been standing, Conant would not have studied Cluny. It was the again the existence of that evocative transept fragment that drew his skills and resources to the site. Because of his vibrant personality, he attracted international attention and a host of visitors. His presentations have influenced all visual conceptions of the site ever since.

Contemporary tourism to Cluny remains within the romantic vision of the Christian Middle Ages that inspired Conant. In fact, his drawings dominate souvenir imagery along with those of Sagot, whose embodiment of the "picturesque" prefigured Cluny's rediscovery as a travel destination. Since the publication of Taylor's *Voyages*, Burgundy has profited from emphasizing her numerous Romanesque structures, mostly dependencies of Cluny. In fact, during the 1860s, the nearby city of Mâcon, which is the seat of the Saône-et-Loire, built a new church dedicated to St. Peter [fig. 7.1]. Following a European trend for the monumental Romanesque that had begun in Protestant Germany during the 1820s, this church is a modern version of the ideal Burgundian Romanesque style. Coming within forty years of the demolition of Cluny's abbey church and dedicated to the same saint, Mâcon's project clearly references the city's famous neighbor.

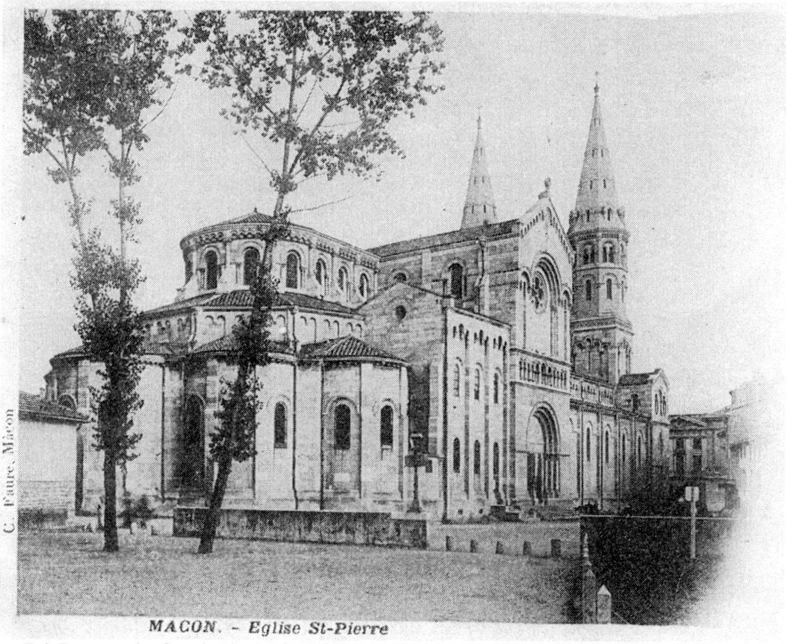

7.1 Postcard of cathedral of Mâcon, built in 1860s and dedicated to St. Peter, around 1901 (Author)

At Cluny, the tension between the medieval accomplishments of the First and Second Estates versus the revolutionaries' successful eradication of their power is perhaps the most acute of that at any French site. The challenge that the town faced, with their cumbersome and useless church ruin and scattered remaining abbey buildings, was to reconcile these conflicting associations into an acceptable representation of French historical culture. This is often the burden assumed by national heritage, to shape collective memory into a source of pride over pain. We saw where Cluny fit into national programs of architectural heritage and historical writing. How the town leaders chose to position themselves vis à vis these trends depended less and less upon their political persuasions or opinions of art and religion. Rather, it became an apparent economic necessity after the rise of the railroads to best position one's town for visitors and thus revive commercial life through hospitality. Perhaps without Conant's romantic vision someone else would have come along to show the town how to re-imagine their ruin. But it was Conant's combination of architectural training, interest in medieval revival designs, and access to American money that served as the magic potion to reintroduce Cluny into both the popular media and academic study.

Notes

[1] Pierre Birnbaum, *The Idea of France*, 1st American ed. (New York: Hill and Wang, 2001). 11

[2] Claude-Marie Bazin, "Industrial Heritage in the Tourism Process in France," in *International Tourism: Identity and Change*, ed. John B. Allcock, Marie-Françoise Lanfant, Edward M. Bruner, *Sage studies in international sociology* (London; Thousand Oaks, Calif.: Sage Publications, 1995). 116

[3] Christopher Woodward, *In ruins*, 1st American ed. (New York: Pantheon Books, 2001). 2

[4] Mary Carruthers, *The Book of memory: a study of memory in medieval culture*, Cambridge studies in medieval literature 10 (Cambridge; New York: Cambridge University Press, 1990); Mary Carruthers, *The Craft of thought: meditation, rhetoric, and the making of images, 400-1200*, Cambridge studies in medieval literature 34 (Cambridge; New York: Cambridge University Press, 1998). Jan Assmann, "Cultural Memory: Script, Recollection, and Political Identity in Early Civilizations," *Historiography East and West* 1, no. 2 (2003).

[5] Quoted and translated in: Alain Schnapp, "Vestiges, Monuments, and Ruins: The East Faces West," in *The Art Historian: National Traditions and Institutional Practices*, ed. Michael F. Zimmermann (New Haven: Yale University Press, 2002). 3

[6] David Lowenthal, "Identity, Heritage, and History," in *Commemorations: The Politics of National Identity*, ed. John R. Gillis (Princeton: Princeton University Press, 1994). 45

[7] Daniel J. Sherman, "Art, Commerce, and the Production of Memory in France after World War I," in *Commemorations: The Politics of National Identity*, ed. John R. Gillis (Princeton: Princeton University Press, 1994). 187

[8] Ibid. 241, 247

[9] Svetlana Boym, *The Future of nostalgia* (New York: Basic Books, 2001). 53-55
[10] Ibid. 49, 15; Avishai Margalit, *The ethics of memory* (Cambridge, Mass.: Harvard University Press, 2002). 60-62
[11] Boym, *The Future of nostalgia*. 42
[12] Janice Mann, "Romantic Identity, Nationalism, and the Understanding of the Advent of Romanesque Art in Christian Spain," *Gesta* 36, no. 2 (1997).
[13] Boym would call this "encasing and classifying…the elusive temporality of longing." Boym, *The Future of nostalgia*. 15
[14] One of Carruthers' examples is Hugh of St. Victor's *De pictura Arche,* which she does not believe was the description of a real painting, but Conrad Rudolph has studied Hugh's texts in depth and disagrees. Carruthers, *The craft of thought: meditation, rhetoric, and the making of images, 400-1200*. 243-6. Conrad Rudolph, *First, I find the center point : reading the text of Hugh of Saint Victor's The mystic ark*, Transactions of the American Philosophical Society, v. 94, pt. 4 (Philadelphia, PA: American Philosophical Society, 2004).
[15] [Jean-Baptiste Lallemand was one of my closest companions for half a century.] Kenneth John Conant, "Sur les pas de Lallemand à Cluny," *Gazette des Beaux Arts* 75 (series 6), no. 1 (1970). 1
[16] Douglass Shand-Tucci and Ralph Adams Cram, *Ralph Adams Cram: life and architecture* (Amherst: University of Massachusetts Press, 1995). Chapter 1, "Pinckney Street"
[17] Maurice Halbwachs, *On collective memory*, The Heritage of sociology, ed. Lewis A. Coser (Chicago: University of Chicago Press, 1992). Reinhart Koselleck, *Futures past: on the semantics of historical time* (New York: Columbia University Press, 2004).
[18] Jan Assmann and Rodney Livingstone, *Religion and cultural memory: ten studies, Cultural memory in the present* (Stanford, Calif.: Stanford University Press, 2006). I was introduced to these ideas in the excellent article by Ann Rigney, "Plentitude, scarcity and the circulation of cultural memory.," *Journal of European Studies* 35, no. 1 (2005).
[19] Jacques Le Goff, *History and memory, European perspectives* (New York: Columbia University Press, 1992). 108
[20] David C. Harvey, "Heritage Pasts and Heritage Present: temporality, meaning and the scope of heritage studies," *International Journal of Heritage Studies* 7, no. 4 (2001). 336, 327
[21] Dean MacCannell, *Empty meeting grounds: the tourist papers* (London; New York: Routledge, 1992). 1
[22] Jan Assmann, "Cultural Memory: Script, Recollection, and Political Identity in Early Civilizations." 157-158
[23] Paul Ricoeur, *Memory, history, forgetting* (Chicago: University of Chicago Press, 2004). 448
[24] Daniel J. Sherman, *The Construction of memory in interwar France* (Chicago; London: University of Chicago press, 1999). 265
[25] Ibid. 24
[26] Jan Assmann, "Cultural Memory: Script, Recollection, and Political Identity in Early Civilizations." 161

[27] Ricoeur stated this another way: "Commemorations seal the incomplete memory and its lining of forgetfulness." Ricoeur, *Memory, history, forgetting*. 451

[28] Herman Lebovics, *True France: The Wars over Cultural Identity, 1900-1945* (Ithaca and London: Cornell University Press, 1992). Pierre Birnbaum, *La France imaginée: déclin des rêves unitaires?* (Paris: Fayard, 1998).

[29] Dominique Poulot, "The Birth of Heritage: 'le moment Guizot'," *Oxford Art Journal* 11, no. 2 (1988). 40

[30] Aleida Assmann, Erinnerungsräume: Formen und Wandlungen des kulturellen Gedächtnisses, C.H. Beck Kulturwissenschaft (München: C.H. Beck, 1999). 18. Also quoted in: Rigney, "Plenitude, scarcity and the circulation of cultural memory.."

[31] E. J. Hobsbawm and T. O. Ranger, *The Invention of Tradition* (Cambridge; New York: Cambridge University Press, 1983). 271

[32] Assmann and Livingstone, Religion and cultural memory: ten studies. 11

[33] Ibid.

APPENDIX

BIBLIOGRAPHY OF KENNETH JOHN CONANT'S WRITTEN WORK ON THE ABBEY OF CLUNY

Compiled by Minott Kerr, 1996, with additions (used by permission)

1928a "La chapelle Saint-Gabriel à Cluny," *Bulletin monumental* 87 (1928) 55-64.

1928b "Five old prints of the abbey church of Cluny," *Speculum* 3 (1928) 401-404.

1929a "Les fouilles de Cluny," *Bulletin monumental* 88 (1929) 109-23.

1929b "Mediaeval Academy Excavations at Cluny: [I] The season of 1928," *Speculum* 4 (1929) 3-26.

1929c "Mediaeval Academy Excavations at Cluny: II Preliminary restoration drawings of the abbey church," *Speculum* 4 (1929) 168-76.

1929d "Mediaeval Academy Excavations at Cluny: III Drawings and photographs of the transept," *Speculum* 4 (1929) 291-302.

1929e "Mediaeval Academy Excavations at Cluny: IV The significance of the abbey church," *Speculum* 4 (1929) 443-50.

1929f "Recent research and excavation at Cluny," *Parnassus* 1:2 (February 15, 1929) 23.

1930a "La date des chapiteaux du choeur de l'abbaye de Cluny," *Bulletin monumental* 89 (1930) 381-85.

1930b "Mediaeval Academy Excavations at Cluny: V The date of the ambulatory capitals," *Speculum* 5 (1930) 77-94.

1930c "The iconography and the sequence of the ambulatory capitals of Cluny," *Speculum* 5 (1930) 278-87.

1930d "Propos d'histoire de l'art: `l'école clunisienne,'" *Annales de Bourgogne* 2 (1930) 321-25.

1931a "Mediaeval Academy Excavations at Cluny: [VI] The season of 1929," *Speculum* 6 (1931) 3-14.

1931b "Le problème de Cluny d'après les fouilles recentes," *Revue de l'art* 2 (1931) 141-54 & 189-204.

1932a "The apse at Cluny," *Speculum* 7 (1932) 23-35.

1932b "Cluny epigraphy," *Speculum* 7 (1932) 336-49. The article is by R. Lloyd with additions by Conant.

1932-33 "Le tombeau presumé de l'abbé Ponce de Melgueil, à Cluny," *Annales de l'Académie de Mâcon* 3me sér. 28 (1932-33) 116-20.

1933a "Excavations at Cluny," *Resumés des communications presentées au XIIIme Congrès international de l'histoire de l'art.* Stockholm: 1933; 104-106.

1933b "A replica of the arcade of the apse at Cluny," *Bulletin of the Fogg Art Museum* Harvard University 3 (November 1933) 5-8.

1938 "Communication sur les fouilles," *Annales de l'Académie de Macon* 3me sér. 33 (1938) xxxi.

1939 "The third church at Cluny," *Medieval Studies in Honor of Arthur Kingsley Porter*, ed. W. R. W. Koehler. Cambridge, Mass.: 1939; II: 327-57.

1940 [Review of Joan Evans, *The Romanesque Architecture of the Order of Cluny*. Cambridge/ New York: 1938], *Art Bulletin* 22 (1940) 276-78.

1940a "Excavations at the Monastery of Cluny," *The American Society of the French Legion of Honor Magazine* (New York) Autumn 1940

1942a "Mediaeval Academy Excavations at Cluny: VII Two new books about Cluny," *Speculum* 17 (1942) 563-65.

1942b "The place of Cluny in Romanesque and Gothic architecture," *Journal of the Society of Architectural Historians* (USA) 2 (July 1942) 3-5.

1942c *A Brief Commentary on Early Medieval Church Architecture with Especial Reference to Lost Monuments*. Baltimore: 1942; 26-34.

1944a "Observations on the vaulting problems of the period 1088-1211," *Gazette des Beaux-Arts* 6me sér. 26 (1944) 127-34.

1944b "Religion in architecture," *The Arts and Religion*, (Ayer Lectures: 1943) ed. A. B. Bailey. New York: 1944; 71-89. Cluny: 85-86.

1948 "Cluny, a center of western monasticism," *Archaeology* 1 (1948) 92-93.

1949 *Benedictine Contributions to Church Architecture*, (Wimmer Lecture: 1947). Latrobe, Pa.: 1949; 18-35.

1949-50 La préparation et la genèse de la grande abbatiale de Cluny," *Bulletin de la Société des Amis des Musée à Dijon* (1949-50) 12-14.

1950a "Cluny I and Cluny II," *Medieval Studies for Rose Graham*, eds. V. Ruffer and A. J. Taylor. Oxford: 1950; 41-50.

1950b "Les églises de Cluny à l'époque de saint Odon et de saint Odilon," *À Cluny, congrès scientifique; fêtes et ceremonies liturgiques en honneur des saints abbés Odon et Odilo*: 9-11 juillet 1949; travaux du congrès.... Dijon: 1950; 37-43.

1952 "El monasterio de Cluny en Borgoña," *Anales del Instituto de Arte Americano e Investigaciones Estéticas* (Universidad de Buenos Aires, Facultad de Arquitectura y Urbanismo) 5 (1952) 9-20.

1954a [Review of Société des Amis de Cluny, ed. *A Cluny--Congrès Scientifique--Fêtes et Cérémonies liturgiques en l'honneur des Saints Abbés Odon et Odilon, 9-11 juillet 1949*. Dijon: 1950] Speculum 29, 1 (1954): 164-65.

1954b "Mediaeval Academy Excavations at Cluny: VIII Final stages for the project," *Speculum* 29 (1954) 1-43.

1955 "Cluny in the tenth century," *Medievalia et Humanistica* 9 (1955) 23-25.

1957a "New results in the study of Cluny monastery," *Journal of the Society of Architectural Historians* (USA) 16:3 (October 1957) 3-11.

1957b "Etudes nouvelles sur l'abbaye de Cluny (Saône-et-Loire)," *Bulletin de la Société nationale des Antiquaires de France* (1957) 164-70.

1957c [Review of Raymond and A.-M. Oursel, *"Les Eglises romanes de l'Autunois et du Brionnais (ancient grand archidiacone d'Autun)* Mâcon: 1956]. Speculum 32, no. 4 (Oct., 1957): 852-54.

1958a [Review of Otto von Simson, *The Gothic Cathedral: Origins of Gothic Architecture and the Mediaeval Concept of Order*. Princeton: 1956], *Speculum* 33(1958): 154-158, esp. 157-58.

1958b "The pointed arch--orient to occident," *Palaeologia* 7:3-4 (November 1958) 267-70.

1959 *Carolingian and Romanesque Architecture: 800-1200*. Harmondsworth: 1959; 82-84 & 115-25. Cf: 2nd edtn., 1966; 3rd edtn., 1973; 4th. edtn, 1978 with changes in 1979: 116-119 & 198-221.

1960 "Données nouvelles sur les restes de l'abbaye de Cluny," *Bulletin de la Société nationale des Antiquaires de France* (1960) 88-91.

1960-61 "Les dimensions systématiques et symboliques à l'église abbatiale de Cluny," *Annales de l'Académie de Mâcon* 3me sér. 45 (1960-61) 2-5.

1961 "Les principes mathématiques à la basilique de Cluny," *Bulletin de la Société nationale des Antiquaires de France* (1961) 185-86.

1962 "Measurements and proportions of the Great church at Cluny," *Beiträge zur Kunstgeschichte und Archäologie des Frühmittelalters: Akten zum VII. International Kongress für Frühmittelalterforschung 21.-28. september 1958*, ed. V. H. Fillitz. Graz: 1962; 220-38.

1963 "Mediaeval Academy Excavations at Cluny, IX: Systematic dimensions in the buildings," *Speculum* 38 (1963) 1-45.

1965 "Cluny II and Saint-Benigne at Dijon," *Archaeolgia* (London) 99 (1965) 179-94.

1966a "Cluny, 1077-1088," *Mélanges offerts à René Crozet à l'occasion de son soixante-dixième anniversaire,* ed. P. Gallais and Y. J. Riou. Poitiers: 1966; 341-45.

1966b "Les rapports architecturaux entre Cluny et Payerne," *L'abbatiale de Payerne; Bibliothèque historique vaudoise*: 39. Lausanne: 1966; 125-38.

1968a *Cluny, Les églises et la maison du chef d'ordre*. Mâcon: 1968.

Reviews

- Crema, *Palladio* n.s. 19 (1969) 189-90.
- Salet, *Bulletin monumental* 127 (1969) 183-86.
- Crozet, *Cahiers de civilisation médiévale* 13 (1970) 149-55.
- Entz, *Acta historiae et artae Hungariae* 16 (1970) 322-324.
- Branner, *Art Bulletin* 53 (1971) 246-48.

1968b The after-life of Vitruvius in the middle ages," *Journal of the Society of Architectural Historians* (USA) 27 (1968) 33-38.

1970a "Sur les pas de Lallemand à Cluny," *Gazette des Beaux-Arts* 6me sér. 75 (1970) 1-10.

1970b "Mediaeval Academy Excavations at Cluny, X," *Speculum* 45 (1970) 1-35.

1971a "La chronologie de Cluny III d'après les fouilles," *Cahiers de civilisation médiévale* 14 (1971) 341-47.

1971b "The history of Romanesque Cluny as clarified by excavations and comparisons," *Monumentum* 7 (1971) 10-33.

1971c "Mediaeval Cluny; Renewed study of the monastic buildings," *Revue bénédictine* 81 (1971) 60-66.

1971d "Observations on the practical talents and technology of the medieval Benedictines," *Cluniac Monasticism in the Central Middle Ages*, ed. N. Hunt. London: 1971; 77-84.

1971e "Early examples of the pointed arch in Romanesque architecture," *Viator* 2 (1971) 203-210. Written with H. M. Willard.

1972a " L'abside et le choeur de Cluny III," *Gazette des Beaux-Arts* 6me sér. 79 (1972) 5-12.

1972b "The background of Gothic architecture in Benedictine building," *Revue bénédictine* 82 (1972) 208-14.

1972c "Deux traditions dans la chronologie du roman bourguignon," *Annales de Bourgogne* 44 (1972) 94-103.

1973 "Le portail monumental en Bourgogne," *Actes des journées d'études d'histoire et d`archéologie organisées à l'occasion du centenaire de la fondation de l`abbaye et de la ville de Charlieu*, 14-16 juillet 1972. [Charlieu: 1973]; 23-25.

1974a "The great transept at Cluny III," *Journal of the Society of Architectural Historians* (USA) 33 (1974) [98]-99.

1974b "The enigma of Abbot Berno's tomb at Cluny," *Ampleforth* Journal 79:part II (Summer 1974): 33-40.

1975a Cluny studies, 1968-1975," *Speculum* 50 (1975) 383-90.

1975b "Edifices marquants dans l'ambiance de Pierre le Vénérable et Pierre Abélard," *Pierre Abélard et Pierre le Vénérable; Colloque internationale du CNRS*, Cluny: 1972. Paris: 1975; 727-32.

1975c "Visite commentée de l'abbaye et des fouilles," *Pierre Abélard et Pierre le Vénérable; Colloque international du CNRS*, Cluny: 1972. Paris: 1975; 69-71.

1976a "The Theophany in the history of church portal design," *Gesta* 15 (1976) 127-34.

1976b [Review of W. Braunfels, *Monasteries of Western Europe*: The Architecture of the Orders. London: 1972] *Art Bulletin* 58 (1976) 287-88.

1977a "A majestic abbey, long destroyed, rises again—on paper," *Harvard Magazine* 79:5 (January-February 1977) 28-33.

1977b [Review of H. E. Kubach, *Romanesque Architecture*. New York: 1975] *Journal of the Society of Architectural Historians* (USA) 36 (1977) 44.

BIBLIOGRAPHY

Académie de Mâcon. Société des arts sciences belles-lettres et agriculture de Saône-et-Loire. *Millénaire de Cluny: congrès d'histoire et d'archéologie tenu à Cluny les 10, 11, 12 Septembre 1910*. 2 vols. Mâcon, France: Protat Frères, 1910.

Adams, Henry. *Mont Saint Michel and Chartres*. New York: Penguin Books, 1986.

Agulhon, Maurice. *The Republican experiment, 1848-1852*. Translated by Janet Lloyd, The Cambridge history of modern France 2. Cambridge: Cambridge University Press; Editions de la maison des sciences de l'homme, 1983.

Alofsin, Anthony. *The Struggle for Modernism: Architecture, Landscape Architecture, and City Planning at Harvard*. New York: Norton, 2002.

Amalvi, Christian. *Le goût du moyen age*, Civilisation et mentalités. Paris: Plon, 1996.

Anderson, Benedict R. O'G. *Imagined communities: reflections on the origin and spread of nationalism*. Rev. and extended, 2nd ed. London; New York: Verso, 1991.

Assmann, Aleida. *Erinnerungsräume: Formen und Wandlungen des kulturellen Gedächtnisses*, C.H. Beck Kulturwissenschaft. München: C.H. Beck, 1999.

Assmann, Jan. "Cultural Memory: Script, Recollection, and Political Identity in Early Civilizations." *Historiography East and West* 1, no. 2 (2003). 154-77.

Assmann, Jan, and Rodney Livingstone. *Religion and cultural memory: ten studies*, Cultural memory in the present. Stanford, CA: Stanford University Press, 2006.

Auduc, Emmanuel. *Les fetes de jubilé de Cluny: Leur preparation, leur celebration, leur conclusion*. Cluny: J. Lamante, 1898.

Baud, Anne. *Cluny, un grand chantier médiéval au coeur de l'Europe*, Espaces mediévaux. Paris: Picard, 2003.

Bazin, Claude-Marie. "Industrial Heritage in the Tourism Process in France." In *International Tourism: Identity and Change*, Sage studies in international sociology 47. Edited by John B. Allcock, Marie-Françoise Lanfant, Edward M. Bruner. London; Thousand Oaks, CA: Sage Publications, 1995.

Benjamin, Walter, *Illuminations*. Edited by Hannah Arendt. New York: Schocken Books, 1986.

Bernard, Auguste, and Alexandre Bruel, eds. *Recueil des chartes de l'abbaye de Cluny*. 6 vols. Paris: Imprimerie nationale, 1876.

Bertelière, Philibert Bouché de la. "Description historique et chronologique de la ville, abbaye et banlieue de Cluny." 1787-1817. Cluny, Municipal Archives.

Birnbaum, Pierre. *La France imaginée: déclin des rêves unitaires?* Paris: Fayard, 1998.

———. *The idea of France*. 1st American ed. New York: Hill and Wang, 2001.

Bizzarro, Tina Waldeier. *Romanesque Architectural Criticism: A Prehistory*. Cambridge: Cambridge University Press, 1992.

Boehm, Barbara Drake. "Body-Part Reliquaries: The State of Research." *Gesta* XXXVI, no. 1 (1997).

Bouché, Jean-Baptiste. *Voyage en Bourgogne; Suivi de Mélanges littéraires*. Paris: Martinon, 1845.

Bourgogne, Association Splendide, ed. *Melanges d'histoire et d'archâeologie offerts au professeur Kenneth John Conant*. Mâcon: Éditions Bourgogne Rhone-Alpes, 1977.

Boym, Svetlana. *The future of nostalgia*. New York: Basic Books, 2001.

Branner, Robert. "K. J. Conant, Cluny, Les eglises et la maison du chef d'ordre." Art Bulletin 53 (1973): 246-48.

Braunfels, Wolfgang. *Monasteries of Western Europe: The Architecture of the Orders*. London; Princeton: Thames and Hudson Ltd., Princeton University Press, 1972.

Bruel, François-Louis. *Cluni : album historique et archéologique, précede d'une étude résumée et d'un notice des planches*. Matiscone: Fratrum Protat, 1910.

Brush, Kathryn. *The Shaping of Art History: Wilhelm Vöge, Adolph Goldschmidt, and the Study of Medieval Art*. Cambridge: Cambridge University Press, 1996.

Byrnes, Joseph F. *Catholic and French Forever: religious and national identity in modern France*. University Park, PA: Pennsylvania State University Press, 2005.

Calo, Mary Ann. *Bernard Berenson and the twentieth century*. Philadelphia: Temple University Press, 1994.

Carruthers, Mary. *The book of memory: a study of memory in medieval culture*, Cambridge studies in medieval literature 10. Cambridge; New York: Cambridge University Press, 1990.

———. *The craft of thought: meditation, rhetoric, and the making of images, 400-1200*, Cambridge studies in medieval literature. 34. Cambridge; New York: Cambridge University Press, 1998.

Carty, Carolyn M. "The Role of Gunzo's Dream in the Building of Cluny III." *Gesta* XXVII, no. 1 and 2 (1988): 113-23.

Centre Cultural de la Fundació Caixa de Pensions, ed. *Josep Puig i Cadafalch: l'arquitectura entre la casa i la ciutat = architecture between the house and the city*: 4 de desembre de 1989 - 11 de febrer 1990. 1. ed. Barcelona: La Fundació, 1989

Champly, Louis Henri. *Histoire de l'abbaye de Cluny*. Mâcon: Legrand/Mme. Ve Félix, 1866.

Champly, Louis Henri, and René Champly. *Histoire de l'abbaye de Cluny*. 3. éd., rev., ed. Paris: Librairie centrale des sciences, 1930.

Charvin, Dom G. "La fin de l'Ordre de Cluny (1789-1791)." *Revue Mabillon* 40 (1950): 29-41.

Chaumont, Louis M. J. *Nouveau guide de Cluny, ou Explications historiques des cartes postales et vues de la ville et de l'ancienne abbaye*. Domois-Dijon,: Impr. de l'Union typographique, 1905.

———. *Recherches historiques sur la persécution religieuse dans le département de Saone-et-Loire pendant la révolution (1789-1803)* t. 4. L'arrondissement de Macon. Chalon-sur-Saone,: E. Bertrand, 1903.

Chavot, Th. "Destruction de l'eglise de l'abbaye de Cluny." *Annales de l'Academie de Macon* (1869): 288-99.

Choay, Françoise. *L'allégorie du patrimoine*, Couleur des idées. Paris: Éditions du Seuil, 1992.

———. *The Invention of the Historic Monument*. Cambridge: Cambridge University Press, 2001.

Clayson, Hollis. *Paris in Despair*. Chicago: University of Chicago Press, 2002.

Cluny, Société des Amis de, ed. *A Cluny: Congrès Scientifique. Fêtes et cérémonies en l'honneur des saints Abbés Odon et Odilon 9-11 Juillet 1949*. Dijon: Imprimerie Bernigaud & Privat, 1950.

Cobb, Richard. *Les armées révolutionnaires*. Vol. 2. Paris: Mouton, 1963.

Conant, Kenneth John. *Benedictine Contributions to Church Architecture*, Wimmer Lecture, 1947. Latrobe, Pennsylvania: The Archabbey Press, 1949.

———. *Carolingian and Romanesque Architecture 800-1200*. Edited by Nikolaus Pevsner and Judy Nairn. Second ed, The Pelican History of Art. Harmondsworth: Penguin, 1959. Reprint, 1974.

———. *Cluny: les églises et la maison du chef d'ordre,* Mediaeval Academy of America. Publication no. 77. Mâcon: Impr. Protat Frères, 1968.

———. "Excavations at the Monastery of Cluny." *The American Society Legion of Honor Magazine* IX, no. No. 2 (1940): 169-74.

———. Review of *Romanesque Architecture,* by Hans Erich Kubach. *Journal of the Society of Architectural Historians* 36 (1977): 44.

———. "Medieval Academy Excavations at Cluny: The Season of 1928." *Speculum* 4 (1929)

———. Review of *Les Eglises romanes de l'Autunois et du Brionnais,* by Raymond and A.-M. Oursel. *Speculum* 32, no. 4 (Oct., 1957): 852-54.

———. Review of *A Cluny--Congres Scientifique--Fetes et Ceremonies liturgiques en l'honneur des Saints Abbes Odon et Odilon, 9-11 juillet 1949*, edited by Société des Amis de Cluny. Speculum 29, no. 1 (January, 1954): 164-65.

———. Review of *Monasteries of Western Europe*, by Wolfgang Braunfels. *Art Bulletin* LVIII, no. 2 (1976): 287-88.

———. "Sur les pas de Lallemand à Cluny." *Gazette des Beaux Arts* 75 (series 6), no. 1 (1970): 1-10.

Conforti, Joseph A. *Imagining New England: explorations of regional identity from the pilgrims to the mid-twentieth century*. Chapel Hill: University of North Carolina Press, 2001.

Connerton, Paul. *How societies remember,* Themes in the social sciences. Cambridge; New York: Cambridge University Press, 1989.

Cowdrey, H. E. J. *The Cluniacs and the Gregorian reform*. Oxford: Clarendon Press, 1970.

Crossley, Ceri. *French historians and romanticism: Thierry, Guizot, the Saint-Simonians, Quinet, Michelet*. London; New York: Routledge, 1993.

Cucherat, François. *Cluny au onzième siècle: son influence religieuse, intellectuelle et politique*. 2e éd. corr., complétée, enrichie de documents inédits. Mâcon: M. Dejussieu, 1873.

Curran, Kathleen. *The Romanesque Revival: Religion, Politics, and Transnational Exchange*, Buildings, landscapes, and societies series 2. University Park, Pa.: Pennsylvania State University Press, 2003.

Dakyns, Janine. *The Middle Ages in French Literature, 1851-1900*. London: Oxford University Press, 1973.

Davis, Michael. "Sic et Non: Recent Trends in the Study of Gothic Ecclesiastical Architecture." *Journal of the Society of Architectural Historians* 58, no. 3 (1999): 414-23.

Day, C. R. "Education, Technology, and Social Change in France: The Short, Unhappy Life of the Cluny School, 1866-1891." *French Historical Studies* 8 (1974): 427-44.

Deschamps, Paul. *French sculpture of the Romanesque period*. Firenze: Pantheon, 1930.

Description historique de l'abbaye de Cluny. Chalon sur.Saône: Imprimerie et lithographie Montalan, 1846.

Desvallées, André. "A l'origine du mot 'patrimoine'." *In Patrimoine et Modernité*, edited by Dominique Poulot, 89-105. Paris: L'Harmattan, 1998.

Duby, Georges. "Le budget de l'abbaye de Cluny entre 1080 et 1155. Économie domaniale et économie monétaire (1952)." *Hommes et structures* (1973): 61-82.

———. *The three orders: feudal society imagined*. Chicago: University of Chicago Press, 1980.

Duparay, Benoit. *Pierre-le-Venerable, abbé de Cluny, Sa vie, ses oeuvres et la société monastique au 12e siecle*. Chalon-sur-Saone: P. Mulcey, 1862.

Dupeux, Georges. *French society, 1789-1970*. London/New York: Methuen; Barnes & Noble, 1976.

Emery, Elizabeth. "Protecting the Past: Albert Robida and the *Vieux Paris* Exhibit at the 1900 World's Fair." *Journal of European Studies* (2005): 65-85

Emery, Elizabeth and Laura Morowitz. *Consuming the past: the medieval revival in fin-de-siècle France*. Aldershot, England; Burlington, VT: Ashgate, 2003.

———. "From the living room to the museum and back again." *Journal of the History of Collections* 16, no. 2 (2004): 285-309.

Etlin, Richard A. *Symbolic Space: French Enlightenment Architecture and Its Legacy*. Chicago and London: University of Chicago Press, 1994.

Evans, Joan. *Prelude and Fugue: An Autobiography*. London: Museum Press Limited, 1964.

Fergusson, Peter. "Medieval Architectural Scholarship in America 1900-1940: Ralph Adams Cram and Kenneth John Conant." In *The Architectural historian in America: a symposium in celebration of the fiftieth anniversary of the founding of the Society of Architectural Historians*. Edited by Elisabeth B. MacDougall. Washington; Hanover: National Gallery of Art; Distributed by the University Press of New England, 1990. 127-42

———. "Necrology—Kenneth John Conant (1895 [sic]-1984)." *Gesta* XXIV (1985): 87-88.

Flanner, Janet. *Men and monuments*. New York: Harper, 1957.

Flanner, Janet, and William Shawn. *Paris journal*. New York,: Atheneum, 1965.

Forest, Alfred. *Histoire d'un jubilé; neuvième centenaire de l'institution par Saint-Odilon, abbé de Cluny (962-1049) de la commémoraison de tous les fidèles trépassés (31 octobre--9 novembre 1898) à Cluny*. Paris: V. Giard, E. Brière, 1899.

———. "Cluny a travers les siècles." In *Programme du Congrès d'Histoire et d'Archéologie du Millénaire de Cluny*: Académie de Mâcon, 1910.

———. *Cluny-guide et ses environs*. Cluny: Truchot, n.d. [1909].

Gandrez, Henri. *Le canton de Cluny en 1900--à travers les cartes postales*. Saint-Seine-l'Abbaye: Éditions de Saint-Seine-l'Abbaye, 1982.

Gerson, Stéphane. *The pride of place: local memories & political culture in nineteenth-century France*. Ithaca: Cornell University Press, 2003.

Gibson, Ralph. *A social history of French Catholicism, 1789-1914*, Christianity and society in the modern world. London; New York: Routledge, 1989.

Gildea, Robert. *Education in provincial France, 1800-1914: a study of three departments*. Oxford [Oxfordshire] London; New York: Clarendon Press ; Oxford University Press, 1983.

———. *The Past in French History*. New Haven and London: Yale University Press, 1994.

Golan, Romy. *Modernity and nostalgia: art and politics in France between the wars*. New Haven: Yale University Press, 1995.

Gooch, G. P. *History and historians in the nineteenth century*. rev. ed. London, New York: Longmans Green, 1952.

Goujon, Pierre. "Cluny, mille ans après." In *L'ouvrier, l'Espagne, la Bourgogne et la vie provinciale*, edited by François Robert et Françoise Bayard, 415-29. Madrid: Presse Université de Lyon, 1994.

Greene, Christopher, M. "Alexandre Lenoir and the Musée des monuments français during the French Revolution." *French Historical Studies* 12 (1981). 200-222.

Guizot, François Pierre Guillaume. *Histoire de la civilisation en Europe depuis la chute de l'Empire romain jusqu'en 1789*. Brussels: Vandooren, 1829-32.

———. *The history of civilization in Europe*. Edited by William Hazlitt and Larry Siedentop. Penguin classics. London; New York, NY: Penguin Books, 1997.

Hahn, Cynthia. "The Voices of Saints: Speaking Reliquaries." *Gesta* XXXVI, no. 1 (1997): 20-31.

Halbwachs, Maurice. *On collective memory*, The Heritage of sociology. Edited by Lewis A. Coser. Chicago: University of Chicago Press, 1992.

Harrigan, Patrick J. *Mobility, elites, and education in French society of the second empire*. Waterloo, Ont.: Wilfrid Laurier University Press, 1980.

Harris, Ruth. *Lourdes : body and spirit in the secular age*. 1st American ed. New York: Viking, 1999.

Harvey, David C. "Heritage Pasts and Heritage Present: temporality, meaning and the scope of heritage studies." *International Journal of Heritage Studies* 7, no. 4 (2001): 319-38.

Hobsbawm, E. J., and T. O. Ranger. The Invention of tradition. Cambridge; New York: Cambridge University Press, 1983.

Hugo, Victor. *Littérature et philosophie mêlées*, Bibliothèque du XIXe siècle 2. Edited by Anthony R. W. James. Paris: Klincksieck, 1976.

Hunt, Noreen. *Cluny under Saint Hugh, 1049-1109*. 1st American ed. Notre Dame, Ind.: University of Notre Dame Press, 1968.

Hurel, Daniel-Odon. "La representation de Cluny chez les auteurs des XVIIe et XVIIIe siècles." *Revue Mabillon* 72 (2000): 115-28.

———. "La Revue Mabillion (1905-1920) dans la correspondence de dom Jean-Martial Besse." *Revue Mabillon* 77 (2005): 55-78.

Iogna-Prat, Dominique. "Cluny, 910-1910 ou l'instrumentalisation de la mémoire des origines." *Revue Mabillon* 72 (2000): 161-85.

———. Études clunisiennes, Les médiévistes français; 2. Paris: Picard, 2002.

Idzerda, Stanley J. "Iconoclasm during the French Revolution," *American Historical Review* 60 (1954) 13-26.

Johnson, Douglas. *Guizot; aspects of French history, 1787-1874,* Studies in political history. London: Routledge & K. Paul, 1963.

Jonas, Raymond Anthony. *France and the cult of the Sacred Heart: an epic tale for modern times*, Studies on the history of society and culture 39. Berkeley: University of California Press, 2000.

———. *The tragic tale of Claire Ferchaud and the Great War*. Berkeley: University of California Press, 2005.

Kaufman, Suzanne K. *Consuming visions: mass culture and the Lourdes shrine*. Ithaca, N.Y.: Cornell University Press, 2005.

Kennedy, Emmet. *A cultural history of the French Revolution*. New Haven: Yale University Press, 1989.

Koselleck, Reinhart. *Futures past: on the semantics of historical time*. New York: Columbia University Press, 2004.

L'Huillier, Albert. *Vie de Saint Hugues: abbé de Cluny, 1024-1109*. Solesmes: Imprimerie Saint-Pierre, 1888.

Le Goff, Jacques, and Jean-Maurice de Montremy. *A la recherche du Moyen Age*. Paris: L. Audibert, 2003.

Le Goff, Jacques. *History and memory*, European perspectives. New York: Columbia University Press, 1992.

Lebovics, Herman. *True France: The Wars over Cultural Identity, 1900-1945*. Ithaca and London: Cornell University Press, 1992.

Lehmann, Richard. *Forschungen zur Geschichte des Abtes Hugo I von Cluny (1049-1109).* Göttingen: Vandenhoeck & Ruprecht, 1869.

Leveque, Pierre. "Le "Déchristianisation" en Mâconnais a l'époque contemporaine: Quelques problèmes." *Mémoires de la Société pour l'histoire du droit et des institutions des anciens pays bourguignons, comtois et romands* 37 (1880): 293-313.

Lorain, Prosper. *Essai historique sur l'Abbaye de Cluny: suivi de pièces justificatives et de divers fragmens de la correspondance de Pierre-Le-Vénérable avec Saint Bernard*. Dijon: Popelain, 1839.

———. *Histoire de l'Abbaye de Cluny depuis sa fondation jusqu'à sa destruction à l'époque de la Révolution française*. Paris: Sagnier et Bray, 1845.

Lowenthal, David. *The past is a foreign country*. Cambridge; New York: Cambridge University Press, 1985.

———. "Identity, Heritage, and History." In *Commemorations: The Politics of National Identity*, edited by John R. Gillis, 41-57. Princeton: Princeton University Press, 1994.

MacCannell, Dean. *Empty meeting grounds: the tourist papers*. London; New York: Routledge, 1992.

Magraw, Roger. *France, 1815-1914: the bourgeois century*. New York: Oxford University Press, 1986.

Mâle, Emile. *Religious Art in France: The Twelfth Century. A Study of the Origins of Medieval Iconography*. Translated by Marthiel Mathews from 1953 corrected edition (by Mâle himself). Vol. XC. 1, Bollingen Series. Princeton: Princeton University Press, 1978.

Mann, Janice. "Romantic Identity, Nationalism, and the Understanding of the Advent of Romanesque Art in Christian Spain." *Gesta* 36, no. 2 (1997): 156-64.

Margalit, Avishai. *The ethics of memory*. Cambridge, MA: Harvard University Press, 2002.

Marguery-Melin, Bruno. *La Destruction de l'Abbaye de Cluny 1789-1823*. Cluny: Centre d'Études Clunisiennes, 1985.

Marquardt, Janet. "The Original Significance of the Gunzo Legend at Cluny." *Comitatus* IX (1978): 55-62.

Mayeur, Jean Marie and Madeleine Rebérioux. *The Third Republic from its origins to the Great War, 1871-1914*. Translated by J.R. Foster, The Cambridge history of modern France 4. Cambridge; New York/Paris: Cambridge University Press; Maison des sciences de l'homme, 1984.

McClellan, Andrew. *Inventing the Louvre: art, politics, and the origins of the modern museum in eighteenth-century Paris*. Berkeley, CA: University of California Press, 1999.

McPhee, Peter. *A social history of France 1780-1880*, Routledge social history of the modern world. London; New York: Routledge, 1992.

Mellon, Stanley. *The Political Uses of History: A Study of Historians in the French Restoration*. Stanford, CA: Stanford University Press, 1958.

Monot, Emile. *Millénaire de Cluny*. Lons-le-Saunier: Lucien Declume, 1911.

Montalembert. *Du vandalisme et du catholicisme dans l'art*. Paris: Debecourt, 1839.

Murphy, Kevin D. *Memory and Modernity: Viollet-le-Duc at Vézelay*. University Park, PA: The Pennsylvania State University Press, 2000.

Nayrolles, Jean. *L'invention de l'art roman à l'époque moderne (XVIIIe-XIXe siècles)*, Collection "Art & société". Rennes: Presses universitaires de Rennes, 2005.

Nochlin, Linda. *The Body in Pieces: The Fragment as a Metaphor of Modernity*. New York: Thames and Hudson, 1995.

Nora, Pierre. *Les Lieux de mémoire*, Bibliothèque illustrée des histoires. Paris: Gallimard, 1984.

Nora, Pierre, and Lawrence D. Kritzman. *Realms of memory: rethinking the French past.* European perspectives, 3 vols. New York: Columbia University Press, 1996.

Orr, Linda. *Headless history: nineteenth-century French historiography of the Revolution*. Ithaca: Cornell University Press, 1990.

Oursel, Charles. *L'art roman de Bourgogne*. Dijon: L. Venot, 1928.

Oursel, Raymond. *Invention de l'architecture romane*. La Pierre-qui-Vire: Zodiaque, 1970.

Ousterhout, Robert. "Architecture as Relic and the Construction of Sanctity: The Stones of the Holy Sepulchre." *Journal of the Society of Architectural Historians* 62, no. 1 (2003).

Pacaut, Marcel. *L'Ordre de Cluny: 909-1789*. Paris: Fayard, 1986.

Penjon, A. *Cluny la ville et l'abbaye*. Cluny,: Mme. Ve. Félix etc., 1872.

———. *Cluny: notice sur la ville et l'abbaye*. 2. ed. Cluny: Imprimerie J.-M. Demoule, 1874.

———. *Cluny; notice sur la ville et l'abbaye.* 3. ed. Cluny: Renaud-Bressoud, 1884.

Perraud, Cardinal. *Le Jubilé de Cluny*. Autun, 1898.

Pignot, J. Henri. *Histoire de l'Ordre de Cluny depuis la fondation de l'abbaye jusqu'à la mort de Pierre-le-Vénérable (909-1157).* Edited by Société éduenne des lettres sciences et arts (Autun France). Autun/Paris: Michel Dejussieu/Libraire Durand, 1868.

Porter, A. Kingsley. *Romanesque Sculpture of the Pilgrimage Roads*. Reprint of 1923 edition in 3 vols. New York: Hacker Art Books, 1966.

Poulot, Dominique. "The Birth of Heritage: 'le moment Guizot'." *Oxford Art Journal* 11, no. 2 (1988): 40-56.

Prévotat, Jacques. "Dom Besse en son temps: sa vision du monde et de l'Église." *Revue Mabillon* 77 (2005): 15-21.

Ricoeur, Paul. *Memory, history, forgetting*. Chicago: University of Chicago Press, 2004.

Rigney, Ann. "Plenitude, scarcity and the circulation of cultural memory." *Journal of European Studies* 35, no. 1 (2005): 11-28.

Rosenwein, Barbara H. *Rhinoceros bound: Cluny in the tenth century*. Philadelphia: University of Pennsylvania Press, 1982.

Rudolph, Conrad. *A companion to medieval art: Romanesque and Gothic in Northern Europe*, Blackwell companions to art history; 2. Malden, MA: Blackwell Publications, 2006.

———. "Bernard of Clairvaux, Apologia as a Description of Clunv, and the Controversy over Monastic Art." *Gesta* XXVII, no. I and 2 (1988).

———. *First, I find the center point: reading the text of Hugh of Saint Victor's The mystic ark*, Transactions of the American Philosophical Society, v. 94, pt. 4. Philadelphia, PA: American Philosophical Society, 2004.

———. *The "Things of Greater Importance": Bernard of Clairvaux's Apologia and the Medieval Attitude Toward Art*. Philadelphia: University of Pennsylvania Press, 1990.

Sackur, Ernst. *Die Cluniacenser in ihrer kirchlichen und allgemeingeschichtlichen Wirksamkeit bis zur Mitte des elften Jahrhunderts*. Darmstadt: Wissenschaftliche Buchgesellschaft/Halle an der Saale, 1892-4, 1965.

Salet, Francis. Review of *Cluny, Les eglises et la maison du chef d'ordre*, by Kenneth John Conant. *Bulletin Monumentale* 127, no. 2 (1969): 183-86.

Salveque, Jean-Denis. "Les batiments conventuels du XVIIIe siecle." *Dossiers d'archeologie* 269 (2002): 88-91.

Schama, Simon. *Citizens: a chronicle of the French Revolution*. 1st ed. New York: Knopf: Distributed by Random House, 1989.

Schnapp, Alain. "Vestiges, Monuments, and Ruins: The East Faces West." In *The Art Historian: National Traditions and Institutional Practices*, edited by Michael F. Zimmermann. New Haven: Yale University Press, 2002. 3-24

Shand-Tucci, Douglass. *Ralph Adams Cram: life and architecture*. Amherst: University of Massachusetts Press, 1995.

Shepard, Mary B. "L'oeuf sacré: Alexandre Lenoir's Courtyard of the Thirteenth Century and the Pointed Arch." In *Medieval Art and Architecture After the Middle Ages*, edited by Alyce Jordan and Janet Marquardt. Newcastle-upon-Tyne: Cambridge Scholar's Publishing, 2008 [forthcoming].

Sherman, Daniel J. *The construction of memory in interwar France*. Chicago; London: University of Chicago press, 1999.

———. "Art, Commerce, and the Production of Memory in France after World War I." In *Commemorations: The Politics of National Identity*, edited by John R. Gillis, 186-211. Princeton: Princeton University Press, 1994.

Sick, Klaus-Peter. "A New Idea of Europe: the Liberal Internationalism of the Nouvelle Revue Française (1919-1925)." *European Political Economy Review* 1, no. 1 (Spring 2003): 105-17.

Sirich, John Black. *The revolutionary committees in the departments of France, 1793-1794*. New York: H. Fertig, 1971.

Soboul, Albert. *Mouvement populaire et gouvernement révolutionnaire en l'an II (1793-1794).* Paris: Flammarion, 1973.

Sorrel, Christian. "Le monachisme masculin en France à la fin du XIXe siècle et au début du XXe siècle." *Revue Mabillon* 77 (2005): 23-54.

Sowerwine, Charles. *France since 1870: culture, politics and society*. New York: Palgrave, 2001.

Spitzer, Alan B. *The French generation of 1820.* Princeton: Princeton University Press, 1987.

Sprigath, Gabrielle. "Sur le vandalisme révolutionnaire." *Annales historiques de la Révolution française.* 52 (1980). 510-535

Stewart, Susan. *On longing: narratives of the miniature, the gigantic, the souvenir, the collection*. Baltimore: John Hopkins University Press, 1984.

Stratford, Neil, Brigitte Chabard and David Walsh. *Corpus de la sculpture de Cluny*. Vol. I. Paris: Picard, forthcoming.

Sutton, Michael. *Nationalism, positivism, and Catholicism: the politics of Charles Maurras and French Catholics, 1890-1914*, Cambridge studies in the history and theory of politics. Cambridge; New York: Cambridge University Press, 1982.

Taylor, Isidore-Justin-Séverin and Charles Nodier. *Voyages pittoresques et romantiques dans l'ancienne France*. Paris: P. Didot l'aîné, 1820.

Terret, Victor. *La sculpture bourguignonne aux XIIe et XIIIe siècles*. Autun/Paris: L'auteur; Librairie d'art catholique, 1914.

Thibaudet, Albert. *Cluny*. Edited by J.-L. Vaudoyer, Portrait de la France. Paris: Éditions Émile-Paul Frères, 1928.

Vauchez, André. "The Cathedral." In *Realms of Memory: rethinking the French past*, edited by Pierra Nora and Lawrence D. Kritzman. New York: Columbia University Press, 1996. 37-68

Verón, Eliseo, Jorge Dana, and Antoinette Franc de Ferrière. *Construire l'événement: les médias et l'accident de Three Mile Island*. Paris: Éditions de Minuit, 1981.

Villard, Monsignor. *Le Millénaire de Cluny (10-12 septembre 1910). Souvenirs religieux et littéraires*. Paris: Lethielleux, 1911.

Virey, Jean. *L'abbaye de Cluny*. Paris: H. Laurens, 1927.

———. *L'abbaye de Cluny*. 4 ed. Paris: H. Laurens, 1957.

———. *Les églises romanes de l'ancien diocèse de Mâcon*. Paris: Picard, 1892.

———. *Les églises romanes de l'ancien diocèse de Mâcon, Cluny et sa région*. Mâcon: Protat, 1935.

———. *Paray-le-Monial et les églises du Brionnais*. Paris: H. Laurens, 1926.

Walsh, David. "The Excavations of Cluny III by K.J. Conant." *Actes du Colloque scientifique international "Gouvernement d'Hugues de Semur à Cluny", Musée Ochier, Cluny 1988*. Mâcon: Buguet-Comptour, 1990. 317-325

———. "An Image of Cluny by Emile Sagot" in *Medieval Art and Architecture after the Middle Ages*, edited by Alyce Jordan and Janet Marquardt Newcastle-upon-Tyne: Cambridge Scholar's Publishing, 2008 [forthcoming]

Weintraub, Karl Joachim. *Visions of culture*. Chicago: University of Chicago Press, 1966.

Werckmeister, O. K. "Cluny III and the Pilgrimage to Santiago de Compostela." *Gesta* XXVII, no. 1/2 (1988). 103-12.

Patrick Young, "Of Pardons, Loss, and Longing: The Tourist's Pursuit of Originality in Brittany, 1890-1935," *French Historical Studies* 30/2. 269-304

Young, Robert J. *Marketing Marianne: French propaganda in America, 1900-1940*. New Brunswick, N.J.: Rutgers University Press, 2004.

INDEX

d'Achery, Luc, 49
Adams, Henry, 150-153, 199
Assmann, Aleida, 256, 259
Assmann, Jan, 256-257, 259
Aubert, Marcel, 167-170, 189, 211, 216, 220, 225, *229*,? 231-232
Auduc, Abbé, 76, 78, 109
L'Autunois, 78, 133-134
Aynard. Édouard, 120

Babelon, Ernest, 121-124, 140
Balzac, Honoré de, 40
Barthes, Roland, 28
Bastille, the, 15
Baud, Anne, 243
Bazin, René, 109
Benjamin, Walter, 13
Berenson, Bernard, 160, 238, 255
Bernard of Clairvaux, Abbot, 11, 23, 48, 152
Berry, Maurice, 222, 236
Berzé-la-Ville, 114, 140, 216, 229
Besse, Jean-Martial, 110, 120, 133, 134
Birnbaum, Pierre, 92, 253, 257, 262
Bolles, John, 209
Boston Evening Transcript, 168
Bosworth, Thomas S., 168
Bouché de la Bertelière, Philibert, 17, 51, 83, 88-89, 237, 244
Bourbon Chapel, 30, 33, 39, 45, 60-65, 67, 69, 70, 84, 89, 97, 121, 135, 258
Bourbon, Palais de Jean de, 17-19, 67, 90
Bourgogne see Burgundy, Burgundian
Boym, Svetlana, 254
Branner, Robert, 237-238
Braunfels, Wolfgang, 6, 7, 12, 23, 235, 240
Brown, John Nicholas, 166-168, 172, 174-175, 189, 196-197, 207, 215, 237
Bruel, Francois-Louis, 112, 140
Bulletin Monumental, Le 164, 216, 238
Bureau of Historic Works *see* Travaux historiques, Comité des
Burgundy, Burgundian, 10, 21, 23, 32, 37-38, 53, 63, 76-77, 80, 84, 87-88, 119, 121, 123, 141, 153, 164, 167, 178, 186, 191, 193, 199, 215, 218, 224, 228, 233, 254, 258, 260-261
Burke, Edmund, 37
Byrnes, Joseph, 73

Cabrol, Ferdinand Michel, 110, 116
Cadafalch *see* Puig i Cadafalch
Carruthers, Mary, 255, 262
Caumont, Arcisse de, 64
Champly, Louis Henry, 79, 83-88, 90
Champly, René, 83, 206
Chateaubriand, François-René,Vicomte de, 30-31
Chaumont, Louis, 67, 87, 136-137
Chavot, Théodore, 51-52, 88
Choay, Françoise, 3, 5, 23, 37, 43
Cluny
- Jubilee (1898), 70, 76-78, 92-93, 95, 109, 140
- Millénaire (1910), 108, 110-113, 115-118, 121-122, 124, 126-133, 135, 137, 140-141, 143
  - *Congrès*, 108-110, 116, 118-119, 123-124, 132-134, 137
- *Fêtes et Cérémonies liturgiques en l'honneur des saints Abbés Odon et Odilon* (1949), 224–33
  - *Congrès*, 225-226, 231-232

Commission of Historic Monuments. *See* Monuments historiques, Commission des
Compostela, Santiago de, 153-154, 160-164, 167, 196
Conant, Isabel Pope, 223, 235
Conant, Kenneth John, 4, 8, 9, 11-13, 22-23, 86, 88, 124, 135, 142, 150–199, 206–247, 254-255, 257, 260-262
Carolingian and Romanesque Architecture 800-1200, 162-163, 198, 234-235, 237, 245
Conant, Marie Schneider, 160, 194, 197, 210, 218
Cousin, Victor, 28, 41
Cram, Ralph Adams, 158, 166-167, 169, 173-174, 207, 255
Crossley, Ceri, 41, 53
Cucherat, François, 81-84, 86-87

Dartein, F. de, 159
Davis, Michael, 243
Day, C. R., 65
Delacroix, Eugène, 30
Delisle, Léopold, 109, 116-119
Dreyfus Affair, 70, 76
Duby, Georges, 10, 232
Dumas, Alexandre, 42
Duréault, Armand, 109-110, 113, 121
Duruy, Victor, 65-68, 110, 125
L'Écho (Lyon), 225
École Nationale Supérieure d'Arts et Métiers, 6, 69, 118, 137, 170, 214, 218, 222
École normale de l'enseignement secondaire spécial, 65, 67, 69, 70, 90, 110, 119, 135-137
Etlin, Richard, 31
Evans, Joan, 192, 206, 216-218, 224-225, 229, 231, 235

Farinier museum, 222-223, 227-229
Félibien, Michel, 49
Fergusson, Peter, 167, 241
Ferry, Jules, 7, 68-70, 92, 107
Flanner, Janet, 225
Fogg Museum, Harvard, 155-156, 158, 208-209, 213-214, 245
Folcher, René, 176
Forest, Alfred, 92-97, 137- 140
Le Figaro, 196

Gandrez, Henri, 124-125
Gelasius, Palace of Pope, 36, 49, 52, 66, 138, 210, 222, 227
Gélis, Paul, 169, 170, 211, 218
Gerson, Stéphane, 31, 71, 81, 109
Gildea, Robert, 37, 65
Golan, Romy, 8
Goldschmidt, Adolph, 160, 163
Goujon, Pierre, 109, 133, 143
Grégoire, Abbé, 14, 28
Gregory VII, Pope, 82, 91
Guizot, François, 28, 40-44, 47, 52-53, 62, 71, 79-80, 108, 110
Gunzo, monk at Cluny, 10, 86

Hahn, Cynthia, 39
Halbwachs, Maurice, 255-257, 259
Hambleton, Toni, 2
Le Haras de Cluny, 60, 63, 67, 69, 135-136, 140, 169-171, 178-179, 197-198, 206, 209, 211, 213, 218, 224, 230
Harvey, David, 256
Hélyot, Pierre, 49
heritage, 3, 5, 7, 23, 32, 37, 39, 40-44, 52-53, 71, 87, 142, 151, 172, 253-254, 256, 258, 260, 262
Hermant, Jean, 49
Héron de Villefosse, Antoine, 120-121
Herrick, Myron T., 167-168
Herriot, Edouard, 169, 171, 231
Historic Monuments, Commission of *see* Monuments historiques, Commission des
Hôtel de Bourgogne, Cluny, 160, 170, 185, 189, 217, 224, 241
Hudnut, Joseph, 245
Huet, J.-C., 38

Hugh, Abbot, 10-11, 81-82, 84, 86-87, 91, 114, 131, 141, 211, 216, 239
Hugo, Victor, 30-31, 40, 44, 84, 95, 111

Imbart de la Tour, Pierre, 120-121
Iogna-Prat, Dominique, 108-109, 116, 143

Le Journal de Saône-et-Loire, 78
Jubilee *see* Cluny (1898) *or* Lourdes (1897)
July Monarchy, the, 30, 40, 42-43, 46, 52-53

Kleinschmidt, Helen, 196-197, 210, 214
Koselleck, Reinhart, 255
Kubach, Hans Erich, 241

Laisné, Charles, 67-70
Lallemand, Jean-Baptiste, 255
Lamartine, Alphonse de, 29, 31, 80-81, 84, 90, 114, 199, 253
La Rochefoucauld, Dominique de, 50
Lassere, Henri, 8
Lasteyrie, Le Comte de, 107, 120, 207
Lebovics, Hermann, 257
Le Goff, Jacques, 60, 97, 111, 256
Lehmann, Richard, 87
Lenoir, Alexandre, 14, 17-18, 21, 31-32, 38, 39
Léon, Paul, 171, 210
Lorain, Prosper, 46-52, 80, 81-87, 89, 92, 122, 137, 139-140, 192
Louis IX, 111, 114, 122-123, 125-126, 132, 260
Louis-Napoléon, Napoléon III, 62-63, 65, 71
Louis-Philippe, 30, 41, 43, 52
Lourdes, 7, 8, 73-76, 92, 96, 97
Jubilee (1897), 74, 76
Lyonnais, André, 134

Mabillon, Jean, 81, 86, 88, 110, 143, 237
MacCannell, Dean, 256
Macdonald, W. A., 168-169
Mâcon
Academy of, 51, 81, 108-110, 112, 114, 116, 119, 123-124, 133, 164, 216, 225, 229
city of, 14-17, 19, 21, 23, 77, 108, 110, 118, 139, 220, 261
Mâle, Émile, 121, 152-154, 160, 244, 246, 254
Malo, Edmund, 136, 164, 169, 170-171, 188, 196, 211, 218
Mann, Janice, 254
Margalit, Avishai, 254, 256
Margery-Melin, Bruno, 17
Marshall, John, 168, 172, 173, 197
Martellange. Etienne, 88
Martin, Henri, 80, 84
Marx, Karl, 40
Mayeul, Abbot, 84
Mazarin, Cardinal, 50
McPhee, Peter, 108, 143
Mediaeval Academy of America, 8, 23, 164, 166-168, 170-174, 179, 183-184, 187-189, 192-196, 199, 206, 209-213, 215-217, 219, 226-227, 235-237, 239, 241, 243, 247
Mérimée, Prosper, 30, 44, 45, 52, 61, 62
Michelet, Jules, 30, 40, 53, 79-80, 122
Mill, John Stuart, 40
Millin, Aubin-Louis, 43
Le Monde, 218
Montalembert, Charles Forbes René, Comte de, 30, 42, 44, 49, 71, 82
Monumens Français, Musée de, 31
Monuments historiques, Commission des, 5, 40, 43-45, 52, 53, 61-62, 64-65, 67-68, 70, 96, 112, 135, 167, 169, 171, 174, 180, 189, 192, 211, 213, 218, 222, 229, 236
Monumentum, 239
Murphy, Kevin, 43
Musée d'art et d'archéologie see Ochier, Musée
Musée Ochier see Ochier, Musée

Nadaud, Gustave, 53
Napoléon Bonaparte, Napoléon I, 12, 15, 90, 124, 231
Napoléon III, *See* Louis-Napoléon
New York Herald Tribune, 188
New York Times Magazine, 168
Nora, Pierre, 12, 253, 258
Nochlin, Linda, 40, 83
Notre-Dame de Cluny, church of, 16, 33, 36, 89, 95, 227-228
Le Nouvelliste, 134

Ochier, Dr. Louis, 45, 61, 64, 67
Ochier, Musée, 171, 179-180, 183, 185-186, 224-225, 238-239
Odilo, Abbot, 3, 7, 76-78, 84, 86-87, 93, 152, 215-216, 224-225, 228, 233
Odo, Abbot, 86, 224-225, 228, 231, 233
Orr, Linda, 80
Oursel, Charles, 155, 164-165, 191-192, 195, 218, 220, 231, 240
Oursel, Raymond, 231, 239

Palais Jacques d'Amboise, 17-19, 230
Palmer, Frederic, 186, 196-197, 209, 214, 238
Paray-le-Monial, 7, 73, 76-77, 81, 88, 97, 116, 244
patrimony, 4-5, 22, 28-31, 37, 41, 43-44, 46, 52-53, 62, 64, 70, 81, 97, 109, 119, 120, 123, 143, 161, 167, 172, 224, 231, 254, 256-257, 260
Penjon, Auguste, 89, 90, 137
Perraud, Cardinal (Bishop of Autun), 77, 93
Peter the Venerable, Abbot, 10, 48, 84-88, 140, 152, 211-212
Le Petit Mâconnais, 225
phylloxera disease, 68, 141
picturesque, 5, 32, 33-34, 37-40, 49
Pignot, J. H., 85-88
Pius X, Pope, 111
Pleindoux, Dr. Charles, 224, 229, 236
Ponce de Melgueil, Abbot, 84-85, 212
Porter, Arthur Kingsley, 153-154, 159-166, 189, 191-192, 208, 210, 213, 215-216, 234, 238, 240, 244, 246-247, 254
Poulot, Dominique, 258
Le Progrès, 78, 133-134, 225, 227, 230-231
Puig i Cadafalch, Josep, 161
Quinet, Edgar, 80

Le Ralliement, 70, 107
Reims cathedral, 172, 174
Réau, Louis, 12, 14
Revue de l'Art, 210
Ricard, E., 63, 90, 91
Richardson, Henry Hobson, 156, 159, 163, 167
Richelieu, Armand Jean Duplessis, Cardinal, 50, 85
Ricoeur, Paul, 256
Roiné, Nadine, 125, 128, 130, 133
Romanesque style, 3, 5, 6, 8-9, 13, 34, 36, 38, 63, 70, 87, 89-91, 97, 119, 121, 133, 136, 153-154, 156, 159-162, 164, 167, 170, 188, 191-192, 194, 198, 222, 235, 244, 254, 258-261
Rosenwein, Barbara, 91

Sachs, Paul, 208, 214
Sackur, Ernst, 8, 91
Sacré Coeur, cult of, 73, 220
Sacred Heart *see Sacré Coeur,* cult of
Sagot, Émile, 32, 34-38, 47-50, 89, 114, 139, 261
Saint-Marcel de Cluny, church of 16, 33, 36, 49
Saint-Maur, Congregation of, 50, 85
Saint Mayeul de Cluny, abbey of, 16, 260
Salet, Francis, 237-239, 245, 247
Sallez, André, 236
Saône-et-Loire, département, 16, 17, 20, 22, 38, 60-61, 66, 70, 73, 78, 79, 243, 261

Schama, Simon, 15
Shepard, Mary, 39
Sherman, David, 256
Siedentop, Larry, 40
Soboul, Albert, 15
Speculum, 159, 163-164, 166, 173, 194, 198, 206, 213, 216, 233, 238-239, 247
Stewart, Susan, 37
Stratford, Neil, 29, 192
Talobre, Joseph, 216, 231-232
Taylor, Baron Isidore-Justin-Séverin, 32-38, 47, 49, 63, 89, 139, 261
Terret, Victor, 119, 191, 210
Thibaudet, Albert, 1, 107, 124, 141, 143
Thierry, Augustin, 40-41, 53, 71, 80
Thiers, Adolphe, 79-80
Tocqueville, Alexis de, 40, 52, 80
Tour Fabri, Cluny, 112, 230
Tour des Fromages, Cluny, 33,136, 220-222
Tour Ronde, Cluny, 33
Travaux historiques, Comité des, 31, 43
Trêve de Dieu (Truce of God) 111, 113
Truce of God see Trêve de Dieu

L'Union républicaine, 78-79, 134, 196
Urban II, Pope, 10, 82

Vaillant, François, 29, 30
vandalisme, 12, 14
Vauchez, André, 12
Ventre, André, 135-136
Verdier, Aymar, 53, 60-64, 88, 171, 181
Vernon, Eliseo, 247
Vézelay, 52, 191, 210, 231, 241
Le Vieux Paris (Exposition Universelle 1900), 92, 111-112
Viollet-le-Duc, Eugène Emmanuel, 41, 44, 52, 60, 84, 86, 88, 192
Virey, Jean, 87-88, 109-110, 119-120, 150, 155, 164, 188, 199, 210, 220, 229, 233-235, 237, 240
Vitet, Ludovic, 41-42, 44-45
Vöge, Wilhelm, 160, 163

Walsh, David, 182, 192
Warren, Herbert Langford, 155-156, 163
Weber, Eugen, 135

Young, Patrick, 77
Young, Robert, 167

Zola, Émile, 96, 97